lonely planet

Provence
& the Côte d'Azur

Alpes-de-Haute-Provence
p259

The Vaucluse
& Luberon
p204

Côte d'Azur
& Monaco
p53

Bouches-du-Rhône
p155

The Var
p116

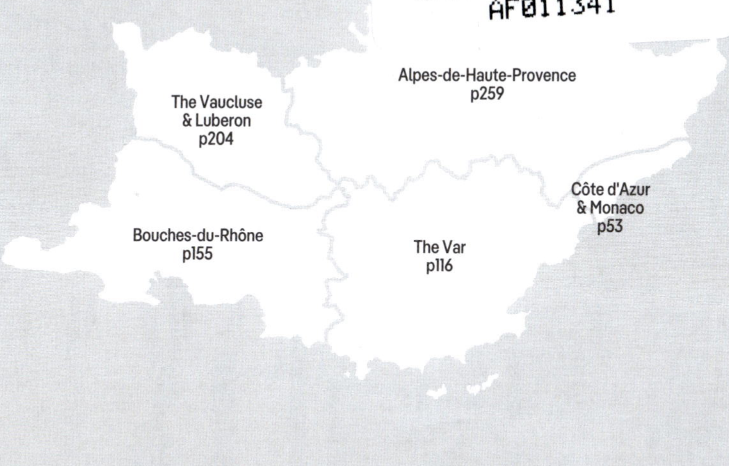

Chrissie McClatchie, Alexis Averbuck,
Michael Frankel, Ashley Parsons

Villefranche-sur-Mer (p73), near Nice

CONTENTS

Plan Your Trip

The Journey Begins Here 4
Provence & the Côte d'Azur Map 6
Our Picks 8
Regions & Cities 24
Itineraries 26
When to Go 36
Get Prepared 38
Lavender Fields of Provence 40
The Food Scene 42
The Outdoors 46

The Guide

Côte d'Azur & Monaco 53
- Nice 58
- Côte d'Azur Beaches 66
- Beyond Nice 73
- Cannes 86
- Beyond Cannes 94
- Monaco 104
- Accommodation 114

The Var 116
- St-Tropez 120
- Beyond St-Tropez 130
- Hyères 136
- Beyond Hyères 140
- Haut-Var 145
- Accommodation 153

Bouches-du-Rhône 155
- Marseille 160
- Beyond Marseille 173
- Aix-en-Provence 178
- Beyond Aix-en-Provence 184
- Arles 188
- Beyond Arles 192
- Stes-Maries-de-la-Mer 198
- Beyond Stes-Maries-de-la-Mer 201
- Accommodation 203

The Vaucluse & Luberon 204
- Avignon 210
- Beyond Avignon 217
- Ventoux Region 224
- L'Isle-sur-la-Sorgue 229
- Beyond L'Isle-sur-la-Sorgue 234
- North Luberon 238
- South Luberon 250
- Accommodation 256

Alpes-de-Haute-Provence 259
- Moustiers-Ste-Marie 262
- Beyond Moustiers-Ste-Marie 270
- Ubaye Valley 276
- Riding the High Passes 280
- Accommodation 282

Toolkit

Arriving 286
Getting Around 287
Money 288
Accommodation 289
Family Travel 290
Health & Safe Travel 291
Food, Drink & Nightlife 292
Responsible Travel 294
LGBTIQ+ Travellers 296
Accessible Travel 297
How to Visit Markets 298
Nuts & Bolts 299
Language 300

Storybook

A History of Provence & the Côte d'Azur in 15 Places 304
A Spotlight on Niçoise Cuisine 308
Facing into Le Mistral Gagnant 311
Beat the Heat in Marseille 314

Tours

Vieux Nice on Foot 71
Drive the Three Corniches 82
Cannes Art Mural Walk 91
Driving The Esterel 98
Monaco F1 On Foot 112
Cruise La Route Du Mimosa 134
Hike the Île De Port-Cros 142
Drive Villages de Caractère 150
Marseille's Le Panier on Foot 170
Follow the Fountains of Aix 180
A Tour of Aix's Vineyards 186
Roman Arles on Foot 190
A Walk Through Old Avignon 215
Hiking the Gorges De La Nesque 226
Cycling through the Monts De Vaucluse 235
Trek Ermitage St-Gens 236
Pedalling the Luberon 242
A Walk in the Forêt Des Cèdres 253
Route Napoléon 268
Mountain Biking the Lure Mountain 273

Parc National du Mercantour (p81)

PROVENCE & THE CÔTE D'AZUR
THE JOURNEY BEGINS HERE

There's the Provence and Côte dAzur of magazine covers and social media posts: vast plains ablaze with lavender, striped beach umbrellas against the dazzling blue of the Mediterranean. Then there's the Provence and Côte dAzur you might not have met yet: little-known ski resorts and alpine villages with rich pastoral traditions.

I've lived in and around Nice for most of my adult life and today, it feels like a whole new side of the region is emerging. It's never been easier for visitors to dive into the hinterland – whether towards the Parc National du Mercantour or the Vallée de la Roya. Both alpine valleys sum up everything that is exciting about the Côte d'Azur right now: a chance to experience lesser-known landscapes and, more importantly, an opportunity to contribute to the efforts of the communities rebuilding their lives after the devastation of Storm Alex in 2020.

Chrissie McClatchie
@chrissie_mcclatchie

Chrissie is a travel writer based in Villefranche-sur-Mer with a background in wine who has tasted her way through most of Provence's great grape appellations. She wrote the Côte dAzur and Monaco chapter.

My favourite experience is a weekend escape in the **Parc National du Mercantour** (p81), where I can swap the crowds of the coast for empty alpine trails in under 90 minutes. Total bliss.

WHO GOES WHERE

Our writers and experts choose the places that, for them, define Provence and the Côte dAzur.

My favourite experience is cycling the **Monts de Vaucluse** (p234). I love the wild valleys and hills on this side of the Monts de Vaucluse, and the quiet villages like Venasque (pictured), which lie at the edge of the typical loop.

Ashley Parsons
@enselle.voyage

Ashley is a travel and adventure writer. She splits her time between Provence and the French Alps. Follow her travels on horseback, bike, foot or by train.

My go-to experience is a local lunch of razor clams and wine in **Les Goudes** (pictured; p166), followed by a walk into the wild and a dive into the Med.

Michael Frankel

Michael is a Marseille-based freelance writer who lives for the slow doors of a hotel room clicking behind him as he makes his way back down to the street.

I love zipping across the waters off Hyères on the ferry to **Île de Porquerolles** (pictured; p140). As the boat slows, we cruise into the island harbour and people disembark, before saddling up on bikes to ride off along forested paths to the beaches.

Alexis Averbuck
alexisaverbuck.com

Alexis paints and writes about her adventures – from living in Antarctica to crossing the Pacific by sailboat – for Lonely Planet, National Geographic UK and others.

RED, WHITE & ROSÉ

When the ancient Greeks planted France's first wine grapes in the soils around newly founded Massalia (Marseille), the seeds of Provence's prized wine tradition were sown. Today, over 80% of all wine made here is rosé, and the pink flows year-round on sunlit cafe terraces. There's so much more to the region's winemaking than one colour, however; it extends from the deep reds of the Vaucluse to boutique 'Made in Nice' whites.

Vineyard Visits

Phone ahead to ensure that someone will be there to welcome you at the cellar door, especially for smaller vineyards. Tasting fees are common.

Co-operative Spirit

If you find yourself short on time but want to get a feel for the region's wines, plan a visit to the local wine co-operative, such as in the Luberon (p241).

Rosé Time

To go to the heart of Provence's famous rosé, visit the Maison des Vins Côtes de Provence (p149) near Les-Arcs-sur-Argens or the Maison des Vins de Bandol (p144).

Vineyard, Montagne Ste-Victoire (p184)

BEST WINE EXPERIENCES

Sip the elixirs of medieval popes at ❶ **Châteauneuf-du-Pape** (p217) and take a new favourite home; these complex reds only improve with age.

Fall under the spell of Beaumes-de-Venise at ❷ **Domaine de Ferme St-Martin** (p221) in the Ventoux. Tastings are hosted by a sommelier.

Take a road trip in the vineyards around Montagne Ste-Victoire outside ❸ **Aix-en-Provence** (p186), including Palette AOC, one of France's smallest appellations.

Meet the small monastic community with a surprising viticultural tradition on the ❹ **Île St-Honorat** (p89) off the coast of Cannes.

Decide for yourself if Coco Chanel really found inspiration for her iconic logo at ❺ **Château de Crémat** (p69) in the hills of Nice.

Canyoning, Gorges du Verdon (p264)

WATER WORLDS

The calm Mediterranean Sea is as pretty as a picture, but don't just admire the view. You can tailor the day's activities to match your mood: relaxed afternoons on a skippered sailing boat; easy swims with a snorkel and mask off undeveloped islands, or deeper dives down to moody shipwrecks.

In Season

Easter is considered the traditional starting point for the diving season, which runs until October. Boats shutter up for winter, though locals swim year-round.

Pointus

A delightful splash of colour and character, *pointus* are the region's traditional wooden fishing boats. Spot them in ports from Marseille to Menton.

BEST WATER EXPERIENCES

Set sail in search of dolphins on a replica 16th-century sailing boat in ❶ **St-Jean-Cap-Ferrat** (p74).

Relax into yachting life or go for a spin on a crewed catamaran in the ❷ **Golfe de St-Tropez** (p125).

BYO snorkelling gear to the ❸ **Écomusée Sous-Marin de Cannes** (p89), where sculptures dot the ocean floor.

Run the rapids of the ❹ **Gorges du Verdon** (p264) for Provence's best rafting and canyoning.

Rig the sails then tuck into a vegetarian brunch on board the *pointu Coco*, departing from ❺ **Marseille** (p160).

CITY LIFE

From the cosmopolitan grit of Marseille to the shiny glitz of Monaco, Provence's urban centres warrant your attention. Inside these bustling cityscapes, you can dine on inventive cuisine, search for street art and relax on a shaded cafe terrace. Expect plenty of history, but also a taste of what the future holds.

BEST CITY LIFE EXPERIENCES

Wake up with an appetite in ❶ **Nice** (p58); from lavender croissants to smashed avo on toast, an inventive breakfast and brunch scene is simmering.

Sink into cafe culture at one of the many outdoor terraces in ❷ **Aix-en-Provence** (p178). Dark sunglasses are a requisite for people-watching.

Find yourself framed by street art on cours Julien in ❸ **Marseille** (p160), where a sunset *apéro* can easily morph into a night out.

Grab a seat at a charming cafe on the canalside rue des Teinturiers in ❹ **Avignon** (p210) and settle in for happy hour.

Join the afterwork crowd for festive Friday-night drinks and organic beer at the harbourfront ❺ **Brasserie de Monaco** (p111).

FROM LEFT: SAKOJ9/SHUTTERSTOCK, ANDREI ANTIPOV/SHUTTERSTOCK

The Principality

Smaller than New York's Central Park and with a population of just 36,000, Monaco (pictured) is the world's second-smallest country and one of its most dense.

Golden Hour

Terrace tables fill up come 5pm with groups of friends catching up for an early evening apéritif, known colloquially as *apéro*.

Home Brew

An exciting craft beer scene is brewing. Swap out your usual choice for a local drop flavoured with regional ingredients, such as lemons from Menton.

ARTS & CRAFTS

Cézanne in Aix-en-Provence, Van Gogh in Arles, Matisse and Chagall in Nice and Picasso here, there and everywhere. The quality of light and the way it colours the landscape has long made Provence a muse for the masters. Marvel at their work in museums, chapels and even the homes they once lived in. A wealth of other arts-and-craft traditions, from fine ceramics to outdoor galleries and even nature's own pigments, awaits.

Handcrafted

Leather sandals in St-Tropez (p122), blocks of *savon de Marseille* in Salon-de-Provence (pictured; p185) and ceramics from **Vallauris** (p97) are all souvenirs to treasure.

Sure Bet

Before the high rollers descend at 2pm, Monaco's Casino de Monte-Carlo (p109) opens for self-guided tours through the lavishly decorated, gilded, Belle Époque gaming rooms.

Wild Art

The Route de l'Art Contemporain (Contemporary Art Route) is an open-air art tour through the prehistoric Réserve Géologique de Haute-Provence (p270), which starts in Digne-les-Bains.

Pottery, Vallauris (p97)

BEST ARTS & CRAFTS EXPERIENCES

Follow in the footsteps of Pablo Picasso, who made the potter's village of ❶ **Vallauris** (p97) and the village of **Mougins** (p97) home.

Spot Frank Gehry's striking ❷ **Luma Arles** (p188) from a distance: it's a steel-clad tower and inspiring cultural palace.

Browse ceramic workshops in the chic village of ❸ **Moustiers-Ste-Marie** (p262). Firing *faience*, or glazed earthenware, is a local tradition that dates back to the Middle Ages.

Hike into the ochre-tinted swirl of cliffs, fairy chimneys, cirques and hills of the terracotta ❹ **Colorado Provençal** (p249).

Join the cool crowd and check out the latest modern art exhibition at ❺ **Villa Noailles** (p138) while taking in the view over Hyères.

Calanque du Jonquier (p177)

ISLANDS & CALANQUES

Get ready to embrace barefoot adventures along powder-white beaches and refreshing swims in shallow waters. Local ferry services shuttle residents and visitors to and from sun-kissed islands, which are blissfully serene and car-free. On the mainland, don't miss Marseille's marvellous *calanques* (coves).

My Calanques

Download the My Calanques app for hiking routes, traffic updates, flora and fauna guides and practical information at your fingertips.

Rubbish- & Plastic-Free

Cannes' Îles de Lérins are garbage bin-free; visitors must take all rubbish back to the mainland with them. BYO water bottle to the Îles d'Hyères.

BEST ISLAND & CALANQUE EXPERIENCES

Sun yourself on the daydream beaches of the ❶ **Île de Porquerolles** (p140) off Hyères.

Hop on the ferry to ❷ **Château d'If** (p168) and Îles de Frioul's rocky islets in the bay of Marseille.

Spend a day in your very own castaway bay in ❸ **Calanque d'En-Vau** (p175).

Catch the Train de la Côte Bleue and skim Marseille's coast to ❹ **Calanque du Jonquier** (p177).

Swap the bustle of Cannes for the pine-fringed hiking trails of the ❺ **Îles de Lérins** (p88), a short ferry ride from the mainland.

INLAND VILLAGES

Medieval builders knew a thing or two about building to last – standing tall over the countryside and witnesses to centuries of history, Provence's hilltop villages have withstood wars and invasions. Today, the only threat to peace comes from tour buses in summer, although many villages in the hinterland remain refreshingly low-key.

Look for This Label

Les Plus Beaux Villages de France is a label that recognises France's most beautiful villages; there are 22 (and counting) in Provence and the Côte d'Azur.

Bistrot de Pays

Taste your way through Provence's rural restaurant scene. The Bistrot de Pays organisation champions rural bistros that serve up local produce at reasonable prices.

High Vantage

High, hard-to-access rocky outcrops were prime real estate in the early Middle Ages as coastal dwellers moved to hilltops to defend themselves against Saracen attacks.

BEST VILLAGE EXPERIENCES

Eat your way through ❶ **Saignon** (p244), a laid-back village perched high above Apt with a generous share of top restaurants.

Hide out in ❷ **Cotignac** (p145), a charming village in the Haut Var with an exciting gourmet and cultural scene.

Scale to the top of ❸ **Ste-Agnès** (p78), the highest coastal village in Europe, where a medieval garden sprouts from 10th-century ruins.

Listen to cicadas as you stroll around the sun-kissed village of ❹ **Eygalières** (p197) in the Alpilles and hike to Chapelle St-Sixte, painted by Vincent Van Gogh.

Unwrap Provence's most famous cheese, the leaf-wrapped ❺ **Banon** (p271), named for the village in the Alpes-de-Haute-Provence where it is made.

NATURE ALL AROUND

No matter where you are in Provence, you're never too far from nature's grasp. Set off on foot along rugged shoreline trails, pause to cool off in the glassy sea, hike to mountain reserves to observe wildlife or tackle majestic mountain summits by bike. At the heart of it all is the sublime Gorges du Verdon, where sport and nature meet.

BEST NATURE EXPERIENCES

Tackle the ride at the top of many cyclists' bucket list, ❶ **Mont Ventoux** (p224), a windswept mountain steeped in centuries of lore.

Go fossil spotting at the ❷ **Réserve Géologique de Haute-Provence** (p270), Europe's largest protected geological reserve.

Take your pick from hiking, cycling, driving, canyoning or rafting the deep ❸ **Gorges du Verdon** (p264).

Breathe in the fresh mountain air and set off in search of alpine wildlife just 1½ hours from Nice in ❹ **St-Martin-Vésubie** (p81).

Slow down in the ❺ **Camargue** (p192), a vast shimmer of salt flats and marshlands where pink flamingos, black bulls and wild horses roam.

Animals Crossing

Wildlife-spotting opportunities include marmots (pictured), chamois and ibex in the Parc National de Mercantour, vultures in the Gorges du Verdon and birds in the Camargue.

Visitor Limits

To preserve the unspoilt feel of the Île de Porquerolles (pictured), visitor numbers are limited to 6000 per day in summer.

Seeing Stars

Sometimes the best experiences stir after dark; low light pollution makes the Alpes-de-Haute-Provence a magnet for stargazers.

Domaine du Rayol (p135)

BEST FLOWER & GARDEN EXPERIENCES

Don't miss Provence's iconic ❶ **lavender fields** (p40) but choose sustainable visits.

Set off on the coastal ❷ **Route du Mimosa** (p134), a 130km winter road trip framed by golden blooms.

Breathe in the scents of the world's greatest perfume flowers at the ❸ **Jardins du Musée International de la Parfumerie** (p101).

Find a peaceful corner of Monaco in the ❹ **Roseraie Princesse Grace** (p107), an English-style garden with over 6000 rose bushes.

Wander ❺ **Domaine du Rayol** (p135), where each corner of the park is cultivated with species from arid ecosystems around the world.

FLOWERS & GARDENS

From rows of purple lavender stretched as far as the eye can see to the delicate rose and jasmine fragrances that underlie the world's most recognisable perfumes, so much of Provence's identity is intertwined with its floral bounty. Breathe in the smells and soak up the traditions in the region's vast fields and manicured gardens.

The Rite of Spring

The gardens of the Côte d'Azur throw open their gates to welcome visitors during the month-long Festival des Jardins de la Côte d'Azur every second year in April.

Purple Power

Hilltop Tourrettes-sur-Loup is known as the village of violets; it breaks out in every shade of purple in early March for the annual Fête des Violettes.

LIVING HISTORY

Wherever you look, you'll find relics of Provence's rich history on display, from the earliest imprints of human settlement carved by hand in caves to imposing Roman arenas where gladiators once fought to the fortified Gothic palace the medieval papacy called home. Belle Époque buildings and art deco detailing are tokens of modern times and tell the story of how the southeastern coast of France grew into a must-visit destination for early travellers.

Boom at Noon

No, you're not hearing things. Every day at midday, a cannon rings out across Nice. A tradition dating from the late 19th century, today's cannonball (pictured) is a firework.

Did You Know?

There is only one team in Marseille: Olympique de Marseille (OM). It was the first French football team to lift the Champions League trophy, in 1993.

True Story

Follow the comings and goings of the emigrants of Barcelonette at the Musée de la Vallée (p278) and in the village's Mexican villas.

FROM LEFT: BERTL123/SHUTTERSTOCK, CLEMENT MAHOUDEAU/AFP VIA GETTY IMAGES, ANDREI ANTIPOV/SHUTTERSTOCK

Palais Princier de Monaco (p105)

BEST HISTORY EXPERIENCES

Wander the UNESCO-World Heritage listed streets of ❶ **Nice** (p58) and step back into an era when winter was the high season for travel.

Scrape back layers of time at the ❷ **Palais Princier de Monaco** (p105), where careful restoration work is revealing Renaissance frescoes.

See if you can answer the mystery surrounding 40,000 enigmatic Bronze Age rock engravings in the ❸ **Vallée des Merveilles** (p84).

Feel the Roman legacy as you walk the streets of ❹ **Arles** (p188) – a one-time economic, political and cultural centre in a sprawling empire.

Lose yourself in the churches, gardens and abbeys that stand testament to the time the papacy swapped Rome for ❺ **Avignon** (p210).

Fête du Citron (p78)

OFF-SEASON SPECIALS

The city of Nice has called it: 'Winter is the New Summer'. As travellers embrace off-season travel, Provence and the Côte d'Azur is a ready-made destination – after all, the region's tourism scene was built on *hivernants*, or winter tourists. Seasonal produce, grape harvests, backcountry cycling and hiking and a busy calendar of festivals are among the delights that reward those who come outside of summer.

Winter Hibernation

Seasonal businesses and activities open, as a rule of thumb, from April to September. In the main centres, you won't feel an impact, but it can mean that the rest of the region feels like your own playground.

Discount Rates

Many activities and excursions are cheaper in shoulder and low-season months. For instance, you can shave nearly €7 off the price of the ferry to the Porquerolles if you travel between November and March.

BEST OFF-SEASON EXPERIENCES

Hit markets where the hottest commodity is black gold – truffles – at ❶ **Carpentras** (p218) and **Aups** (p147) in winter.

Savour sea urchins pulled fresh from the sea by local divers in ❷ **Nice** (p58) and during February's **Oursinade** (p43) in Carry-le-Rouet.

Tuck into *gardiane de taureau*, a slow-cooked Provençal bull stew, on winter menus in the ❸ **Camargue** (p192).

Pedal the backroads with fewer cars to share the road with: the ❹ **Haut-Var** (p145) and **Monts de Vaucluse** (p234) are delightful.

Whittle away a day under a flowering lemon tree at ❺ **La Ferme des Citrons** (p77) in Menton in February's **Fête du Citron** (p78).

FRESH FINDS

The biggest overhaul in half a century of Cannes' iconic La Croisette is approaching completion, while Monaco is suddenly 3% bigger. This is a region that doesn't like to sit still, constantly innovating new experiences and activities that showcase its tradition, culture, gastronomy or future-forward vision. Think you've done all Provence has to offer?

BEST NEW EXPERIENCES

Study the work of women artists at ❶ **FAMM** (p97) in Mougins, the first private museum in Europe dedicated to female art.

Learn about the role seagrass plays in the Mediterranean ecosystem at ❷ **Posidonia – Espace Mer et Littoral** (p96) in Antibes.

Enjoy trout from the Sorgue at ❸ **JU Maison de Cuisine** (p247), Bonnieux's newly annointed Michelin-starred restaurant.

Step inside in a 17th-century fort shuttered for decades, the ❹ **Fort du Pradeau** (p139) on the Presqu'île de Giens.

Climb to the restored ❺ **Grotte de Ste-Marie-Madeleine** (p152), a cave in the Massif de la Ste-Baume that sheltered Mary Magdalene.

Growth Spurt

Monaco officially increased in size by six hectares in December 2024, when its newest neighbourhood was inaugurated. Mareterra (pictured; p108) has risen on land reclaimed from the sea.

Olympic Buzz

Expect to feel Olympic fever rising, with the French Alps the host of the 2030 Winter Olympics. The closing ceremony will be held on Nice's **Promenade des Anglais** (pictured).

Guinguette Gems

France is rekindling its love affair with guinguettes, or summer al-fresco drinking, dining and dancing spots. In the Vaucluse, soak up the seasonal ambiance at la Guinguette de la Colline in Orange (p221).

FLAVOURS OF PROVENCE

Whether you're hungry for gastronomic dining or street food that sets your taste buds sizzling, Provence and the Côte d'Azur's kitchens have you covered. Marseille overflows with global flavours, while chefs in Nice are reinventing the city's traditional cuisine. Fresh, seasonal flavours rule the coast; inland, the mountain air is paired with heartier fare. Whether breakfast, brunch, lunch or dinner, there's always someone bringing something new to the table. So make sure you pack your appetite.

Black Gold

The truffle season runs from mid-November to mid-March; an estimated 70% of French truffles (pictured) sprout from the soils of the Vaucluse. Carpentras (p218) is the truffle hub.

Markets

Provence knows how to throw a market, from fragrant weekly events to speciality markets that shine a spotlight on a particular product in season.

Book Ahead

It's becoming increasingly advisable to reserve in advance to guarantee a seat at the table at your preferred restaurants, even out of season in bigger cities.

Chez Bruno (p149), Lorgues

BEST FOOD EXPERIENCES

Spoil your senses at the temple of truffles, ❶ **Chez Bruno** (p149), in a wonderfully rustic Provençal *mas* (farmhouse) in Lorgues.

Confuse your sweet tooth with a scoop of charcoal-flavoured vanilla ice cream at ❷ **Vanille Noire** (p170) in Marseille.

Immerse yourself in the Camargue's rice culture during a visit to the ❸ **Maison du Riz** (p196). You can even stay the night.

Warm up after a day on the slopes with a delightfully decadent ❹ **fondue de l'Ubaye** (p276) created from three alpine cheeses.

Feast on catch-of-the-day from the last of Monaco's traditional fishermen, Eric Rinaldi, at ❺ **U Luvassu** (p105).

REGIONS & CITIES

Find the places that tick all your boxes.

The Vaucluse & Luberon

MOUNTAINS, WINE & SUNSHINE

Avignon blends papal history with modern theatre. Too-pretty-to-be-true Gordes is the essence of Provence in a bottle. Saddle up to summit Mont Ventoux or slow down on country lanes weaving through scented lavender fields. Fill your basket with fresh produce at markets in Carpentras and sip your way through Châteauneuf-du-Pape.

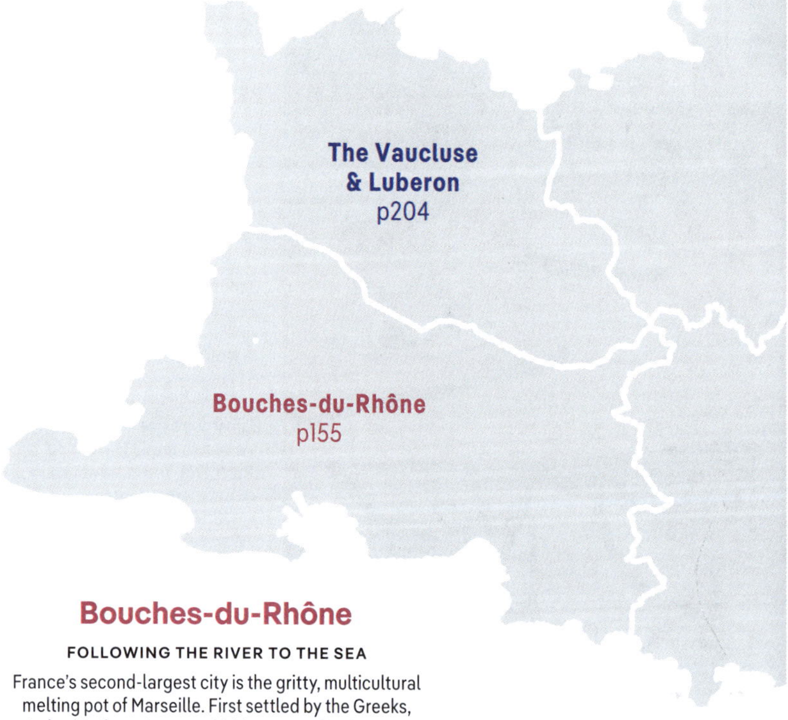

The Vaucluse & Luberon
p204

Bouches-du-Rhône
p155

Bouches-du-Rhône

FOLLOWING THE RIVER TO THE SEA

France's second-largest city is the gritty, multicultural melting pot of Marseille. First settled by the Greeks, today it's the gateway to hidden coastal *calanques* (coves), Aix-en-Provence's cafe culture, the wetlands of the Camargue, Arles' Roman monuments and a timeless landscape that inspired Van Gogh and Cézanne.

Alpes-de-Haute-Provence

FROM ALPINE VALLEYS TO LAVENDER FIELDS

Buckle up for white-knuckle adventure in the Gorges du Verdon, bike past shepherd's huts on the Lure mountain, trace fossilised footprints in the Réserve Géologique de Haute-Provence and ski the slopes of the Ubaye Valley. The southern Alps is Provence like you never imagined.

Alpes-de-Haute-Provence
p259

Cote d'Azur & Monaco
p53

Côte d'Azur & Monaco

WHERE THE MOUNTAINS MEET THE MEDITERRANEAN

Nice is the big city coming of age while Cannes and Monaco deliver all the five-star glamour. Mougins, Èze and other perched villages conceal artists' studios and fine-dining tables. The gardens of Grasse perfume the world. The mountain scene is gloriously off-radar.

The Var
p116

The Var

TURQUOISE SEA, BEACHES AND HILLTOP VILLAGES

From the blingy beach clubs of St-Tropez to the laid-back surfer vibe of Hyères Presqu'île de Giens, there's a beach to suit everyone in the Var. Pale pink rosé flows from inland vineyards while the Haut-Var brims with stylish villages and lush green landscapes.

Lavender fields, Saignon (p244)

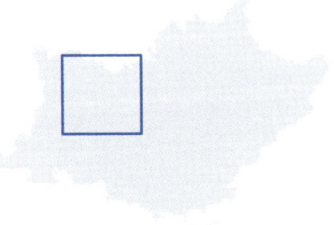

ITINERARIES

Hilltop Towns & Villages

Allow: 5 days **Distance**: 105km

The Vaucluse and the Luberon are storybook Provence: dreamy hilltop villages, vineyard-strewn plains, buzzing produce markets and vintage 2CVs chugging along country lanes. From Carpentras, this unhurried route coils east through antique towns, lavender-framed abbeys and serene frescoed churches towards sweet Reillanne.

❶ CARPENTRAS ⏱ 1 DAY

Your Luberon road trip starts with a gastronomic bang in the shady squares of **Carpentras** (p218) where aromas of fresh truffles and juicy strawberries fill the air, depending on the season, and a bright Provençal market pops up every Friday morning, no matter the time of the year. Spend the afternoon among the sun-drenched vineyards of the Ventoux, just a short drive out of town.

❷ L'ISLE-SUR-LA-SORGUE ⏱ 1 DAY

Where cobblestones meet canals, **L'Isle-sur-la-Sorgue** (p229) oozes charm. Traditional boats and waterwheels stand testament to the town's rich past while the antique shops lining the narrow streets speak of its status as one of France's top destinations for antiques.

🚗 *Detour: Uncover the source of the River Sorgues in Fontaine de Vaucluse.* 🚌 *5 hours*

❸ GORDES ⏱ 1 DAY

In a country not lacking in the beautiful villages department, **Gordes** (p240) is often voted as the most attractive of all. Decide for yourself if this Luberon stunner takes your top place, although be prepared to share the winding lanes with busloads of tourists in summer.

🚗 *Detour: Stretch your legs on the 3km walk to the* **Abbaye Notre-Dame de Sénanque** *(p240), a 12th-century abbey surrounded by lavender.*

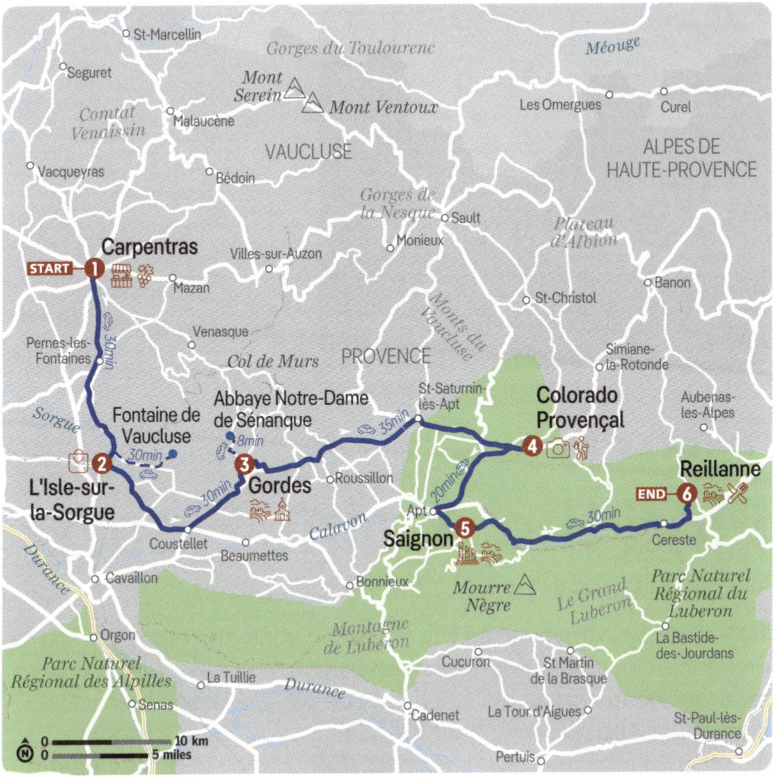

④
COLORADO PROVENÇAL
⏱ 1 DAY

Beat the heat by setting off early for the **Colorado Provençal** (p249), an awe-inspiring landscape of chimneys and desert rocks tinted rust, crimson and burnt orange between Roussillon and Rustrel. A busy ochre quarry from the 1880s to the late 1950s, the site is now a hiking destination with two family-friendly (but not pram-friendly) trails.

⑤
SAIGNON ⏱ ½ DAY

Get a feel for traditional Provençal life in **Saignon** (p244), a lovely village above Apt that overlooks the Luberon and beyond to Mont Ventoux. Capture the best views by following the short trail up to the castle ruins and the Rocher de Bellevue, then wind back down to admire fading frescoes inside the 12th-century Église Notre-Dame de Pitié. Stock up on picnic supplies in the village.

⑥
REILLANNE ⏱ ½ DAY

Raise a toast to the end of the journey at Café du Cours, a lively restaurant-cafe in the centre of **Reillanne** (p245) with a popular live music programme. Sunday's Grand Marché de Reillanne is one of the best in the region and transforms the quiet perched village into a feast of zero-kilometre produce: olive oil, farm-fresh eggs, chickpeas and melt-in-the-mouth tomatoes.

FROM LEFT: EGAL/GETTY IMAGES, JENIFOTO/SHUTTERSTOCK, RICHARD SEMIK/SHUTTERSTOCK

Gorges du Verdon (p264), Moustiers-Ste-Marie

ITINERARIES

Find the Alpine Heart

Allow: 6 Days **Distance**: 214km

Take roads less travelled as you drift deeper into the Alpes-de-Haute-Provence. Cut across sun-drenched plateaux bursting with purple lavender, contemplate brilliant night skies, kit up for white-knuckle adventures and recover in thermal cures as you embark on this action-packed drive that curves north from Banon to Barcelonnette.

❶ BANON ½ DAY

Begin this inland itinerary in **Banon** (p271), an attractive hilltop village overlooking lavender fields and best known for its eponymous goat's cheese (pictured) wrapped in chestnut leaves. Pick up a parcel at either the Tuesday or Saturday morning markets; add in a baguette, tomato, charcuterie and some in-season fruit and voilà, your picnic lunch *à la provençale* awaits.

❷ ST-MICHEL-L'OBSERVATOIRE ½ DAY

The small village of **St-Michel-l'Observatoire** (p272) is a stargazer's delight. See what constellations you can spot with the naked eye, or spend a summer night in the company of English-speaking astronomers at the Centre d'Astronomie.

🐦 *Detour: Watch for birds of prey along the 13km hiking trail that starts and ends in Revest-des-Brousses.*
🚗 *3 hours*

❸ VALENSOLE 1 DAY

For a few weeks in late June and early July, the vast 800-sq-km **Plateau de Valensole** (p266) explodes in the purple hues of lavender bloom – your chance to snap the quintessential Provence photo. Lavender farms are open year-round for distillery tours, souvenir shopping and to explain the key differences between the region's two main crops: *lavande* and *lavandin*.

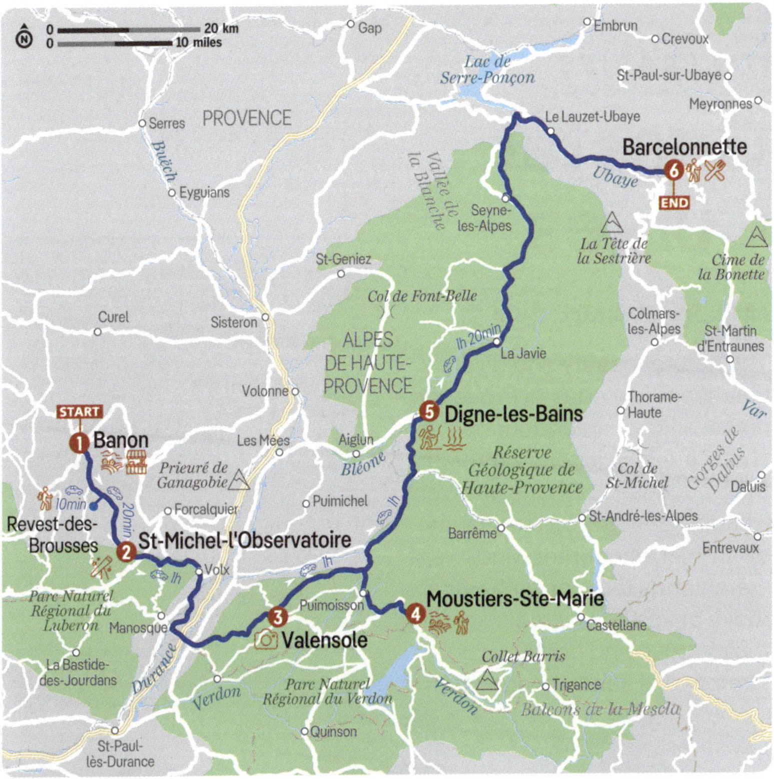

④ MOUSTIERS-STE-MARIE ⏱ 2 DAYS

Huddled beneath sheer cliffs, the stonewashed village of **Moustiers-Ste-Marie** (pictured; p262) oozes Provençal chic. Devote a day to mooching around cobbled streets and learning more about the local ceramic traditions. Set off early for an action-packed second day in the **Gorges du Verdon** (p264), whether hiking, cycling, rafting or canyoning.

⑤ DIGNE-LES-BAINS ⏱ 1 DAY

Choose your own adventure in **Digne-les-Bains** (p270): either relax in the famous healing baths that once cured Napoleonic soldiers or set off in search of the Dalle aux Ammonites, containing over 1500 fossilised ammonites (pictured). The capital of the Alpes-de-Haute-Provence was also the home of female traveller Alexandra David-Néel. Book a visit in advance to her villa-museum, Samten Dzong.

⑥ BARCELONNETTE ⏱ 1 DAY

Take in the dramatic alpine views as you cross over mountain passes en route to **Barcelonnette** (p277), the friendly village dotted with sumptuous Mexican villas – so named after emigrants to Mexico who returned in the late 19th century. Set off on a hike into remote pastures. Once the sun sets, tuck into one of the valley's famous three-cheese fondues.

FROM LEFT: TOMAS MAREK/SHUTTERSTOCK, BRUNO M PHOTOGRAPHIE/SHUTTERSTOCK, BTWIMAGES/SHUTTERSTOCK

ITINERARIES

Coastal Curves

Allow: 7 days **Distance**: 314km

The natural beauty and diverse landscapes of coastal Provence reveal all their splendour on this shore-hugging itinerary through the Bouches-du-Rhône and Var. Heading east from Stes-Maries-de-la-Mer, encounter windswept marshlands teeming with wildlife, rocky coves, towns rediscovering their groove and endless stretches of sandy beaches.

❶ STES-MARIES-DE-LA-MER ⏱ 2 DAYS

Begin in **Stes-Maries-de-la-Mer** (p198), a seaside town of wide beaches, pretty shops and Roma pilgrimages. Hire a bike to pedal deep into the haunting landscapes of the Camargue wetlands, with pink flamingos and cowboys for company. Track birds of prey at the Parc Ornithologique du Pont de Gau nature reserve.

 Detour: Break for a lunch with a side serving of Roman history when you pass through Arles. 🚗 5 hours

❷ CARRY-LE-ROUET ⏱ 1 DAY

Next stop is the Côte Bleue (Blue Coast), a pine-scented coastal stretch of limestone coves, walking trails and long-horned goats west of Marseille. Base yourself in **Carry-Le-Rouet** (p177), a quiet fishing port that's now a popular holiday resort and the spot to feast on hand-plucked *oursins* (sea urchins), particularly during February's beloved Oursinades celebrations. Cool off in the Parc Marin Côte Bleue, a designated marine park.

❸ CASSIS ⏱ 1 DAY

Bypass busy Marseille for laid-back **Cassis** (p173), a chic fishing village and the gateway to the majestic Parc National des Calanques. Lace up your hiking boots (and pack your swimsuit) to tackle the trail to Calanque d'En-Vau and back. Reward your efforts with a glass of AOC Cassis, Provence's first wine appellation, on a terrace overlooking the photogenic waterfront.

④ HYÈRES ⏱ 1 DAY

Visitors too often drive straight through Hyères on their way to the Îles de Porquerolles – it's their loss. Today, the hip Villa Noailles modern art gallery and a cluster of cool dining options are bringing this resort town back to life. Don't miss the medieval *vieille ville* high above the modern centre.

🚢 *Detour: Ditch the car for the Île de Porquerolles (p140), a short ferry ride from Hyères.*
⛴ *1 day*

⑤ GRIMAUD ⏱ 1 DAY

Seven kilometres separate **Grimaud** (p128) from Port Grimaud and a full day allows you to see both. Quilted in bright bougainvillea (pictured), medieval Grimaud is perched high above the Golfe de St-Tropez; the modern pleasure port dates from the 1960s and is a pretty place to spend a few hours mooching around its canals and bridges.

🚢 *Detour: Hop on a Bateaux Verts for a day trip to St-Tropez.*
⏱ *1 day*

⑥ ST-RAPHAËL ⏱ 1 DAY

Savour this last length of road (in winter, a stretch of the scented Route du Mimosa) as it clings to the coast through lovely Ste-Maxime, energetic watersports hub St-Aygulf, and Fréjus with its impressive Roman ruins. Where Fréjus ends, **St-Raphaël** (p135) begins. Lounge on the lively town's buttercream beach and decide whether to push on to Cannes along the show-stopping Corniche d'Or.

Villefranche-sur-Mer (p73)

ITINERARIES

Côte d'Azur Classics

Allow: 4 days **Distance**: 97km

Tick off the classics as you journey from one end of the Côte d'Azur to the other, starting at cinematic Cannes. This itinerary arcs inland to pause at arty hilltop villages surrounded by fragranced gardens, before edging back to the coast and Menton on the Italian border.

❶ CANNES ½ DAY

Spend the morning soaking up the main sights in glitzy **Cannes** (p86): walk along the palm-lined Croisette beachfront past the superyachts moored in the Vieux Port and stop for a snack at the covered Marché Forville. Push on towards Le Suquet, Cannes' oldest neighbourhood, brimming with colourful houses.

↪ *Detour: Escape the bustle on the tranquil Îles de Lérins.*
⏱ *1 day*

❷ MOUGINS ½ DAY

Polished stones and cascading flowers make **Vieux Mougins** (p97) an artist's dream; it's on a vast estate not far from the hilltop village where Picasso spent the last 12 years of his life. You can peek into the estate from the cypress-flanked Chapelle de Notre-Dame de Vie next door. Dine on gastronomic fare on an al-fresco terrace in the heart of the old village.

❸ GRASSE 1 DAY

Wrap yourself in the world of fragrance in **Grasse** (p99), a town synonymous with perfume, stretched across the hillside high above Cannes. Tour grand perfumeries where you can try your hand at making your own scent, linger in interactive museums inside historic houses and set foot in enchanting gardens where rose, jasmine, violet, iris and other aromatic flowers grow.

④ VILLEFRANCHE-SUR-MER ⏱ 1 DAY

Drop back down to the coast in **Villefranche-sur-Mer** (p73), a fishing village next to Nice that has graced the covers of endless travel magazines. Practise the art of being a *flâneur*, or leisurely stroller, along attractive alleyways that lead down to a row of harbourfront restaurants.

↪ *Detour: Visit the smallest cathedral in France in Vence.*
🚗 *3 hours.*

⑤ ÈZE ⏱ ½ DAY

On a coastline scattered with captivating jewels, eagle's nest **Èze** (p74) can claim to be the most dazzling of them all. Follow the winding lanes towards the summit where a tranquil cactus garden sprouts in the ruins of the old château. Be sure to have plenty of battery left in your phone or camera – from this height, the views across the Mediterranean Sea are out of this world.

⑥ MENTON ⏱ ½ DAY

Menton (p77) defies the stereotype of unappealing border towns; just footsteps from Italy, the pastel-painted old town rising up from the Mediterranean Sea is a setting that has energised artists, writers and culinary stars like celebrated Argentinian chef Mauro Colagreco. Book a table at one of his three local restaurants or taste juicy local lemons on sunny terraced fruit groves.

FROM LEFT: ARNDALE/SHUTTERSTOCK, TUUL & BRUNO MORANDI/GETTY IMAGES, EQROY/SHUTTERSTOCK

TUUL & BRUNO MORANDI/GETTY IMAGES

Toulon (p143)

ITINERARIES

Provence by Train

Allow: 6 days **Distance**: 260km

No car? No problem. This slow-travel itinerary propels you from Aix-en-Provence to Nice via charming coastal spots on the region's excellent Zou! rail network. Each segment is a direct route, so doesn't involve any complicated changes. Sit back, relax and enjoy the view.

① AIX-EN-PROVENCE ⏱ 1 DAY

Aix-en-Provence (p178) is the university town that cool Parisians dream of moving to, with its leafy streets, cafe culture and high-end shopping. Get your bearings by using its numerous fountains as reference points on a walking tour, before hitting Atelier des Lauves, Paul Cézanne's studio for a culture fix. Tuesday, Thursday and Saturday are market mornings.

② MARSEILLE ⏱ 1 DAY

Football is the religion that unifies multicultural **Marseille** (p160), alongside specialities such as panisse and *pizza moitié-moitié*. Locals are also proud of the spectacular coastline and its dazzling network of *calanques* (coves). Save time to wander through Le Panier, the oldest neighbourhood in the city.

↳ *Detour*: Savour spectacular views on the Train de Côte Bleue.
🚆 *2 hours*

③ BANDOL ⏱ 1 DAY

The pretty coastal village of **Bandol** (p144) has beaches and restaurants but is best known for being Provence's great red wine terroir. The appellation's vineyards dot the countryside, but on foot, the Oenothèque de Bandol in the centre is a great start. If grapes aren't your thing, there's an excellent 12km coastal trail that leaves from its port. Plan four hours.

④ TOULON ⏱ 1 DAY

Toulon (p143), France's second-largest naval port, has a gritty charm. Push past the high-rise blocks on its harbour to access a perfumed produce market and some cool concept stores. A guided boat tour of the bay takes in plenty of military sights and WWII history.

🚗 *Detour: Connect with the pine-scented l'Île de Porquerolles from Toulon's port.*
⏱ *1 day.*

⑤ FRÉJUS ⏱ 1 DAY

Arriving into Gare St-Raphaël Valescure, walk 15 minutes along the beach to neighbouring **Fréjus** (p135). Here Roman history is on display with its amphitheatre and aqueduct. After, claim a spot on the sand. Sunny and laid-back, Fréjus might just be the perfect resort town.

🚗 *Detour: From St-Raphaël just next door, catch a ferry across the bay to St-Tropez.*
⏱ *1 day.*

⑥ NICE ⏱ 1 DAY

The end of the line, this time, is **Nice** (p58). No city in the region has undergone such a transformation over the last decade or so. Belle Époque facades have a fresh lick of paint and whole city blocks of concrete are coming down to make place for urban parkland.

🚗 *Detour: Hop aboard the Train des Pignes for a journey into the Nice hinterland.*
⏱ *1 day.*

FROM LEFT: FREDP/SHUTTERSTOCK, ADRIEN LE TOUX/GETTY IMAGES, KIRK FISHER/GETTY IMAGES

WHEN TO GO

Most visitors come between May and August, but for many others, the charm lies in sunny winters and warm spring and autumn weather.

Winter – today's low season – was once the high season, particularly in the Var and on the Côte d'Azur, when everyone from aristocrats to artists flocked here for their share of New Year sun. The winter months still pack a punch, from the ski slopes of the Alpes-de-Haute-Provence to the coastal Route du Mimosa, which explodes with golden blooms come January. Visit in spring or autumn to breathe in fresh air on mountain hikes and cycling trails, or to move freely through galleries and museums. It can feel like a switch has been flicked around Easter, as sleepy villages wake up from their off-season slumber with the first of the new season's tourists. Expect a party mood during the sweltering summer months, as visitors from around the world crowd out beaches and the narrow streets of the region's perched villages.

Accommodation Lowdown

As a general rule, accommodation prices are lowest in November and January. Expect a spike around Christmas and New Year, as well as during February festivals. July and August command top dollar – as do marquee events such as the Cannes Film Festival (May) and the Monaco Grand Prix (June).

I LIVE HERE

EXPLORE THE GORGE

The locals of Verdon know the Gorges du Verdon like the backs of their hands.
@lesfillesduverdon

The Verdon is hugely popular in the middle of summer, but those who live here know that every season is magic. Our favourite is spring, the moment when nature awakens. This is the best time for running, walking or cycling from site to site, far from the rest of the world. Our absolute favourite thing? A traditional game of *jeu de paume* (court tennis) in Artignosc.

Racing yachts, Les Voiles de St-Tropez (p128)

LE MISTRAL

Legends swirl around the mistral, France's famous wind. This cold, sustained wind gusts for days on end through the Rhône Valley, into Provence and out to the Mediterranean Sea. It can occur throughout the year, but it's most common in winter and early spring.

Weather through the Year: Nice

JANUARY	FEBRUARY	MARCH	APRIL	MAY	JUNE
Avg. daytime max: **13.1°C** (74°F)	Avg. daytime max: **13.6°C** (73°F)	Avg. daytime max: **15.4°C** (60°F)	Avg. daytime max: **17.3°C** (63°F)	Avg. daytime max: **21.2°C** (70°F)	Avg. daytime max: **24.8°C** (76°F)
Days of rainfall: 5	Days of rainfall: 4	Days of rainfall: 4	Days of rainfall: 4	Days of rainfall: 5	Days of rainfall: 4

SNOW FLURRIES

Snow flurries are a rare sight on the coast, but the first dusting of snow blankets the ski resorts of the Côte d'Azur and Alpes-de-Haute-Provence in early December. Snow cover is at its most abundant in January; by March, much has melted away.

Plan in Advance Festivals & Events

Monaco goes motorsport crazy when the F1 roadshow rolls into town. The legendary **Monaco Grand Prix** (p112) is now joined on the event calendar by the **Monaco ePrix** and, every second year, the **Grand Prix Historique de Monaco**. **May/June**

Classic and modern sailing yachts with a fiery competitive streak hoist their sails for over a week of racing – and the chance for serious bragging rights – during the **Voiles de St-Tropez** (p128) in the Golfe de St-Tropez. **September**

Avignon turns 'on' and 'off' as papal courtyards, gardens and chapels transmute into stages for the annual **Festival d'Avignon** (p213) performing arts fest. **July**

Film stars from around the world dress in their red-carpet best for film screenings and press calls during the **Festival de Cannes** (p86). The atmosphere is electric. **May**

Celebrate Culture & Tradition

Mandelieu-La Napoule goes mimosa mad when the soft golden pom-poms burst into bloom. The **Fête du Mimosa** (p94) is a five-day festival of flower parades, evening animations and fireworks. **February**

The Camargue breaks out in an explosion of guitars, dancers and mounted cowboys as itinerant communities of Romanies, Manouches, Tziganes and Gitans converge for the annual **Pèlerinage des Gitans** (p199). **May**

The impromptu street-corner acoustic gigs and bigger DJ parties of the **Fête de la Musique** mark midsummer across France; in Provence and the Côte d'Azur you can party till dawn in Nice and Marseille. **June**

The population of Barcelonnette celebrates its links with Mexico in costume and through colourful parades and street performances during the annual **Fête des Mortes** (p277) celebration. **November**

I LIVE HERE

SPRING AND AUTUMN ARE IDEAL

Jeany Cronk is a winemaker and cofounder of the Maison Mirabeau in Cotignac. @maisonmirabeau

The shoulder seasons, when it's sunny but less busy, are perfect for a visit. In early summer the vineyards are lush, the sea is warm enough for a swim and long lunches beckon. The light in September has a gorgeous intensity and everything is bathed in its soft rays. It's ideal for a tour along the Côte d'Azur.

Autumn sun in the Camargue (p192)

AUTUMN STORMS

October and November are the rainiest months in the region; the changing seasons can also bring heavy storms. In 2020, Storm Alex burst river banks and washed away homes (and lives) in the mountain communities of the Côte d'Azur. The scars are still visible.

JULY	AUGUST	SEPTEMBER	OCTOBER	NOVEMBER	DECEMBER
Avg. daytime max: **27.4°C** (81°F)	Avg. daytime max: **27.8°C** (82°F)	Avg. daytime max: **24.6°C** (76°F)	Avg. daytime max: **21.1°C** (74°F)	Avg. daytime max: **19.6°C** (70°F)	Avg. daytime max: **13.7°C** (57°F)
Days of rainfall: 2	Days of rainfall: 3	Days of rainfall: 5	Days of rainfall: 7	Days of rainfall: 6	Days of rainfall: 5

Côte d'Azur, Nice (p58)

GET PREPARED FOR PROVENCE & THE CÔTE D'AZUR

Clothes

Evening wear Pack a fancy frock and dress shirt for a big night out in Monaco, Cannes and St-Tropez, but the rest of Provence and the Côte d'Azur is refreshingly relaxed about dress code.

Layers Summer nights in coastal Provence are sultry, but sunny spring and autumn days can quickly turn cold after dusk, so keep a warm jacket handy. The villages of Alpes-de-Haute-Provence are always a few degrees cooler, so layer up, even in July and August.

Shoes Flip-flops are standard uniform for beach days, but if you're planning a mountain scramble or bike ride, sneakers or hiking shoes are a must. Nice's pebbly beaches are notoriously uncomfortable; shops facing the Promenade des Anglais sell plastic jelly shoes.

Hats In a region that's blessed with 300 days of sunshine, a hat is always recommended.

Manners

Covid-19 may have put a pause on **la bise** (the cheek-to-cheek air kiss), but the classic French custom is back. Just so there's no confusion, in Provence it's a peck on both cheeks.

Toast to new friendships by looking directly in the eyes of your companions as you clink glasses. **Santé!**

The **middle finger** is considered extremely offensive in France.

READ

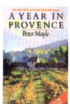 **A Year in Provence** (Peter Mayle; 1989) Mayle's humorous account of moving to Provence is the stuff dreams are made of.

 **The Man Who Planted Trees** (Jean Giono; 1953) Manosque-born Giono's tale is a powerful environmental allegory.

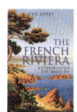 **The French Riviera** (Ted Jones; 2004) The Côte d'Azur through the eyes of the authors and artists who have made it home.

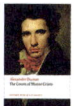 **The Count of Monte Cristo** (Alexandre Dumas; 1844) The Château d'If is Dantès' island prison in this epic tale of revenge.

Words

As this is the second-most-visited destination in the world's most-visited country, chances are that the local you're conversing with has better English than your French.

But that doesn't mean that your effort with a few basic words won't go unnoticed. The accent here can be vastly different to what you've been learning online. Near Marseille, see if you can make out the distinctive Provençal twang, or what sounds like an 'ang' at the end of words ending in -ain, such as *pain* (bread) and *demain* (tomorrow).

Here's a basic vocabulary to get you started:

Bonjour (bon-zhoor) means 'good day' and is how you say hello in France.

Bonsoir (bon-swah) means 'good evening' and is how you say hello after around 6pm.

Au revoir (o-rer-vwa) means 'goodbye', but is very formal. The increasingly universal *ciao* is more casual.

A bientôt (ah-byen-toe) means 'see you soon', even if soon is next week.

Ça va? (sa va) means 'How are you?' and is also repeated as a reply: 'I'm fine'.

S'il vous plaît (seel-voo-play) means 'please'.

Merci (mair-see) means 'thank you'.

De rien (der-ree-en) means 'you're welcome'.

Je m'appelle … (zher ma-pel) is how to say 'My name is …'.

Parlez-vous anglais? (par-lay voo ong-glay) is how to politely ask 'Do you speak English?'

 WATCH

To Catch a Thief (Pictured; Alfred Hitchcock; 1955) The film that brought Grace Kelly to Prince Rainier III's Monaco.

La Gloire de Mon Père (Yves Robert; 1990) Based on Marcel Pagnol's coming-of-age classic.

Brice de Nice (James Huth; 2005) A bleached-blond surfer longing for the perfect wave in Nice's flat sea; a cult comedy.

Marseille (Netflix; 2016) Gérard Depardieu takes the lead role in this French political drama.

Le Gendarme de St-Tropez (Jean Girault; 1964) Slapstick classic that pits policeman Louis de Funès against a nudist community.

LISTEN

Riviera Radio Tune to FM 106.5 between Menton and St-Tropez for the Côte d'Azur's only English-language radio station.

Mon Paradis (Christoph Maé; 2007) Carpentras-born Maé's guitar-driven French pop is the perfect summer soundtrack.

La Solitude (Léo Ferré; 1971) Melody and melancholy in equal measure from the celebrated Monegasque singer-songwriter-poet.

13'Organisé (Jul; 2020) An album that brings together 50 rappers from Marseille; the lead single *Bande Organisée* broke French streaming records.

Lavender field, Abbaye Notre-Dame de Sénanque (p240)

TRIP PLANNER

LAVENDER FIELDS OF PROVENCE

Violet brushstrokes of lavender, set against glorious sky blues: it's the image that has become synonymous with Provence. The vast plateau of Valensole might be the most famous of the region's lavender fields, but there are other places to visit to get your lavender fix.

Where to Go

VALENSOLE

At an altitude of 590m, this 800 sq km **plateau** (p266) between Manosque and Moustiers-Ste-Marie in the Alpes-de-Haute-Provence is considered lavender central in the region. **Lavandes Angelvin** and **La Ferme du Riou** (p267) are among the farms offering free visits and on-site boutiques. The area can be crammed with tour buses in season.

SAULT

Northwest of Valensole in the Vaucluse, **Sault** (p228) is snug at the foot of the legendary Mont Ventoux. Lavender and lavandin grow in this *terroir* to create a patchwork of purples and blues. Trails criss-cross the landscape and invite active discovery. Pedal through the landscape on a mountain bike or e-bike, or set off on foot along the Chemin des Lavandes, a 5.3km marked trail with information panels. Don't forget your hat, sunscreen and a bottle of water.

GORDES

If you've stuck a picture of a stone abbey surrounded by lavender on your travel mood board, chances are it's taken at the **Abbaye Notre-Dame de Sénanque** (p240) just outside Gordes, the beloved village in the Luberon. The monks who still inhabit this 12th-century Cistercian abbey produce and sell lavender honey, lavender sweets and essential oils,

📅 WHEN TO GO

June Consider mid-June as a safe starting date to see lavender in bloom, particularly around Apt and Gordes.

July Early July is the best time to visit Valensole. If you're in the region later in the month, make a beeline for Sault. At a higher altitude, the season runs later.

August You might just catch the crop in early August in Sault before harvest.

Rest of the Year Many farms are open year-round. Pick up scented souvenirs, such as essential oils, soaps and perfumes, from the source at on-site boutiques.

among other products. A nine-minute drive from Gordes, or just under an hour's walk.

PLATEAU DES CLAPARÈDES

Dodge the crowds on the Plateau de Valensole by heading towards the **Plateau de Claparèdes** (p247) instead. Near the Luberon villages of Saignon and Buoux, the field here is less manicured and more wild – and made more atmospheric by the presence of *bories*, traditional farmers' cabins made from stone built among the fields.

ALSO CONSIDER

Sentier des Plantes (p142) in Port-Cros or **Jardins du MIP** (Musée International de la Parfumerie; p101) in Mouans-Sartoux.

LAVENDER, RESPONSIBLY

Don't dismiss tousled crops, where grass and other plants push through the soil in between the lavender rows. Provence's lavender is a crop under threat and the practice of planting cover crops is one of the ways some growers are able to nurse the soil back to health as they adapt agroecology practices in response to climate and environmental challenges. Backing them are organisations like the Fonds de Dotation Sauvegarde du Patrimoine Lavandes en Provence (Fonds SPLP).

GOOD TO KNOW

Museums, Festivals & More

● **Musée de la Lavande Luberon**, Cabrières-d'Avignon, a conservatory of Provence lavender, organises visits and hosts workshops.

● **MEA Provence**, Valensole, is a producer with a 2-hectare park where educational display panels explain the essentials of production.

● The **Corso de la Lavande** at Digne-les-Bains in early August can attract up to 15,000 people a day over four days.

● **Routes de la Lavande** maps out 1500km of fragranced roads to plan your perfect itinerary. See *routes-lavande.com*.

Lavender vs Lavandin

● Real lavender grows at altitude, is slightly greyer and a key ingredient in perfume.

● Lavandin is a long-stemmed hybrid used to scent household products.

Day Tours

● Not close by? No worries. A whole industry has cropped up offering half-day and full-day tours from Aix-en-Provence, Marseille, Cannes, Antibes and Nice.

Best Practice

● Do: use more than one of your senses – it's not just a scene to capture on your iPhone. Listen to the hum of bees and sound of birdsong, signs of a healthy ecosystem. Breathe in the herbal fragrance of the crop in bloom.

● Don't touch – the one sense to hold back on.

● Remember, these crops are more than a photo shoot, these are people's livelihood. Be careful not to tread on plants and definitely don't pick any flowers.

Lavender, Plateau de Valensole (p266)

Ratatouille

THE FOOD SCENE

Colourful homespun ingredients rich in flavour: Provençal cuisine brings a taste of sunshine to every bite.

The cuisine of Provence reflects its snug geographic location at the intersection of two great food cultures. The ingredients that spring to mind when you think about northern French food, such as lashings of butter or thick cream, are notably absent; in their place are the olive oils and wild herbs more associated with Italy. Focaccia and chickpea-based street-food snacks also share more similarities with their neighbour. No great surprise, when you consider how fluid the modern-day borderlines have been.

Flavour-rich seasonal produce – peppers, courgettes, leafy greens and aubergines – that can thrive in dry Mediterranean soils form the base for many regional specialities, served alongside small fish caught from the shore, or, more infrequently, meat. Slow-cooked stews and soups that soften cheaper cuts of meat or bony fish have become culinary classics; something you'll agree with after your first bowl of bouillabaisse in Marseille.

In essence, this is simple, fresh, local cuisine at its best. Today, that's to everyone's tastes.

The Home Pantry

Peek inside the cupboards of a Provençal kitchen and you'll find staples such as a bottle of olive oil, most likely pressed from local olive groves and picked up at the weekly

---

Best Provençal Dishes

AÏOLI
Garlicky mayonnaise that accompanies a variety of dishes.

ARTICHOKES À LA BARIGOULE
Artichoke stew that can be savoured as a main or a side.

DAUBE
A slow-cooked beef stew, often accompanied by polenta.

RAVIOLIS NIÇOIS
Fresh pasta stuffed with *daube* and Swiss chard.

produce markets. Alongside it, other essential ingredients include coarse salt from the Camargue, to use in cooking and to sprinkle over summer tomatoes cut into wedges. Somewhere on the shelves, you'll spot a jar or two of tapenade, a spread made of finely chopped olives, with other variations including chickpeas and anchovies. In the fridge, sheets of fresh *raviolis niçois* (beef filling) are on hand for quick and tasty lunches, while a pretty ceramic fruit bowl brims with garden lemons.

Vegetarians, Vegans & Gluten-Free Diets

Made from little more than chickpea flour, water, olive oil and salt, Provence's two quintessential street snacks, *socca* and panisse, are suitable for vegetarian, vegan *and* gluten-free diets. But a lack of ingredients doesn't equate to a lack of flavour – something you'll realise the first time you bite into either, whether it's a thin and crispy slice of *socca* or a chip-like portion of panisse. The chickpea has taken to the coastal soil, and this cheap but nutritious legume features heavily in salads and soups – it's even pureed into spreads.

In fact many of Nice's traditional dishes are suitable for vegetarian diets. Another beloved local dish, ratatouille, is a simmering delight and bursts with the flavours of the summer harvest: red and yellow peppers, courgettes, aubergines, onions, tomatoes, garlic and basil, seasoned with lashings

FOOD & WINE FESTIVALS

Fête du Citron (p78) Menton celebrates its juicy golden lemons during this February carnival celebration, complete with fabulous floats made out of citrus (pictured).

Oursinade (p177) Feast on fresh sea urchins by the sea on the first three Sundays in February at Carry-le-Rouet on Marseille's Côte Bleue.

Fête des Vendanges (p128) Toast to the new vintage of Provence rosé at Ste-Maxime's grape harvest festival held the first weekend of September.

Fête du Fromage (p272) Every May, the lavender-fringed village of Banon throws a huge party in honour of its eponymous goat's cheese wrapped in a chestnut leaf.

Fête de la Châtaigne (p130) Aromas of roasting chestnuts fill the air and sweet chestnut liqueur fills glasses in Provence's chestnut capital, Collobrières, on the last three Sundays in October.

Bouillabaisse **(fish stew)**

BOUILLABAISSE
Rust-coloured fish stew; *the* emblematic dish of Marseille.

SOUPE AU PISTOU
Rustic legume- and vegetable-packed soup.

LES PETITS FARCIS NIÇOIS
Colourful market vegetables stuffed with mince and herbs.

RATATOUILLE
Slow-cooked veggie classic, brimming with seasonal produce.

Pissaladière (caramelised onions and anchovies on bread)

of salt, pepper and olive oil. *Pissaladière*, or slow-cooked caramelised onions served on a base of focaccia-like bread, is another street-food staple to look out for. The classic take is for the onion topping to be layered with a slice of anchovy, but nowadays the anchovy is completely optional and most stalls will create two separate versions.

Meat & Cheese

Provence's culinary traditions are notably free of two mainstays in French cuisine: beef and cow's milk cheeses. That's because this is a region where sheep and goats are the principal livestock, reared in alpine pastures.

Lamb from Sisteron in the Alpes-de-Haute-Provence is a quality marker around the country, especially at Easter, while in the Vallée de la Roya, the Brigasque is a milk-producing breed of sheep valued for its dairy products. The most famous cheese of the region hails from the small village of Banon in the Alpes-de-Haute-Provence. Known by the same name, this creamy goat cheese comes wrapped in chestnut leaves and has been made since the Middle Ages.

Truffles

A whopping 70% of all France's *Tuber melanosporum* (black truffles) are grown in the rich soils of the Vaucluse. Carpentras is considered the capital of truffles and its Friday morning truffle market between November and March attracts chefs and wholesale dealers out to secure the best finds of the season.

Aups in the Var is another truffle hotspot – Thursday is the designated market day for truffles in winter. Plenty of fine-dining tables in the region serve truffles on the menu; none do them better than **Chez Bruno** (p149) in Lorgues. The milder, nuttier flavoured summer truffle is in season from May to September.

Summer Guinguettes

In the 17th century, *guinguettes* (pronounced 'gang-get') emerged in Paris as cheap and cheerful neighbourhood taverns or bars.

Over the last few years, the concept has enjoyed a rebirth as these wonderfully atmospheric and cheap pop-up al-fresco drinking spots took off around the country, usually serving their first drink in May, with last orders normally poured around September.

Expect food and merriment too. Look out for them in rural settings in particular. Favourites in the region include **La Guinguette de la Colline** (p221) above the hills in Orange and in the eco-village of **Montrieux-le-Vieux** (p152).

Local Specialities

Street Food & Snacks
Pissaladière Pizza topped with caramelised onions, olives and anchovies; served by the slice.
Socca Thin chickpea-flour pancake baked in wood-fired ovens across Nice.
Panisse Chickpea-flour fritters: crispy on the outside, creamy on the inside.
Pizza moitié-moitié Half anchovies, half emmental cheese – a must in Marseille.
Barbajuan Bite-sized fried ravioli; Monaco's national dish.

Sweet Treats
Tarte Tropézienne A brioche filled with two types of cream and dusted with pearl sugar.
Tourte aux blettes sucrée Savoury Swiss chard in a sweet tart.
Nougat Chewy honey-and-almond confection from Sault.
Tarte des Alpes Looks like a lattice-crust pie filled with jam.
Calissons d'Aix Diamond-shaped almond-and-fruit sweets from Aix-en-Provence.

Dare to Try
Saucisson de taureau Bull sausage is a trademark of the Camargue.

Calissons d'Aix

Pieds paquets Slow-cooked lamb trotters and tripe stew.
Merda de can Get past the name (dog poo) and you've got a plate of fresh green gnocchi in Nice.

Local Liqueurs
Génépi Fiery herbal liqueur that warms up mountain communities.
L'Orangeraie Zesty liqueur made from Monaco's very own bitter orange trees.
Pastis The aniseed drink Provence has exported to the world.
Liqueur de Lavande Provence's emblematic lavender crop in a bottle.

MEALS OF A LIFETIME

Auberge La Fenière (p252) Nadia Sammut's wonderfully rustic Luberon table is the world's first gluten-free restaurant to receive a Michelin star.

Le Mirazur (p78) Mauro Colagreco's three-Michelin-star address is just metres from the Italian border in Menton. Menus change according to the cycle of the moon.

La Chassagnette (p191) Michelin-star dining in the middle of the Camargue; the farm-to-table setting is Provençal perfection.

La Petite Plage (p123) Oysters, caviar and Champagne cocktails on the yacht-lined harbour. When in St-Tropez...

Villa Morelia (p278) A grand dining room in the heart of the Ubaye Valley serving up refined, market-fresh cuisine.

BELOW, FROM LEFT: DANITA DELIMONT/SHUTTERSTOCK, BARMALINI/SHUTTERSTOCK, MARCO CURABA/SHUTTERSTOCK, SLOWMOTIONGLI/SHUTTERSTOCK

THE YEAR IN FOOD

SPRING
Greens from Provence include asparagus, beans and Swiss chard. Look for the telltale purple tips on *violet de Provence* artichokes (pictured), considered the cream of the crop. Families feast on Sisteron lamb at Easter.

SUMMER
Markets explode with the reds, yellows and oranges of freshly picked strawberries, tasty cantaloupes and juicy tomatoes of all shapes and sizes. Peppers, courgettes and aubergines abound for classic ratatouille.

AUTUMN
Chestnuts crackle on open fires. Pumpkins and squashes of all colours sprout; scoop out the seeds and stuff them with *cèpes* (porcini mushrooms) from the Luberon. Olive trees are shaken and pressed for a new vintage.

WINTER
Foodies hunt out truffles (pictured) in the Luberon, sea urchins in Marseille, and Nice and Menton's beloved lemons. The rich aroma of *daube (stew)* fills the air. Christmas is celebrated with oysters, foie gras and a total of some 13 desserts.

Hiking, Île de Porquerolles (p140)

THE OUTDOORS

Hike majestic mountains, cycle lavender-scented plains and enjoy the glistening sea: in Provence and the Côte d'Azur, the good life is outdoors.

Where the Alps tumble into the Mediterranean Sea, outdoor enthusiasts are spoilt for choice no matter the experience level. Add in a mild off-season climate and you've got hiking and cycling trails to set off on, no matter the month. In winter, the low-key ski resorts of the Alpes-de-Haute-Provence come alive with the first snowfall. Spring signals the start of a new watersports season, from high-octane rafting and canyoning in the Gorges du Verdon to leisurely swimming and sailing along the Côte d'Azur.

Cycling

Home to bucket-list climbs such as the Col de la Madone de Gorbio, Col de la Bonette and, of course, the holy grail, Mont Ventoux, Provence is quite literally the training ground for the world's best road cyclists. You don't have to be an Olympic athlete to enjoy the view from the saddle, however: the quieter back roads of the Luberon and Provence Verte snake through fragranced fields and postcard-pretty villages, although you're never too far from the next incline. The TransVerdon is one of France's classic mountain-bike trails. In summer, the ski runs behind Nice and in the Alpes-de-Haute-Provence turn into shaded off-road routes.

Road bikes *(vélo de route)*, mountain bikes *(VTT, vélo tout-terrain)* and e-bikes are available to hire across the region. Alongside local tourist offices for maps and guides, bike cafes *(cafés vélo)* are emerging as hubs

---

Thrills & Spills

ROCK CLIMBING
The limestone cliffs of **Buoux** (p244) rise high above the Luberon and are a legendary destination for climbers.

CANYONING
Jump, slide and rappel down ravines and waterfalls in the **Gorges du Verdon** (p264) and the **Gorges du Loup** (p101).

KITESURFING
For kitesurfers, the wild landscape of the lagoon beach, **Plage de l'Almanarre** (p139), on the presqu'île de Giens is one of pure beauty.

FAMILY ADVENTURES

Aspiring cowboys and cowgirls saddle up for horse-riding adventures with **Domaine de la Palissade** (p193) through the flamingo-speckled wetlands and beaches of the Camargue.

Swim with shoals of dreamfish and skim over lazy sea cucumbers during summer's guided snorkel tours at **Domaine du Rayol** (p135).

Step into a real-life wildlife documentary at the **Parc Ornithologique du Pont de Gau** (p200) nature reserve in the Camargue.

Spot cute marmots and striking chamois as you hike into the **Parc National du Mercatour** (p81) from St-Martin-Vésubie.

Paddle a canoe downriver through tunnels of trees and over gentle rapids to **L'Isle-sur-la-Sorgue** (p229).

Snowshoe through enchanting snow-dusted forests in **Le Sauze** (p278) in the Ubaye Valley.

---

to connect with fellow cyclists, learn about local routes, sign up for group hikes and sip a seriously good coffee.

Hiking

Provence and the Côte d'Azur's postcard landscape of high hills, dizzying gorges and rocky coastlines is a delight to navigate on foot, from sweeping mountain treks across long-distance GR *(Grande Randonnée)* trails to short but steep coastal scrambles and flat island paths that weave through fragrant pine forests. Even in the bigger cities, you're never too far from a *sentier balisé* (marked path); the local tourist office hands out maps and guides, and will also point out accessible hiking trails.

Being prepared is essential; hiking shoes, water, hat and sunscreen are a must. A phone signal isn't guaranteed. The most popular trails are hot and busy in summer – high wildfire risks shutter some forested paths as well. Spring and autumn days enjoy ideal temperatures and conditions.

Skiing

In the Alpes-de-Haute-Provence, the Ubaye Valley is a sleeper of a ski hotspot where those in the know find snow even during dry winters. With 180km of runs, Pra Loup (1600m) is the largest resort in the valley and also has snowshoeing and cross-country skiing trails, as well as modern facilities. The station connects with Foux d'Allos (1800m).

The Côte d'Azur is one of the rare places where you can swim in the morning and be on the slopes by lunch, with the closest resorts just 1½ hours from Nice. From the summit of Isola 2000 (2610m), you can see the Mediterranean Sea. As unlikely as it might sound, Provence might become your next favourite winter sports destination.

BEST SPOTS
For the best outdoor spots and routes, see the map on p48.

Rafting, Gorges du Verdon (p264)

RAFTING
The whitewater rapids of the **Gorges du Verdon** (p264) and the **Ubaye** (p277) promise wonderful thrills and spills.

DIVING
Wreck diving doesn't come much better than the *Grec* and *Donator* sites off the **Île de Porquerolles** (p140).

SWIMMING
Monaco's **Solarium** (p111) is made of concrete, but this swimming and sunning spot on the harbour is totally unique.

KAYAK
Why catch the ferry from Cannes to the **Îles de Lérins** (p88), the duo of pine-shaded islands, when you can get there on a kayak?

Walking/Hiking
1. Calanque d'En-Vau (p175)
2. Gorges du Verdon (p264)
3. Moustiers-Ste-Marie (p262)
4. Réserve Naturelle de la Plaine des Maures (p131)
5. Île de Porquerolles (p140)
6. Sentier Nietzsche (p76)
7. Gordes (p240)

Cycling
1. Stes-Maries-de-la-Mer (p199)
2. Gorges du Verdon (p264)
3. Ubaye Valley (p276)
4. Île de Porquerolles (p140)
5. Haut-Var (p145)
6. Mont Ventoux (p225)
7. Coustellet (p242)

ACTION AREAS

Where to find Provence & the Côte d'Azur's best outdoor activities.

PROVENCE & CÔTE D'AZUR

THE GUIDE

Alpes-de-Haute-Provence
p259

The Vaucluse
& Luberon
p204

Côte d'Azur
& Monaco
p53

Bouches-du-Rhône
p155

The Var
p116

Basilique Notre-Dame de la Garde (p171), Marseille
THEO GIACOMETTI/LONELY PLANET

Above: Monaco (p104) from Roquebrune; Right: Alpine chamois, Parc National du Mercantour (p81)

Researched by
Chrissie McClatchie

Côte d'Azur & Monaco

WHERE THE MOUNTAINS MEET THE MEDITERRANEAN

A world-famous coastline, entrancing hilltop villages and an emerging hinterland scene: the Côte d'Azur and Monaco are eternally chic, but there are new surprises waiting.

What's in a name? In 1887, the French writer Stéphen Liégeard set off on a journey across France's eastern Mediterranean coastline, chronicling his experiences in the book *La Côte d'Azur*. Until just a few decades before, this corner of the country had acted as little more than a stopover point for intrepid travellers en route to Italy, but that was changing as a new train line unfurled from the north, bringing with it foreigners waving doctors' prescriptions for a healthy dose of the region's winter sun.

Nobility, artists and royalty soon followed, ready to flaunt their best dress on waterfront promenades and in the black-tie casinos. Liégeard's 'Azure Coast' cast a wide net from Marseille to Genoa, but the name he coined stuck.

There's still no hard-and-fast starting and finishing point – you'll see the Côte d'Azur defined as stretching all the way to St-Tropez or Hyères in the Var – but what's not debated is that the sweep from Cannes to Menton, or the boundary of the Alpes-Maritimes region, as it is known administratively, is France's glittering blue coast.

Princely Monaco lies in its embrace. The Côte d'Azur maintains its glorious allure with its intoxicating mix of sun, sea, culture, food and wine, and the green mountain interior beckoning today's batch of adventure travellers.

THE MAIN AREAS

NICE
Beaches, architecture and a blossoming foodie scene. **p58**

CANNES
Flashy festivals and refreshingly quiet spaces. **p86**

MONACO
Small in size, big in glamour. **p104**

Find Your Way

Tucked into the southeastern nook of France, the lively resort towns along the coast quickly give way to perched inland villages. Behind them, vast national parks stretch across mountain landscapes.

TRAIN
The scenic TER Sud Provence Alpes-Côte-d'Azur train line connects the region's main seafront destinations between Cannes and Menton (including Monaco) and beats taking the car every time. A train service also links Grasse to the coast.

CAR
Driving is a hassle in Nice, Cannes and Monaco, and parking can be pricey, but your own transport is the best way to see the Côte d'Azur that exists beyond these busy destinations.

Monaco, p104
With a princely palace and glitter-ball casino framing the yacht-lined harbour, Monaco is a postage-sized principality that packs a punch.

Nice, p58
The capital of the Côte d'Azur, Nice's richly coloured Belle Époque streetscapes are recognised by UNESCO, while foodies are waking up to the city's cuisine.

BUS
Cheap and comprehensive, the Zou! intercity bus network links Cannes and Nice with smaller towns both along the coast and further inland, although expect longer travel times than the train when faced with a choice between the two.

Cannes, p86
A busy calendar of global events gives Cannes a year-round buzz, although neighbourhoods like Le Suquet and the Marché Forville add a low-key flavour.

Plan Your Time

Get your share of both beach and culture along the coast and make easy day trips to pretty perched villages. Cool down in the mountain landscapes of the Côte d'Azur backcountry with hiking and wildlife spotting.

Villefranche-sur-Mer (p73)

Weekend Break

● Base yourself in **Nice** (p58) and get a taste for the city over a long brunch at **Marinette** (p68) before setting off on a walking tour of **Vieux Nice** (p71).

● Hop on the bus for the short ride around the headland to the charming fishing village of **Villefranche-sur-Mer** (p73) – or walk the 3km **Sentier du Littoral** (p75) coastal trail starting at Port Lympia – and wander the alleyways that lead down to a shimmering bay.

● Return to Nice for a sunset **apéro** (p70) followed by dinner at one of the **Vieux Nice's cosy bistros** (p62) and perhaps some late night **live music** (p72).

● The next day, after a **morning cycle along the Promenade** (p59), catch the train to the world's second-smallest country, **Monaco** (p104).

SEASONAL HIGHLIGHTS

Winters are sunny and mild and the heat of summer is punctuated by sea breezes. Spring sees the region's gardens at their best, while autumn's cooler days are bliss.

JANUARY
The **Route du Mimosa** (p134) bursts into bloom around Mandelieu-La Napoule and along the Corniche d'Or into the Var. Ski season is in swing at a swag of family-friendly resorts just an hour from Nice.

FEBRUARY
A frenzy of festivals including the **Carnaval de Nice** (p68), **Fête du Citron** (p77) in Menton and the **Fête du Mimosa** (p94) in Mandelieu-La Napoule light up the last days of winter.

MAY
May is a mammoth month of public holidays. The region rolls out the red carpet for the **Cannes Film Festival** (p86), while Grasse's famous rose gardens are awash with pastel-pink flowers ready to be picked for the world's perfume houses.

Five Days to Travel Around

- Still based in Nice for the first few days, you can learn more about its newly minted UNESCO status, visit **a bar in a church** (p65) and **marvel at masterful art** (p62).

- Day trips allow you to extend your reach towards lemon-scented **Menton** (p77) on the Italian border, the artists' village of **St-Paul de Vence** (p78), and even into the alpine hinterland at **St-Martin-Vésubie** (p81).

- Swap Nice for artsy **Antibes** (p94) as a base for the last two days of your stay. Understand why Picasso chose to make this part of the world home in **Vallauris** (p97) and **Mougins** (p97).

- Don't leave without setting foot on one of the **Îles de Lérins** (p88), the pine-scented islands off the coast of Cannes.

Longer Than a Week

- After Nice and Antibes, add a few nights in **Cannes** (p86), where the handprints of Hollywood stars are permanently cast outside the famous **Palais des Festivals et des Congrès** (p86).

- Pick up a picnic at **Marché Forville** (p92) before the short ferry ride to **Île Ste-Marguerite** (p88), where the 'Man in the Iron Mask' was incarcerated.

- Take a day to drive the spellbinding coastal **Corniche d'Or** (p98), or see the craggy coast from the **water** (p133). Loop up towards perfumed **Grasse** (p99) to escape the crowds for a day or two.

- The **Gorges du Loup** (p101) is also on your doorstep. From there, you could push into the **Parc Naturel Régional des Préalpes d'Azur** (p103), retracing the famous **route** Napoléon took in 1815 (p100).

JUNE	JULY	SEPTEMBER	DECEMBER
In 2026 the **Monaco Formula One Grand Prix** (p104) officially moves to the first week in June. The summer solstice is celebrated in style: **La Fête de la Musique** is a France-wide affair on 21 June but particularly rocks in Nice.	Every weekend buzzes with outdoor events: fireworks, music, cinema. The region is packed to the rafters, especially around **Bastille Day** (14 July). Markets brim with juicy strawberries and tomatoes; pair with a Provence rosé for beach picnics.	The last days of summer are a dream for hiking the backcountry, particularly near St-Martin-Vésubie and deep into the **Vallée des Merveilles**. Boat shows mean accommodation fills up fast in Cannes and Monaco.	First flurries of snow and first mugs of mulled wine at **Christmas markets**, particularly in Nice, Antibes and Monaco. Shops shut early on 24 December, although it's back to business as usual from 26 December.

Nice

BEACHES | ART | FOOD

The capital of the Côte d'Azur, Nice has undergone a complete refresh in the last decade or so, with investments in a smart tram network, upgraded civic areas and new hotels – and the pace of change doesn't look like it's going to slow down anytime soon. Don't be surprised to find certain landmarks from past visits closed for renovation, or even torn down, as concrete makes way for greenery in France's fifth-largest city.

As the UNESCO Winter Resort Town of the Riviera, the city has a new purpose and swagger. Nice is no longer living off its reputation for beaches, palm trees and sunshine. An exciting food scene is simmering, bringing local produce and traditional cuisine to the fore, alongside cool wine bars and independent boutiques in trendy yet local neighbourhoods such as the Port and Libération. Visit today and you'll realise that Nice is finally growing into its nickname, Nissa la Bella.

Nice's Protected History
A UNESCO World Heritage Site

Nice's UNESCO heritage can be seen in around 800 buildings across the city and their art deco detailing and Belle Époque flourishes can be admired from the street. The excellent Explore Nice Côte d'Azur app *(explorenicecotedazur.com/en/discover-the-unesco-heritage-routes)* organises some of the most noteworthy sites into a series of self-guided neighbourhood walks, complete with a pop-up historical outline of each building listed. You can also deep dive into this protected heritage at the **Musée Massena** *(massena-nice.org; adult/child €10/free)* on the Promenade des Anglais. Much of the permanent collection is dedicated to the history of Nice; the 19th-century romantic landscapes of the city and its surrounds painted by the trio of Trachel brothers are particularly worthy of contemplation.

GETTING AROUND

Ditch the car on your visit to Nice; driving in the centre is a frustrating experience. Many of the main highlights can be navigated on foot – although Ligne d'Azur's tram line and extensive bus network are also reliable.

Tickets (€1.70 single fare) are paperless, so be prepared to fork out an extra €2 on your first trip for the city's transport card, La Carte, available at ticket machines and booths (Android users can download a card directly on the Ligne d'Azur app).

Also, note that, from the airport, the tram fare is €10 return. Near the airport, the Grand Arénas has emerged as the main transport hub, where most intercity bus lines begin. Gare de Nice St-Augustin-Aéroport is also on the site for trains to Cannes and Menton, and stations in between.

Musée Massena

Cycling the Prom
Take Nice's public e-bikes for a ride

The combo of Nice's **public e-bike fleet** and the dedicated, flat bike lane that extends the entire 6km length of the Promenade des Anglais (and then some) is one of the city's best pairings. The Prom is scattered with bike pick-up and drop-off points. Propelled by the battery and the fresh sea air, you'll reach Nice Côte d'Azur airport in less than 20 minutes (if starting out at the eastern end opposite the arcades of Vieux Nice), but you can easily stop along the way and lock your bike on the app until you're ready to get cycling again. If you're in the groove, push further west on the same path for pretty beachside towns St-Laurent du Var or Cagnes-sur-Mer. In fact, you can pedal all the way to Antibes – a total distance of 20km.

Nice's First Settlement
Ruins with a view

The Ancient Greeks didn't set up base on the **Colline du Château** for the sea views, but the site of Nice's original settlement offers up the best panorama of the city. The rocky outcrop that sits snugly between Vieux Nice and Port Lympia has witnessed every era of the city; during the Middle Ages, a fortified settlement was built here and, later, today's *vieille ville* (old town) grew at its base. Louis XIV ordered the destruction of the castle in the early 18th century, and

☑ TOP TIP

The tram from Nice Côte d'Azur Airport to the centre is a flat €10 return fare. If you're travelling light, consider walking the 6km along the Promenade des Anglais. The wide, beachfront pedestrian promenade is a delightful introduction to Nice's outdoor lifestyle. There's also a bike lane – pick up a shared e-bike at the airport.

Continues on p62

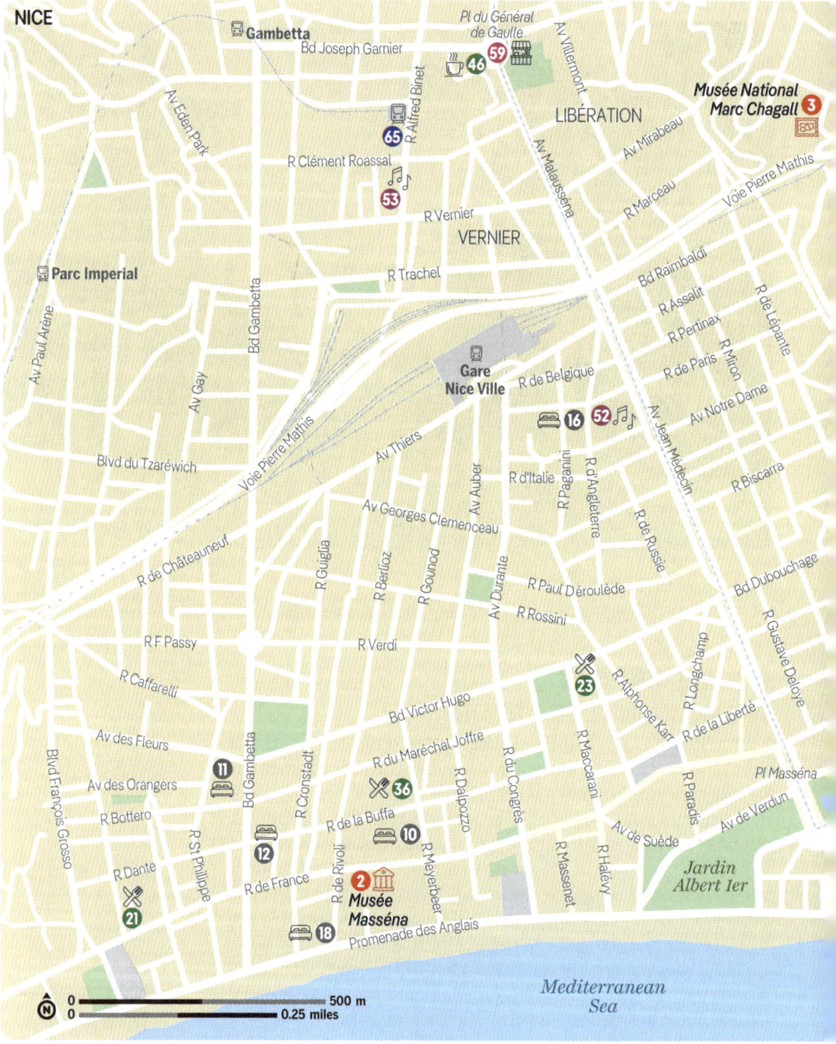

NICE

⭐ **HIGHLIGHTS**	7 Palais Lascaris
1 Colline du Château	8 Promenade du Paillon
2 Musée Masséna	● **ACTIVITIES**
3 Musée National Marc Chagall	9 Les Petits Farcis
	● **SLEEPING**
● **SIGHTS**	10 Hostel Meyerbeer Beach
4 La Tour Bellanda	11 Hôtel Amour
5 Musée d'Art Moderne et d'Art Contemporain	12 Hôtel Arome
6 Palais Caïs de Pierlas	13 Hôtel du Couvent
14 Hôtel du Pin	23 Chez Davia
15 Hôtel La Pérouse	24 Chez Palmyre
16 Hôtel Ozz	25 Chez Pipo
17 Hôtel Rossetti	26 Chez René Socca
18 Le Negresco	27 Chez Thérésa
● **EATING**	28 Comme un Dimanche
19 Acchiardo	29 Flaveur
20 Babel Babel	30 Jan
21 Boulangerie Roy Le Capitole	31 Kalös
22 Café Paulette	32 La Gratta
	33 La Merenda

34 Lavomatique	**41** Cave de la Tour
see **30** Le Bistrot de Jan	**42** Comptoir Central Électrique
35 Le Bistrot de Serruriers	**43** La Boulisterie Club
36 Le Canon	**44** La Civette du Cours
see **18** Le Chantecler	**45** La Part des Anges
37 Marinette	**46** L'Altra Casa
38 ONICE	**47** Le Bethel
39 Zielinska	**48** Le Café des Chineurs
	49 Rouge
🟢 **DRINKING & NIGHTLIFE**	**50** SuperBar
40 Cave Bianchi	

51 Wayne's Bar	**58** Maison Auer
	59 Marché de la Libération
🔴 **ENTERTAINMENT**	**60** Nicolas Alziari
52 La Cave Romagnan	**61** Pêche Locale
53 La Zommé	**62** Puces de Nice
54 Opéra de Nice	**63** Village Ségurane
55 Shapko	
	🔵 **TRANSPORT**
🟠 **SHOPPING**	**64** Colline du Château Lift
56 Cours Saleya flea market	**65** Gare de Nice-CF de Provence
57 La Boulisterie Store	

Monastère Notre Dame de Cimiez

WHEN WINTER WAS THE HIGH SEASON

Before the Côte d'Azur became the place to sun yourself in summer, this stretch of the Mediterranean coast was the winter destination *du jour* for royalty, politicians, aristocrats and artists from Britain, northern Europe and Russia, who flocked here for its mild climate and winter sun and to stroll in their glad rags along the newly paved Promenade des Anglais (English Promenade).

The most famous visitor was Britain's Queen Victoria; so beloved were her sojourns here that, on her deathbed in England, she apparently remarked, 'If only I was in Nice, I should recover'.

The architectural legacy from this period (1760-1940) saw Nice inscribed on the UNESCO World Heritage list in 2021 as the Winter Resort Town of the Riviera.

Continued from p59

it became a park at the end of the 19th century. The site reveals its secrets as you follow its shaded pathways towards a grassy plateau that is a favourite picnic spot for locals; think centuries-old stone walls covered by climbers, as well as the occasional excavation site. The views over the terracotta-red rooftops of the city are what steal the show, particularly from **La Tour Bellanda** viewpoint. Plenty of staircases sprout from the back alleys of Vieux Nice to the hilltop; there's also the free **Colline du Château Lift**, operating 10am to 5.25pm.

Chagall & Matisse in Nice
Two masters and their museums

It is a truth universally acknowledged that the light on the Côte d'Azur has an allure unlike anywhere else in the world. Countless artists have been drawn to the region in search of it: two in particular have left their mark (or, perhaps it's the other way around?): Marc Chagall and Henri Matisse. Dedicated museums to both artists occupy sprawling grounds in Cimiez, the leafy residential neighbourhood in the north of Nice, and can be visited on the same day. Start at the **Musée National Marc Chagall** (*musees-nationaux-alpesmaritimes*

EATING IN NICE: VIEUX NICE BISTROS TO BOOK AHEAD FOR

Acchiardo: Atmospheric, family-run favourite in the heart of the old town with local specialities like *merda de can* on the menu. *noon-2pm & 7-10pm Mon-Fri* €

La Merenda: Rustic dining room with only 24 seats and a blackboard of Niçois specialities. Book: lamerenda.net or @lamerendanice. *noon-1.45pm & 7-9pm Tue-Fri* €

Chez Palmyre: Oozes charm and tradition and its three-course lunch menu for €25 is incredible value. *noon-1.30pm & 7-9.30pm Mon, Tue, Thu, Fri* €

Le Bistrot de Serruriers: Hidden among the residential streets of the old town. The menu is small but packed full of flavour. *11am-9.30pm Wed-Sun, to 10pm Fri & Sat* €

fr/chagall; adult/child €10/free), where the most extensive public collection of the Belarusian artist's work hangs. The 12 monumental canvases depicting scenes from the Old Testament are spellbinding in colour and detail and will linger in your memory long after you've left. A further 20 minutes' walk (or Ligne d'Azur bus 5) and you'll arrive at the **Musée Matisse** *(musee-matisse-nice.org; adult/child €10/free)*. The array of paintings, sculptures, drawings and prints trace the artist's love affair with Nice. The setting, in a coral-red Genoese villa dating from the 17th century, is magic, with olive groves and ancient ruins. Matisse is buried in the **Monastère Notre Dame de Cimiez** at the eastern end of the parkland. The serene monastery gardens are worth a detour, too. Both museums are closed Tuesdays.

Coulée Vert
A green oasis cuts through the city

Like a lush green carpet that unfurls through the heart of Nice, the **Promenade du Paillon** is a playground-and-shade-blessed urban park that has emerged from the demolition of a bus station, car park and even the city's dated 1960s convention centre. A series of parks within a park make it an ideal pit stop for families looking to break up a busy day of sightseeing: parents can cool down under the cover of trees while their kids splash around under water jets in the mirror pool or scramble up imaginative wooden climbing structures and make new friends. While the first stretch from the Promenade des Anglais to MAMAC (the Musée d'Art Moderne et d'Art Contemporain, currently under renovation) has been a beloved part of the landscape for over a decade now, the second part, which extends further inland, is a work in progress and much of it still a jumble of concrete at the time of writing. Local officials are promising a 20-hectare urban forest with over 1500 trees. But it hasn't come cheap, reportedly costing the city €75 million.

Morning Markets
Antiques and fresh produce

Bright and bustling, Nice's morning markets are worth waking up early for. On Mondays, the **Cours Saleya flea market** takes over Vieux Nice's busy restaurant-lined thoroughfare, filling every corner with antique stands peddling vintage posters, tableware and other curios. Don't be afraid to bargain

LIME VS PONY

You'll notice two different brands of shared bikes being pedalled around: Lime *(li.me)* and Pony *(getapony.com)*. Both are unlocked and locked via their own apps, which also show the closest available bikes to you.

Both bikes come with a convenient saddle at the back, should you need to carry a passenger. Pay per ride: for e-bikes, the rate is set at €1 to unlock and between €0.23 and €0.26 per minute. Pony's option to rent a bike for four hours for €19.99 or 24 hours for €29.99 is a good choice.

Save for the colour, there's little discernible difference between either the quality of the bikes or their availability at designated pick-up and drop-off spots, so download one app and stick with it.

EATING IN NICE: BEST FOR A MICHELIN-SPLURGE

Jan: Jan Hendrik van der Westhuizen's menu blends methods learnt in his grandmother's kitchen in South Africa with local ingredients. *7-10pm Tue-Sat €€€*

Le Chantecler: Housed in a sumptuous Regency dining room inside the Hôtel Negresco; each delicate course is a story of local provenance. *7-10pm Wed-Sun €€€*

Onice: Florencia Montes and Lorenzo Ragni learnt from the master, Mauro Colagreco, at Le Mirazur in Menton. Menu based on daily catch and season. *7-8.30pm Wed-Sun €€€*

Flaveur: Nice's most celebrated address with two Michelin stars; expect foams, reductions and all the fine-dining flourishes. *noon-1.30pm & 7.30-9.15pm, Tue-Sat €€€*

Cours Saleya flea market (p63)

MAMAC ON TOUR

Nice's star art gallery, Musée d'Art Moderne et d'Art Contemporain (MAMAC), shuttered in early 2024 for renovations as part of the extension of the Promenade du Paillon. At the time of updating this guide, there was no official date for its re-opening.

The museum is particularly celebrated for its collection of works from the École de Nice (School of Nice), a movement most associated with avant-garde and experimental art and artists such as Yves Klein and Niki de Saint Phalle. During the closure, star pieces of the museum's collection are popping up in various places across the Côte d'Azur, as part of the MAMAC Hors Les Murs (MAMAC Outside the Walls) tour, including Palais Lascaris in Vieux Nice and Musée Matisse. Consult the website *(mamac-nice.org)* for up-to-date exhibition locations.

– strongly – if something takes your fancy. From Tuesday to Sunday, the *brocante* is swept away, replaced by baskets brimming with fresh fruit, veg and flowers. Do like the locals and shop according to the season, so sweet pears in autumn and juicy tomatoes in summer. These prices, however, are fixed. For the city's quintessential market experience, make a beeline for the **Marché de la Libération** in the Libération neighbourhood in the north of Nice. Long considered the city's best because it serves locals every day but Monday, no matter the season. All markets start around 7am and are packed away just before 1pm.

Antiques & Curios
Search for vintage treasures

Everything from old linens to perfume bottles and costume jewellery is on sale at the **Puces de Nice** (@lespucesdenice), a collection of old fishing shacks turned flea market stalls across from Port Lympia and open Tuesday to Saturday. This is the spot to pick up precious one-of-a-kind souvenirs that will fit snugly into your hand luggage. It's okay to haggle a little on the price, too. A similar collection of *brocante* (second-hand shops) cluster in the nearby antiques arcade, **Village Ségurane**, although the opening hours of individual shops can be unpredictable. This entire neighbourhood is known as the *quartier des antiquaires* (antiques quarter); it's a lovely

 EATING IN NICE: OUR PICKS

Lavomatique: Trendy bistro in Vieux Nice where shared plates are cooked in an open kitchen and washed down with natural wines. *hours vary* €€

Babel Babel: Cuisine from around the Mediterranean. Don't miss the panisse with homemade za'atar. *10am-midnight, Mon, Thu, Sun, to 2am Fri & Sat.* €€

Le Bistrot de Jan: More casual sibling to the Michelin-starred Jan next door. The decor is straight from a design magazine. *noon-3pm & 7-12.30am Tue-Sat, 11am-3pm Sun* €€

Le Canon: Unpretentious neighbourhood favourite with a hyper-local focus: each farmer is named on the menu. *noon-2pm Mon, Tue, Thu, Fri, 7.30-11.30pm Mon-Fri* €€

part of the city to indulge in some window shopping; the street-facing boutiques are pricey.

Nice's Last Fishers
The early bird catches the worm

Nice's two remaining fishermen sell their morning's catch at the **Pêche Locale** stands just across from the Puces de Nice on Port Lympia every day from 10.30am to 12.30pm. Arrive a little early; not only because it's first-in-first-served, but also to enjoy the theatre of the fishing folk arranging their precious haul on to wide counters filled with ice. The golden rule? Don't come for anything specific; adapt to what the morning has delivered. Depending on the season that could be inky cuttlefish, small Mediterranean rockfish for soups, or red mullet. Between mid-December and mid-April the real treats are the spiky purple sea urchins, collected by divers and brought back fresh in netted sacks. Do as locals do and order a dozen for €20 to eat fresh on makeshift tables fashioned out of big fishing boxes for lunch. BYO bread and crisp white wine.

The Coolest Street in Town
Bars, restaurants and the LGBTIQ+ scene

The strip and the surrounding streets around **rue Bonaparte** are Nice's hip LGBTIQ+ district, having earned the nicknamed *le petit Marais*, a nod to Paris' famous bohemian gay quarter. A part of the road is painted in blue, à la San Francisco's Castro District, and the stretch between place Garibaldi and place du Pin is now fully pedestrianised. This is where you should head if you are looking for a guaranteed evening buzz, as new bars or restaurants are always opening – just remember that you're still in the provinces, and even the most lively bars shutter by 1am, particularly out of season.

A Bar Within a Church?
Nice's holy watering hole

Duck through an unmarked side passage in the nave of the Église du Gesù in Vieux Nice to enter **Le Bethel** *(@bethel_riviera)*, easily the most unexpected setting for a bar in the city – even perhaps the country. If it feels sacrilegious to order a drink in a church, rest assured you have the blessing of the parish priest, Father Frédéric. In fact, the idea to transform a small internal courtyard at the rear of the 17th-century church into a cosy, intimate garden bar was his! With its decor of climbing plants, string lights, mismatched chairs and glowing candles, the vibe is wonderfully bohemian and just a little spiritual. Open evenings except Monday from late May to the end of September. The bar is entirely volunteer-run, with no reservations possible.

THE BOOM AT NOON

Nice's midday cannon – a loud boom at noon that rings out across the city – makes most visitors jump out of their skin the first time they hear it. The noisy custom was originally instigated by a wintering Brit, Thomas Coventry, in the 19th century.

The cannon of yesteryear has now been replaced by a small colourless firework that is set off rain, hail or shine in a small gated yard near the Israelite Cemetery on the Colline du Château by either Philippe or Kelly Arnello, a father-and-daughter duo and trained pyrotechnicians.

For the city's residents, the sound is the signal to stop for lunch. There's only one day when the cannon doesn't go off at noon: 1 April.

HELP ME PICK:

Côte d'Azur Beaches

It can almost feel like the whole of France has decamped south to the Côte d'Azur in the warmer months, so swarming with bodies are its main beaches. That said, there are ways to ensure a relaxing, rather than harried, experience: arrive early in the morning and be gone before lunch, fork out for a sunlounger at a private beach, or make the effort to access out-of-the-way local haunts. As soon as you slip into the refreshing Mediterranean Sea, you won't want to leave it.

Where to swim if you love…

Loungers & Cocktails

Baia Bella in Beaulieu-sur-Mer is France's first carbon-neutral private beach, according to Allcot, and uses organic ingredients, solar panels to heat water and rainwater to water plants. *baiabella.com*

Plage Keller On Cap d'Antibes' legendary Plage de la Garoupe, once the playground of Hemingway, Picasso and Fitzgerald. *plagekeller.com*

Castel Plage Nice's oldest private beach is LGBTIQ-friendly and catches the day's last rays of sunshine. *castelplage.com*

La Guérite The only way to access this beach club on the Île Ste-Marguerite is by boat. Expect a glam crowd, with the odd celeb mixed in. *restaurantlaguerite.com/cannes*

La Réserve de Mala (pictured left) Tucked below sheer cliffs, this hidden cove in Cap d'Ail is far from the crowds but the sunloungers here are some of the priciest on the coast. *lareservedelamala.com*

Public & Free

Plage des Sablettes Menton's beloved beachfront strip, where the sand is fringed by restaurant terraces, a playground and a wide, smooth footpath for rollerblading and scooters.

Plage des Marinières Finer pebbles than Nice and a train station just footsteps away make Villefranche-sur-Mer's public beach prime real estate on summer days.

Plage Publique de l'Opéra Play volleyball by day or lay out a picnic with friends at night on this popular, pebbly stretch of public beach across from Vieux Nice.

Plage du Midi Cannes' westernmost beach is this long strip of sand towards Mandelieu-La Napoule. Outfits organise boat trips and boat hire, as well as parasailing and more, at **Port du Béal** (p93).

Sssh… Locals Only

Crique des Pêcheurs (p111) This hidden cove at the foot of Monaco-Ville is bliss for a refreshing dip at low tide.

Coco Beach It's not your classic beach, but the translucent water at Nice's craggy eastern edge is ideal for snorkelling.

Plage de la Darse Pebbly beach sheltered from the cruise-ship crowds near the port of Villefranche-sur-Mer. Also great for snorkelling.

Calanque de Maubois (p98) Hidden cove along the Corniche d'Or with crystalline waters and red pebbles that match the ochre-red Esterel mountains that frame it. Accessed by steep steps.

PRINCELY POOLS

Dive into Monaco's urban swim spots on p111.

Plage des Sablettes

HOW TO

When to go Private beaches dust off their sunloungers for another season from around April. By October, everything is packed neatly back away until next summer.

Book ahead Beach loungers fill up, particularly in July and August, so make sure you phone in advance to guarantee your space.

Budget The cost of a sunlounger is inching ever higher: be prepared to pay anywhere upwards of €25 for a day.

Another tip? Expect to shell out more if you want prime front-row placement. Most private beaches also offer half-day bookings, too.

Pebbles or sand?

Rather than soft sand, Nice's beach strip is covered in smooth pebbles, some as big as the palm of your hand. Intriguingly, the city trucks in whole container loads to cover the beach afresh every March. Their official name is *galets* (note, one of the private beaches are named for them). These *galets* aren't particularly comfortable to walk on, nor, to be honest, to lie on, which is why a pair of jelly shoes and a thick straw beach mat are smart investments before your summer vacation to the city.

Further towards Italy, especially around Villefranche-sur-Mer and Beaulieu-sur-Mer, the *galets* make way for smaller, softer stones. If you find any sand, such as along Monaco's Larvotto beach, it's safe to assume that it's been imported. If your holiday dreams hinge on buttercream sandy beaches, the best bet is to base yourself somewhere west of Antibes. Fluffy fine sand can be found in Antibes Juan-les-Pins and Golfe-Juan, as well as along La Croisette and the glorious (and popular) stretch from Cannes west towards Mandelieu-la-Napoule.

Despite their proximity to the cinematic centre, the beaches on the Îles de Lérins are closer to Nice in their pebbly nature: here, swimming from rocks in coastal coves reigns supreme.

One more tip: it can be frustratingly hard to find sunscreen in supermarkets before April, so pack some in your suitcase.

BEST EVENTS IN NICE

Carnaval de Nice: For two weeks in late February and early March, floats and flower battles take over the streets. One of Europe's brightest carnivals, running since the Middle Ages.

Lou Queernaval: France's first queer carnival runs adjacent to the Carnaval de Nice; expect glitter, dazzling floats and drag queens.

Nice Jazz Festival: Jam-packed four-night calendar of performances in Jardin Albert Ier and fringe concerts popping up all around town.

Pink Parade (Pride): Crowds swarm Nice's main streets for July's Pink Parade (Pride); the afterparty lasts all night.

Noël à Nice: Sip bubbles with fresh oysters and ride on a giant Ferris wheel: Nice lights up in festive delight during December.

Sample the Niçois Culinary Renaissance
Move over, salade Niçoise

Nice's street-food culture is based on the colourful vegetables and legumes that thrive in the poor, water-deprived soils of the Mediterranean coastline. It feels closer to Italy in nature and flavour than the heavier, sauce-based cuisine of northern France. The city today brims with cheap and cheerful street-food stops, as well as more classic local *bistrots*. If you see the *Cuisine Nissarde* sticker displayed proudly at a restaurant's entrance, you know their dishes respect local culinary traditions. Beyond the traditional addresses, a new wave of trendy chefs is putting a fine-dining twist on local dishes, elevating them to a semi-gastronomic standing. So knowledgeable is Canadian-born Nice resident Rosa Jackson about Niçois cuisine that she wrote the book about it, literally. She also runs wonderful market tours and cooking workshops in her Vieux Nice kitchen, **Les Petits Farcis** (petitsfarcis.com; from €210).

 EATING IN NICE: BEST FOR BREAKFAST & BRUNCH

Marinette: It's a strictly pancakes, granola and cookies affair until 11am at this pastel-pretty address tucked down a Vieux Nice backstreet. *8.30am-6pm, Wed-Sun* €

Boulangerie Roy Le Capitole: Unassuming bakery with an exquisite claim to fame: the only bakery in France to craft a delicate lavender croissant. *hours vary* €

Zielinska: Historian and baker Dominika Zielinska is bringing long-forgotten local flours, such as *pétanielle noire de Nice*, back to her bakehouse. *hours vary; closed Wed* €

Comme un Dimanche: In Port Lympia, Marie and Stéphane serve up a brunch menu inspired by their three years living in Australia. *10.30am-3pm Wed-Sun* €

Château de Bellet

Taste Nice Wine
Nice's hidden vineyards

Interspersed between the Provençal villas of Nice's western flank are nine boutique vineyards that form the Bellet AOC. Not only is this postage-stamp-sized appellation – with just 50 hectares of vines – one of France's smallest, but it's also the only one in the country to fall within city limits. Two grape varieties grown here – folle noire and braquet – don't grow anywhere else in the world. These aren't the sprawling estates you'll find in major wine regions, and many still have a *'vin de garage'* feel. The two largest producers offer a delightful perspective of the city's history alongside a comprehensive visitor experience. **Château de Bellet** *(chateaudebellet.com)* is the oldest of the Bellet vineyards, and 45-minute tours in English run daily (€20, including three wines, book ahead) and start from an intimate private chapel built by the Barons of Bellet in 1873. **Château de Crémat** *(chateaucremat.com)* is housed in a towering, terracotta-red, faux-medieval fortress

WHEN BOULES BECAME COOL

Despite its image as an old person's pastime, boules (or *pétanque* as it is also called) is anything but.

Walk past a *terrain de boules* (boules court) and you'll see people of all ages taking part in the quintessential French afternoon sport. To play after dark – and to see just how cool boules has become first-hand – plan an evening at **La Boulisterie Club** *(laboulisterie.com)*, a bar and indoor boules court inside an airy converted garage on rue Lascaris in the Port. Here, you'll be able to add all-important accompaniments such as chilled Provence rosé and panisse (chickpea fries) to your game.

The same team is behind the hipster boules and clothing store in Vieux Nice, **La Boulisterie Store**, which designs the cool *Pastis et Pétanque* T-shirts you'll spot people wearing around the city.

 EATING IN NICE: BEST NIÇOIS ADDRESSES

La Gratta: This unassuming food truck in Port Lympia makes what many refer to as the best *pan bagnat* in town. *9am-5pm Mon-Fri, 8.30am-6pm Sat & Sun* €

Chez Pipo: The point of reference for fresh-from-the-oven *socca* in Nice for over 100 years. *11.30am-2.30pm & 5.30-10pm Wed-Sun* €

Chez Réné Socca: This cheap and cheerful Vieux Nice institution is the classic Niçois street-food stop. *9am-9pm Tue-Sun* €

Chez Davia: Book to savour chef Pierre Altobelli's interpretation of classics such as *soupe au pistou* and ratatouille. *12.30-2pm & 7.15-9.30pm Wed-Sat, from noon Sun* €€

A GLOSSARY OF NIÇOIS CUISINE

Socca Thin (gluten-free, vegan) chickpea-flour pancake from a wood-fired oven.

Pan bagnat This 'wet bread' in local dialect is a *salade niçoise* in a sandwich.

Barbajuan Fried raviolis stuffed with Swiss chard. Monaco's national dish.

Petits farcis Range of courgettes, peppers, onions, stuffed with meat.

Pissaladière Focaccia with caramelised onions and anchovies.

Beignets de fleurs de courgettes Who knew battered courgette flowers could taste so good?

Panisse This thicker version of *socca* is a serious challenger to the French fry.

Tourte de blette sucrée Sweet pastry with Swiss chard.

Daube Provençal Rich, slow-cooked beef stew.

Merda de can Green gnocchi (also based on Swiss chard).

Wine from Château de Crémat (p69)

dating from 1906. Its interlocking C motif is said to have inspired the logo of Coco Chanel, who is known to have spent glamorous evenings on its vast terrace during the Roaring Twenties. You can decide if the tale is fact or fiction, but the possibility does make a fascinating theme for the 1½-hour-long tour through the property. The visit concludes with a tasting – how many wines dictates the price of the tour (three for €30, six for €35).

Happy Hour
Sunset drinks in the city

Come 5pm, under the glow of the late afternoon sun, Nice's residents flock to the nearest terrace for an *apéro*, as the pre-dinner apéritif is more colloquially known. It's an easy habit to slip into during your visit. Prime *apéro* spots can be broken down into four main areas. Along the cours Saleya in Vieux Nice, chilled rosé and thirst-quenching pints are served with a side of people-watching, particularly in the cluster of

Continues on p72

 EATING & DRINKING IN NICE: RUE BONAPARTE PICKS

Comptoir Central Électrique: With its bohemian vibe, exposed walls and mismatched seating, this is the bar that started it all on rue Bonaparte. *9am-12.30am*

SuperBar: Super-stylish newbie with a cocktail menu that goes well beyond the tried and tested. *5pm-1am*

Kalōs: Soak up the buzz on the cheap at this Mediterranean street-food eatery specialising in oh-so tasty pitas. *11.45am-2.45pm & 6.30-10.30pm, closed Sun* €

Café Paulette: Perennial favourite, partly because it's whatever you need it to be: cool cafe, lively lunch spot or chic wine bar. *8am-12.30am Tue-Sat, 9.30am-5pm Sun* €€

A COLOURFUL MEANDER THROUGH VIEUX NICE ON FOOT

A wander through the pastel-pretty Vieux Nice, the city's pedestrian old town, on foot is one of the highlights of any trip to the Côte d'Azur.

START	END	LENGTH
14 rue St-François de Paule	place St-Augustin	1km; 30min

This colourful meander through Nice's charming old town starts outside the warm yellow facade of ❶ **Nicolas Alziari**, a local olive-oil producer whose distinctive blue tins grace the region's top restaurant tables. The flat stretch of street surrounding the grand 19th-century ❷ **Opéra de Nice** is home to some speciality shops worth browsing for a local souvenir. Continue straight ahead to the ❸ **cours Saleya**, the city's lively restaurant-lined strip and setting for fragrant fresh produce and flower markets and an antique market. Take a left turn to head deeper into the busy, labyrinth-like alleyways. On rue Doite, the wood-fired oven at ❹ **Chez Thérésa** has been baking *socca* since 1925 (fresh platters are also cycled down to a stand at the cours Saleya markets). The gentle rise is barely noticeable as you continue towards ❺ **Palais Lascaris**, a fresco-adorned 17th-century noble house turned museum and wonderfully preserved example of Baroque architecture. At the next corner, another history lesson awaits, if you can spot it. The heavy ❻ **cannonball** attached to the wall was fired by Turkish forces in 1543 during the Siege of Nice. The city managed to repel the forces and history has turned a local washerwoman called Catherine Ségurane into the heroine of the victory. In ❼ **place St-Augustin**, after a slight uphill stretch, you'll find a plaque in her honour.

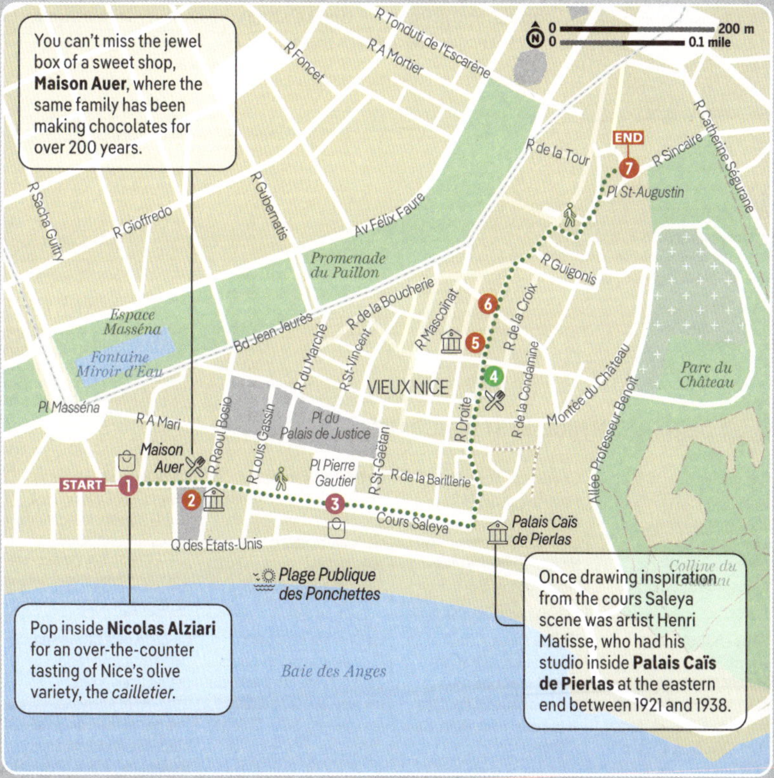

You can't miss the jewel box of a sweet shop, **Maison Auer**, where the same family has been making chocolates for over 200 years.

Pop inside **Nicolas Alziari** for an over-the-counter tasting of Nice's olive variety, the *cailletier*.

Once drawing inspiration from the cours Saleya scene was artist Henri Matisse, who had his studio inside **Palais Caïs de Pierlas** at the eastern end between 1921 and 1938.

LIVE MUSIC IN NICE

Did Kwo is a local guitarist and songwriter who has played in bars and restaurants across the city. He shares his top spots for live music in Nice.

Wayne's Bar
In this fun English pub in Vieux Nice you'll find cover bands playing party songs to get people dancing.

Shapko
A great late-night bet in Vieux Nice for jazz, soul, R&B and blues. An all-ages crowd.

La Cave Romagnan
This wine bar near Gare Thiers offers early-bird jazz on Saturday night.

La Zonmé
An underground venue in Libération with an eclectic lineup; keep an eye on its social media account for what's on.

Continued from p70

cafes and restaurants at the eastern end. Just outside, along Les Ponchettes, a series of beachfront bars have balconies positioned perfectly to catch the last of the afternoon sun: many people find nothing beats a DIY *apéro* on the beach. For a local vibe, head to the Libération neighbourhood above the main train station.

A Trip into Nice's Hinterland
The perfect rail day trip

A charming train trip to consider into Nice's forested hinterland is the Chemins de Fer de Provence *(cpzou.fr)*. The commuter route connects **Gare de Nice-CF de Provence** with Digne-les-Bains in 3½ hours (with a bus from St-André-les-Alpes for the last stretch to Digne-les-Bains), following the bends of the Var River through sleepy hamlets that feel a world away from the bustle of the coastal resorts. Entrevaux (1½ hours from Nice) makes a good stop for a day trip. The well-preserved fortified village is still reached from the main road by a mighty stone bridge. Expect to be kept busy while you wait for the return train: there's a sporty ascent to the 17th-century Citadelle, with splendid views over the river and a tempting selection of shady bistro terraces among its picturesque medieval streets.

DRINKING IN NICE: BEST WINE BARS & APÉRO SPOTS

Rouge: Sleek spot just back from Port Lympia serving up stylish, modern tapas plates, served with organic wines. *noon-10.30pm*	**Cave de la Tour**: A soundtrack of 1940s jazz, an interior that has hardly changed since then and Nice wine by the glass. *8am-2.30pm & 6-8.30pm Tue-Sat, 8am-12.30pm Sun*	**La Part des Anges**: A treasure trove of natural and organic wines in the city centre voted best wine bar in France in 2020. *10am-8.30pm, closed Sun*	**Cave Bianchi**: History seeps out of every nook of this atmospheric Vieux Nice wine shop and bar across from the Opéra. *9.30am-7.30pm, to 10.30pm Fri & Sat*
Babel Babel (p64): The spot along Les Ponchettes to sip an inventive cocktail as the sun sets. *10am-midnight, Mon, Thu, Sun, to 2am Fri & Sat*	**L'Altra Casa**: Cool Italian joint in the Libération neighbourhood mixing the best Aperol spritzes in the city. *6am-11pm, from 9.30am Mon*	**La Civette du Cours**: The terrace of this cours Saleya favourite packs out for rosé on ice and *demis* (half beers). *8am-12.30am*	**Le Café des Chineurs**: Boho vibe and tapas plates draw a hip after-work crowd to this bar at the corner of place Garibaldi and rue Bonaparte. *10am-12.30am*

Beyond Nice

Nice's surrounds brim with postcard-pretty resort towns, eagle's-nest villages, energising hiking trails and unexpected alpine experiences.

You don't have to travel too far from Nice to feel like you've left the big city behind; in fact, the pace turns down a few notches as soon as you arrive in Villefranche-sur-Mer, a charming fishing village joined to Nice at its eastern hip. The trio of sublime corniches, or coastal roads, layered between Nice and Monaco weave through Belle Époque coastal resorts, pass eagle's-nest villages and open onto lush hiking trails. They merge together in Italianate Menton, the last town before the border.

Northwest of Nice, St-Paul de Vence and Vence are an artist's idyll. Nice's backcountry, and the dramatic pre-alpine landscapes of the Parc National du Mercantour, are having a moment, too.

Places
Villefranche-sur-Mer p73
St-Jean-Cap-Ferrat p74
Èze p74
Roquebrune-Cap-Martin p76
Menton p77
Ste-Agnès p78
St-Paul de Vence p78
Vence p79
St-Martin-Vésubie p81
Vallée de la Roya p84

Villefranche-sur-Mer

TIME FROM NICE: 20min

La flânerie in Villefranche-sur-Mer

Irresistibly photogenic Villefranche-sur-Mer starts at Nice's eastern edge but is a world away from the buzz of the big city. This is small village life, where locals catch up on gossip at the Wednesday and Saturday morning produce markets or play *pétanque* in the shadow of the high-walled 16th-century **Citadelle St-Elme**. The pedestrian streets of Villefranche's old town are ideal to awaken your inner *flâneur* – someone who strolls in a leisurely manner. Start by admiring the green thumbs of residents along rue Volti and rue Baron de Brès, who have turned their pastel-palette facades into delightful street gardens that have become impromptu settings for social media shoots. Staircases down to the water frame views of the glistening sea.

Just before the waterfront, **rue de Poilu** is a hub of activity with restaurants and small, lavender-fragranced boutiques selling floaty dresses and wide-brimmed straw hats. One street down, **rue Obscure** is a 130m-long vaulted alley that offers a shadowy glimpse into the village's medieval past. The whimsical brushstrokes of Jean Cocteau cover the walls and ceilings of the must-see **Chapelle St-Pierre**, telling the story of Villefranche's fishing traditions.

GETTING AROUND

When the train runs to timetable, the TER Sud line makes small work of travel times between Nice and coastal stops and takes a supremely scenic track built right on the coast. The bus network is best for inland villages like St-Paul de Vence, Vence and St-Martin-Vésubie. To explore the lower alpine areas you'll need your own car or bike.

WHY I LOVE VILLEFRANCHE-SUR-MER

Chrissie McClatchie, writer

When the hit Netflix show *Emily in Paris* came to the Côte d'Azur in season 2, it was clear many of the scenes passed off as St-Tropez were actually filmed in Villefranche-sur-Mer. For residents like me, it affirmed what we already knew: our colourful seaside village outshines its more glamorous and better-known coastal neighbours.

There's the obvious natural beauty of the deep bay; add in the pastel-hued buildings cascading into the sea and you have one of the classic Côte d'Azur scenes.

Yet the feel here is more low-key than jet-set; there's no blingy nightlife or designer boutiques, just wine bars in small candlelit village squares and local faces behind bars and in shops, who have now become friends.

St-Jean-Cap-Ferrat

TIME FROM NICE: **30min**

Belle of the Belle Époque

There's nowhere better to appreciate the ornate Belle Époque beauty of the Côte d'Azur than at **Villa Ephrussi de Rothschild** *(villa-ephrussi.com; adult/child €18/12)*, one of the great architectural treasures of the coast. As soon as you set foot inside the pink-and-white villa, sitting high atop the leafy – and incredibly wealthy – peninsular of Cap-Ferrat, which juts out into the Mediterranean with the bays of Villefranche-sur-Mer and Beaulieu-sur-Mer on either side, you'll be swept back to a time when Louis XVI furniture and Fragonard paintings were the height of fashion. Commissioned by socialite and art collector Baroness Béatrice Ephrussi de Rothschild and completed in 1912, the elaborate two-storey residence is frozen in time with original furnishings and decorations, which a free audio guide provided at the entrance explains in detail. Don't rush the nine themed gardens that fan out from the villa, an enchanting landscape of sweeping stone staircases, rose-covered pergolas and even a theatrical fountain. The sea views framed by crumbling stone pillars and olive groves are sublime.

See the Sea

Plenty of boat rental and excursion outfits can get you out on the water beyond Nice, but few and far between are those that offer the opportunity to sail up to 35km off the coast on board a replica 16th-century wooden Mediterranean trading boat – and help safeguard the ocean along the way. For over three decades, local association **SOS Grand Bleu** *(sosgrandbleu. asso.fr)* has fought for the protection of dolphins and whales in the Mediterranean. In 2005, it took possession of the 23m *Santo Sospir* sailing yacht. For €65 per person (€45 for children under 12), you can jump on board this beautiful vessel for a full-day group outing (maximum 20 passengers) in search of these majestic marine animals. Pack a picnic, sunglasses, hat, sunscreen and swimming costume. April to November only.

Èze

TIME FROM NICE: **30min**

Exotic flowers and sweeping views

Although you'll increasingly need to swerve around selfie-stick-wielding visitors as you meander through it, the **Jardin Exotique d'Èze** *(jardinexotique-eze.fr; adult/child €5/free)* is still one of the region's most delightful experiences. Around

---

🍴 EATING IN VILLEFRANCHE-SUR-MER: OUR PICKS

La Voile Bleue: From April to early autumn, this simple shack on the beach serves some of the best *pan bagnat* on the coast. *9am-10.30pm, to 7.30pm Sun & Mon €*

Lou Bantry: Of the water's-edge restaurants, Lou Bantry stands out for its menu of Niçois classics and reasonable prices. *8am-6pm, to 7pm Sat & Sun €€*

Bistro de l'Étoile: A village favourite set back from the waterfront with a sunny terrace and a fresh menu of home-cooked treats. *noon-2pm & 7-10pm Tue-Sat €€*

Achill's: Good grub, but the real star here is the rooftop terrace that grooves until the small hours on hot summer nights. *9-1.30am €€*

Jardin Exotique d'Èze

the ruined 12th-century château above the terracotta rooftops of the village, a peaceful cactus garden grows: it's more than worth the entry fee for the sweeping sea views that extend beyond Cannes alone.

Perfume pause

If you can't make it high in the hills to Grasse (p99), Èze serves as as the perfume capital's understudy, with two of the region's historic perfumeries carving out a presence here. English-speaking guided tours through the sunflower-yellow **Parfumerie Fragonard** *(usines-parfum.fragonard.com; free)* take 30 minutes; they also run every 30 minutes (no reservation required). The space is big and bright and you'll be inducted into the secrets of perfume, as well as see its the workshops where the historic brand creates its cosmetics and sweet-smelling soaps. Enter the on-site boutique at your own risk: the range of fragrances, skincare, candles, even fashion is so exquisitely presented that it takes great willpower to leave without a purchase. Consider yourself warned. Across the road, **Galimard** *(galimard.com; free)* feels slightly dated by comparison but a small exhibition explaining the history of perfume behind the boutique can be visited at your own pace. A 30-minute guided tour, including a short workshop, costs €18, but the opportunity to blend your own eau de cologne by choosing three scents from a selection of 10 is a particularly kid-friendly activity.

BEST COASTAL HIKES

Promenade Maurice Rouvier: This flat, paved 1.3km path links Beaulieu-sur-Mer with St-Jean-Cap-Ferrat and is accessible for all. Perfect pre- or post-lunch walk.

Sentier de Cap d'Ail: A 5km track leading from Plage Marquet at the edge of Monaco to the hidden bay of Plage Mala.

Tour du Cap-Ferrat: This rocky 7km trail around Cap-Ferrat starts at Plage Passable, facing Villefranche-sur-Mer, and passes hidden coves and a lighthouse.

Sentier Le Corbusier: A 5km path from the train station at Roquebrune-Cap-Martin towards Menton. Views back towards Monaco are sublime.

Sentier du Littoral: Swimmers and sneakers are recommended on this rugged 3km trail between Nice and Villefranche-sur-Mer.

 EATING IN ÈZE & CAP FERRAT: OUR PICKS

| **Le Cabanon Cap Ferrat:** Among all the mansions is this no-frills light bites kiosk on the coastal path in St-Jean-Cap-Ferrat. Summer only. *10am-7pm* € | **Deli' Èze Village:** Atmospheric alfresco salad bar near the entrance to the Jardin Exotique d'Èze. Walk-ins only; be prepared to wait for a lunch table. *9am-6pm* € | **Château Eza:** : Michelin-starred modern French cuisine and jaw-dropping views. *The* special occasion spot on the Côte. *noon-2pm & 7.30-9.30pm* €€€ | **Restaurant Béatrice:** The original dining room of the Villa Ephrussi de Rothschild is delightful for a light lunch or afternoon tea. *11am-5.30pm, to 6.30pm Jul & Aug* €€ |

OVERTOURISM

With its dizzying cliffside setting 400m above the sea and spellbinding coastal panorama, Èze is one of the Côte d'Azur's most spectacular sites.

Thanks to its convenient location halfway between Nice and Monaco, the eagle's nest medieval village is also one of its most touristy: up to 5000 visitors a day crowd into its small, dense, clifftop alleys. This foot traffic is great news for the artists and shopkeepers, but for the people who call it home, not so much.

Officials are said to be considering measures to regulate visitors, while a new underground car park has upped the parking capacity from 90 to 350. The best time to visit the village is before 10am or after 4pm, but note the closing time of the garden between November and March is 4.30pm.

The most similar experience without the crowds is **Ste-Agnès** (p78).

Jardin Serre de la Madone

Hike the Nietzsche trail

You can drive the three corniches (p82), or you can scramble up them on foot on the **Sentier Nietzsche**, an old mule track connecting Èze-bord-de-Mer and Èze Village. Named for German philosopher Friedrich Nietzsche, who found inspiration to complete the third part of *Thus Spoke Zarathustra* while walking it, the 3.8km trail can be tackled from top down, but the classic departure point is across the road from the Èze train station on the Basse Corniche. BYO water: it's a steep ascent from the coast on a well-defined yet rocky path that winds through Mediterranean shrub and feels far from civilisation. After about 45 minutes, you'll emerge at the base of medieval Èze Village on the Moyenne Corniche. To return, hike down to the train station or catch the Ligne d'Azur bus 82 back to Nice from Èze Village, bearing in mind that this is probably the busiest bus stop along the whole of the Côte d'Azur.

Roquebrune-Cap-Martin TIME FROM NICE: 30min

Le Corbusier's château

Le Corbusier called it his Château on the Côte d'Azur: a small 14 sq m pinewood cabin at the water's edge in Cap Martin. Now a UNESCO World Heritage Site, the **Cabanon Le Corbusier**, as it's known, remains the only structure that the Swiss-born architect designed for himself. It was built as his summer residence in 1952 on a strip of land adjacent to **Villa E-1027**; the latter was designed by his friends, Irish interior decorator Eileen Gray and Romanian-born architect Jean Badovici. An early example of modernist architecture, the villa dates from 1929 and has been meticulously restored to Gray's original vision, down to a faithful replica of the door handles. The ensemble of the site – including the Étoile de Mer, the neighbouring bar shack owned by Thomas Rebutat, and its five holiday cabins designed by Le Corbusier – now goes by the name of **Cap Moderne** *(capmoderne.monuments-nationaux.fr; adult/child €19/10)*. An excellent two-hour guided tour of the four buildings departs on foot daily at 10am and 2pm from a hangar at the Gare Cap-Martin-Roquebrune train station between April and October. Arrive 15 minutes early to have a chance to browse the informative exhibition inside. Booking well in advance is encouraged; make sure you select the English-language visit. Le Corbusier had a heart attack swimming off the rocks outside his cabin in 1965 and is buried in the cemetery in medieval Roquebrune village.

Menton

TIME FROM NICE: **40min**

A day at the lemon farms

Arguably the most delightful way to while away a day on the Côte d'Azur is by visiting Menton's lemon farms, where the warm golden yellows of the sun and the fruit set against the bright blues of the sky and the sea are a superb, all-natural mood enhancer. Block off a whole day to visit **La Ferme des Citrons** *(lafermedescitrons.fr; adult/child €39/25)*. The excursion starts at a central meeting point in Menton in the morning, where a 4WD awaits you for a short yet steep drive to the farm. After an hour-long guided tour through avocado trees, olive groves and, of course, lots of lemon trees, you are allowed ample time to relax on a sunny terrace with a shaded children's play area and nature's best views. A tasty Niçois lunch is included in the price of the visit, before your 4WD transfer back to town mid-afternoon. Request an English-speaking guide when booking.

Trickier to get to, unless you have your own wheels, is **Maison Gannac** *(lamaisonducitron.com; adult/child €12/free)*. Tours through its nursery and orchard above Menton's pastel-pretty old town leave at 9am and 1pm Tuesday to Saturday and last 1½ hours. Learn about different varieties of citrus, from thin finger limes to puckered bergamot, and even take home some tips to ensure your plants thrive at home. The visit finishes with a 30-minute tasting of its products.

Enchanting gardens

Considered the green lung of the Côte d'Azur, Menton dazzles with its remarkable gardens. Those with evergreen opening hours include **Jardin Botanique du Val Rahmeh** *(jardinbotaniquevalrahmehmenton.fr; adult/child €8/6)*, just back from the beach towards the Italian border, where over 1700 different species bloom in this 120-year-old terraced garden, originally designed for British general Sir Percy Radcliffe (closed on Tuesdays). From the waterfront, a narrow road snakes towards the entrance to **Jardin Serre de la Madone** *(serredelamadone.fr; adult/child €15/11)* on the road to Gorbio. Ponds, pergolas and plenty of statues decorate this charming garden, which dates to 1924, when Anglo-American Laurence Johnston started planting flora here collected from his world travels. A handful of other delightful gardens are open sporadically and for guided visits only – visit Menton's **tourist office** for up-to-date programming and availabilities.

MENTON'S PRECIOUS LEMONS

There's something about the mountains-meets-sea climate of **Menton**, the last curve of France before the Italian border, that encourages lemon trees to thrive.

Historically a mainstay of the town's economy, a combination of factors saw the decline of production in recent years. Happily the crop is undergoing a renaissance and today the *citron de Menton* is feted anew for its sweet taste and impressive size.

During February's annual **Fête du Citron** celebrations, the streets around the waterfront light up yellow and orange. Tickets are required for the street parades of floats and flamboyantly dressed dancers, but you won't need to pay a cent to admire the giant citrus displays sculpted to a different theme every year in the central Jardins Biovès.

Ste-Agnès

TIME FROM NICE: **1hr**

Medieval garden in the sky

As it clings to a rock face 800m above Menton, all roads leading to Ste-Agnès share tight bends and narrow lanes. It claims to be the highest coastal village in Europe, and from the pretty paved alleyways of the quaint village, a 10-minute climb up stairs will lead you to the original settlement at an even dizzier altitude. The 10th-century château lies in ruins, but the site is passionately maintained by a volunteer association that has planted a small but colourful medieval garden behind the ramparts. It's free to enter, but a donation is greatly appreciated. The panorama is showstopping – the trucks that plough the busy A8 motorway are mere specks below – but those wary of heights may feel a little squeamish, particularly atop the rickety ruined fort with a 360-degree view. Think Èze, but without the gloss or crowds – and therein lies the real charm.

St-Paul de Vence

TIME FROM NICE: **1HR 10min**

Walking walls & ramparts

Deep in the Côte d'Azur hinterland, the artists' village of St-Paul de Vence is another of Provence's almost-too-pretty-to-be-true hilltop villages – but this magazine-spread perfection means it's also a particular magnet for tour buses. Dodge the crowds inside the walls by following the **Sentier des Fortifications Henri Layet**, a 30-minute walk around the base of the western ramparts that tells of the village's history as both a military stronghold and an agricultural heartland. Cast your gaze down the flanks and you'll notice neat rows of vines. Further along, an orchard bursts with bitter orange trees while birdcalls fills the fragrant air. The path ends at the southern part of the thick medieval walls. From there, you can head into the village – but before you do, pay your respects to Marc Chagall, who is buried in the local cemetery.

Boutique wine

Those vines you saw as you walked the base of the fortification? It's a teeny vineyard, cultivated by Domaine des Claus, a boutique biodynamic winery whose grapes are mainly grown in nearby Tourrettes-sur-Loup (p103). While this particular plot is not open for visitors, you can taste the wine, or buy a souvenir bottle, at **La Cave de Saint-Paul** (*cavesaintpaul.com*) inside the village. If only the walls of this subterranean

---

BIKE CLUB

For serious road cyclists, the mountain passes behind Nice are bucket-list rides. The most mythical of all is the **Col de la Madone**, which rises 925m near Ste-Agnès. The route was made famous as Lance Armstrong's pre-Tour de France fitness test.

Cafés vélos, or cyclist cafes, are popping up across France as places not only for good coffee, but also to connect with others who are passionate about the sport and to participate in scheduled rides.

In Nice, **Café du Cycliste** (*cafeducycliste.com*) is the original bike cafe. Join in on a weekly group ride or set off on your own on an itinerary that starts from its doorstep into the hinterland. Road and gravel bikes are available to hire. Also on sale is the cafe's branded stylish sportswear.

 EATING IN MENTON: OUR PICKS

| **Le Mirazur**: A mere 20m from the Italian border, Mauro Colagreco's three-Michelin-star address is farm-to-table perfection. *12.15-2pm Thu-Sun, 7.15-10pm Wed-Sun* €€€ | **Halles Municipales**: Pick up a feast of seasonal fare at Menton's covered food market near the seafront. *8am-1pm* € | **Le Bistrot des Jardins**: *Bistronomique* (fine dining in a bistro setting) with a delightful patio garden and seasonal flavours. *hours vary.* €€ | **Mitron**: Colagreco's organic bakery is bringing France's forgotten flours back to the bakehouse; a divine lemon tart is another speciality. *8am-7pm Tue-Sat, to 3pm Sun* € |

Vence

cavern could talk: dating from the 14th century, it once housed the local lords' wine stash. Oenophiles will still feel like they've stumbled into an Aladdin's cave. Fine wines and rare vintages are crammed into every inch of space; pull up a stool among them while you swirl and sip a trio of the village wines for €20 (or €9 for a single glass). No reservations for this tasting necessary, but be aware this small space fills up quickly.

Vence

TIME FROM NICE: 1hr

Vence walking tour

Unlike nearby St-Paul de Vence, tourists don't overwhelm Vence: the fact that there's no space for tour buses to park is deliberate, explains local Steve Wilkerson (*steveandcarolein vence.com*). During Wilkerson's 90-minute walking tours inside the walls of the old city *(adult/child €10/free)*, you'll quickly understand why the American has fallen under the charm of this well-preserved walled town: although more lived-in than its Disney-perfect neighbour, there are centuries of history on every corner, a lively market most mornings (busiest on Friday and Saturday) and an impressive concentration of foodie addresses for its size, many spilling out onto atmospheric squares. Along with pinpointing the blink-and-you'll-miss-it details, such as Roman columns and medieval doorways, along with the historic 'Hell' neighbourhood, Wilkerson also introduces you to many of Vence's 20 fountains. So reputed

BEST OF THE REST: PERCHED VILLAGES

Gorbio: Shaded by a 300-year-old elm tree in the main square, Gorbio is a classically beautiful Provençal village.

Castillon: Quirky artists' village rebuilt on a new site in the 1950s after it was destroyed first by an earthquake and then war. A rock-climbing paradise.

Castellar: This Italianate hilltop village brims with local flavours at its Sunday-morning market. *Barbajuans* – the national dish of Monaco – are a speciality.

Peillon: Half the adventure is getting to Peillon, in the Nice hinterland, on a twisty mountain road. Book ahead for lunch at **Auberge de la Madone**.

Roquebrune: A splash of orange buildings and terracotta rooftops seemingly stuck to the cliffside. Views to Monaco – and France's oldest tree.

EATING AROUND MENTON: OUR PICKS

Le Righi: The views from this Ste-Agnès institution might be the best of any restaurant on the Côte d'Azur. Best for big plates of pasta. *9am-6pm Thu-Tue* €

L'HarTmonie: This *bistrot de pays* in Castillon supports employment for people with disabilities. Emphasis on regional cuisine. *9am-4pm Wed-Sun, 6-10pm Sat* €

Le Beauséjour: Local fare in a beautiful dining room overlooking Gorbio's beloved elm tree. *noon-2.30pm Thu-Tue Mar-Oct, dinner service Jul-Aug* €€

La Grotte & l'Olivier: Prince Albert of Monaco is known to frequent this bistro built into a rock in Roquebrune's medieval village. *10am-11pm Wed-Mon, closed Wed lunch* €€

BEST ART EXPERIENCES IN ST-PAUL DE VENCE & VENCE

La Colombe d'Or: You have to book a table or a room to admire the art at this five-star inn, where Picasso and Matisse once paid their bills with canvases.

Chapelle Folon: This intimate chapel glimmers in gold and pastel mosaic, the last work of Belgian artist Jean-Michel Folon.

Fondation Maeght: Find a who's who of 20th-century artists inside this gallery. The avant-garde building and sculpture gardens are a delight.

Chemin Ste-Claire: Artists once took this delightful short path to the Fondation Maeght: a handful of tiny chapels break up the walk.

Chapelle du Rosaire: Matisse viewed this chapel in Vence as his masterpiece. The museum traces its creation through sketches, photos and texts.

is the pure water from the local spring, La Foux, that it was nearly bottled in the early 1900s. Had that happened, the name Vence just might be as globally known as Evian.

The smallest cathedral in France

If you're a fan of quirky trivia facts, here's a new one for you. Where in France can you find the country's smallest cathedral? Right here in Vence. While not dollhouse-sized by any stretch of the imagination, the **Cathédrale Notre-Dame de la Nativité** *(vence-tourisme.com/cathedrale-notre-dame-de-la-nativite; free)* is still tiny compared to other cathedrals you'll visit around the country, especially as only the facade is visible. Dating from the 10th century (and the seat of a bishop until the French Revolution), it packs a punch despite its size. Treasures to admire inside include papal relics (Pope Paul III was the bishop of the town before his promotion to Rome) and one of Chagall's last ever works, the *Moses Saved from the Waters* mosaic.

EATING IN ST-PAUL DE VENCE: OUR PICKS

Le Saint Paul: The €19 *plat du jour* out of season is stunning value at this elegant Relais & Châteaux property. *noon-2.30pm* €€€

Le Tilleul: A shady terrace and a menu of fresh flavours beckon you to settle in for a long lunch on the ramparts of the village. *noon-2.30pm & 7-11pm* €€

Café Timothé: Cute hole-in-the-wall organic cafe serving light lunch bites as well as pick-me-up cakes and cookies. *10am-6pm Mon-Sat* €

La Colombe d'Or: Considering the artwork on display in the dining room, if this isn't worth a once-in-a-lifetime splurge, little else is. *12.30-1.30pm & 7.30-9.30pm* €€€

Parc National du Mercantour

St-Martin-Vésubie

TIME FROM NICE: 1hr 10min

Indoor & outdoor adventure

The coastline and the sea blues might steal the limelight, yet over 80% of the Alpes-Maritimes, the French *département* which lies in the Côte d'Azur's embrace, is actually mountain terrrain. Pretty St-Martin-Vésubie is a hiking haven and a great jumping-off point into the Côte d'Azur's alpine interior. From here, you can pick up numerous trails through the flora- and fauna-rich valleys of the **Parc National du Mercantour**, a magnificent national park that encompasses 679 sq km, stretching from the Côte d'Azur into Haute-Provence. In the company of friendly English-speaking guides from **Guides06** *(guides06rando.com)*, you'll uncover the best mountain paths to get up close to majestic chamois and whistling marmots. The village is also home to the excellent **Vésubia Mountain Park** *(puremontagne.fr/en/to-see/vesubia-mountain-park; prices vary depending on activity),* an indoor adventure-sports centre where kids and adults scale climbing walls, kit up for canyoning or tackle the rooftop adventure course.

Mountain beer

Decide for yourself if the spring water from the River Vésubie is what makes the local brew from **Brasserie du Comté** *(brasserieducomte.fr)* so refreshing: the taphouse has been completely rebuilt on a new site just outside the village after the storm washed away the original one. Operational since 2012, this brewery is considered the premier of the Côte d'Azur's

Continues on p84

BEST WINTER SPORTS DESTINATIONS

The Côte d'Azur is one of those magical places where you can swim in the morning and be on the slopes by lunch, if you dare. Five starting points for winter sports within 1½ hours of Nice Côte d'Azur Airport are:

Auron: Bucketloads of alpine charm and a lively après-ski scene.

Isola 2000: The good: great slopes with Mediterranean views from the summit. The bad: uninspiring 1970s architecture.

Valberg: The first ski resort on the Côte d'Azur and a firm favourite with weekend skiers from Nice.

La Colmiane: The 30km of ski runs include some gentle beginners' slopes.

Le Boréon: Hire snowshoeing and cross-country ski equipment from Parc Alpha and head into snowy trails through larch forests.

DRIVING TOUR

Follow the Three Corniches

Three corniches (coastal roads) cling to the cliffs between Nice and Monaco: the Basse, Moyenne and Grande Corniche (in order, the lowest, middle and highest). With a new favourite vista around every bend, the views of the Mediterranean can be a distraction, but thankfully there are plenty of lookout points. You could drive this route without stopping in under an hour, but that would mean skipping many of the Côte d'Azur's crown jewels.

1 Mont Boron

Begin at Nice's wooded eastern fringe, the Parc Forestier du Mont Boron. This urban forest is a hikers' favourite, but you can park close to the 16th-century Fort du Mont Alban for scene-stealing views across the bay of Villefranche-sur-Mer – a taster for the road ahead.

The Drive: This fairly flat 5km stretch of the Basse Corniche hugs the coast. Stop for photos at the Mémorial Princesse Grace viewpoint at the entrance to Villefranche-sur-Mer.

2 Villefranche-sur-Mer

Villefranche-sur-Mer's Citadelle St-Elme looms tall at the entrance to the small harbour, but don't let the immense walls scare you off: inside, a charming sculpture garden blooms under the nurturing touch of the Mediterranean sea breeze.

The Drive: Continue along the low road for a further kilometre, before turning left onto av Léopold II, a narrow road that winds up to the Moyenne Corniche. Settle in for a scenic 5km stretch to Èze.

Mont Boron

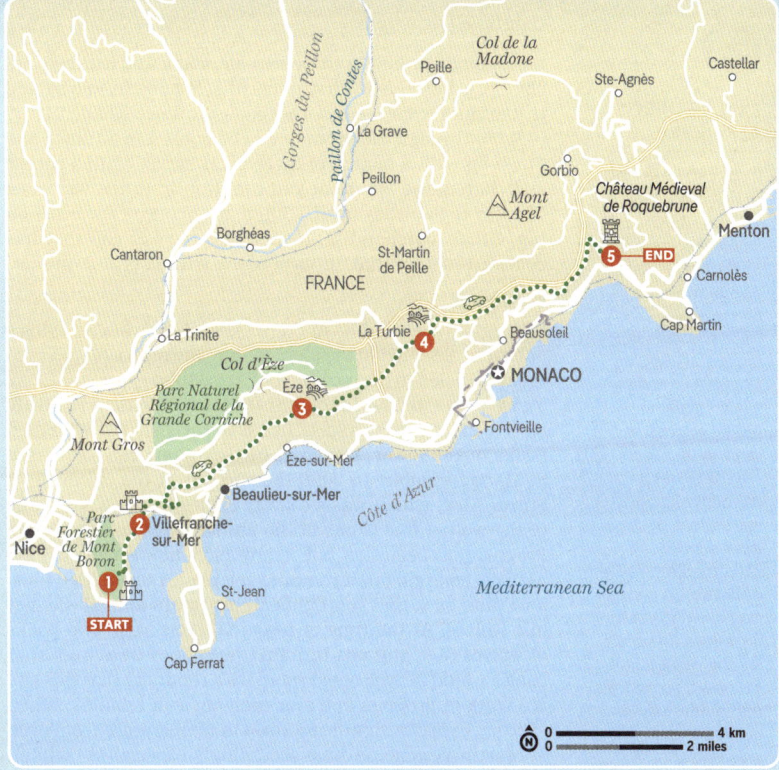

3 Èze

Parking can be tricky but this isn't a stop to miss: snuggled into a rocky nest nearly 500m above the sea, Èze is a Côte d'Azur sparkler where the narrow medieval streets all lead to one place, the **Jardin Exotique d'Èze** (p74), a multi-level garden that sprouts among the ruins of the old château.

The Drive: Not long after leaving the village, turn left onto the route de la Turbie to head even higher above the sea. At the top, merge onto the Grande Corniche and La Turbie will appear around the first bend.

4 La Turbie

So high is La Turbie that the village often sits in a soft cloud. When it clears, you can clearly make out three countries from the **Tête du Chien** viewpoint: France, Monaco and Italy. You can't miss the **Trophée d'Auguste**, a victory monument raised for Roman emperor Augustus. Even better: the buttery croissants at **Ma Première Boulangerie**, some of the best in the region.

The Drive: Staying on the Grande Corniche, the road twists and turns for 5km as you sweep around Monaco.

5 Roquebrune-Cap-Martin

A huddle of rich red and warm yellow buildings clinging to the cliffside, Roquebrune-Cap-Martin's medieval village is another of the Côte d'Azur's most charming perched sites, just without the hordes of tourists like Èze.

Park up at the entrance then head off on foot to explore the warren of alleyways: look out for the signs leading to the 10th-century château (and France's oldest tree).

Continued from p81

increasingly prolific craft-beer scene; you'll find its range, including a deliciously thirst-quenching lemonade, in bars and restaurants from Menton to Aix-en-Provence. Guided tours (€21.50) through the brewery can be booked in advance and finish up with a tasting of three beers served with a cheese and charcuterie board, or you can drop in to the bar, open Monday to Saturday until 5.30pm, to sip one of the beers on tap. Other merchandise, including a trucker cap that has become the unofficial uniform of the village, is also on sale.

Wolf pack

Wolves had been extinct in France since 1930 when, in 1992, a pair were observed in the Mercantour. The return of wolves to French soil led to the creation of **Parc Alpha** *(puremontagne .fr/en/to-see/parc-alpha; adult/child €14/10)*, a wildlife reserve in Le Boréon, a speck of a ski resort beneath the jagged peaks of the lower Alps 8km further along the road from St-Martin-Vésubie. In 2020 the site was at the epicentre of Storm Alex, which washed away enclosures and set many of the wolves free (some of the animals were never found). Progress has been slow but steady and a new version of Parc Alpha is emerging that you can explore on a self-guided tour: a wildlife park that spotlights all mountain animal life, not just wolves. At the time of research, there were two packs of wolves (five animals in total), but hopes were high that babies would be welcomed soon. It's a reminder that this site is a work in progress and ever evolving as it rebuilds. When visiting, expect a significant drop in temperature from even St-Martin-Vésubie, so dress accordingly, especially in winter, when snow boots are a requisite to visit.

Vallée de la Roya

TIME FROM NICE: **1HR 30min**

Valleys of wonder

Tens of thousands of engravings – some of horned animals and others of humans – dating from the Neolithic and Bronze Age, are carved into stone in two mysterious valleys around 2000m above sea level north of Nice: the **Vallée des Merveilles** and **Vallée de Fontanalba**. These smooth rock canvases are framed by a majestic landscape of mirror lakes and rocky slopes. It's a setting that gives the name the Valley of Wonders a dual meaning. The carvings can be visited from the end of

---

EXPLORE NICE'S ALPINE SIDE

If you only have time to visit one village in Nice's alpine hinterland, make it St-Martin-Vésubie, also known as *La Suisse Niçoise* (Nice's Switzerland) for its green setting and pretty wooden chalets situated 1000m above sea level north of Nice.

In 2020, lives were lost and buildings and bridges washed away when Storm Alex struck the Vallée de la Vésubie and the neighbouring Vallée de la Roya. The scars are still very evident, as you will notice from the boulder-strewn landscape and presence of bulldozers and other construction equipment, but the community is showing its mountain spirit as it rebuilds after the devastation.

Your support and spending is an enormous boost to their efforts – but you'll get something back, too.

EATING IN VENCE: OUR PICKS

Les Petits Tabliers: Rustic wine bar and bistro. Menu changes weekly, with local produce, including fish. Shaded rear terrace. *9.30am-10.30pm Tue-Sat* €€

Le Michel Ange: Long-standing local favourite serving up Niçois classics on a fountain-clad square. *noon-2pm Tue-Sun, 7-9.30pm Fri & Sat* €€

La Cassolette: *Bistronomique* fare that leans into the seasons served on a sunny terrace outside the *mairie* (town hall). *noon-1.30pm & 7-9.30pm Thu-Mon* €€

Trattoria al Lubio: Delightful Italian trattoria with tables spilling out onto a charming square. Antipasti, pasta, the likes. *noon-2pm & 7-9.30pm Thu-Mon* €€€

May to the beginning of October and are reached after two (Fontanalba) to four hours (Merveilles) of walking from car parks in Les Mesches or Casterino near Tende in the Vallée de la Roya. Plan and book ahead to stay overnight at the refuge de Merveilles (*refugedesmerveilles.ffcam.fr*) and Fontanalba (*refugedefontanalbe.com*). You can hike two marked discovery trails independently, although to really experience the full scope of the whole site, including engravings not on the hiking routes, arrange a registered guide (*see vallee-merveilles.com*).

Tende, the French village with an Italian flavour

Welcome to France's most easterly nook! Tende is the end of the line, quite literally – from here, Piedmont in Italy beckons through the 3km-long Col de Tende tunnel which, when it opened in 1882, was the longest tunnel in the world. Passed like a hot potato between France and Italy until 1947, when it became definitely French, this amphitheatre-shaped village still feels torn between the two countries. The ornate Baroque facade of the **Collégiale Notre-Dame de l'Assomption** can be spotted from most angles and is accessed through a warren of pedestrian streets. Don't miss the **Musée des Merveilles** (*museedesmerveilles.departement06.fr; free*) just across from the train station, with its large visual displays and artefacts that trace the history of the prehistoric carvings of the Vallée des Merveilles.

France's Sistine Chapel

A 20-minute drive from Tende, just outside the village of La Brigue, the **Sanctuaire Notre-Dame-des-Fontaines** (*adult/child €4/free*) is an astonishing 15th-century church nestled in nature. It has been dubbed the Sistine Chapel of the Southern Alps for the detailed frescoes that cover every inch of the 220 sq metre interior. There's no electricity or lighting, which only adds to the ethereal atmosphere inside the intimate chapel – although you need to time your visit before daylight starts to fade. Visits must be reserved in advance with **La Brigue Tourist Office** (*menton-riviera-merveilles.fr*) so someone can be on site to meet you. From the tennis court in the village, a marked walking trail leads to the chapel if approaching on foot. Plan for 1½ hours each way from the village.

TRAIN DES MERVEILLES

The commuter train that connects Nice with the communities of the Vallée de la Roya is known as the **Train des Merveilles** (Train of Wonders), and for good reason.

The route carves a dazzling course through deep gorges, pine forests and rushing cascades, and feats of engineering include dizzying viaducts, plenty of tunnels and spiral loops. Completed in 1928, the track once connected Nice with Italy, but now French trains only go as far as Tende.

In late 2024 the line closed for maintenance; while replacement buses are running, they don't compare with the beauty of the train line, which should be operational again in mid 2026. When it is, here's hoping the live commentary in both French and English also returns.

 EATING IN THE VÉSUBIE: OUR PICKS

Le St Mart': This wine bar and bistro in St-Martin-Vésubie serves up all the classics, executed to perfection. Book ahead. *hours vary* €

Relais des Merveilles: Mountains-meets-Niçois classics at this cosy hikers' inn in the Vallée de la Vésubie. Opens Easter to mid-October. *noon-2pm & 7.30-9.30pm.* €

L'Air du Temps: Creative cuisine in St-Martin-Vésubie's four-star Pure Montagne Resort. Chef Julien Matheret is from the valley. *Tue-Sat 7.15-9pm, Sat-Sun noon-1.30pm* €€€

La Prairia: Stock up on goat and sheep cheeses for a mountain picnic at this shop in St-Martin-Vésubie. The family's flock graze the Mercantour. *hours vary, Fri-Sun* €

Cannes

ISLANDS | CINEMA | BEACH

GETTING AROUND

The centre of Cannes is mostly flat and, with La Croisette as a point of reference, easily walkable – although the landscape does get a little hilly around Le Suquet and the furthest neighbourhoods. Between them, the Gare de Cannes train station and Hôtel de Ville bus stops serve the majority of the city's Palm Buses; to be dropped at the base of the Californie, catch line 21. If you're driving, don't rely on street parking.

☑ TOP TIP

Over 140 annual festivals and events, including June's Cannes Lions International Festival of Creativity and the MIPs (MIPCOM, MIPIM and MIPTV), mean accommodation books up early and hotel prices often rise sky high. If there's an event on during your visit, consider staying outside of town.

Cannes is the host with the most; not content to hold just one world-leading industry affair a year – yes, Cannes Film Festival, we're looking at you – the conference and event schedule is so busy that dates spill out from the calendar most months. It's a place that always feels on and dressed in its global party best, pushing local traditions and experiences into the wings as a consequence.

Yet despite first impressions, including superyachts crowding the bay and luxury cars double-parked outside the designer boutiques of La Croisette, Cannes is an old Provençal soul, as the traditional fishing boats bobbing in the harbour or the battered courgette flowers cooked fresh in the Marché Forville bear witness to. And, in a world now celebrating what makes each destination unique, this understudy is starting to shine.

Festival Fever

Roll out the red carpet

For two weeks every May, Cannes rolls out the red carpet for a galaxy of stars during the annual **Festival de Cannes** (the Cannes Film Festival). The harbourfront **Palais des Festivals et des Congrès** is the epicentre. For the remainder of the year, the gloss barely fades. Follow the trail of over 400 stars who have cast their handprints in stainless steel along the Chemin des Étoiles (path of stars) outside the Palais. Dates for tours *(adult/child €6/3)* inside the Palais are only scheduled six weeks in advance by the **tourist office** (conveniently housed in the building), depending on the upcoming event calendar, and are only in French. When visits do run, you're given a 1½-hour behind-the-scenes insight into one of cinema's most legendary venues.

Île Ste-Marguerite

Îles de Lérins

When you're shoulder-to-shoulder with crowds on La Croisette, it's hard to believe that a pocket of Cannes exists where the buzz of doing business is replaced by the sweet smell of pine and the gentle sound of waves. Yet such a spot exists and, if you look up and out to sea, you'll spot it: the **Îles de Lérins**, the two islands off the mainland.

DON'T MISS

Fort Royal

Musée du Masque de Fer et du Fort Royal

Écomusée Sous-Marin de Cannes

Abbaye de Lérins

Vineyards of Île St-Honorat

Forteresse de St-Honorat

Action-Packed Île Ste-Marguerite

Of the duo, Île Ste-Marguerite feels more action-packed, and that's not only because it's inside the 17th-century **Fort Royal** where the mysterious Man in the Iron Mask was incarcerated under the orders of King Louis XIV. You can stand inside the exact cell – and learn about the island's strategic importance – when you visit the **Musée du Masque de Fer et du Fort Royal**, which is an easy walk from the ferry pier.

The island is much bigger than its monastic neighbour; the coastal loop is 9km long, although wide pine-scented alleys cut through its centre, too. The best swim spots are on the southern side, facing Île St-Honorat. Weekends are particularly popular with families and groups of friends making the crossing from Cannes to picnic and swim in shallow waters.

PRACTICALITIES
- cannes-france.com/decouvrir-visiter/iles-de-lerins/sainte-marguerite
- cannes-ilesdelerins.com
- Accessible year-round

Underwater Museum

At depths of 3m to 5m below sea level, an underwater gallery of seafloor sculptures by Jason deCaires Taylor sits off the southern coastline of the Île Ste-Marguerite. The six submerged statues of the **Écomusée Sous-Marin de Cannes** stand 2m high and depict the faces of residents of the city.

The renowned British underwater sculptor has chiselled their profiles out of pH-neutral marine-grade cement, a textured material on which marine life can set up home. Located between 84m and 132m from the shore, the site can be accessed for free from the island. BYO mask and snorkel.

Serene Île St-Honorat

By contrast, peaceful Île St-Honorat is privately owned by a community of monks. A group of 25 work and pray away from prying eyes and, although much of the 19th-century Abbaye de Lérins is closed to the public, you are allowed into the church and to participate in Mass (11.25am Tuesday to Saturday and 9.50am Sunday).

Plan about an hour to complete the shady, eucalyptus-fringed loop that skims the circumference of the island, passing small chapels scattered amid the woodland and even two furnaces built at the command of Napoléon Bonaparte to heat cannonballs. After extensive renovations, the **Monastère Fortifié**, what remains of the original monastery, re-opened in summer 2025. Jutting protectively into the sea at the southern edge of the island, it dates from the 11th century.

Holy Wines

Unlike on its bigger neighbour, vines thrive in St-Honorat's soil. Once a month, you can learn why during a short vineyard tour and tasting of two wines. Book your tickets for this **Journée Vignes-Vins** *(cannes-ilesdelerins.com; €25)* in advance on the website. The price includes the return ferry.

Getting There & Away

Boats leave Cannes from the western side of the harbour and take 15 to 20 minutes. Due to construction works, the three ferry operators are based in temporary structures on quai St Pierre just opposite the Canopy by Hilton Cannes hotel. **Trans Côte d'Azur** and **Horizon** run ferries to Île Ste-Marguerite *(adult/child €18.50/12.50)*, while **Planaria** *(cannes-ilesdelerins.com; adult/child €22/14)* shuttles back and forth from Île St-Honorat.

Ferry times vary depending on the season; check the websites for latest timetables. Frustratingly, there's no inter-island ferry, so to visit the pair of them, you have to return to Cannes first.

SLEEPING & EATING OPTIONS ON THE ISLANDS

Centre International de Séjour Îles de Lérins: This hostel inside Île Ste-Marguerite's fort is mainly for school groups, although the general public can reserve a bunk on weekends from April to early November.

La Tonnelle: The only restaurant on Île St-Honorat. The feet-in-the-sand setting comes with fine-dining prices. Reserve in advance (there's also a snack bar inside for takeaway paninis and drinks).

TOP TIPS

- **Book online:** Horizon and Planaria offer cheaper ferry tickets (a euro or so less) if bought in advance online.

- **Take your rubbish with you:** Neither island has any rubbish bins, so be prepared to leave with everything you came with.

- **Limited food in low season:** Apart from a small snack bar on Île Ste-Marguerite, most food outlets shutter over winter, so pick up a picnic from Marché Forville before you board the ferry.

- **Kayak:** If you prefer to tackle the 1.3km that separates Île Ste-Marguerite from Cannes' Palm Beach yourself, **Sea First Kayak** *(seafirst.fr)* rents out kayaks. A full day's hire costs €35.

Le Suquet

CANNES FILM FEST LIKE A PRO

How to do the Cannes Film Festival like a pro? If you're prepared to stand for hours in smart dress outside the Palais, you may find someone willing to offload a ticket for a screening they can no longer attend. A makeshift sign stating what you want to see will increase your chances.

After sunset, everyone is invited to **Cinéma de la Plage**, the free open-air cinema that runs for the duration of the festival on Plage Macé. Mostly showing classics, with the occasional world premiere, you may rub shoulders with a member of the cast or crew.

Arrive early for the best seats. If you're a true cinephile, submit an application at festival-cannes.com to be one of the lucky few selected for a pass to access screenings.

La Croisette, Renewed
Breathing new life into Cannes' beachfront boulevard

The scaffolding is coming down in autumn 2026 on **La Croisette**, after the iconic waterfront strip completes its biggest renovation since the 1960s. The trendy (and pricey) beach bars and designer boutiques haven't changed, nor have the quick and easy food kiosks and the public chess boards. New features to watch out for as you stroll the palm-shaded strip include public benches in the form of waves, much more greenery and a new event space, Le Théâtre de la Mer. Look down at the ground: the all-new pavers reflect the rich red of the Massif de l'Esterel mountains that frame Cannes' western edge.

A Village in a Town
Art and viewpoints

Meaning 'summit' in Provençal, **Le Suquet** is Cannes' oldest neighbourhood and relaxes with its sleepy charm. Feel the crowds and the big-name bling of La Croisette fade into the distance as you wander the quiet streets stretching up from the western edge of Le Vieux Port. Loops of colourful

Continues on p92

   EATING IN CANNES: OUR PICKS

Poissonnerie Forville: Bustling fish counter outside Marché Forville serving fresh-from-the-sea treats such as oysters and sea urchins. *7am-2.30pm, Tue-Sun* €€

Mido: Mouthwatering Nikkei cuisine and excellent sushi in a stylish setting, tucked down a restaurant-lined alley. *7pm-midnight* €€

La Casa di Nonna: Popular restaurant-tearoom for breakfast, lunch and afternoon tea. Fresh pasta and homemade cakes. *8am-7.30pm, Mon-Sat* €€

Le Pompon: A menu of creative small plates that changes daily with the season. Colourful ingredients and beautiful presentation. *lunch & dinner Tue-Sat* €€

ART MURAL WALK

Follow a trail of bright murals dedicated to cinema – what the French consider the seventh art – on this city-centre walking tour.

START	END	LENGTH
Gare de Cannes	place Cornut-Gentille	1.6km; 30min

Looking right from the Gare de Cannes, the first painted wall is easy to spot, atop the rise on place du 18 Juin, on the corner of rue du Maréchal Joffre. It's named ❶ **Le 7ème Art**. Look at the figures closely. Do any look familiar?

Drop down rue du Maréchal Joffre for 100m or so, then onto rue Meynadier on your right. Continue until you arrive at **Marché Forville** (p92). At the western extent of the market, take a right at rue du Dr Pierre Gazagnaire. At the top of the street, turn left onto bd Victor Tuby. You are close to number 29 and ❷ **Buster Keaton** bursting from the wall. Just next door, at 7 rue des Suisses,

❸ **L'Envers du Décor** shows a behind-the-scenes view of a director's set.

Leave the traffic behind as you enter Le Suquet (p90), Cannes' calm, pedestrianised old quarter. On place du Suquet, the neighbourhood's central square, you'll quickly spot the mural named ❹ **Hôtel de la Plage**. The *trompe l'oeil* ❺ **Le Barbarella** is facing west on the side wall of the building opposite.

From there, it's a quick drop down rue du Suquet to the most photographed mural of all at place Cornut-Gentille: ❻ **Cinéma Cannes**, depicting some of Hollywood's most iconic characters.

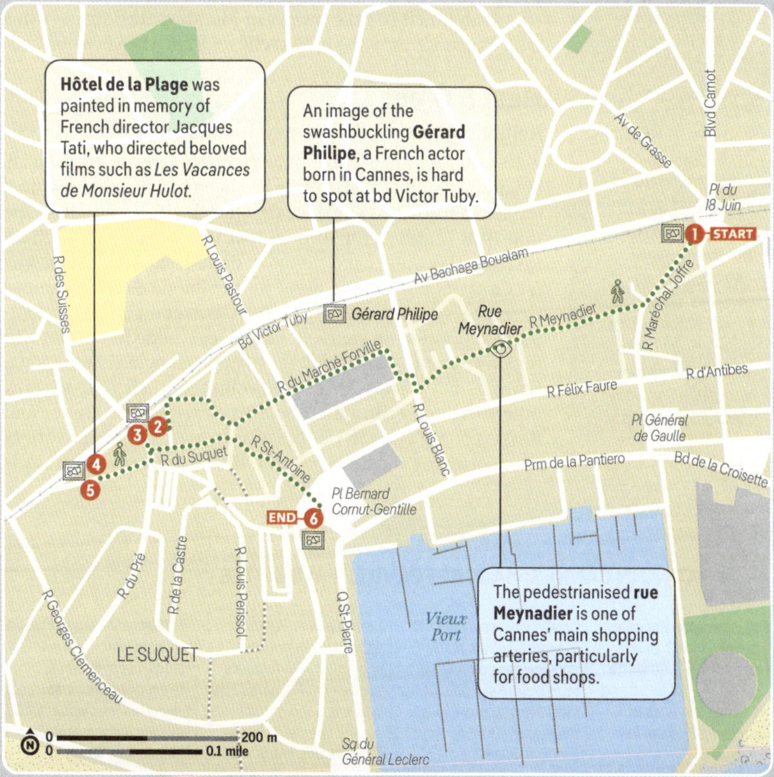

Hôtel de la Plage was painted in memory of French director Jacques Tati, who directed beloved films such as *Les Vacances de Monsieur Hulot*.

An image of the swashbuckling **Gérard Philipe**, a French actor born in Cannes, is hard to spot at bd Victor Tuby.

The pedestrianised **rue Meynadier** is one of Cannes' main shopping arteries, particularly for food shops.

Continued from p90

village houses with floral balconies are crowned by a cluster of historic attractions, including the medieval castle of the monks of the Îles de Lérins that now, as the **Musée des Explorations du Monde** *(cannes.com; adult/child €6.50/free)*, harbours treasures from all four corners of the world. Outside the entrance, the Cannes selfie sign is deliberately angled to capture a stunning view of the bay, although you can go one better by scaling what's left of the castle ramparts in front of the 17th-century **Église Notre-Dame de l'Espérance** around the corner.

Shop like a Local
Cannes' covered market

Skip the supermarket and make your way instead to **Marché Forville**, behind Le Vieux Port. Open Tuesday to Sunday from 7.30am to 1pm, Cannes' covered produce markets are an explosion of juicy fruit, plump vegetables and food stalls serving up cuisine from around the world, although upgrades currently underway mean half the space is cordoned off. Seasonality rules, so depending on the time of year, fill your basket to the brim with ruby-red strawberries from nearby Carros or pungent black truffles snuffled out from the neighbouring Var – or grab lunch to take away. On Mondays, the space brims with curios for the weekly **Marché de Brocante** flea markets.

Meet & Greet
Neighbourhood walks and new friends

A 20-minute walk east from the centre of Cannes, the hillside neighbourhood of **Californie** has been one of the city's most exclusive addresses since the first lavish villas went up in the mid-19th century. You'll break out in a sweat on the climb up from the waterfront along av de la Favorite. 'That's why *les Cannois* don't come here,' jokes Simone Revel, a Cannes Greeter *(cannesgreeters.com; free)*. You can pound the footpaths of Californie yourself, but a local guide like Revel will regale you with the anecdotes a quick Google search won't. Greeters networks – locals who volunteer their time to show others their city through their eyes – exist across France and Revel is one of eight in Cannes who propose, for free, a variety of experiences in the city. From little-trodden nature trails

BEST ARTS EXPERIENCES

Festival d'Art Pyrotechnique: International teams compete to win the best firework show crown. Six nights in summer. *(festival-pyrotecnique-cannes.com)*

Les Plages Électroniques: Epic three-day dance festival on the beach with eight stages and over 50,000 festivalgoers. In August. *(plages-electroniques.com)*

Musée Bonnard: Neo-impressionist painter Pierre Bonnard (1867–1947) was known as the Painter of Happiness, and Le Cannet was his happy place. *(museebonnard.fr)*

Le Suquet des Artistes: A small but avant-garde exhibition space in the ex-city morgue that brings local artists to the fore, with four in workshops on site. *(@suquetdesartistes)*

EATING IN CANNES: MARCHÉ FORVILLE FAVOURITES

Rotisserie de Forville: Between March and late October, courgette flowers are battered and deep-fried in front of your eyes. *7.30am-1pm Tue-Sun* €	**Soupe Poisson Forville**: Alexandre Serre starts cooking big pots of fish stew before sunrise for the morning trade (pre-order bouillabaisse). *7.30am-1pm Tue-Sun* €	**Socca'nnes**: Panisse – either *au nature* (plain) or infused with flavours such as truffle, herbes de Provence and green olives – is the speciality here. *7.30am-1pm Tue-Sun* €	**Dr Mezze**: Aussayd Mando escaped war in Syria to build a life in Cannes. He's brought recipes from home; his fried aubergine sandwich is incredible. *7.30am-1pm Tue-Sun* €

Église Notre-Dame de l'Espérance

at its outer edges to La Croisette, but seen through the lens of a Cannes native, the two to three hours you spend with your Greeter will give you a whole new perspective of the city.

Watersports HQ

Zippy Zodiac excursions and water toy hire

A cluster of boat tour and watersport operators emerge from their off-season hibernation at the start of April around **Port du Béal**, on the sandy stretch of beach heading west out of Cannes. Think of the small marina as your adrenaline HQ. For parasailing adventures and to play captain for the day by taking out a small boat *sans permis* (without a licence) – even as far as the **Îles de Lérins** (p88), there's BoatEvasion *(location-bateaux-cannes.com/port-du-beal)*; for superhero-inspired eFoils, head to eFoil Côte d'Azur *(efoilcotedazur.fr, €150/hour)*. Most fun for all the family are Black Tenders' 12-seater semi-rigid Zodiacs that zip in and out of the secluded rust-red coves along the Corniche d'Or on a 1½-hour excursion *(blacktenders.fr; €45)* stopping along the way for refreshing swims in peacock-coloured waters. Departures are late afternoon and early evening to avoid the heat of the summer sun.

CLAY COURT LEGENDS

Legend has it that clay court tennis was born in Cannes in the 1880s when two-time British Wimbledon winners, the Renshaw brothers, found that grass courts couldn't handle the heat of the Côte d'Azur.

Turning to ground-up terracotta pottery from nearby Vallauris, the duo covered their courts with this inventive material. Just like that, tennis had a new surface.

While arguably no more than a great story, what isn't debated is that the **Carlton Cannes**, the iconic Belle Époque hotel on La Croisette, hosted the match of the century between France's Suzanne Lenglen and America's Helen Wills on this surface in 1926 (Lenglen won, if you're wondering).

You'll find fine terracotta powder encased under the glass reception desk, among other nods to this sporting history.

 DRINKING IN CANNES: OUR TIPS

Bar Fouquet's: Many a business deal is done at the Hôtel Barrière Le Majestic over a cocktail where homemade bitters and edible perfumes are standard. *10am-midnight*

Maison Grenache: Atmospheric wine bar next to the Marché Forville with ultra-knowledgeable owners. *9am-5pm, to 10.30pm Fri & Sat*

The Quay's: This friendly harbourside Irish pub is a long-standing Cannes institution with cold beer, happy hours and a sunny terrace. *4pm-midnight, to 2am Wed-Sat*

Le Hive: It's about drinking, eating and gaming (board games included) at this bohemian neighbourhood bar with regular DJ sets. *6pm-12.30am Wed-Sat*

Beyond Cannes

Let Cannes be your springboard into perfumed villages bathed in a light that has inspired generations of artists.

Places
Mandelieu-La Napoule p94
Antibes p94
Juan-les-Pins p97
Vallauris p97
Mougins p97
Grasse p99
Gorges du Loup p101
Parc Naturel Régional des Préalpes d'Azur p103

The coastal roads out of Cannes lead either towards the mimosa-scented Mandelieu-La Napoule, which once exported these floaty yellow flowers to the furthest corners of Europe, or Antibes and Juan-les-Pins, neighbouring resort towns that groove to the smooth beats of jazz come summer. The pine-shaded landscapes of this coastal stretch have long been a magnet for artistic types, and this heritage can still be felt in irresistibly pretty inland villages such as Mougins, where Picasso saw out the last years of his life. Rising up behind them, Grasse's flowers scent fragrances sold around the world, while the landscape of the Gorges du Loup and Préalpes that neighbour it are simply out of this world.

GETTING AROUND

The train links Cannes and Mandelieu-La Napoule, with hourly departures; top reach Vallauris, hop on Palm Bus 9 from the station. Public transport between Cannes and Mougins Vieux Village is surprisingly poor; a taxi should cost around €20 each way. The train ride between Cannes and Grasse takes 30 minutes. It's a 15-minute walk uphill to the perfumeries. The train is best for Antibes. For the Gorges du Loup your own wheels are recommended.

Mandelieu-La Napoule
TIME FROM CANNES: **10min**
A festival of winter flowers

Mandelieu-La Napoule, the resort town at the western end of the Baie de Cannes, is considered the mimosa capital of the Côte d'Azur and is the halfway point along the **Route du Mimosa**. The main event to note in your calendar during the golden mimosa bloom is February's **Fête du Mimosa** *(mandelieu-tourisme.com)*, a four-day celebration with flower parades, evening animations, fireworks and a party mood. You can also join in on daily hikes deep into the Massif de Tanneron, considered Europe's largest mimosa forest, with qualified local guides such as the wonderfully knowledgeable Maddy Poloméni *(maddypolomeni.com, €19)*. Outside of the mimosa flowering season, she also leads a busy calendar of walks into the hills around Mandelieu and beyond.

Antibes
TIME FROM CANNES: **15min**
Markets & megayachts

Antibes is the quintessential Riviera resort town and mixes traditional village charm with flashy wealth: its marina, Port Vauban, is Europe's largest. You can spend a fabulous day simply pottering about in **Vieil Antibes**' colourful pedestrian streets and sampling what is arguably the Côte d'Azur's best coffee scene. The **Marché Provençal** beckons for a DIY lunch; juicy olives, garlicky tapenades (olive spreads), gooey

Marché Provençal, Antibes

cheeses and Corsican charcuterie are just some of the produce to tempt your taste buds (Tuesday to Sunday, daily in July and August). A walk along the ramparts offers up sublime snowcapped peaks-meets-Mediterranean sea views and leads around to the harbour. Barriers separate mere mortals from the gigayachts on the appropriately named Quai des Milliardaires (Billionaires Quay), but if you are in the mood for some yacht spotting, you can ogle them from the **Bastion St-Jaume**. Here, the 8m-tall *Nomade* (2010) sculpture of a figure looking out to sea is just as attention-grabbing as the shiny boats below.

Picasso in Antibes

'If you want to see the Picassos from Antibes, you must come to Antibes to see them', the great Spanish artist famously quipped, so do as he instructed. Picasso set up his studio inside the imposing 14th-century Château Grimaldi in the old town in 1946; it became the **Musée Picasso** (*antibesjuanlespins.com/en/discover/the-must-sees/picasso-museum; adult/child €12/free*) in 1966. The mesmerising *Ulysses and Sirens* is the headline act, although a series of still lifes depicting platters of octopus, cuttlefish and sea urchins are a charming insight into the memorable meals he enjoyed on the coast.

MIMOSA & MANDELIEU

In winter, the western extent of the region explodes in a thick yellow brushstroke of mimosa, a plant that is said to have arrived on the Côte d'Azur from Australia via the luggage of visitors.

At the start of the 20th century, local growers would pack cut mimosa flowers inside baskets woven from cane and willow for export to flower markets in London and Moscow. Today, the handful of remaining *mimosistes*, as the growers are known, are based at the foothills of the Massif de Tanneron in Pégomas, directly north of the town.

At La Colline des Mimosas (*lacollinedes mimosas.fr*), you're welcome to drop in to buy freshly cut flowers or to learn more about the technique of forcing flower buds to open in hot, humid rooms called *forceries*.

EATING & DRINKING IN ANTIBES: OUR PICKS

Lilian Bonnefoi: Hip, child-friendly brunch spot on a quiet square next to the ramparts with photogenic plates. *hours vary Wed-Sun €*

Le Zinc: Small, stylish wine bar and bistro just steps from the Marché Provençal. *7-10pm Mon-Sun, 10.30am-2pm Wed-Sun €€*

Absinthe Bar: Put on a funny hat and sip the green fairy at this dimly lit cellar bar, an Antibes institution. Live music at weekends. *9am-2am*

Le Bistrot de Curé: Lunch on salads and Niçois classics at this garden bistro next to the Phare de la Garoupe lighthouse. *9am-5pm Tue-Sun €*

PANORAMIC PRÉALPES

A natural terrace overlooking the coast, the **Parc Naturel Régional des Préalpes d'Azur** is a national park that extends across a vast territory almost 900 sq km in size and encompasses towns including Vence, Tourettes-sur-Loup and Grasse.

The **Route Napoléon** (p100) passes through it. A diverse landscape of forests, gorges, garrigue (dry Mediterranean shrubs), wildflower-covered plains and limestone plateaus is criss-crossed by hiking trails, while the roads are popular with packs of cyclists and motorbikers, as well as the odd supercar at speed.

Villages include Gréolières, with a buzzy Saturday market that attracts local growers and honey producers; Caussols, a mountain commune that, according to local folklore, possesses the ideal terrain for UFO landings; and Gourdon, another medieval eagle's-nest village with sublime views.

Mougins

A master glassblower

The Antibes region has a rich tradition of glassblowing; try your hand at the craft with **Didier Saba – Maître Verrier** (didiersaba.fr). Saba, a master craftsperson with a rock star attitude, keeps the door to his old town atelier wide open, so those who are passing can pause and watch him (with no obligation to buy) conjure up delicate vases and patterned glasses from little more than a scoop of pure glass and a couple of well-timed puffs. For €20, you can blow your own Christmas bauble with Saba as your teacher. Book in advance, but be aware that the glass needs time to set once fired in the sizzling furnace, so you'll have to come back the next day to collect it.

Lighthouse views

To reach the top of the **Phare de la Garoupe** (free) at the highest point on leafy Cap d'Antibes, you need to climb 116 spiral steps – but the reward for your effort is sweeping 360-degree views of the coast from Italy to St-Tropez. After being off-limits to the public for a quarter of a century, the lighthouse is now open Saturday and Sunday from 10am to 5pm. Visits are every 20 minutes by groups of ten; you'll be allocated a time when you arrive, with the last entry at 4.40pm.

A spotlight on the sea

The all-new **Posidonia – Espace Mer et Littoral** (antibes.fr/posidonia; adult/child €12/6) at the tip of Cap d'Antibes is difficult to label. Part exhibition space, part aquarium, part pine forest, the common thread is the marine habitat and what we can do to better protect it. As the name suggests, the star of the show is *Posidonia* (seagrass), a vital ingredient in the Mediterranean ecosystem. It's designed to appeal to all ages: young kids will enjoy the interactive exhibits and coral-filled aquarium, and the 10-plus group will get the biggest buzz from the virtual diving experience (€3 extra). Between June and September, you can also set off on guided kayak and snorkelling tours from the site; book in advance on the website.

Juan-les-Pins

TIME FROM CANNES: **10min**

Jazz in Juan

Juan-les-Pins is the sleepy resort neighbour of Antibes that rouses for a summer of partying along its beachfront bars and beach clubs, particularly around July's **Jazz à Juan** *(jazza juan.com)* festival, one of the oldest jazz festivals in Europe. On the beachfront Pinède Gould stage, surrounded by pines, evenings groove late to some of the biggest names in music: Ray Charles, Ella Fitzgerald and Carlos Santana are some of the greats to have performed here since the first edition in 1960. Side events held around the event, which typically runs for 10 days, include emerging jazz musician performances and late-night jam sessions.

Vallauris

TIME FROM CANNES: **40min**

Picasso's purple patch

There are prettier spots on the Côte d'Azur, but Vallauris is a worthwhile stop to browse local ceramic studios. So intertwined is the name Vallauris with ceramics that many of the street name signs are *petit* works of art. The town's most famous disciple is (you guessed it) Picasso, who came here to learn about the craft. After an hour inside the **Musée National Picasso 'La Guerre et la Paix'** *(musees-nationaux-alpesmaritimes.fr/picasso; adult/child €6/free)*, you emerge with an understanding of just how much of a natural the artist was with clay, firing more than 4000 pieces. The entrance ticket grants access to three museums in one and, while ceramics is the medium most celebrated, the most moving work is his immense *Chapelle La Guerre et la Paix* (War and Peace Chapel), a small, windowless 12th-century chapel with an incredible mural he painted covering every surface but the floor.

Mougins

TIME FROM CANNES: **20min**

Fine dining & fine art

Wound as tightly as the swirl on a snail shell, Mougins' hilltop old town is a photographer's delight for snapping dreamy Provençal scenes. This sunny spot is the place for art and gastronomy, so plan enough time to indulge in both – and bring a little extra cash, as fine dining here doesn't come cheap. The polished-to-perfection medieval alleys brim with galleries and studios; the one to bookmark is **FAMM** (Female Artists

---

HOW TO HIRE YOUR OWN BOAT

Fancy a slice of the superyacht lifestyle on a tight budget? Every coastal spot has a boat rental outfit.

Self-drive No boat licence is needed to hire a boat under 5m in length, with a maximum capacity of 5 people. The boat is very basic and you won't be able to cruise very far from the port, but, trust us, it's enormous fun. Expect to pay around €200 for the day.

With licence If you have a boat licence, your options are great with lots of boats in the 5m to 8m range. Hire costs are higher, starting from €450 plus deposit.

Captain and crew The sky is the limit when it comes to a crewed charter. Platforms like Click & Boat *(clickandboat. com)* offer a range of boat styles and prices.

 EATING & DRINKING IN MOUGINS: OUR PICKS

| **Le Petit Fouet**: Frogs legs, terrines, foie gras and duck: classic French in a relaxed setting. Also popular for breakfast. *9am-1.45pm & 6.30-9.45pm, Fri-Tue* €€ | **Resto des Arts**: Artsy restaurant serving up cool cocktails and modern-French cuisine. *7-10pm Mon-Sun, noon-12pm Sat & Sun* €€ | **La Cave de Mougins**: Chic wine bar with a sunny terrace at the entrance to the village; tasting boards to nibble on. *11am-late, from 6pm Wed* € | **Bohème**: Fabulous fine dining at the entrance to the village. Fine cuts of beef cooked on embers a speciality. *noon-2pm & 7-10pm Tue-Sat* €€ |

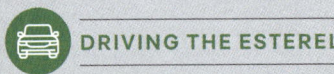

DRIVING THE ESTEREL

Drive sweeping coastal curves through the striking, ochre-red Massif de l'Esterel on this classic Côte d'Azur road trip.

START	END	LENGTH
Château de la Napoule	Agay	22km; 1hr

Start this drive along the Corniche d'Or (Golden Coast) at ❶ **Château de la Napoule**, a medieval fortress turned art foundation in Mandelieu-La Napoule, just west of Cannes. Continue west; the road lights up in gold in winter as part of the Route du Mimosa. Depending on traffic, you'll reach Théoule-sur-Mer in a few minutes.

The soft sand of the public ❷ **Plage du Suveret** beckons for a refreshing swim, although parking is a lottery in the height of summer. Pushing on, the landscape transforms as you enter the Massif de l'Esterel, the mountain range that frames the eastern edge of the Alpes-Maritimes. The road mimics the twists and turns of the craggy coastline, cutting through the rich red rocks that cascade into the translucent sea below. The scattered neighbourhood of ❸ **Le Trayas** is said to be the Côte d'Azur's most beautiful, with waterfront homes overlooking sparkling *calanques* (small coves). Many are only accessible by boat, although the sheltered ❹ **Calanque de Maubois** has a small car park.

You can also park up at ❺ **Pointe de l'Observatoire**, just around the bend, for a wide panorama back towards the Îles de Lérins (p88) and Cap d'Antibes beyond. The route continues all the way to St-Raphaël (p135), but without a 4WD you can't drive past the ❻ **Agay** beachfront strip with its many cafes and watersports options.

> The gardens of the **Château de la Napoule** (lnaf.org; adult/child €4/free) open from April to September (closed Mondays).

> The strange pink building in Théoule-sur-Mer is the **Palais Bulles**, a bubble house once owned by Pierre Cardin (closed to the public).

of the Mougins Museum; *famm.com; adult/child €16/5)*. The four floors form an incredible visual journey celebrating pioneering women in art. Standout canvases include the impressionist works by Monet's step-daughter and daughter-in-law Blanche Hoschedé-Monet.

Picasso in Mougins

Picasso spent the last 12 years of his life in Mougins and passed away in 1973 at his home, a sprawling 800 sq m farmhouse called Notre Dame de Vie in the leafy hills that surround the *vieux village*. It's now privately owned, but you can peek into the estate from the **Chapelle Notre Dame de Vie** *(mougins tourisme.com; free)* next door.

Flanked by tall Tuscan cypresses and an olive grove, this peaceful 12th-century chapel is worth a short visit for the small but fascinating collection of black-and-white photographs of Picasso at home, as well as the bronze Minotaur sculptures by contemporary artists in the gardens. It's a nine-minute drive (or 30-minute walk) from the village itself; road access for the last few hundred metres is paved but narrow. Open daily in July and August.

Grasse

TIME FROM CANNES: **35min**

Follow your nose in Grasse

Grasse's status as the world capital of perfume was cemented with the awarding of UNESCO's Intangible Cultural Heritage status in 2018. A trio of local fragrance houses dominate this sprawling town stretched out high in the hills above Cannes. With its historic factory at the entrance to the pedestrianised old quarter, **Fragonard's Usine Historique & Musée du Parfum** *(fragonard.com)* is the most visible. See original extraction and distilling equipment up close during the free 20-minute guided visits of the factory floor, while the two upper levels of the building are given over to a gorgeous boutique and small self-guided perfume museum.

An easy 10-minute walk away on bd Victor Hugo, the cherry-red *bastide* (country house) of **Molinard** *(molinard.com)* features a glass roof constructed by Gustave Eiffel and a similar complimentary tour. Heading out of town, the **Galimard** *(galimard.com)* factory along the route de Cannes also offers free guided visits. Hands-on experiences are the real highlight when in Grasse, allowing you the chance to play perfumer for anywhere between 20 minutes to an hour. You

Continues on p101

BEST GRASSE MUSEUMS

Musée International de la Parfumerie: A must-see, even if you're not a perfume lover, presenting three millennia of perfume history in a variety of ways: sight, sound, smell and even touch – a hit with children.

Musée Provençal du Costume et du Bijou: In a former *hôtel particulier* (mansion) at the start of the old town, this Fragonard-owned museum showcases traditional Provençal clothing and jewellery. Prepare to fall in love with the gorgeous fabrics.

Musée Jean-Honoré Fragonard: Celebrates Grassois painter Fragonard (1732–1806), even though, during his lifetime, the subject of his work shocked French society.

Musée d'Art et d'Histoire de Provence: Feel like you've stepped back into a 18th-century Provençal noble's home, inside a grand *hôtel particulier*.

EATING IN GRASSE: OUR PICKS

Les Délicatesses de Grasse: Part-restaurant, part-deli on place aux Aires with gorgeous tasting boards of cheese, charcuterie and tapenade. *10am-10pm €*

Taverne de l'Oratoire: A meat-heavy medieval-themed tavern in Grasse's old town. *6pm-midnight Mon-Sun, noon-3pm Fri-Sun €*

Auberge du Vieux Château: With your own wheels, this classic in nearby Cabris is wholly worth the detour. Great location and views. *lunch & dinner Wed-Sun €€€*

L'Imprévu: Opposite the Musée International de la Parfumerie with something for everyone and a sunny rooftop terrace. *11am-4pm Mon-Fri, 10.30am-5pm Sat & Sun €*

TOP EXPERIENCE

Route Napoléon

On 1 March 1815, Napoléon escaped exile on the island of Elba and landed on the Côte d'Azur with the intention of marching to Paris and reclaiming the French throne – which he did, albeit briefly. The legendary Route Napoléon retraces the 325km he marched from Golfe-Juan, on the coast between Cannes and Antibes, to Grenoble. It's one of France's epic road trips.

Colonne Napoléon

Golfe-Juan to Grasse

A small **sign**, *'Ici commence la Route Napoléon'*, just across from the marina in Golfe-Juan, signals the start of the Route Napoléon, although you'll struggle to find any further reference until Le Cannet, when the start of the N85, as the road is officially known, is signposted. This first stretch passes in a disappointing blur of urban sprawl. You could almost skip it entirely and start in Grasse – unless a short detour into the pretty town of **Mougins** (p97) is on your to-do list.

Grasse to Séranon

Leaving the built-up landscapes of the Côte d'Azur behind, the Route Napoléon comes into its own. It's a short hop from Grasse to St-Vallier de Thiey where the **Colonne Napoléon** commemorates where the emperor stood under a tree. The 17km stretch of balcony road between St-Vallier and Escragnolles is a thing of beauty. From there, the route opens out into grassy plains around sleepy Séranon. **La Bastide du Broundet**, where Napoléon spent a night – legend says too fearful of being poisoned to eat – stands across from the **Auberge de Seranon** (p101). It's in ruins but is still worth a short visit. Just after Séranon, you'll cross into the Alpes-de-Haute-Provence where the dramatic balcony roads of the Côte d'Azur give way to lavender-scented plateaux.

(See also: Hiking the Route Napolen, p268)

TOP TIPS

● La Route Napoléon à Cheval (Route Napoléon by horse) is a trail from Grasse to the outskirts of Grenoble. See route-napoleon-a-cheval.com.

● On the first weekend in March, Golfe-Juan hosts a reenactment of Napoléon's arrival on its shores. See vallauris-golfe-juan.fr.

● The **Réserve Biologique des Monts d'Azur** (p103) is a 20-minute drive east of Séranon.

PRACTICALITIES

● route-napoleon.com
● open year-round
● suits two wheels (motorbike) and four wheels

Continued from p99

can reserve workshops at all three perfume houses online; Molinard's setting is particularly atmospheric. In a high-ceiling, monochrome-tiled room, you'll mix and match dozens of top, middle and base notes to create a custom scent to take home. A short *Petit Parfumer* experience *(ages 4 to 8, €32)* offers children an introduction to the wonder of scent.

Grasse's perfumed gardens

The 20-minute drive from Grasse to nearby Mouans-Sartoux to visit the enchanting **Jardins du MIP** *(jardins dumip.museesdegrasse.com; adult/child €4/free)*, the gardens of the Musée International de la Parfumerie, is more than worth it. In this tactile garden, the world's greatest perfume flowers grow: its particularly lovely in spring when the Rose de Mai is in full bloom.

In the village of Plascassier, 7km southeast of Grasse, the sweet-scented **Domaine de Manon** *(domainedemanongrasse.com)* supplies Centifolia roses, jasmine and tuberose exclusively to Chanel; tours are held Tuesdays at 9am during flowering seasons: May for roses; late August to mid-October for jasmine and tuberose. Book in advance.

Gorges du Loup

TIME FROM CANNES: **50min**

Scenic villages along the Loup River

From the mountain plains high above Cannes, the Loup River runs all the way down to the Mediterranean and is at its most dramatic northeast of Grasse, snaking through a landscape of plunging cliffs, perched villages, refreshing waterfalls and thick forest, an area known as the Gorges du Loup.

Meaning 'wolf' in English, the Loup has given its name to a cluster of delightful villages, starting with sun-kissed Le Bar-sur-Loup, which has a rich tradition of cultivating bitter oranges. The next wolf along, Le Pont du Loup, is more hamlet than village, but the craft beer brewed at **Bacho Brewery** *(bachobrewery.com)* attracts a crowd from Nice and beyond. Set on a terrace of orange trees lit by fairy lights, this atmospheric microbrewery is the place for a quiet drink or a party night, depending on your mood. Just down the road, you can learn how clementines, rose petals and violets are crystalised and candied during a short tour at the Côte d'Azur's equivalent of Willy Wonka's chocolate factory, **Confiserie Florian** *(confiserieflorian.com, free)*.

CANYONING IN THE GORGES DU LOUP

Lionel Richard is a guide with Bureau des Guides LesGeckos (lesgeckos.eu). Here, he explains why the Gorges du Loup is paradise for outdoor sports.

Le Pont du Loup is the launching pad for incredible hiking, swimming, rock climbing and canyoning adventures. Most of the rock-climbing sites are for experienced climbers, although the Belvédère site is suitable for beginners. Canyoning is our most popular activity during summer. On a half-day excursion, we begin at the bottom of the Courmes waterfall and abseil into the gorge, followed by plenty of jumps and slides – at one point, you get to plunge 8m into the water below! Our half-day tours take about three hours and are for ages eight and up.

 EATING IN THE PRÉALPES & ON THE ROUTE NAPOLÉON: OUR PICKS

| **Auberge de Seranon**: Bistro classics like pizza and steaks rule in this rural restaurant. The open fire in winter is a delight. *hours vary* € | **La Bergerie**: Bright lunch spot in St-Vallier de Thiey with sunny patio. Light bites, but made from local and mostly organic ingredients. *9am-6pm Tue-Sat* € | **Restaurant Les Chasseurs**: Pizzas and a sunny terrace with a wide-angled view get a big thumbs up at this family restaurant in Andon. Reserve. *hours vary* € | **La Vieille Auberge**: Delightful restaurant inside the village of Gréolières, serving up family favourites on a shady tree-lined square. *noon-2pm Wed-Mon* € |

BEST DIVING SPOTS

Alex Diamond, PADI course director and freelance instructor, shares his favourite spots to dive on the Côte d'Azur.

Beginner: La Lauve off the Cap d'Antibes is a magical place to first experience scuba diving. The rock formations are beautiful and just beneath the surface awaits a shallow plateau teeming with life.

Intermediate: The Dromadaire and L'Enfer de Dante off La Fourmigue in Golfe Juan. Spectacular rock formations and underwater cliff faces with grouper, barracuda, dentex and gardens of gorgonian coral.

Advanced: The wrecks of *The Grec* and *Donator* off l'Île de Porquerolles are something else. The decks are 40m deep and the sea bed is simply awesome – it's so rich in marine life!

Scorpionfish, wreck of the *Donator* off l'Île de Porquerolles

Tourrettes-sur-Loup, closer to Vence, is known as the village of violets, particularly when the flower blooms between October and March. Find out why at the charming **Bastide aux Violettes** *(tourrettessurloup.com/la-bastide-aux-violettes-horaires-visites, adult/child €2/free)*, 10 minutes' walk from the centre of town.

Parc Naturel Régional des Préalpes d'Azur

TIME FROM CANNES: 1hr 15min

Into the wild

In 1993, Dr Patrice Longour, a French veterinarian, established the **Réserve Biologique des Monts d'Azur** *(reserve-biologique.com)* in order to achieve his long-held vision: rewilding mammals at risk of extinction, such as the European bison, Przewalski's horse and elk (moose). The 700-hectare reserve is located in Thorenc in the Parc Naturel Régional des Préalpes d'Azur.

Visit and you'll quickly get the sense that the fences are more to keep people from going in rather than the animals from coming out. Access to the sprawling reserve is either on foot (two hours) or on a horse-drawn cart (75 minutes). Both tours must be booked in advance and are led and narrated by a qualified guide well versed in tracking the park's resident three-legged wild boar and judging just how close visitors can get to the majestic herd of 50 bison.

The cluster of buildings at the entrance once formed part of a small hamlet and now functions as a variety of visitor services, including a snack bar serving up hot drinks and crêpes, a children's play area, a small open-air museum and a restaurant where organic ingredients shine. Stay overnight in one of the prairie-facing glamping tents (May to October only) or well-appointed rooms (year-round). Autumn's *brame du cerf* (rutting season) is a particularly memorable time to pay a visit.

Hike with a view

Towering nearly 800m above sea level, the eagle's-nest village of **Gourdon** dangles high above the Gorges du Loup with uninterrupted Mediterranean views. There's no shortage of restaurants inside its thick walls, so why not work up an appetite first on one of the Côte d'Azur's highest hikes? Take the D12 road north from the village for 2km, where a gravel car park to your right denotes the start of the **Plateau de Cavillore** hike.

The trail appears steep to look at, but the switchbacks that lead towards the summit are fairly gentle, making it a popular family outing. With each curve that you take, the views are better than the last. The whole loop is 5.7km and takes around 2½ hours; for many people it's enough to reach the summit and turn around: for that, plan an hour and a half.

TENDER IS THE NIGHT

A century ago, before it became the postcode of choice for the world's elite, Cap d'Antibes was a playground for the Lost Generation of American Writers including Ernest Hemingway and F Scott Fitzgerald. They whiled away days at **Plage de la Garoupe**, the starting point for the fabulous 5km coastal footpath, the **Sentier de Tirepoil**.

The Cap's legendary five-star **Hôtel du Cap Eden Roc**, immortalised as the Hôtel des Étrangers in Fitzgerald's *Tender is the Night*, was another favourite hang. Fitzgerald's tome was actually written in a waterfront villa in Juan-les-Pins, which would become another five-star lodging: **Hôtel Belles Rives**.

Inside the art deco stunner, the street-level Bar Fitzgerald is still furnished with some original pieces from the era.

Monaco

GLITZ | MOTORSPORTS | ROYALTY

GETTING AROUND

On foot is the best way to get around Monaco with no distances longer than an hour's walk, but the terrain can be very steep. Skip the stairs – and catch your breath – with one of the principality's 79 public lifts or its around 35 escalators.

The Compagnie Autobus de Monaco operates six bus lines that serve all corners of the principality; tickets can be purchased on board the bus (cash or card) for €2; you can purchase up to six tickets with one credit/debit card.

MonaBike is Monaco's excellent electric bike-sharing scheme; register in advance on the Monapass app. If driving, avoid commuter hours. Public parking fills up fast and can be pricey during daytime hours, although the hourly rate drops significantly come evening.

Monaco is constantly evolving. Towering cranes are as ubiquitous as superyachts and sports cars as the principality stretches up and out to sea to maximise every inch of its limited space. Nowhere else on the Côte d'Azur feels so built up, but in fact over 20% of Monaco's territory is made up of gardens. Spearheaded by HSH Prince Albert II, the principality harbours even greater green ambitions with a goal of carbon neutrality by 2050.

'Green is glam' (as Monaco's sustainable push with a luxury twist is known) is the latest chapter in the Hollywood history of the world's second-smallest country, whose reputation was built on a lavish Belle Époque casino and sealed with the marriage of a Grimaldi prince, Rainier III, to a silver-screen princess, Grace Kelly. The glitz is as pervasive as ever, but is now balanced out by local experiences – and flavours – that add another side to Monaco's real identity and culture.

Racing Weekends
Fast cars, three ways

For the Monaco **Formula One Grand Prix** 2026 is a marquee year: the traditional late-May race weekend has been swapped for the first weekend in June, a date that's now fixed in the calendar until 2031. How you feel about being in town when the Formula One roadshow rolls in depends on how you feel about cars racing around in circles. Most residents leave, but if you're a fan, there's no place better to be. Tickets for the four days of racing go on sale on the **Automobile Club de Monaco**'s online portal *(acm.mc)* around six months ahead of the race. You can nab a seat at Thursday's practice sessions for €30 but expect to pay from €550 for even the cheapest seats for Sunday's race day. Even if you don't have a ticket, it's still worth coming to Monaco on the weekend. The echoes of engines reverberate off every building and the excitement builds with every driver appearance at the fan zone on place

Grand Prix Historique de Monaco

d'Armes in La Condamine. Many restaurants stream the race live so you don't miss any of the action. Unfortunately, it's almost impossible to find anywhere to view the circuit for free anymore.

An abridged version of the famous street circuit has become an annual May fixture on the ePrix calendar. Tickets for the **Monaco ePrix** cost €30 to €45, depending on the stand.

If you prefer vintage classics over modern iterations, the **Grand Prix Historique de Monaco** is held every second year in April (2026 and 2028 are the next dates). Watch champions from yesteryear compete for a variety of trophies – and bragging rights. Tickets start from €50, also via the Automobile Club de Monaco.

Uncovering a Palace's Past
Hidden Renaissance frescoes

From the **Palais Princier de Monaco** (visitepalaisde monaco.com; adult/child €10/5) high up in Monaco-Ville, the Grimaldi family has ruled over the principality since the late 13th century. As it's still the official residence of the sovereign

Continues on p108

> ☑ **TOP TIP**
>
> If you're planning on spending a decent amount of time in Monaco, download and register on the Carlo app before you arrive. This popular homegrown app offers a 5% cashback on purchases made at numerous businesses in the Principality, even multinationals like McDonalds. A nice little pot can accumulate quickly; just ensure you spend it at a participating store before you leave. See carloapp.com.

 EATING IN MONACO: OUR PICKS

Les Perles de Monte-Carlo: Tuck into oysters reared on site at this marine research centre turned seafood counter in Fontvieille. *hours vary* €€

Il Terrazzino: Business lunch spot serving up Neapolitan favourites near Casino Square. A taste of the Amalfi in Monaco. *noon-2.30pm & 7-10.30pm Tue-Sat* €

Sexy Tacos: Fiery Mexican cuisine and zesty margaritas make this the hottest address on the Larvotto beach strip. *noon-10.30pm* €€

U Luvassu: The speciality here is the catch of the day, fresh from *Diego*, the fishing boat of Eric Rinaldi, Monaco's last fisher. *noon-2pm Mon-Sat* €€

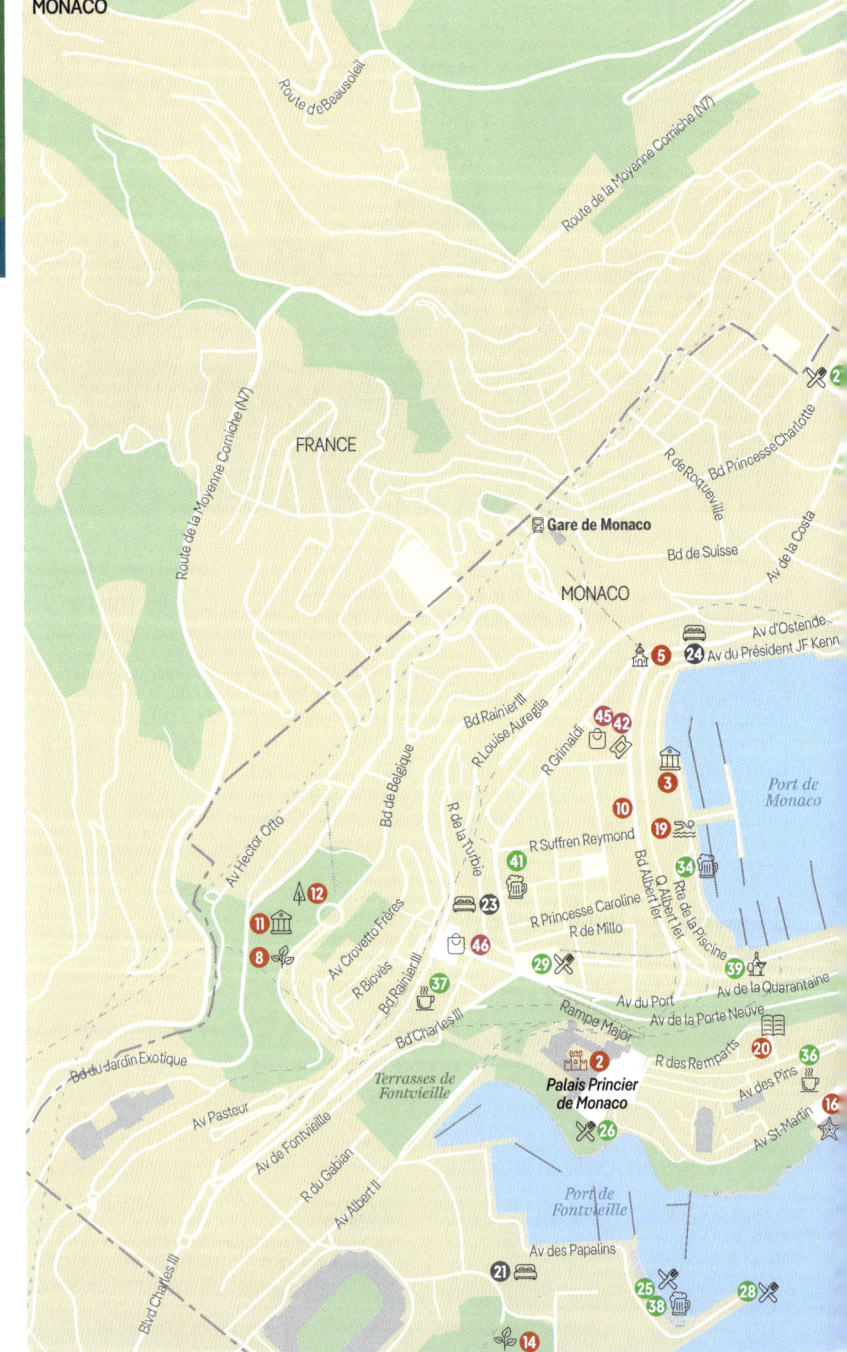

★ HIGHLIGHTS
1. Casino de Monte-Carlo
2. Palais Princier de Monaco

● SIGHTS
3. Collection de Voitures de SAS le Prince de Monaco
4. Crique des Pêcheurs
5. Église Ste-Dévote
6. Espace de Méditation
7. Fairmont Hairpin
8. Jardin Exotique
9. La Grotte Bleue
10. Monaco Grand Prix starting grid
11. Musée d'Anthropologie Préhistorique de Monaco
12. Parc Princesse Antoinette
13. Place du Casino
14. Roseraie Princesse Grace
15. Tunnel Louis II

● ACTIVITIES
16. Musée Océanographique de Monaco
17. Plage du Larvotto
18. Plage du Solarium
19. Stade Nautique Rainier III
20. The Princess Grace Irish Library

● SLEEPING
21. Columbus Monte-Carlo
22. Hôtel Capitole
23. Hôtel de France
24. Hotel Miramar

● EATING
see 29 A Roca
25. Beefbar
26. Castel Roc
see 29 Chez Roger
27. Il Terrazzino
28. Les Perles de Monte-Carlo
see 29 Maison des Pâtes
29. Marché de la Condamine
see 29 Mitron Bakery
30. Sexy Tacos
31. Song Qi
32. U Luvassu
33. Zeffirino Restaurant

● DRINKING & NIGHTLIFE
34. Brasserie de Monaco
35. Café de Paris
36. Chocolaterie de Monaco
37. Costadoro Social Coffee Monaco
38. Gerhard's Café
39. La Rascasse
40. Le Teashop
41. Slammer's

● ENTERTAINMENT
42. Automobile Club de Monaco
43. Monaco Open-Air Cinema
44. Théatre Princesse Grace

● SHOPPING
45. La Boutique de l'Automobile Club de Monaco
46. La Distillerie de Monaco

THE GUIDE

MONACO CÔTE D'AZUR & MONACO

GET TO KNOW MONACO'S NEIGHBOURHOODS

Despite being used interchangeably with Monaco, **Monte Carlo** is just one of the principality's neighbourhoods, albeit its most famous, with sites such as the **Casino de Monte-Carlo** (p109) inside its limits.

La Condamine, around Port Hercules, has a distinctly local flavour and hosts the place d'Armes **market** (p111). A huddle of colourful buildings high above the port, **Monaco-Ville,** also known as Le Rocher, is Monaco's historic heart, with narrow streets and covered passages fanning out from the **Palais Princier de Monaco.**

Like Mareterra, Monaco's newest neighbourhood, **Fontvieille** has risen out of the sea at the western edge. The **Larvotto** beachfront strip is one of the most expensive slices of real estate in the world.

Continued from p105

family, only the Grands Appartements, or staterooms, are open to public eyes – and only between April and October for self-guided visits with an audio guide (except for the Formula One Grand Prix weekend). These formal rooms, which still have a ceremonial function, display a princely penchant for heavy drapery, extensive gold-leaf panelling and fine art. The entire experience has been elevated with the uncovering of over 600 sq metres (and counting) of captivating Renaissance frescoes that depict three heroes from antiquity – Hercules, Odysseus and Europa – hidden for centuries under layers of paint. The work is ongoing, as the metres of scaffolding attest, using natural solvents and environmentally friendly solutions to gradually restore walls and ceilings to their original decoration. It's a project those at the palace believe will last the lifetime of the current sovereign, His Serene Highness, Prince Albert II. Time your visit around the changing of the guards, daily at 11.55am.

Morning, Mareterra!
A new neighbourhood rises from the sea

Although primarily residential, Mareterra, Monaco's newest neighbourhood, is still worth a mosey, if anything to appreciate the marvels of land reclamation. You can't access all corners, but you get sensational views across to Italy along a smooth, 500m-long seafront promenade that connects with the Larvotto beachfront at the eastern end. Look out for two unmarked doors along the way that open onto a couple of the Principality's most curious attractions: a cavern of pink crystals styled as an **Espace de Méditation**, or public meditation space, and **La Grotte Bleue**, a sliver of the 26m-high foundations left exposed for public viewing. It's a nice idea, but the room is unlit and little more than a concrete railing separates you from the drop into the sea, so the whole experience ends up eerie rather than engaging.

Made in Monaco Drinks
Taste the local spirit

Agriculture was the lifeblood of Monaco's economy until the mid-19th century when the Grimaldi family ceded 95% of its territory to France. Today, if you look closely enough, there are still clues to this heritage, such as the 600 bitter orange

Continues on p110

 EATING IN MONACO: BEST MIDWEEK LUNCHTIME SET MENUS

Song Qi: Cool Shanghai art deco design and three different menus: noodle, dim sum or a choice of a meat or fish dish. *noon-2.30pm & 7-10.30pm, to 11pm Fri & Sat* €€

Beefbar: Legendary carnivore emporium in Fontvieille serving a starter and beef tartare or tagliata with chips. *noon-2.30pm & 8-11pm, to 11.30pm Fri & Sat* €€

Zeffirino Restaurant: Genoese fine dining near Larvotto, famed for its pesto. *noon-2.15pm & 7.30-10.30pm, to 11pm Fri & Sat* €€

Castel Roc: A+ for location, just steps from the palace. Food is traditional French. Go all in with three courses for €38. *noon-3pm* €€

TOP EXPERIENCE

Casino de Monte-Carlo

Built on an arid plateau where citrus trees once prospered, the **Casino de Monte-Carlo** is the ornate Belle Époque marvel that put the principality on the map for Europe's high rollers when it first opened in the 1860s. Yet this gilded address is so much more than a spot for a flutter – in fact, it's one of the region's architectural treasures.

More than a Gambling Den

In the morning, you can ogle the ornate marble and gold-leaf-clad *salons privés* without risking a cent on a self-guided tour through the gaming rooms. Take your time and admire the intricate styling of each of the 10 rooms you pass. An audio guide, included in the entrance fee, weaves in history and entertaining anecdotes while pointing out the incredible decorative detail.

Even the fittings and fixtures are works of art. In Salle Europe, the oldest gaming room, roulette wheels spin underneath eight dazzling Bohemian crystal chandeliers, weighing 150kg each. Salle Blanche, a private den, sparkles with mosaic detailing and caryatids.

The Empire-style Salle Médecin, where the casino's original high rollers played away from prying eyes, is also a silver-screen star, with two Bond movies, *Golden Eye* and *Never Say Never Again*, shot here.

Fancy Flutter

Fun fact: Monaco nationals are not allowed to gamble. For all other nationalities, you must be at least 18 years and have a photo ID to enter the gaming rooms after 2pm. There's a strict dress code: think smart attire rather than shorts, sportswear and flip-flops.

TOP TIPS

● Between October and March the group visits thin out.

● Don't miss the back of the building: the sea-facing rear facade is wonderfully elaborate, too.

● Fancy a flutter? The minimum bet in the Salle Europe is €5 for roulette.

PRACTICALITIES

● montecarlosbm.com/en/casino-monaco/casino-monte-carlo
● adult/child €19/free
● 10am-1pm; last entrance at 12.15pm (for visits). Gaming starts at 2pm.

MONACO'S PEACEFUL CONQUESTS

How do you expand your land when you're surrounded by France and the Mediterranean Sea? With a territory similar in size to New York's Central Park and a population of 39,000, it's a question Monaco has long puzzled over.

The answer is land reclamation: under Prince Rainier III and now Prince Albert II, Monaco has swollen from 150 to 202 hectares through this peaceful form of conquest. As a result, entire new areas and districts have been built, including Port Hercules, the Larvotto waterfront and the Fontvieille port and business district.

Now the landscape has changed once again with a new neighbourhood, Mareterra, rising from the sea in front of Monte-Carlo in 2025. The 'eco-district', as Mareterra has been billed, has added 3% to Monaco's territory.

Continued from p108

trees that line some of the principality's main boulevards (particularly rue Grimaldi behind Port Hercules). Rather than confining the fruit to waste, Philip Culazzo saw an opportunity to transform this tangy citrus into a punchy orange liqueur, called L'Orangeraie. Since opening **La Distillerie de Monaco** *(distilleriedemonaco.com)* in 2020 across from La Marché de la Condamine, the Irish national has added three more distinctly Monégasque drinks to his made-in-Monaco spirits cabinet: Carruba, a rich, velvety chocolate liqueur made from Monaco's national tree, the carob; a seven citrus Gin aux Agrumes; and the newest release, a rum made in partnership with the Prince.

You can swing by the distillery to buy a bottle, but book ahead for a 15-minute tasting (€9) or a 25-minute tour and tasting (€27) – much of the price difference comes down to how many miniatures you are given to take home (one versus three).

DRINKING IN MONACO: CAFE CULTURE

Costadoro Social Coffee Monaco: Whatever your coffee preference, this Italian cafe in La Condamine serves it. *7.30am-7.30pm Mon-Sat, 9am-7pm Sun.*

Chocolaterie de Monaco: Chocolate emporium with cafe at the back specialising in hot chocolate. On Le Rocher. *9.30am-noon & 1-6pm Mon-Tue & Thu-Sat*

Le Teashop: Cute neighbourhood cafe on bd des Moulins, with 100-plus teas plus plenty of tea-adjacent finds. *9am-1pm Mon-Sat, 2-6pm Mon-Fri*

Café de Paris: You're paying as much for the setting on Casino Square as the coffee – and it's top dollar. *8am-1am*

Port Hercules, Monaco

Where the Locals Lunch
A small square and big market

Despite its glitzy image, the good news is that you don't have to take out a loan to eat well in Monaco. You can find a hub of cheap and cheerful eats inside the bustling **Marché de la Condamine** on place d'Armes.

This lively square, just back from Port Hercules in La Condamine neighbourhood, bursts with fresh flowers and colourful fruit and vegetables from just across the border in Italy. The covered market rises early to cater to the breakfast trade, although the real buzz is at lunch when workers from nearby offices flood in to tuck into plates piled high with fresh pasta and other tasty, quick eats. Note, the food hall is shuttering in January 2026 for an extensive 13-month upgrade that La Condamine residents hope won't strip away the market's charm. While the works are underway, you'll find the stallholders installed in temporary chalets on the square.

BEST SWIM SPOTS IN MONACO

Plage du Larvotto
Pricey private beach clubs and a public beach to lay down your towel for free at Monaco's eastern edge.

Stade Nautique Rainier III
Open-air Olympic-sized pool among the superyachts in Port Hercules. The extra €6 for a sunlounger is worth it.

Plage du Solarium
An unlikely swim spot that has emerged on the concrete outer wall on the western side of the harbour. The steps are an ideal jumping-off point to cool down on a hot day. Note: the water here is deep and unpatrolled.

Crique des Pêcheurs
This hidden half-moon of pebbly beach snuggled into the cliff face is bliss at low tide – but not when the sea is up.

 DRINKING IN MONACO: LOCAL HAUNTS

La Rascasse: Legendary bar on the F1 corner of the same name. Chilled happy hours, loud late-night parties. *4.30pm-3.30am Tue-Thu, 6.30pm-4.30am Fri & Sat*

Slammer's: Small pub with big sports screens and a reputation for atmosphere, especially on Grand Prix weekend. *4pm-1am*

Gerhard's Café: Long-running German pub on Fontvieille's bar and restaurant strip with a laid-back atmosphere and friendly vibe. *8am-3am, from 11am Sun*

Brasserie de Monaco: Boisterous microbrewery on Port Hercules pours organic pale ales and wheat beers brewed on site, alongside typical pub grub. *noon-2am*

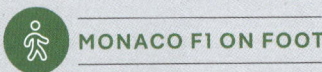

MONACO F1 ON FOOT

Visiting outside of race day? Set the pace on a walking tour of the legendary street circuit – and familiarise yourself with many of Monaco's sights along the way.

START	END	LENGTH
Port Hercules	Port Hercules	3.4km; 1½hr

Begin this tour in pole position, literally, at 17 bd Albert 1er on Port Hercules, aka the ❶ **Monaco Grand Prix starting grid**. A few doors down at number 23 is race organiser, the ❷ **Automobile Club de Monaco** (ACM); it's a member's-only address, but you can browse the memorabilia on display in the windows.

The Ste Dévote bend is named after the ornate ❸ **Église Ste-Dévote**, a church so small compared to the tall apartment blocks around it that it looks like a decorative figurine. You'll next start the climb towards ❹ **place du Casino**, the world's glitziest car park for supercars, before descending to the ❺ **Fairmont Hairpin**, the slowest corner of any F1 circuit.

Follow the footpath down to ❻ **Tunnel Louis II**. Once you have walked through it, you'll emerge at the ultra-exclusive Yacht Club de Monaco. The rest of the route is flat, following the harbourfront.

Next stop is the ❼ **Collection de Voitures de SAS le Prince de Monaco**, Prince Rainier III's shiny automotive stockpile, including vintage F1 and rally racers. In F1 terms, ❽ **La Rascasse** (p111) is the tight corner just before the pit lane entrance, but in Monaco it's also the name of the popular bar in the same place. Happy hour runs from 6pm to 8.30pm. You're so close to the finish you could call it a day here, or sweep back around to the starting line to close the loop.

Before dipping into the Tunnel Louis II, look out towards **Mareterra** (p108), the principality's newest neighbourhood that has risen from the sea.

Make a quick pit stop inside **La Boutique de l'Automobile Club de Monaco**, the sleek merchandise shop run by the ACM.

At **La Rascasse** (p111), happy hour runs from 5pm to 11pm, or quench your thirst with a made-in-Monaco brew at the nearby **Brasserie de Monaco** (p111).

Best Meal of the Day
Brilliant bargains at lunch

Although still considered pricey compared to most other destinations, Monaco's high-end restaurant menus that veer towards exorbitant for dinner are often more wallet-friendly for weekday lunch, when restaurants are out to court the business crowd. Expect to pay around €30 per person for a set lunch menu with a glass of wine – a price that wouldn't cover the main course come sunset.

Catch Some Cinematic Highlights
Making movies an event in Monaco

Going to the movies might not be the first thing you think about when visiting a new country, but Monaco has two cinemas that can claim to be destinations in their own right – and have a solid program of movies in VO (*version originale*, or original language) to boot. In a building dating from 1932, the two-screen Cinema des Beaux-Arts inside the **Théatre Princesse Grace** makes a trip to the cinema feel like a real event. At this antithesis to today's sprawling megaplexes, you can admire photos of Grace Kelly on the wall or have a pre-film drink at the old-school bar and lounge area with superb views over the port.

A Hollywood-worthy setting on a ledge jutting out over the sea at the foot of Le Rocher almost steals the limelight at the **Monaco Open-Air Cinema**. Movies start at sunset, but doors open half an hour before the film and there's a small bar. Open June to September. See what is showing in both at *cinemas2monaco.com*.

ENJOY MONACO WITH KIDS

Musée Océanographique de Monaco: This world-class marine museum on Le Rocher includes an aquarium and shows.

Parc Princesse Antoinette: A multitude of play areas suitable for kids of all ages.

Musée d'Anthropologie Préhistorique de Monaco: Small anthropology museum with rows of bugs, butterflies and beetles in glass cases, plus a mammoth skeleton.

Roseraie Princesse Grace: A pastel-pretty English-style garden in Fontvielle where 6000 rose bushes burst into bloom in spring.

Princess Grace Irish Library: Guardians of Grace Kelly's tomes of Irish literature on Le Rocher. The kids' corner on rainy days is a welcome shelter.

 EATING IN MONACO: BUDGET BITES AT MARCHÉ DE LA CONDAMINE

Mitron Bakery: Monaco outpost of Mauro Colagreco's organic bakery in Menton. Freshly baked breads and sweet lemon tarts. *7.30am-1.30pm Tue-Sun* €

Chez Roger: So renowned is the *socca* and *pissaladière* at Chez Roger that there's little need to sell anything else. *9.45am-1.30pm Tue-Sat* €

Maison des Pâtes: The lunch crowd flock with good reason to this pasta spot for strings of fresh tagliatelle or pouches of ravioli. *7am-3.30pm Mon-Sun, 6-9.30pm Tue-Sat* €

A Roca: The spot for *barbajuans*, tasty fried ravioli considered the principality's national dish. *8.30am-2.50pm Tue-Sat, 8am-1pm Sun* €

Places We Love to Stay

€ Budget €€ Midrange €€€ Top End

Nice
Map p60

Hostel Meyerbeer Beach € Friendly hostel with a cracking city-centre location, just three minutes from the beach. Dorms are mixed.

Hôtel Ozz € A decor that pops, bunks with curtains, female-only dorms and a lively bar, all a stone's throw from Nice-Ville train station.

Hôtel Arome €€ This secure, centrally located hotel run by a wonderful Franco-Italian couple is popular with solo women.

Le Saint Paul €€ Across from the breakwater in Port Lympia, this church-run choice has the best-value seafront rooms in Nice.

Hôtel Rossetti €€ Charming three-star boutique hotel with seven rooms in the shadow of Cathédrale Ste-Réparate in Vieux Nice. The hidden terrace is lovely.

Hôtel du Pin €€ An unbeatable location among the bars and restaurants on rue Bonaparte, even if the rooms are lacking on the space and storage front.

Hôtel La Pérouse €€€ Clinging to the Colline du Château with a hidden pool and sea views, this delightful four-star hotel is one of Nice's finest.

Hôtel Amour €€€ Uber hip address slightly off centre in the Fleurs neighbourhood with an eclectic boho-chic styling and the trendiest hotel bar for miles.

Le Negresco €€€ The grande dame of Nice's hotels set across from the beach. Each room is unique and styled to a theme. The art collection is priceless.

Hôtel du Couvent €€€ A lemon-shaded courtyard, on-site herbalist and thermal baths: the five-star address that has emerged from an abandoned 17th-century convent in Vieux Nice chooses serenity over glitz.

Villefranche-sur-Mer

La Régence – Chez Betty € Top-value find in the centre of town with charming, Provençal-styled rooms, a family feel and a bar where you'll get chatting to locals.

Hôtel de la Darse €€ Basic but smart two-star choice across from the water in the quiet port neighbourhood. Sea-view rooms with sunny balconies.

Welcome Hôtel €€€ Jean Cocteau, Pablo Picasso and Winston Churchill are among the names who have slept at this legendary burnt-orange hotel on the harbour.

St-Jean-Cap-Ferrat & Èze

Hôtel Brise Marine €€ Three generations of the Maîtrehenry family have run this lemon-yellow three-star hotel with garden steps from the beach.

Château Eza €€€ Fourteen rooms scattered throughout Èze's atmospheric alleys, many with sublime sea and coast views. If you're looking to propose, few settings are more memorable.

Menton

Hôtel Lemon € Comfortable rooms shaded the colours of Menton near the train station. The citrus garden and organic breakfast are highlights.

La Fabrique à Poupées €€ Three rooms and one apartment in a clay-red villa that, until 2002, produced folkloric dolls for souvenir shops. Stylish with a great location.

St-Paul de Vence

Camping Pinèdes € Shaded pitches and mobile homes, with a swimming pool and wild river swimming on the doorstep. Ten minutes' drive from St-Paul de Vence.

Hôtel Les Messugues €€ Dreamy Provençal *mas* (stone house), surrounded by olive groves of the Fondation Maeght. Quirk: doors have come from prison cells.

Orion Treehouses €€ Four cedar-wood treehouses around a wild swimming pool. An utterly enchanting and unique setting. Reservations Saturday to Saturday in summer.

Vence

Domaine de la Bergerie € Tranquil campsite nestled in woodland between Vence and St-Paul de Vence with pitches and mobile homes, restaurant, small supermarket and pool.

La Maison du Frêne €€ A real *coup de coeur* for this richly decorated B&B in the centre of Vence that reflects the passion of the owners, Thierry and Guy, for Baroque and pop art.

St-Martin-Vésubie

Relais des Merveilles € Cosy hikers' inn with dorms and doubles, as well as animal spotting, half an hour out of town. Open from late April to October.

La Bonne Auberge € Delightful three-star find in the centre of

St-Martin-Vésubie, run by the same family since 1946. The 12 rooms have chalet vibes. Breakfast is excellent.

Pure Montagne €€€ Swanky spa resort that brings more than a sprinkling of alpine glam to the backcountry. A top choice for families (and Monaco residents on weekend getaways).

Cannes   Map p87

Banana's Camp € Clean and bright mixed and female dorms in a buttermilk-yellow villa less than 10 minutes' walk from the train station.

Hôtel de Provence €€ This leafy oasis in central Cannes is a real find, but fills up fast. Opt for room 12, 14 or 15.

Hôtel Jardin Croisette €€ Just next door to the Hôtel de Provence, with an inviting tropical garden and bright, modern rooms.

Hôtel Villa Claudia €€ Cosy, high-ceilinged rooms drip with character in this 19th-century pastel-pink villa and garden close to the train station. On-site parking for €18 a day.

Hôtel Le Mistral €€ The friendliness of owner Jean-Michel and the nightly price makes up for some dated decor. Unbeatable location near the Palais des Festivals et des Congrès.

Mandelieu-la-Napoule

Bungalows du Golfe Camping Les Pruniers € A bit hemmed in by holiday apartments, but you won't find a friendlier campsite closer to Cannes or the beach. Particularly good for motorhomes.

Hôtel Casarose €€ This fun hotel brings a funky California vibe and bright decor to the Côte d'Azur. An Instagram favourite.

Antibes

Le Relais du Postillon €€ Three-star hotel on a popular square at the edge of the old town. Rooms are snug but full of Provençal charm.

Hôtel Josse €€ For a more summer vibe, this low-slung, whitewashed, 27-room hotel just across from the beach is a top choice.

Mougins

La Lune de Mougins €€ With a pool, spa, tennis court, restaurant and kids' play area, this spacious three-star is recommended.

Le Manoir d'Étang €€ A sprawling, plant-covered 19th-century residence on a five-hectare estate overlooking parkland, this is the definition of a peaceful Provençal oasis.

Grasse

Auberge les Arômes € Simple yet spacious rooms, on-site parking, a delicious Greco-Armenian restaurant and a family touch lacking in most hotels nowadays.

Domaine de la Cascade Parfumée €€€ Romantic suites with luxe trimmings in a canary-yellow *bastide* (country house) behind Grasse, fully renovated in 2024.

Gorges du Loup

Auberge des Gorges du Loup € This great-value find in Pont du Loup has oodles of Provençal charm. Pet friendly and hugely popular with motorbikers.

Hôtel Particulier des Jasmins € Rustic yet romantic rooms inside an old perfumer's house with deep valley views in Le-Bar-sur-Loup.

Route Napoléon

Le Relais Imperial € Friendly, family-run hotel in St-Vallier de Thiey. Rooms seem dated, but rather than being off-putting, it all feels wonderfully nostalgic.

Gîte Bastide Napoléon €€ Of the two rustic roadside *gîtes* just outside Seranon, 'La Grange' is particularly family friendly with a billiards table and shelves full of board games.

Monaco   Map p106

Hôtel de France € Cheapest hotel in Monaco with 26 well-appointed rooms and airy high ceilings. There's no lift.

Hotel Capitole € Technically in the French town of Beausoleil, but one street away from the Monaco border. Simple rooms, some with sea glimpses, with less of the Monaco price tag.

Columbus Monte-Carlo €€€ This stylish three-star hotel in Fontvieille punches above its weight with a pool and great views.

Hôtel Miramar €€€ Boutique hotel with a superb location opposite Port Hercules, a chic nautical theme and a cool rooftop bar. Watch out for last-minute discounted rates.

Researched by
Alexis Averbuck

The Var

TURQUOISE SEA, BEACHES, HILLTOP VILLAGES

From famous St-Tropez, golden beaches and the sparkling Mediterranean to chestnut-packed forests and the perched villages of the Haut-Var, southern Provence shines brightly.

Glamour and sophistication along the Golfe de St-Tropez…family-friendly beach access near Hyères…charming villages looking across world-class vineyards… the Var has it all.

Is bling your thing? Prioritize St-Tropez, where an historic fishing village meets the finest beaches, cocktails and hotels – luxury yachts included. The umber lanes thrum with high-end shopping and art; plus, foodies, the coast is your hot spot for seafood. Boats ply the waters all around, making easy jumping-off points to further adventure.

Looking for a more laid-back scene? Hike the red-rock Corniche de l'Estérel or venture inland to the forests of Massif de la Ste-Baume and Massif des Maures for chestnuts, monasteries and serenity.

The palm-lined, understated city of Hyères is a vibrant pleasure, and its Presqu'île de Giens beaches are tops for wind sports. Or go bird-watching for flamingos in its former saltpans. You'll love the Îles d'Hyères – Porquerolles, Port-Cros or Levant – by bicycle, with a snorkel or on foot.

To the west of St-Tropez, exalt in flower-redolent breezes at Mediterranean gardens, and come in winter to revel in the mimosa flowering season. Inland, Haut-Var villages such as Cotignac – with its cliffs, caves and main street crammed with restaurants – will make you want to move here. Raise a glass of rosé to toast the sunset. From the hills to the coast, the Var is yours.

THE MAIN AREAS

ST-TROPEZ
Capital of glitz and glamour. **p120**

HYÈRES
Medieval city with out-of-this-world islands. **p136**

HAUT-VAR
Perched villages and top rosé. **p145**

For places to stay in The Var, see p153

THE GUIDE

THE VAR

Left: Salema porgy fish, Parc National de Port-Cros (p141); Above: Cotignac (p145)

Find Your Way

THE VAR

THE GUIDE

In summer, it's best to get around urban areas using public transport. The largest train stations are in Hyères, St-Raphaël and Les Arcs–Draguignan.

Haut-Var, p145
Escape the crowds and heat in rolling vineyards and hilltop villages, each with its own vibe.

Hyères, p136
All the elements of a classic Côte d'Azur town, without the rush or bling. Islands nearby, too.

St-Tropez, p120
The capital of hot summer nights; come here to live out your French Riviera dreams, beach or harbourside.

BOAT
On the Golfe de St-Tropez, Les Bateaux Verts ferries cross between Ste-Maxime, Grimaud and St-Tropez. Les Bateaux Bleus serve St-Raphaël. Ferries connect La Tour Fondue and Île de Porquerolles. Excursion boats serve other coastal cities and islands.

CAR
The pros: get around the Haut-Var easily. The cons: the coastal road is a traffic-clogged nightmare, and parking in coastal towns comes with a gold-plated price tag. Park on the fringes and walk or ferry. Everything is easier in low season.

0 — 10 km
0 — 5 miles

Vieux Port, St-Tropez (p121)

Plan Your Time

Can't move to the south of France? We'll help you plan your time without stretching it too tight. After all, the luxuriating pace is part of the joie de vivre.

Weekend in St-Tropez

● In the morning explore the **harbour and old town** (p121), then go for lunch at a club on **Plage de Pampelonne** (p124). Dance till dawn at one of St-Tropez' **bars or clubs** (p124). Sleep off last night on a lounger or a **catamaran** (p125), or take in the views from **Ramatuelle and Gassin** (p126), then hit St-Tropez' **fashion boutiques** (p122) and **galleries** (p123).

Four Days Inland

● Connect with nature in the chestnut groves of **Monastère de la Verne** (p130) and **Collobrières** (p130) before going **winetasting** (p143). Then dine and sleep below the cliffs of **Cotignac** (p145). Take a **driving tour through Haut-Var villages** (p150), stopping at **markets** (p147), then hit the coast at **Hyères** (p136) and **Île de Porquerolles** (p140).

SEASONAL HIGHLIGHTS

SPRING
Fewer crowds and mild weather. Drive the Rte du Mimosas in late winter and early spring when they're blooming.

SUMMER
Reserve all lodging well ahead. In early summer, snorkel in Île de Porquerolles before crowds intensify.

AUTUMN
Weather and crowds soften. Les Voiles de St-Tropez (p128) takes over the gulf and port for ten days.

WINTER
Days are shorter, but it's the best time to cycle the Haut-Var – calm roads, mild temps. It's also truffle season.

St-Tropez

GORGEOUS TOWN | HOT BEACHES | GLAMOUR

☑ TOP TIP

Not planning to party till dawn? Then late May and June are great times to visit, as most beach clubs will be open for day-lounging, but with a chiller vibe. Reservations are essential in high season; many restaurants and hotels close in winter.

Sexy St-Tropez is the most desired destination on the French Riviera. Sail the gulf, dine in glitzy restaurants, sunbathe on Plage de Pampelonne beach-club loungers and dance till dawn. Stroll the Vieux Port, with yachts jostling for millionaire moorings. Meander cobbled lanes in the old fishing quarter of La Ponche, watch people play *pétanque* beneath plane trees on place des Lices, or walk in splendour from beach to beach along the coastal path. Dig deeper still and you'll get your art, shopping and festival fix, too.

St-Tropez is busy, it's flashy, and in the summer months, it's also jam-packed. Explore Ramatuelle and Gassin, precious villages with great views, and the beach at nearby Gigaro. Across the gulf you can escape to laid-back Ste-Maxime, perfect for families and those not wanting to spend a bling-bling budget on a single cocktail. The French Riviera is what you make of it, so make it fabulous, no matter the time of year or your budget.

GETTING AROUND

During high season, those in the know avoid horrendous four-hour traffic bottlenecks on the one road into St-Tropez (and €40 scarce parking) by parking in Port Grimaud, Ste-Maxime or Cavalaire and taking a **Les Bateaux Verts** shuttle boat. **Les Bateaux Bleus** serves St-Raphaël, Fréjus and Agay. **Vedettes Îles d'Or et Le Corsaire** runs boats to St-Tropez and Îles d'Hyères from Le Lavandou, Cavalaire-sur-Mer and La Croix-Valmer. **Trans Côte d'Azur** has ferries to Nice and Cannes. Pricey **sea taxis** *(taxi-boat-saint-tropez.com)* serve the gulf.

Free and cheap shuttle buses (p126) connect St-Tropez' neighbourhoods and beaches. Zou buses *(zou.maregionsud.fr; €2.10)* connect St-Tropez **bus station** with Ramatuelle (35 minutes) and St-Raphaël (1¼ to three hours, depending on traffic) via Grimaud and Port Grimaud, and Fréjus. Bus 878 to Toulon (two hours) stops at Le Lavandou (one hour) and Hyères (1½ hours). Bus 873 serves Toulon-Hyères airport (1½ hours). Var Express *(varexpress.eu; from €50)* serves Nice Airport.

By train, the most convenient station is St-Raphaël.

ST-TROPEZ

⭐ HIGHLIGHTS
1. Citadelle de St-Tropez
2. La Ponche
3. Vieux Port

● SIGHTS
4. Bailli de Suffren Statue
5. Chapelle de la Miséricorde
6. Église de St-Tropez
7. Musée de l'Annonciade
8. Place des Lices
9. Plage de la Fontanette
10. Plage de La Ponche

● ACTIVITIES
11. Les Bateaux Verts
12. Sentier du Littoral

● SLEEPING
13. B Lodge Hôtel
14. Hôtel Byblos
15. Hôtel Ermitage
16. Hôtel Le Colombier
17. Hôtel Lou Cagnard

● EATING
18. Au Caprice des Deux
19. Gourd'l Saint-Tropez
20. La Petite Plage
21. La Ramade
22. La Tarte Tropézienne
23. Le Sporting
24. Le Traiteur de l'Auberge des Maures

● NIGHTLIFE
25. Gaïo
26. Hôtel Bar Le Sube
27. Le Tigrr
28. Les Caves du Roy
29. Sénéquier

● SHOPPING
30. Bel-Air Fine Art
31. K Jacques
32. La Cabane d'Anoé
33. La Pause Douceur
34. La Vielle Mer
35. Le Dépôt
36. Les Galeries Tropéziennes
37. Market
38. Rondini

● TRANSPORT
39. Bus Station
40. Les Bateaux Bleus
41. Trans Côte d'Azur

Stroll Central St-Tropez
Soak up the history and glamour

Start your visit by promenading along the quays at the richly charming **Vieux Port** (old port), where yachts line the harbour and denizens sip coffees or cocktails at waterfront cafes. Sable-coloured townhouses glow in the sun; and the **Bailli de Suffren statue** of a 17th-century naval hero, cast from a 19th-century cannon, peers out to sea.

MARKET DAYS AROUND THE GOLFE DE ST-TROPEZ

Bountiful markets are a mainstay around the region, and fill town squares with farmers and makers selling everything from organic food to readymade meals, clothing and antiques. Find out more at golfe-saint-tropez-information.com. Weekly markets follow and tend to run 8am to 1pm:

Tuesday: St-Tropez
Wednesday: Cogolin (inland village)
Thursday: Grimaud, Ramatuelle
Friday: Ste-Maxime, Rayol-Canadel-sur-Mer (April to September)
Saturday: St-Tropez, Cogolin
Sunday: La Croix-Valmer, La Garde-Freinet (inland villages), Port Grimaud, Ramatuelle

Tarte Tropézienne

Once you've snapped all the pics you want, shrug off the harbour's buzz and wander back into St-Tropez' historic fishing quarter, **La Ponche**, to the northeast. Place Garrezio sprawls east from 10th-century Tour Suffren to place de l'Hôtel de Ville. From here, rue Guichard leads southeast to sweet-chiming **Église de St-Tropez**, a quintessential St-Tropez landmark. Building began in Italian baroque style in the 17th century and was completed in 1784. Inside, look for the bust of St Torpes, namesake and patron of the city.

Follow rue du Portail Neuf south to the 1645 **Chapelle de la Miséricorde** and continue on to St-Tropez' legendary, charming central square, **place des Lices**, studded with plane trees and cafes. Linger and watch the *pétanque* players, and jostle with the crowds at the twice-weekly **market** (from 8am to 1pm Tuesday & Saturday), jam-packed with everything from fruit and veg to antique mirrors and sandals.

St-Tropez Fashion Spree

Indulge in stylish elegance

Most global luxury brands have a boutique somewhere in the narrow streets of St-Tropez. But look past the flashy names and you'll discover some unmissable shopping spots. As in Capri and Menorca, St-Tropez has its own signature sandal: **Rondini**

EATING & DRINKING IN ST-TROPEZ: WITHOUT BREAKING THE BANK

Au Caprice des Deux: Traditional *maison de village* (stone townhouse) is a local fave, with award-winning chef Stéphane Avelin. *7.30pm-midnight Wed-Mon* €€

Gourd'l Saint-Tropez: Friendly Italian *épicerie* (grocery), where daily pasta specials and charcuterie platters are always delish. *9am-10.30pm* €€

La Ramade: Old-fashioned Provençal hospitality at this terraced bistro with great French service. *noon-3pm & 7pm-1am Tue & Sat, 7-9pm Mon, Wed-Fri & Sun* €€

Le Sporting: There's a bit of everything on the menu at this always-packed bar–bistro, and it's one of St-Tropez' more reasonably priced spots. *7am-2am* €

(rondini.fr). For over 80 years, the Rondini family has been crafting high-quality leather sandals. Their flagship model, the gladiator, is available in both low-cut and ankle-wrap versions and is exclusively made-to-measure.

It's a good alternative to **K Jacques** *(kjacques.fr)*, hand-crafting sandals since 1933 for such clients as Picasso and Brigitte Bardot.

Les Galeries Tropéziennes *(galeriestropeziennes.com)* has been a mainstay in St-Tropez shopping life since 1903. On one side, a practical space brings together everyday accessories (haberdashery, metre fabrics, brushes, household linen), the other side is an emblem of St-Tropez elegance (swimsuits, espadrilles, cashmere sweaters, straw hats and tableware). Bargain hunters should visit **Le Dépôt** *(ledepot-saint-tropez.com)*, a chic boutique of secondhand and vintage designer clothes and accessories.

Stock Your Picnic Basket
Delectable delicacies

St-Tropez' twice-weekly **market** (p122) is a must, but don't leave town without sampling *tarte Tropézienne*, an orange-blossom-flavoured double sponge cake filled with thick cream, created by Polish baker A Mickla in 1955. His smart, lively cafe–bakery **La Tarte Tropézienne** *(latartetropezienne.fr)* is the originator, and you'll see branches all over the region.

For a more rarefied experience, visit **La Pause Douceur** *(instagram.com/la_pause_douceur_st.tropez)*, run by a local family. This irresistible little shop sells delicious homemade chocolates, biscuits and sweet treats. The praline chocolate is a favourite of chef and cookery writer Nina Parker.

To stock your picnic basket with more than just sweets, pop over to **Le Traiteur de l'Auberge des Maures** *(instagram.com/le.traiteur.de.lauberge)*, where you can browse the homemade takeaway meals, from charcuterie to potatoes *gratin* and buy by the kilo.

Explore Riviera Art
Get your culture fix

Art lovers will easily find inspiration throughout the village. Whet your appetite at **Musée de l'Annonciade** *(saint-tropez.fr; adult/child €6/free)* which showcases an impressive collection of modern art infused with that legendary Côte d'Azur light. In a gracefully converted 16th-century chapel you can

WINERIES

Mas de Pampelonne *(masdepampelonne.com)*: Excellent, crisp rosé from 15 hectares of the verdant St-Tropez peninsula. Find it a few hundred metres inland from Pampelonne beach.

Château de Chausse *(chateaudechausse.fr)*: Another superb rosé producer, near La Croix-Valmer.

Vignobles de Ramatuelle *(vignoblesderamatuelle.com)*: Modern tasting room in the heart of St-Tropez wine country, also specialising in rosé.

Château Minuty *(minuty.com)*: Family-run winery with a warm welcome, just north of Gassin.

Les Maîtres Vignerons de la Presqu'île de St-Tropez *(maitresvignerons.com)*: Not a tasting opportunity, but a shopping roundup of regional vineyards, near roundabouts west of St-Tropez.

 EATING & DRINKING AROUND ST-TROPEZ: OUR PICKS

La Vague d'Or: Triple-starred gastronomic temple from chef Arnaud Donckele at Cheval Blanc St-Tropez. *7.30-9.30pm Thu-Tue May-Sep* €€€

Chez Camille: Former 1913 fishing cottage turned beachside restaurant famous for wood-grilled fish and bouillabaisse. *noon-2.30pm & 7-10pm Apr-Sep* €€€

La Petite Plage: Luxurious, cool dishes, an oyster bar and caviar in boho-chic style, smack on the harbourfront. *noon-2.30pm & 7pm-3am* €€€

Hôtel Bar Le Sube: Nab a table on the balcony overlooking the harbour to see the swishy action while sipping a sunset *apéro*. *8am-1am*

Sentier du Littoral

PAMPELONNE BEACH CLUBS

Le 1051 *(le1051.com):* One of the newer clubs (2018) and popular for some of the best food on Pampelonne and a more chill vibe.

Cabane Bambou *(maisoncabanebambou.com):* It's the best club for early birds, offering breakfast service.

La Réserve à la Plage *(lareserve-plage.com):* Start with a glass of rosé at this bohemian chic club then move on to lunch and artful cocktails.

Le Club 55 *(leclub55.fr):* Longest-running Pampelonne club, originally the crew canteen during *And God Created Woman*. Caters to incognito celebs.

Nikki Beach *(nikkibeach.com/saint-tropez):* Favoured by dance-on-the-bar glitterati, and those who just want to be seen, Nikki can become a beachside bacchanal.

browse the collection, from pointillist Paul Signac (who bought a house here in 1892 and introduced other artists to the area) to cubists George Braque and Picasso, and Fauvist artists including Derain and Matisse (who spent the summer of 1904 here).

Keep on the contemporary trend by popping into **Bel-Air Fine Art** *(belairfineart.com)*, part of the largest fine-art gallery groups in Europe. Pieces are curated to meet St-Tropez tastes, while still highlighting trends in the international art world.

If marine nostalgia is more your vibe, delve into La Ponche's narrow lanes to reach **La Vieille Mer** *(06 74 07 91 46)*, a cavern of treasures from the sea. Ships' lanterns, wheels, telescopes, clocks and all forms of marine memorabilia are on display.

Generally, art shops and galleries are open April to October.

A Guide to St-Tropez' Beach Clubs

Get your toes in the sand

Beach clubs first took off in St-Tropez in the 1950s, when a 22-year-old Brigitte Bardot turned the town into a popular destination for the rich and famous. Since then, there's been no turning back. This seaside scene revolves around sandy clubs and restaurants, all with their own style. Most are open May to September, and advance bookings are highly recommended. Beaches also have public areas where you can lay down your towel.

The 5km-long, celebrity-studded **Plage de Pampelonne** is the most famous of the beaches and has the largest selection of exclusive clubs and restaurants. It's the place to see and be seen – you'll want to reserve a lounger and lunch. Lined with clubs, it's about as 'hot European summer' as you can get, with neat rows of picture-perfect parasols and chairs lining the coast. Atmosphere? Indulgence, glitz and relaxation.

Looking for a quieter beach experience without sacrificing luxury? Book ahead for **La Cabane Méditerranée** *(lacabanemediterranee.com; loungers from €30)*, on the edge of **Plage d'Héraclée**. About 10km further south from St-Tropez, the beach is wilder than Pampelonne, and the club is tucked into the edge of a rock.

Hit the Open Seas
Set sail at sunset

Get out on the water to take in the gorgeous coast. It can be as easy as taking a ride on **Les Bateaux Verts** (p120), with boat excursions throughout the region. Or opt for a water-skimming catamaran on Golfe de St-Tropez at sunset with **Sport Decouverte** *(sport-decouverte.com; €40)*, where you can sip an *apéro* suspended in the nets of the catamaran, sandwiched between the blues of the sea and the sparkling sky.

Coastal Walks
Amble the Sentier du Littoral to Gigaro

For a more active holiday, embark on the spectacular coastal path, **Sentier du Littoral**, as it wends past rocky outcrops and hidden bays 35km south from St-Tropez, around the peninsula to the beach at **Cavalaire-sur-Mer**. In St-Tropez, the yellow-flagged path starts at **La Ponche** (p122), immediately east of Tour du Portalet, and curves around Port des Pêcheurs, past the citadel. It then leads past the walled Cimitière Marin, Plage des Graniers and more lovely, less-crowded beaches. The tourist office has maps with distances and walking times (eg Plage des Salins is 8.5km or around 2½ hours' walk).

You can also pick it up in **Gigaro**, on the southeastern coast of the Presqu'île de St-Tropez. This seaside hamlet harbours a sandy beach, some lovely eating and sleeping options, and a watersports school. From the far end of the beach, a board maps the portion of the Sentier du Littoral that works its way around the coast to Cap Lardier (4.7km, 1½ hours) and past Cap Taillat to L'Escalet (9km, 2¾ hours).

> **FAMILY-FRIENDLY BEACHES**
> St-Tropez is a notorious partygoing, luxury vacation spot. For family beach days, try **Ste-Maxime** (p129) or **Presqu'île de Giens** (p139) instead.

EATING IN RAMATUELLE, GASSIN & GIGARO: OUR PICKS

Saveurs Sincères, Ramatuelle: Classic French fare at this family run restaurant. *noon-2.30pm & 7-10pm Tue-Fri, 11.30am-10pm Sat, 9am-5pm Sun* €€

Qui l'Eût Cru..., Ramatuelle: Creative fusion-flavoured organic and vegan platters pair well with smoothies and desserts in the village heart. *9am-5pm Thu-Tue* €

Le Pescadou, Gassin: Favourite for refined French fare, with set-price *(adult/child €45/15)* menus. *noon-2pm & 7-9.30pm Tue-Sun* €€

Le Refuge, Gigaro: Proprietors cook up tasty grills at the start of the coastal path. *noon-3pm & 7-11.30pm* €€

TRANSPORT TO THE BEACHES

Traffic on the peninsula is a nightmare in summer. Bike or take a shuttle to the beaches. The year-round **shuttle** *(saint-tropez.fr; ticket €0.50)* from place des Lices serves Plage de Bouillabaisse and Plage des Salins and, from May to October, one includes Pampelonne. Download the Pysae app for real-time info. From mid-June to mid-September there's a free beach shuttle from Ramatuelle *(ramatuelle.fr)*, serving Pampelonne and L'Escalet, near Gigaro. Taxis from St-Tropez cost €30 and up.

The northern edge of Pampelonne begins 4km southeast of St-Tropez with an area dubbed Plage de Tahiti. Find public access and parking *(€1.20 per hour from 11am to 5pm)* at one of six access points.

Sunset Spots on the Coast
Watch the day melt into night

At sunset, St-Tropez transitions from lazy beach days to wild nights. Plan the sunset moment in advance so you'll have the best seat in the house. **Plage de Gigaro** near La Croix Valmer (17km south of St-Tropez) is hands-down the best sunset beach. In town, **Plage de la Bouillabaisse** is convenient for a sunset cocktail before heading home to change for dinner. But since beach bars here are usually packed, you'll only get a spot if you've been here all day.

Plage de La Ponche and **Plage de la Fontanette** make for easy town-based views. And, for the more adventurous sunset spotters, bring your own snack and bottle to the historic **Cap Camarat lighthouse,** perched on the edge of the peninsula, a one-hour walk from Pampelonne on the Sentier du Littoral.

Village Views from Ramatuelle & Gassin
The peninsula's sweetest villages and vistas

Spend a half-day, high in the hills, starting at sweet **Ramatuelle** *(ramatuelle-tourisme.com)*, a labyrinthine walled village with a tree-studded central square where you can people-watch while lounging in **Café de l'Ormeau** *(indiegroup.fr/cafedelormeau)*. The village got its name from 'Rahmatu'llah', meaning 'Divine Gift' – a legacy of 10th-century Saracen rule. Jazz and theatre fill the tourist-packed streets during August's **Festival de Ramatuelle** *(festivalderamatuelle.com)* and June's **Jazz Fest** *(jazzaramatuelle.com)*.

Ramatuelle

If you follow the **rte des Moulins de Paillas** up over the hilltop then 2.5km towards Gassin, you'll take in grand views, especially from the historic **Moulins de Paillas** *(ramatuelle. fr)* where you can look off each side of the ridge. Check online or at the Ramatuelle tourist office for occasional weekend tours of the mill.

Once you reach medieval **Gassin**, 11km southwest of St-Tropez atop a rocky promontory, ascend the narrow streets to the village church (1558). But for sure, Gassin's most compelling feature is its 360-degree view of the peninsula, St-Tropez bay and islands Port-Cros and Levant, as well as the Maures forests. To go deeper, take a free guided walk from the **tourist office** *(gassin.eu)* on Monday afternoons April to October, or download the map online.

BEACHES OF PRESQU'ÎLE DE ST-TROPEZ

Plage de Pampelonne: Luxurious, long white-sanded beach lined with celebrity-rich beach clubs.

Plage des Salins: A 600m-wide pine-fringed beach at the southern foot of Cap des Salins; served by a shuttle year-round.

Plage de Tahiti: Famous nudist beach is also a naturally magnificent sandy stretch, 4km southeast of St-Tropez.

Plage de Gigaro: Local favourite for unscripted beach days on the southern edge of the peninsula.

Plage de la Bouillabaisse: Just west of town, it can get busy, but it's convenient and kid-friendly.

Plage de La Ponche & Plage de la Fontanette: More for views than swimming; start of **Sentier du Littoral** (p125).

DRINKING IN ST-TROPEZ: SUNSET COCKTAILS

Pearl Beach, **Plage de la Bouillabaisse:** Keep things classic with an Apérol spritz at this chic beach bar perfect for a sunset drink. *10am-4pm*

La Cabane Méditerranée (p125), **Plage d'Héraclée:** Try a Cabana spritz with curaçao, lime and prosecco; near Gigaro. *10.30am-7pm, to 9.30pm Fri & Sat*

Hôtel Cheval Blanc, **Plage de la Bouillabaisse:** Pricey cocktails but a once-in-a-lifestyle mixology experience, with a rarified sunset view. *9am-late*

Le Tigrr, St-Tropez: Escape the crowds at laid-back Ermitage Hotel, with enchanting views of the rooftops of old St-Tropez and the sea. *5pm-midnight Apr-Oct*

FESTIVALS AROUND ST-TROPEZ

Bravade de Saint-Tropez (May) Since 1558, locals have turned out in costume for an ear-splitting army of musket-firing bravadeurs.

Bravade des Espagnols (June) Re-enactors mark victory over the Spanish who attacked Marseille in 1637.

Fête des Vendanges Late August or early September, join the party honouring the grape harvest in Ste-Maxime.

Fête de la Libération (Aug) Enjoy fireworks on 15 August to mark Ste-Maxime's liberation in WWII.

Fête de la St-Pierre des Pêcheurs (Aug) St-Raphaël honours its patron saint with fishers jousting from flat-bottomed boats.

Les Voiles de St-Tropez (Sep–Oct) Largest sailing festival. Sailors, find a captain on *vogavecmoi.com*.

Lighthouse, Citadelle de St-Tropez

Live Music at La Citadelle
Catch a concert at St-Tropez' fortress

Sure, the beach clubs have DJs that keep the tunes pumping all summer long. But music lovers should absolutely check what's on at the **Citadelle de St-Tropez** *(saint-tropez.fr; adult/child €5/free)*. Built in 1602 to defend the coast against Spain, the fortress dominates the hillside overlooking St-Tropez to the east. Walk up for fantastic views, and try to spot the exotic peacocks wandering the grounds. Or delve into its dungeons, home to the excellent **Musée de l'Histoire Maritime**, focussing on Tropézienne and Provençal seafarers. But if you're into music, the star is the outdoor concert hall, which hosts concerts and mini festivals throughout the year.

Photo-Ops in Grimaud & its Port
Charming canals and floral villages

If you're looking to get out of town and post some likeable pics, **Port Grimaud**, between St-Tropez and Ste-Maxime, is a ready for its close-up: canals and pleasure port with photogenic footbridges and motorboats. Up the hill 7km, **Grimaud**

DRINKING AROUND ST-TROPEZ: AFTER-BEACH BARS

Gaïo: Since 1958, the stars have come here to hit the dance floor. Order Nikkei cuisine from the kitchen if you need extra fuel. *8pm-5am*

Les Caves du Roy: Bar at legendary **Hôtel Byblos** (p153) is champion of St-Tropez nightclubs. Dress to impress. *11pm-5am Fri & Sat Apr-Oct, daily Jul & Aug*

Sanctum: Can't stumble back to town? Stay on Plage de Pampelonne in July and August when resident DJs take it all night long. *midnight-6am*

Sénéquier: Lounge in the iconic red chairs, harbourside, day and night, with pricey drinks and white-linen service at this St-Tropez classic. *8am-1am*

itself is a medieval hilltop village surrounded by vineyards, olive trees and the oak-and-beech-clad foothills of the Massif des Maures. In spring, make a beeline for **rue de la Treille** to get a shot of the exploding blooms, then capture **Pont des Fées** from below to make this tiny, well-preserved footbridge seem larger than life. And keep your eyes open for Hermann's tortoises (p149).

Grimaud comes alive twice a year (check *grimaud-provence.com* for dates) when international street artists participate in an outdoor art festival. And the on-beat vibe in July and August continues with **Les Grimaldines** *(les-grimaldines.com)*, a world music and street performance festival.

Bus 877 connects St-Tropez to Grimaud village. To get to Port Grimaud, it's easiest to take a **Les Bateaux Verts** ferry.

Family Fun, Promenades & Ports

Play all around Ste-Maxime

Ste-Maxime *(sainte-maxime.com)* lies just across the gulf from St-Tropez and offers its own long, white-sand beaches. Unlike the beach clubs of St-Tropez, Ste-Maxime has a more egalitarian atmosphere, making it ideal for a more a more laid-back day out with family and friends.

For children, the private **Barco Beach** *(barcobeach.fr; day pass from €22)* has a special kids' corner and runs activities all summer long. If you're a nature-lover, **Plage de la Madrague** is a must for its marine life. Don a snorkelling mask and gaze at the rockfish flitting around the coves. You can reserve ahead for a free guided swim *(golfe-sainttropez.fr)* on Friday mornings in July and August off the nearby **Sentier Marin de la Pointe des Sardinaux**. You must bring your own gear. Check other underwater circuits and Gulf activities at *amusezvous.net*.

In town, stroll beneath pine trees on **Promenade Aymeric Simon Lorière** near the port, where you'll find an antique market on Wednesdays, and on summer evenings there's usually free live music.

Port de Ste-Maxime is always alive with movement and marine activity, with its more than 800 boats – from sailboats and fishing trawlers to motorboats and mega yachts. Nearly every evening during summer, **Théâtre de la Mer**, at the port's edge, stages free musical or theatrical entertainment.

To get between Ste-Maxime and St-Tropez, take a **Les Bateaux Verts** *(bateauxverts.com; 15 minutes)* shuttle boat.

THE ST-TROPEZ PRICE TAG

As the jet-set destination of the Côte d'Azur, St-Tropez can take a chunk out of your holiday fund if visiting on a budget: the glamour dust sprinkled on fish and chips doesn't come cheap.

Hotels in the city start at around €200 a night, while beach-club loungers run from €50 to €150 (and some require you to eat lunch or dinner at the establishment). Looking to keep the finances balanced?

Skip the lounger at Pampelonne by arriving early to claim a space on one of the stretches of public beach. And to eat on a budget, reserve a table at **Le Sporting** (p122) bistro – pizzas start at €13.

EATING IN GRIMAUD & STE-MAXIME: WALLET-FRIENDLY CHOICES

| **Chez Jeff et Ju, Grimaud:** For a culinary adventure, head to this cosy tapas restaurant serving unique small plates. *10am-2.30pm & 7-10pm* €€ | **J'aime les Glaces, Port Grimaud:** Stroll the canals with a delicious ice cream in flavours from coffee to *licorne* (unicorn). *10am-11pm Apr-Oct* € | **La Maison Bleue, Ste-Maxime:** Enjoy comfy seating and inspired cuisine, like octopus with chorizo or Provençal aïoli. *noon-1.45pm & 7-10pm Wed-Mon* € | **La Casa Mia, Ste-Maxime:** Large portions and convenient to beaches northeast of town. *7am-7pm Mon & Tue, to 11pm Wed-Sat, to noon Sun* € |

Beyond St-Tropez

Explore chestnut forests and a monastery inland, then the coast for flower-rich villages, gardens and vibrant red mountains.

Places
Massif des Maures p130
Corniche des Maures p133
Fréjus & St-Raphaël p135

A wild range of wooded hills, Massif des Maures is a pocket of surprising wilderness just a few miles from the Côte d'Azur hustle. Shrouded by pine, chestnut and cork oak trees, its near-black vegetation gives rise to its name, derived from Provençal *mauro* (dark pine wood). Traditional products are made around Collobrières and Monastère de la Verne, and hiking trails offer spectacular views of surrounding coastline.

Want flower power to guide you? The region's gardens and winter mimosa blooms are unrivalled along the coastal Route du Mimosa around the village Bormes-les-Mimosas.

East of St-Tropez, St-Raphaël and Fréjus are good matches for families and budget-conscious travellers. Adventurers hunt for the perfect rocky cove or mountain hike along the red-rock Massif de l'Estérel.

Massif des Maures
TIME FROM ST-TROPEZ: **1hr**

Chestnut tasting & more at Collobrières
Hidden in the Massif des Maures forests, roughly an hour from St-Tropez, Hyères and Brignoles, the leafy village of **Collobrières** is *the* place to sample chestnuts. Local producer **Confiserie Azuréenne** *(confiserieazureenne.com)* has a well-stocked shop of *marrons glacés* (candied chestnuts), chestnut ice cream, *crème de marrons* (chestnut cream) and chestnut liqueur. There's also a small, free museum showing how chestnuts are processed.

Across the 11th-century bridge, the **tourist office** *(mpm tourisme.com)* can help you join the October chestnut harvest, celebrated with the **Fête de la Châtaigne**, or join a guided forest walk. And one of the best Provençal markets takes place in the centre on Thursday and Sunday mornings. Branch out further at **Meni & Fils**, which make an astonishing array of sausages, terrines, cured meats and preprepared dishes. Or drop into the **Gourmands et Gourmets** *(facebook.com/gourmandsetgourmets)* for cakes and cookies.

Retreat to a dreamy monastery
Don't miss, the majestic 12th-century Carthusian **Monastère de la Verne** *(bethleem.org; adult/child €7/5)* perched on a forested ridge 15km east of Collobrières. You'll see it rising like

GETTING AROUND

Fréjus blends into St-Raphaël and the centres are walkable. Further afield, a car is simplest, but in summer you'll spend time and money parking. Zou! bus 878 runs between St-Tropez and Toulon. Bus 876 goes from St-Raphaël train station to St-Tropez, and 90 goes to Nice Airport. Public transport is nonexistent in the hills, except for bus 881 connecting Collobrières and Toulon.

Réserve Naturelle de la Plaine des Maures

an island of honeyed stone in a carpet of green, with views to the sea. It was founded in 1170, possibly on the site of a temple to the goddess Laverna, protector of the bandits who hid in the Maures. It has been ravaged by fire and rebuilt several times – a 20-minute video details the restoration. The monastery now houses a community of approximately 30 Sisters of Bethlehem. You'll get to visit their austere Romanesque church, the prior's cell (with small formal garden and workshop), the bakery and the olive mill.

The nuns live partially off the shop, which sells honey, leatherwork and brilliant ceramics they've made. Trails lead from the monastery through ancient *châtaigneraies* (chestnut groves), and when you alight at the car park, you'll walk the final 700m on an unpaved road, with the rustle of the breeze in the oaks and chestnut trees and streams cascading down the hills. The monastery is closed January and Tuesdays.

Walk a wild refuge

Looking for a fun, daylong outdoor activity to do with the family? Try hiking the 12.6km loop trail in the **Réserve Naturelle de la Plaine des Maures** *(snpn.com)*. As you walk through the reserve, passing parasol pines, cork oaks and maquis scrub, try to spot the animals that call the area home: wild boars, foxes, deer and many birds, including migratory

---

TIPS FOR WALKING IN MASSIF DES MAURES

Walking in the Massif des Maures and its Fôret des Maures is a delightful rural escape. Local tourist offices (such as *bormeslesmimosas.com*) supply hiking guides. Collobrières (*mpmtourisme.com*) hikes include one to Châtaignier de Madame (the biggest chestnut tree in Provence: 10.4m circumference) or one to the two biggest menhirs in the Var, heritage-listed monuments raised between 3000 BCE and 2000 BCE.

From June to September, access to many areas can become limited due to the risk of forest fire. Depending on the risk, trails are graded yellow, orange, red and black, with yellow meaning some minor restrictions at certain times of day, and black meaning total closure. Ask at a tourist office before you set out.

 EATING & DRINKING IN MASSIF DES MAURES: OUR PICKS

La Petite Fontaine, Collobrières: Book ahead for wild boar stew and lamb with candied vegetables. For dessert: chestnut ice cream. *noon-2pm Tue-Sun* €€

La Farigoulette:, Collobrières Local produce, especially chestnuts, feature at this small, welcoming restaurant. *noon-2pm Thu-Mon* €€

Ferme de Peïgros: Farm restaurant 1.8km along a gravel track from top of Col de Babaou (8km from Collobrières). *noon-2pm Sun, Mon, Thu & Fri, 7-9pm Fri* €€

Auberge de la Môle:, La Môle No-frills village inn, with legendary terrines, pâtés and feisty pickles. *9.30am-1.30pm & 7.30-10pm Tue-Sat, 9.30am-2pm Sun* €€

CORNICHE DES MAURES BEACHES

Plage de Cavalière: As the D559 hugs the coast, you'll reach the beautiful beach at **Cavalière** (not to be confused with Cavalaire-sur-Mer).

Plage du Layet: Rocky point Layet has its own minute sandy arc hidden from view.

Plage du Rayol: Tiny, particularly enchanting beach backed by pine trees, with a restaurant on the sand.

Cap de Brégançon: Scenic peninsula with imposing 11th-century **Fort de Brégançon** (bormeslesmimosas.com; adult/child €12/10; reserve 72 hours ahead).

Plage du Lavandou: Small but intact old town **Le Lavandou** has 12km of golden sand backed by family-oriented beach resorts. Boats sail to Îles des Hyères.

species nesting near beautiful **Lac des Escarcets**, a highlight of the trail. The lake is surrounded by reeds and rushes, providing a habitat for waterfowl, such as ducks and coots.

Driving the Route des Crêtes

For breathtaking views of sea, islands and forests, follow **Route des Crêtes** as it winds through maquis-covered hills some 400m above the water. From Bormes-les-Mimosas, follow the D41 uphill (in the direction of Collobrières) past the Chapelle St-François and, 1.5km north of the village centre, turn immediately right after the sign for Col de Caguo-Ven (237m).

You can take a break at **Relais du Vieux Sauvaire**, a restaurant and pool with dreamy 180-degree views. Past the restaurant, rte des Crêtes joins the final leg of the panoramic **Col du Canadel** road. On the *col* (mountain pass), turn left to descend into the heart of the forested Massif des Maures, or right to the sea and the coastal Corniche des Maures (D559).

EATING ON CORNICHE DES MAURES COAST: REGIONAL SPECIALITIES

Le Jardin, Bormes-les-Mimosas: Refined menu of delicate dishes: everything from truffles to edible flowers in a cool garden. *noon-2pm & 7-9.15pm Wed-Sun* €€€

La Rastègue: Menu of superb Provençal fare, inviting dining room, sensational sea-view terrace and open kitchen. *7.30-9pm Tue-Sun Apr-Nov* €€€

L'Estagnol, Plage de l'Estagnol: Built in *guinguette* (outdoor tavern) style. Specialities: wood-grilled lobster and fish. *noon-2.30pm & 7.30-10pm Jun-Sep* €€

Chez Jo, Plage du Layet: Summer seafood shack buzzes with barefoot beach-lovers, sipping Bandol whites and devouring seafood. *noon-3pm May-Sep* €€

Corniche des Maures

Corniche des Maures
TIME FROM ST-TROPEZ: **45min**

Bormes-les-Mimosas, the 12th-Century Floral Village

The Corniche des Maures (D559) unwinds beautifully southwest from La Croix-Valmer to Le Lavandou along a shoreline trimmed with sandy beaches ideal for swimming, sunbathing and windsurfing. Slightly inland, **Bormes-les-Mimosas** is the jewel in its crown. It's named after the 100-plus species of mimosa growing here, which bloom between January and March, filling the town and surrounding countryside with bursts of vibrant yellow colour. Every February, **Le Corso Fleuri Festival** celebrates the flower with bloom-covered floats.

The town's love affair with the mimosa began in the 19th century when the flower was introduced from Australia, where it's known as the yellow wattle. Today, many local businesses use the flower in products such as perfumes, soaps and candles. Explore the cobbled streets of this 12th-century village to find boutiques selling these, like **Savonnerie de Bormes**

WATER ACTIVITIES

Les Bateaux Bleus: Great coast trips through the coves of Corniche de l'Estérel (€60), Marseille's calanques (€70) and Île de Porquerolles (€48 to €65; lesbateauxbleus.com).

Diving: Corniche de l'Estérel is a leading dive centre: WWII shipwrecks, pristine waters, protected coast (fauna and flora are abundant).

Euro Plongée: Reputable, family-friendly dive club with CMAS accreditation, dives, courses and two-hour snorkelling tours (europlongee.fr).

Plage d'Agay: One of the best beaches along the Corniche de l'Estérel for activities (beach volleyball, kids' clubs, watersports etc).

Corniche de l'Estérel, Sentier du Littoral: Running 11km between Agay and Port Santa Lucia, this coastal path (yellow markers) accesses scenic swim spots.

EATING & DRINKING AROUND ST-RAPHAËL: OUR PICKS

Chez Gaston, St-Raphaël: Pavement tables, a wall of wines and hearty dishes (steak *Béarnaise*; fish soup). *11.30am-2pm Tue-Fri, 7-9.30pm Tue-Sat* €€

L'Entrée des Artistes, Fréjus: Brothers run this intimate bistro with a front terrace overlooking a square in the historic centre. *noon-2pm & 7-9pm Tue-Sat* €

Le Palais du Fromager, Fréjus: Friendly cheesemongers sell great cheeses and prepare charcuterie platters on street-side tables. *9am-7pm Tue-Sat* €

Villa Matuzia, Agay: Provençal house serving elaborate Mediterranean cuisine, some of the best on the Estérel coast road. *noon-1.30pm & 7-9.30pm Wed-Sun* €€

CRUISE LA ROUTE DU MIMOSA ALONG THE COAST

Scenic 60km La Route du Mimosa *(routedumimosa.com)* is a fragrant journey along the Côte d'Azur, showcasing all the beauty of the winter coastline.

START	END	LENGTH
Bormes-les-Mimosas	Tanneron	115km; 5hr

Start your journey in the quaint village of ❶ **Bormes-les-Mimosas** (p133), just inland, where the large nursery has 90 varieties of mimosas, especially resplendent from January to March when mimosas bloom. The thin D559 winds along the coast to ❷ **Domaine du Rayol** (p135), where you can descend through its abundant gardens all the way to the sea. Detour up to the mountain pass at ❸ **Col du Canadel** (p132) for a prime sea view where the panorama stretches all the way to Hyères' three islands.

Continuing east on the D559 you'll skirt the western edge of St-Tropez and its peninsula swathed in vineyards, and you can stop at the cheerful seafront town of ❹ **Ste-Maxime** (p129) for a snack break or a quick dip. Alternatively, continue along, watching the red spires of the Massif de l'Estérel approach, and stretch your legs instead with a hike at ❺ **Calanque d'Anthéor** on the edge of Corniche de l'Estérel. The trail winds down the sinuous Route de la Corniche d'Or on the cliffside to reach the water's edge.

If you still have energy left, drive the last 33km (about 1 hour slow driving) along the spectacular corniche to wrap up inland at ❻ **Tanneron;** its large mimosa festival *(facebook.com/ TanneronEnFete)* kicks off in late January.

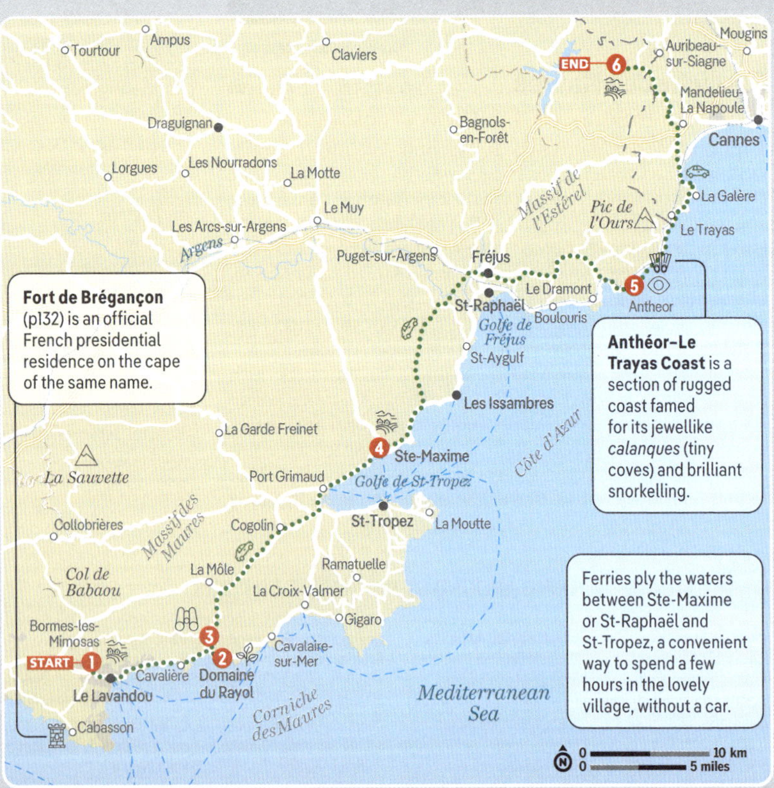

Fort de Brégançon (p132) is an official French presidential residence on the cape of the same name.

Anthéor–Le Trayas Coast is a section of rugged coast famed for its jewellike *calanques* (tiny coves) and brilliant snorkelling.

Ferries ply the waters between Ste-Maxime or St-Raphaël and St-Tropez, a convenient way to spend a few hours in the lovely village, without a car.

(savonnerie-bormes.com). Arts and crafts shops include glassmaker Stéphane Marchioni's **À l'en Verre** *(alenverre.com)* and **Les Bibis du Midi** *(06 22 70 13 31)*, where hatmaker Clémence Grisot crafts hats for all occasions.

Botanical world tour at Domaine du Rayol

Spend a few hours in **Domaine du Rayol** *(domainedurayol. org; adult/child €14/10)*, a unique botanical garden started in 1910 that showcases the landscapes of the world with a climate similar to the Mediterranean. The dense flora cascades down the hillside to the sea, and while the flowers are at their best in April and May, it's always worth a visit.

What makes a Mediterranean garden special is its ability to thrive in a hot and dry climate, and these gardens often feature drought-resistant plants, such as succulents and cacti, as well as fragrant herbs and flowering shrubs. The garden is also home to a marine snorkelling garden that is open during summer for visitors ages eight and up. The estate's relaxed Café des Jardiniers, open from noon, serves light organic lunches and refreshing hibiscus-peach infusions.

Reserve ahead for activities, including children's programmes, yoga classes and open-air concerts. In July and August, a free shuttle runs from the nearby town of Rayol-Canadel-Sur-Mer.

Fréjus & St-Raphaël

TIME FROM ST-TROPEZ: 1hr

Coastal city vibes with beaches

Fréjus and St-Raphaël are two beach towns merging into one another 37km east of St-Tropez. Easygoing, they're worth a day's exploration.

Founded by Julius Caesar in 49 BCE, **Fréjus** is dotted with Roman ruins, including an amphitheatre, **Les Arènes** *(frejus.fr; free)*, and aqueduct, well explored at its **Musée Archéologique** *(ville-frejus.fr; adult/child €3/free)*. Visitors can also walk the town's medieval quarter, where narrow streets and picturesque buildings include 13th-century Gothic **Cloître de la Cathédrale de Fréjus** *(cloitre-frejus.fr; adult/child €7/free)*, housing a unique collection of medieval ceiling frescoes. Fréjus is particularly worth a visit on Wednesday or Saturday morning, when the old-town market is in full swing. **Plage de St-Aygulf** is a popular spot for swimming and sunbathing, while **Plage de Port-Fréjus** is super central, with calm waters, sandy shores and views of St-Raphaël.

St-Raphaël briefly flourished as a Jazz-Age hang-out during the 1920s and 1930s, but urban sprawl has somewhat obscured its charm. It's a handy base for exploring Massif de l'Estérel – and a lot cheaper than Cannes. Take a break in the town's lively marina area or on its long stretch of sandy **Plage Beaurivage**, perfect for swimming, sunbathing and watersports. And not to be outdone, it has its own good **Musée Archéologique de St-Raphaël** *(ville-saintraphael.fr; admission free)*. St-Raphaël's train station is the most convenient for the region, and **Les Bateaux Bleus** (p133) runs boats to/from St-Tropez.

TIPS FOR HIKING & MOUNTAIN BIKING MASSIF DE L'ESTÉREL

Local tourist offices have leaflets detailing popular walks of **Massif de l'Estérel** *(circuits.esterel-cote-dazur.com)*, including Pic de l'Ours (496m) and Pic du Cap Roux (452m) and mountain-bike rides. Buy IGN's *Carte de Randonnée* (1:25,000) No 3544ET *Fréjus, Saint-Raphaël & Corniche de l'Estérel* for more serious walks. For a more informed hike, sign up for a three-hour guided walk with a forest ranger at **St-Raphaël tourist office** *(saint-raphael.com)*. Access to the range is prohibited on windy or particularly hot days because of fire risks; check with the tourist office before setting off. The waterfront Corniche de l'Estérel also has a **Sentier du Littoral** (p133).

Hyères

MEDIEVAL TOWN | ART STUDIOS | BEACH BLISS

GETTING AROUND

Toulon-Hyères Airport is 3km south of Hyères and 25km east of Toulon. From the airport, Réseau Mistral *(reseaumistral.com; tickets €1.40)* bus 102 runs to Hyères (10 minutes) and the train and bus station in Toulon (40 minutes). To reach other Var towns, including St-Tropez, use Zou! buses *(zou.maregionsud.fr; tickets €2.10)*. Coastal trains serve **Gare de Hyères**. Central Hyères is best on foot. **Transport Littoral Varois** *(tlv-tvm.com)* runs year-round ferries to the offshore islands.

☑ TOP TIP

Transport Littoral Varois *(tlv-tvm.com)* runs ferries from La Tour Fondue to Île de Porquerolles *(return €24 May-Sep, reduced rest of year, 20 minutes)* and from Port d'Hyères to Île de Port-Cros *(return €29, one hour)* and Île du Levant *(return €29, 1½ hours)*.

Hyères, once a rightly acknowledged gem of the Var with rich history and a sparkling beach scene, has become a bit under-appreciated in the glamour-seeking mind of today's Riviera sun-chaser. Odd, when you consider Hyères' thriving, compact *vieille ville*, garden-clad heights, and proximity to the many beaches, watersports and abundant birdlife of the Presqu'île de Giens...not to mention the fantastic Îles d'Hyères (p140).

Driving down the busy streets of modern Hyères, lined by stately palm trees, you could be forgiven for completely missing the medieval old town above. Make sure you don't. And appreciate all the creative artist studios and eclectic restaurants hidden within – this is a prosperous town, year-round.

For families, Presqu'île de Giens offers many old-fashioned campsites located just steps from the sea. Kids will love spending their days on the beach and exploring the stunning natural beauty of the region or cycling its flat lanes.

Soak up Hyères on Foot
Spend the day ambling through the city

Over 2400 years of fascinating history, and you've only got time for a day in Hyères? Here's how to hit the highlights.

Begin by exploring the **vieille ville** (old centre), packed with picturesque streets, colourful facades, monuments and historical sites. Enter on the western side of place Georges Clemenceau through the 13th-century **Porte Massillon** and walk rue des Porches, with its polished flagstones and shady arcades.

Ascend beyond the **Tour des Templiers** *(free)*, originally built by the Knights Templar, where you can check to see if there's a temporary exhibit. Continue up beyond the **Vieux Lavoir** (old washhouse; *free*) to **Collégiale St-Paul** *(free)*, where you should duck inside to see its moving collection of ex votos, paintings made in thanks for miracles and cures rendered.

HYÈRES

★ HIGHLIGHTS
1 Salin des Presquiers
2 Vieille Ville

● SIGHTS
3 Château d'Hyères
4 Collégiale St-Paul
see 5 Fort du Pradeau
5 La Tour Fondue
6 l'Almanarre
see 6 Olbia
7 Parc Castel Ste-Claire
8 Plage de la Bergerie
see 6 Plage de l'Almanerre
9 Plage du Pradeau

10 Porte Massillon
11 Tour des Templiers
12 Vieux Lavoir
13 Villa Noailles

● ACTIVITIES
see 6 Flyboard Hyères
see 6 Hyères Windsurf Organisation
14 MF Kitesurf
15 Rte du Sel
16 Sentier du Littoral

● SLEEPING
17 Hôtel Les Orangers
18 Lilou

● EATING
19 Au Fil de l'Eau
20 La Salle
21 Le Cadet 83
22 Le Café-Bohème
23 Restaurant La Cabane
24 Snack de la Bergerie
25 Vola Cafe

● SHOPPING
26 Artdanh
27 Atypique Provence
28 Diweye Créations
29 L'Atelier d'Aurélia
30 Sous les Palmiers

31 Tuesday & Saturday Market
32 Valeria Tarroni Créatures en Terre Ceramic
33 Vévédentelles

● TRANSPORT
34 À Motos & Vélos
35 À Vélo 83
36 Gare de Hyères
37 Toulon-Hyères Airport
see 5 Transport Littoral Varois

PRESQU'ÎLE DE GIENS ACTIVITIES

Hyères Windsurf Organisation (hyereswindsurforganisation.fr): Windsurf and wind-foil rentals and lessons.

Flyboard Hyères (flyboard-hyeres.com): Zoom on a Flyboard above the water.

MF Kitesurf (mfkite.com): Rent equipment or learn to kitesurf.

Sentier du Littoral (Coastal path): Trail along the south of the peninsula.

Bird-watching: Flamingos dot **Salin des Presquiers** (p139). Hyères tourist office (provencemed.com) guides bird walks.

Rte du Sel (Salt Rd): Spectacular western sandbar road (May-Oct).

Cycling: À Vélo 83 (avelo83.com) and **À Motos & Vélos** (amotos.fr) hire out standard and e-bikes.

Windsurfing, Plage de l'Almanarre

Climb to the 10th-century **Château d'Hyères**, on the heights of Castéou Hill, before descending back to **Parc Castel Ste-Claire** (provencemed.com; free) with its superb neo-Romanesque mansion built on the foundations of an old convent by Olivier Voutier, a naval officer who discovered the Venus de Milo. It was later home to American writer Edith Wharton. The adjoining park overflows with 6500 sq m of flowers and tropical vegetation.

Wrap up at the cubist **Villa Noailles** (villanoailles-hyeres.com; free), an interesting national art centre hosting art and photography exhibitions, designed by Robert Mallet-Stevens. The garden was designed by Gabriel Guévrékian.

Creativity from Ateliers to Markets
Support local artists and producers

One of the treats of Hyères is the mass of creative artists and craftspeople who work here. They have banded together in the Parcours des Arts (provencemed.com), mapping out the myriad studios and shops you can visit. Some examples include **Artdanh** (artdanh.com) with edgy art and accessories. **Sous les Palmiers** (souslespalmiers.net) features upcycled arts and crafts. For ceramics, visit **L'Atelier d'Aurélia** (instagram.com/aureliabelnetpoterie) and **Valeria Tarroni Créatures en Terre** (valeria-tarroni.com). Nearby, **Vévédentelles** (instagram.com/vevedentelles) feels like a flashback,

EATING & DRINKING ALONG THE COAST: OUR PICKS

L'Oursinado, Cap de Carqueiranne: Secluded fantasy, on a cliff where sea views are pure Med magic and the seafood is sublime. *hours vary* €€€

Le Cadet 83, Port d'Hyères: Soak up the sun and enjoy a fish-forward menu including sashimi and *tataki*. *noon-2pm Wed-Mon & 6.30-9.30pm Wed-Sun* €€

Le Café-Bohème: Caribbean cabana vibes and cocktails pair well with cheerful, creative dishes, from steak to ravioli. *10am-10.30pm Tue-Sat, to 3.30pm Sun* €€

Snack de la Bergerie, Plage de la Bergerie: Delicious burgers and homemade sandwiches – eat at pavement tables or picnic on the beach. *9am-6pm* €

with all the detailed needlework. For African textile fashion, **Diweye Créations** *(diweyecreations.fr)* is the place. Pop across the street where **Atypique Provence** *(atypiqueprovence.com)* produces natural soaps and unguents.

Still want more? The large **Tuesday & Saturday Market** fills the city centre from 6am to 1pm, bringing abundant food to the mix.

Ancient Greek Settlement

The waterfront ruins of Olbia

History fans should make their way 5km south of town to the coastal Greek ruin of **Olbia** *(provencemed.com; adult/child €4/free)*. From April to October you can walk the ruined walls of a 325 BCE fortified city founded by people from the Greek settlement of Massilia (now Marseille).

Beach Days on the Presqu'île de Giens

From windsurfing to wading

Presqu'île de Giens is the promontory due south of Hyères, facing Île de Porquerolles. The peninsula is home to stunning but low-key beaches and historic **Salin des Presquiers**, saltpans used to harvest sea salt. Although the flats are no longer productive, bird-watchers will love walking the **Rte du Sel**, where many seasonal species – including herons, egrets, teals, cormorants and Provence's famous flamingos – feed in the lagoons.

Windsurfers and kitesurfers flock to **Plage de l'Almanarre** – the western shore of the 'leg' connecting to the peninsula's foot. With white sand and shallow water, this beach is also safe for swimming. **Plage du Pradeau**, near the peninsula's heel, is only accessible on foot or by boat, and it's sheltered from the wind. From here you can walk the coastal path to 17th-century **Fort du Pradeau** *(portcros-parcnational.fr; adult/child €6/3)*, renovated in 2022 to contain a **Parc National de Port-Cros** (p140) interpretation centre, tipping the promontory at **La Tour Fondue**.

Handiplage at **Plage de la Bergerie**, along the eastern shore, is a wheelchair-accessible beach equipped during summer with amphibious wheelchairs, assistance for entering the water and adapted restroom facilities. Little **Port d'Hyères** bobs with boats. Visit for its lively restaurants and day trips to the Îles d'Hyères.

ARTISTIC INSPIRATION

Hyères has all the elements of a decadent holiday in the south of France and, best of all, it remains a relatively unsung destination. For some, the fact that the distractions of the trendier cities are out of reach make it that much more appealing.

In addition to the many working artists in Hyères now, generations of writers and artists have travelled up here to work. Among the anglophones, we have Joseph Conrad who mentions the peninsula in his final work, *The Rover*, and F Scott Fitzgerald who corrected the manuscript of *The Great Gatsby* here. Robert Louis Stevenson wrote several of his novels, including *Prince Otto*, at the Grand Hôtel des Îles d'Or. And Edith Wharton lived here for years at **Castel Ste-Claire**.

 EATING & DRINKING IN HYÈRES: CASUAL & CREATIVE

Au Fil de l'Eau: Book ahead for refined seafood (good catch-of-the-day selections) in the *vieille ville*. *noon-2pm Tue-Thu, 7-11pm Tue. & Wed* €€

La Cabane: Fun small bistro near Porte Massillon serving inventive French with a distinct Mediterranean twist. *noon-2pm & 7-10pm Tue-Sat* €

La Salle: French fare with Asian highlights in a charming restaurant that doubles as a *brocante* (vintage shop). *noon-2pm & 7-10pm, closed Sun & Wed* €€

Vola Cafe: Local favourite up by Collégiale St-Paul, with a leafy terrace. *9am-2pm & 5-9pm Mon, Thu & Fri, 10am-10pm Sat & Sun* €

Beyond Hyères

Offshore from Hyères, the Îles d'Hyères are in the Parc National de Port-Cros, a wonderland for hiking, swimming and snorkelling.

Places
Île de Porquerolles p140
Île de Port-Cros p143
Toulon p143
Sanary-sur-Mer p144
Bandol p144

The Îles d'Hyères are also known as Îles d'Or (Islands of Gold) – not only for their mica-rich rock but also for golden beaches fringing their forested hinterland. Just a short ferry ride from Hyères, Île de Porquerolles is the largest, and a paradise for outdoor enthusiasts. Rent a bike and explore the island's many beaches, coves and hiking trails. For a more adventurous experience, nearby Île de Port-Cros offers fantastic snorkelling and some of the best hiking in the region, with stunning views of the Med and the surrounding islands.

West of Hyères, Toulon makes a fascinating day-trip for its rich nautical life, and on the coast further west still, you'll find lovely Sanary-sur-Mer and wine-rich Bandol.

GETTING AROUND

Réseau Mistral (*reseaumistral.com*) bus 67 connects Hyères and its ports for the islands. Vedettes Îles d'Or et Le Corsaire has ferries from Le Lavandou, Cavalaire-sur-Mer and La Croix-Valmer.

Toulon's **TGV train station** is in the city centre. Reseau Mistral and Zou! (*zou.maregionsud.fr*) buses radiate out from Toulon. Corsica Ferries has services to Corsica and Sardinia. In summer Bateliers de la Côte d'Azur (*bateliersdelacotedazur.com*) goes to Îles d'Hyères and St-Tropez.

Île de Porquerolles

TIME FROM LA TOUR FONDUE: **20min**

Paradise with bikes & bathing suits only

Jaunt just offshore from Presqu'île de Giens to **Île de Porquerolles,** a magnet for families and nature lovers. It fosters its own chilled-out personality, and you can only visit on foot or with a bicycle. Despite the huge influx of summer day trippers (up to 6000 a day in July and August), it remains largely unspoilt. Two-thirds of its sandy white beaches, pine woods, maquis and eucalyptus are protected by **Parc National de Port-Cros** (*portcros-parcnational.fr*), and a wide variety of indigenous and tropical flora thrive. April and May are the best months to spot some of the 114 bird species.

Pottering along the island's rough unpaved trails on foot or by bicycle, breaking with a picnic lunch on the beach and a dip in crystal-clear turquoise water, is heavenly. The southern edge of the island is the most dramatic and uncluttered, but the inland vineyards and olive groves have a magic of their own, as do the gorgeous beaches of the northern coast.

The main village circles the wide **Place d'Armes** and from there it's easy to walk up to **Fort Ste-Agathe** (*adult/child €6/3*). Inside, the 16th-century fortification contains historical and natural-history exhibits, and its tower has sweeping island views. If you take a **guided tour** (*adult/child €12/6*) you can also visit the nearby windmill **Moulin du Bonheur**. Wild camping and cars are forbidden throughout the archipelago.

Île de Porquerolles

Botanical gardens & national park centre

While you're in town, pop into the wonderful ornamental **Jardin Emmanuel Lopez** *(free)*, planted with palms, cypresses, vanilla and grenadier trees, cactus and bamboo, sweetly scented jasmine, and every herb known to grow under the Provençal sun. It's also home to the **Parc National de Port-Cros Maison du Parc** *(portcros-parcnational.fr)*, where you can pick up maps and information or book guided tours.

Snorkel crystalline waters

France's first marine national park, founded in 1963, **Parc National de Port-Cros** has exceptional marine fauna and flora, which makes it a snorkelling paradise. The French call snorkelling *randonnée palmée,* or 'hiking with flippers.' **Calanque de Brégançonnet** is easily accessible if you have gear and want to go on your own. Otherwise, book a boat and a guide with **Iléo Porquerolles** *(ileo-porquerolles.fr; €45)* and spend several hours discovering the vibrant and delicate underwater ecosystem off the coast. Most frequently spotted fish include tiny Blenny fish, shiny mendoles and the large black-headed sea bass.

BEACHES ON ÎLE DE PORQUEROLLES

Plage de la Courtade: Gorgeous crescent of sand 800m east from the port (follow track uphill behind the tourist office).

Iléo Porquerolles *(ileo-porquerolles.fr)* watersports May-Oct.

Plage d'Argent: West of the village, popular with families with summer cafe, lifeguards, toilets.

Plage de Notre Dame: Largest and said to be the most beautiful beach, 3.5km east of the port.

Plage du Langoustier: Secluded beaches at former lobster farm 4.5km from village, with watersports May-Oct.

Calanque de Brégançonnet (southwest) **& Calanque de l'Oustaou-de-Diou** (southeast)**:** Spots to swim, snorkel, dive on cliff-lined, more dangerous southern coast.

 EATING & DRINKING AROUND PORQUEROLLES: OUR PICKS

L'Orangeraie, Île de Porquerolles: Sip local wines on a deck overlooking swaying masts and enjoy plenty of fresh seafood. *8am-11pm Wed-Mon* €€

Fly Deck, **Île de Porquerolles:** Cheerful bistro with small front terrace and friendly staff serving generous French fare. *noon-2pm & 7.30-9.30pm Tue-Sat* €€

Au dé Lisse, Sanary-sur-Mer: Well-made pasta, meat and fish; on a pedestrianised lane in the heart of town. *noon-2pm Tue-Sun, 7-10pm Tue-Sat* €€

L'Espérance, Bandol: Reserve ahead to get a spot in this tiny Provençal restaurant run ably by a husband-and-wife team. *noon-1pm & 7-9pm Wed-Sun* €€

HIKE THE PRISTINE ÎLE DE PORT-CROS

Circle between historic forts and remote beaches on this untouched island at the centre of France's oldest marine park.

START	END	LENGTH
Port-Cros port	Plage du Sud	15.8km; 5–7hr

The national park doesn't even allow bicycles on the well-marked trails of this undeveloped little island, so strap on your boots and bring a towel and swimsuit for great swims along the way. Add a picnic, water and sunblock (bring it all from the mainland) and you're good to go.

When you arrive at ❶ **Port-Cros port**, pick up a map at **Maison du Parc** (p143) *(portcros-parcnational.fr)* then walk up to ❷ **Fort du Moulin**, an 18th-century fortification that overlooks the harbour and offers stunning views of the sea and surrounding cliffs. The ❸ **Sentier des Plantes**, surrounded by wild lavender and rosemary, is actually the beginning of the trail.

The path runs alongside ❹ **Plage de la Palud** (p143) and rocky cliffs on the north side of the island, providing a refreshing sea breeze and broad views of the Med. Around 5km into the hike, you'll reach ❺ **Plage de Port Man**, a quiet bay perfect for a break and a dip. Detour onto the point to ❻ **Fort de Port Man**, built to monitor passages between Port-Cros and Île du Levant.

The trail then turns south, where you'll see ❼ **Fortin de la Vigie**, built on the island's highest point. Spend the rest of the day at popular ❽ **Plage du Sud**, with wide shores and shallow waters, before heading back to the port.

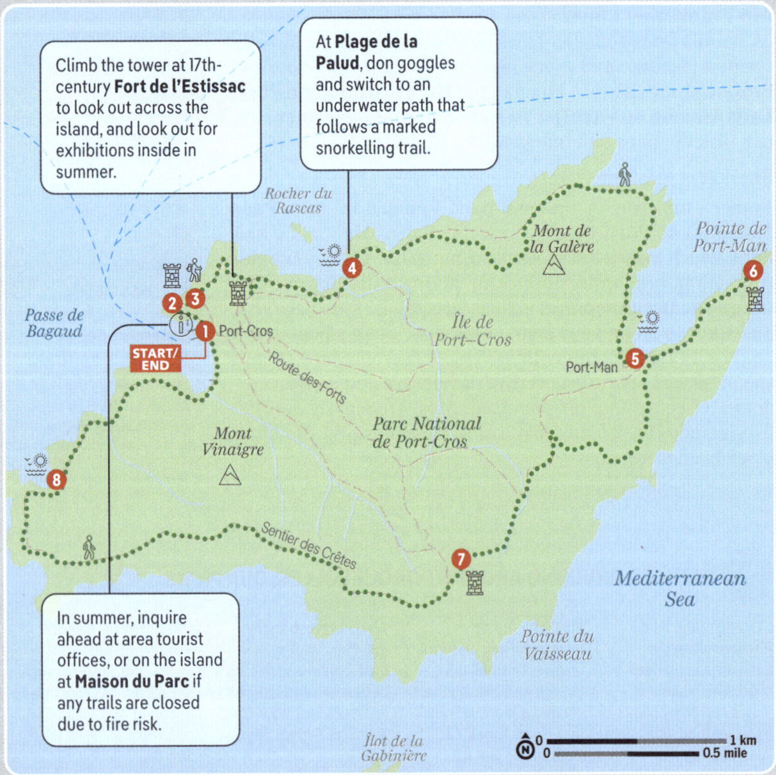

> Climb the tower at 17th-century **Fort de l'Estissac** to look out across the island, and look out for exhibitions inside in summer.

> At **Plage de la Palud**, don goggles and switch to an underwater path that follows a marked snorkelling trail.

> In summer, inquire ahead at area tourist offices, or on the island at **Maison du Parc** if any trails are closed due to fire risk.

Sip local wines

Pick up a bottle of rosé for your picnic at **Domaine de la Courtade** *(lacourtade.com; tours/tastings from €15/5)*, which also offers tastings if you book ahead online. Or if you're in town, **Domaine de l'Île** *(domainedelile.com)* offers tastings by appointment in its town-based **boutique** and restaurant.

Modern art mansion & sculpture garden

Art lovers should check out what's on at dazzling **Villa Carmignac** *(fondationcarmignac.com; adult/child €16/free)*, from May to November. Not only will you get to see cutting-edge art, but you can get inside the bespoke home, with an aquatic ceiling, of Fondation Carmignac and its elaborate sculpture gardens. It's a 15-minute walk or 5-minute cycle east of town.

Île de Port-Cros

TIME FROM LA TOUR FONDUE: **1hr**

Swim an underwater guided path

In addition to great walking, Île de Port-Cros offers you the chance to swim **Sentier Sous-Marin**, a 35-minute underwater circuit offshore at **Plage de la Palud**. Fishing is prohibited on the island, and the bay is home to 180 species, plus 500 types of algae.

The *sentier* (trail) is marked by buoys with explanatory panels, and **Maison du Parc** *(portcros-parcnational.fr)* at the port sells a waterproof leaflet *(€5)*. Rent equipment from portside **Sun Plongée** *(sun-plongee.com; dives from €48)*. Check to see if there are jellyfish before diving in!

Toulon

TIME FROM HYÈRES: **25min**

Maritime experiences in a great port

Built around a *rade* (sheltered bay lined with quays), France's second-largest naval port, **Toulon,** stands distinct from the glitter of the Côte d'Azur. It's got a certain rough charm, and with its long naval history, and importance as a commercial and military port, it makes an interesting half-day visit.

Portside **Musée de la Marine** *(musee-marine.fr; adult/child €7/free)* is an excellent, modern seafaring museum with exhibits, models and paintings illustrating the town's rich naval pedigree. Then, take a guided boat tour around the *rade*, with **Les Bateliers de la Rade** *(lesbateliersdelarade.com; adult/child €16.50/11.50)*. Commentary fills you in on the local events of WWII. (It also runs excursions to Île de Porquerolles from May to September, and from La Londe to Île de Porquerolles, Île de Port-Cros or St-Tropez.)

Wrap up above the town atop **Mont Faron** (589m), accessible by **téléphérique** *(telepherique-faron.fr; return adult/child €9/7)*, where, near the summit, **Mémorial du Débarquement de Provence** *(memorialdumontfaron.fr; adult/child €6/free)* commemorates the Allied landings of Operation Dragoon, which took place along this coast in August 1944.

HOW TO CYCLE ÎLE DE PORQUEROLLES

To cycle the gorgeous isle, hire a bike or e-bike at one of the many outfits in town. Prices are pretty uniform *(adult/child €19/15 per day, e-bike €45)*; we recommend reliable **Le Cycle Porquerollais** *(velo-porquerolles.fr)*, which has a slight discount if you book online.

Or, if you're planning ahead you can reserve your bike rental with the round-trip ferry tickets through the tourist office for a deal *(provencemed.com/loisirs/pack-bateau-vtt-porquerolles)*.

The **tourist office** *(porquerolles.com)* map illustrates four cycling itineraries, from 6.5km to 14km long. More detail can be found in *cyclo-guide* (€7), a French-language publication, available at the Maison du Parc.

Sanary-sur-Mer

WHAT'S THE STORY WITH ÎLE DU LEVANT?

Île du Levant, an 8km strip of an island, has a split personality. A closed military camp comprises 90% and the remaining pocket of **Héliopolis** *(iledulevant.com.fr)*, on the island's southwestern edge, is a nudist colony.

Baring all is not obligatory except on beaches… from the port, walk in the direction of Plage de Sable Levant along Sentier Georges Rousseau, and signs reading '*Nudisme Intégral Obligatoire*' mark the moment you have to strip.

The hotels, holiday homes, cafes and hotels are clustered around the central square 1km uphill from the port along rte de l'Ayguade. From there a nature trail leads east into the **Domaine des Arbousiers**, a nature reservation in the eastern part of the colony sheltering rare island plants.

Sanary-sur-Mer

TIME FROM HYÈRES: **35min**

Waterfront dreams

Pretty as a picture, seaside Sanary-sur-Mer fulfills the dream of a small Riviera harbour. Watch the fishers unload their catch on the quay, or admire the traditional fishing boats from one of the seafront cafes. Wednesday's colourful market draws crowds from miles around, and shops line interior streets. The broad white sweep of neighbouring **Plage de Bonnegrâce** gets jammed in summer.

Want more? From mid-April to September, jump on a **Croix du Sud V** *(croixdusud5.com)* boat tour to explore the *calanques* east of Marseille, or go to Île de Porquerolles. Or take a boat excursion to **Île des Embiez** from the small port at Le Brusc, a beach resort 5km south of Sanary-sur-Mer.

Bandol

TIME FROM HYÈRES: **45min**

Sample brilliant wines, seaside

Bandol's old fishing-port charm has been overshadowed by high-rise apartment blocks, but plentiful restaurants, cheap-and-cheerful shops and beach facilities make it a favourite for holidaymakers from Toulon and Marseille. For most others, it's best for a quick lunch stop or a spot of winetasting at one of 49 vineyards under the regional Bandol appellation. To stock up, visit **Oenothèque de Bandol** *(maisondesvins-bandol.com)* or the mothership **Maison des Vins de Bandol** *(vinsdebandol.com)* in Le Castellet, 12km north. This little oenophile's playground provides tastings and can direct you to surrounding vineyards.

To walk off your indulgences, a yellow-marked **Sentier du Littoral** (coastal trail) runs 12km (allow four hours) from Bandol's port to La Madrague in St-Cyr-les-Lecques, with the beautiful Calanque de Port d'Alon roughly halfway. Off Bandol, **Île de Bendor** *(lesilespaulricard.com)* is closed for renovations at the time of writing.

Haut-Var

HILLTOP VILLAGES | FOREST WALKS | WINETASTING

The northern half of the Var *département* (north of the A8), called the Haut-Var, is vastly different from its coastal counterpart. Peaceful hilltop villages drowse beneath the midday sun, and are within easy reach of the wild Gorges du Verdon (p264). Even in the busier seasons, when you head for the hills, a slower pace of life, lush vineyards, earthy black truffles and a bounty of gastronomic delights await. Rosé is the word of the day here, too, where you can taste at the vineyards producing the finest in France. Bike routes link up these communities, and cyclists, especially those with kids, will appreciate pedalling away from the main road.

Then, discover the chestnut forests and cork groves in the Massif de la Ste-Baume nature reserve, laced with sparkling rivers and dotted with flowering shrubs. The mountain range also contains Mary Magdalene's cave and an innovative eco-village.

With a mild Mediterranean climate – hot summers and softer winters – the Haut-Var can, and should, be enjoyed all year long.

Cliff-Face Dwellings in Cotignac & Villecroze
Caves, from wine to monks

Sheltered beautifully under a towering 400m-long sienna tufa cliff-face, the stone village of **Cotignac** is a real picture. The River Cassole and tree- and bistro-lined promenade cours Gambetta run through its heart, but above are **Grottes Troglodytes de Cotignac** *(adult/child €2.50/free)*: dwellings cut directly into the rockface. The **Tuesday-morning market** is lively, and the tourist office has maps of area walks, including to **Shrine of Our Lady of Graces**, a minor place of pilgrimage. After you've explored, pop into **Les Vignerons de Cotignac** *(vigneronsdecotignac.com)* collective to taste and buy local rosé. Northeast 20km, legends swirl about the caves that formed 700,000 years ago. The Benedictine monks settled in them in the 9th century, and today you can explore **Les**

GETTING AROUND

Renting a car is simplest, but if you're staying in a village for a few days, renting an e-bike (from €35 per day) is a great ecofriendly option. Brignoles, Les Arcs and Draguignan are the main hubs for Zou! buses *(zou.maregionsud.fr)* in the Haut-Var, running to many of the towns you may wish to visit. Les Arcs is a very handy hub for onward bus connections within Var. **Les Arcs–Draguignan train station** is served by both regional and TGV trains.

☑ TOP TIP

If you're thinking of reserving a villa inland and driving down to the coast every day, think again – you'll hit the dreadful littoral traffic jam. Best to spend half your stay beachside, and then book a few days inland to explore. For Haut-Var ideas: Visit Var *(visitvar.com)* and Provence Verte *(provenceverte.fr)*.

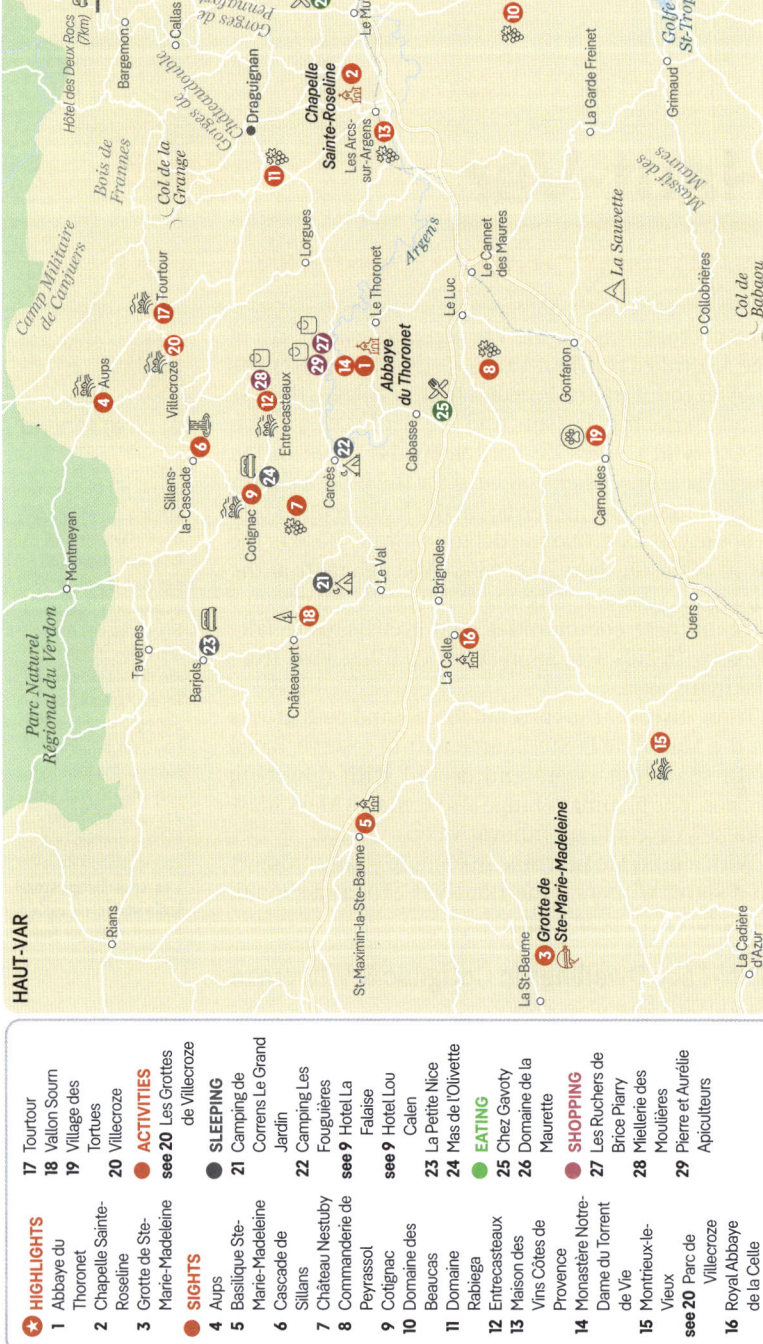

HAUT-VAR

★ HIGHLIGHTS
1 Abbaye du Thoronet
2 Chapelle Sainte-Roseline
3 Grotte de Ste-Marie-Madeleine

● SIGHTS
4 Aups
5 Basilique Ste-Marie-Madeleine
6 Cascade de Sillans
7 Château Nestuby
8 Commanderie de Peyrassol
9 Cotignac
10 Domaine des Beaucas
11 Domaine Rabiega
12 Entrecasteaux
13 Maison des Vins Côtes de Provence
14 Monastère Notre-Dame du Torrent de Vie
15 Montrieux-le-Vieux
see 20 Parc de Villecroze
16 Royal Abbaye de la Celle
17 Tourtour
18 Vallon Sourn
19 Village des Tortues
20 Villecroze

● ACTIVITIES
see 20 Les Grottes de Villecroze

● SLEEPING
21 Camping de Correns Le Grand Jardin
22 Camping Les Fouguières
see 9 Hotel La Falaise
see 9 Hotel Lou Calen
23 La Petite Nice
24 Mas de l'Olivette

● EATING
25 Chez Gavoty
26 Domaine de la Maurette

● SHOPPING
27 Les Ruchers de Brice Piarry
28 Miellerie des Moulières
29 Pierre et Aurélie Apiculteurs

Grottes de Villecroze *(grottes-villecroze.fr; €5)* and learn about their history (as long as you can climb stairs and are over six years old). Be sure to walk through the surrounding **Parc de Villecroze** gardens, with waterfalls and sculptures.

Walk to Hidden Double Falls
Sillans-la-Cascade's namesake waterfalls

Wondering how Sillans-la-Cascade got its name? You won't be able to tell from the roadside. Park at the **Place du 8 Mai 1945 lot** on the D560 southern edge of the village, and walk 550m on a clearly marked, level walking path, to the wide trail descending to **Cascade de Sillans** on the River Bresque. You'll zigzag another 300m down through lush forest and hear them well before you arrive. Stand in the mist of the towering double falls and behold them in all of their thundering glory.

Dig into Aups' Famous Truffles
The truffle capital of the Var

Amber-hued Aups, a gateway to the Gorges du Verdon (p264) to the north, has a history older than even its quaint streets suggest, having been a Celtic *oppidum* (fortified settlement), Roman town, and a Moorish stronghold. Now it's best known for precious black gold: *Tuber melanosporum* (black truffles). These alien-looking nuggets of revered fungus end up on many a Michelin-starred table. From November to late February they mature beneath the area's frigid ground and you can see them (and buy them) at the Thursday-morning **truffle market** on the central plane-tree-studded square. It generally runs 9am to noon (closing earlier if they sell out) from late-November to late March; but check the website, as markets end when that year's harvest ends.

Maison de la Truffe *(maisondelatruffe-verdon.fr; Truffle Adventure adult/child €2.50/1.50)*, attached to **Aups tourist office** *(aups-tourisme.com)* sells truffles in various forms (whole, in pastes and pastas). It's also home to Truffle Adventure, an interactive space exploring the precious fungus, its history and gastronomy. Check online for truffle-hunting and other activities.

Actually want a truffle-enhanced meal? Reserve at **Restaurant des Gourmets** *(restaurantdesgourmets.com)*, one of the best places in Aups to try them, even in the form of truffle ice cream.

Tastings and truffle-hunting demonstrations lure a crowd on the fourth Sunday in January during the annual **Fête de la Truffe Noire**.

VAR VILLAGE MARKET DAYS

Most Var villages hold a weekly market; a window into local life, and the best way to build a picnic. Markets set up from 7am and pack up by noon/1pm.

Monday Bormes-les-Mimosas.

Tuesday Bandol, Callas, Cotignac, Fayence, Hyères, Lorgues.

Wednesday Aups, Bormes-les-Mimosas, La Garde Freinet, Salernes, Sanary-sur-Mer, Tourtour.

Thursday Aups (truffles, in winter), Bargemon, Callas, Collobrières (July and August), Fayence, Hyères, Ramatuelle.

Friday Entrecasteaux, La Motte.

Saturday Aups, Carcès, Claviers, Cogolin, Draguignan, Fayence, Hyères, Tourtour.

Sunday Ampus, Cavalière, Collobrières, Gassin (April to Oct), La Garde Freinet, Ramatuelle, Salernes, Vidauban.

 EATING & DRINKING IN COTIGNAC: QUALITY & VARIETY

Picotte Provence: On a sunny day, opt for the clifftop terrace in the back; top wines and regional specials. *noon-2pm Thu-Sun & 7-9.30pm Wed-Sat* €€

Le Bistro: Choose between the elegant dining room or the people-watching terrace under the plane trees. *noon-2pm daily & 7-9pm Mon-Wed, Fri & Sat* €€

Le Clos des Vignes: Seek out this farmhouse for the home-cooked cuisine and the warm welcome. Terrace by the vines. *noon-2pm & 7-10pm Tue-Sat, noon-2pm Sun* €€

La Tuf: Brewery making craft beers, from pale ales to sours and porters, and occasional live music. *5-10pm Tue & Wed, to midnight Thu-Sat*

ENTRECASTEAUX HONEY FARMS

Just like you can sample and buy wines, olive oils and cheeses with the producers, you can also visit the Var's excellent honey farms. Here are some of our favourites around Entrecasteaux (or find them at local markets p147):

Miellerie des Moulières *(remy-mielleriedes moulieres.fr)*: North of Entrecasteaux off the D31, specialising in honeys like rosemary, chestnut and lavender.

Pierre et Aurélie Apiculteurs *(pierreetaurelie.com)*: Southeast of Entrecasteaux off the D62; carry similar varieties and also a delicious thyme honey, olive oil and soaps.

Les Ruchers de Brice Piarry *(brice-piarry.com)*: Nearby; also make honey with notes of the shrubs maquis and garrigue and acacia (mimosas).

Callas

Soak in a Tourtour Sunset
Thrilling panoramas

Make your way to the best sunset in the Haut-Var, at little Tourtour. Known as the village in the sky, the amber-stoned village is perched on a hilltop with a churchyard stretching across a promontory with panoramic views. The centre of this medieval town is pedestrian-only, and its cobbled lanes filled with galleries and shops make it a relaxing evening (with or without children).

Taste Olive Oil at a Grove in Callas
Four generations of olive oil production

The largely 18th-century hill village of Callas sits 400m above prime olive- and grape-growing country, with the natural beauty of the Pennafort Gorge and its waterfall 8km south. Callas is a charm to wander, admiring fountains of pitted stone and venerable churches, and from the central village square you get a stunning panorama of the red-rock **Massif**

EATING & DRINKING IN THE HAUT-VAR: VINEYARD DINING

La Table de St-Roux: Market-sourced creations at the chic indoor dining room or the shaded terrace of the **Château St-Roux**. *noon-2pm & 7-9pm* €€

Le Patriarche: Between Thoronet and Carcès at **Château Ste-Croix**, *prix-fixe* truffle and asparagus ravioli. *noon-2pm daily & 7-9.30pm Fri & Sat* €€€

Chez Gavoty: Each Friday in summer, visit for cocktail hour: music, tapas, and winetasting. Off the A8, south of Cotignac. *7pm-midnight Fri Jun-Aug* €€

Domaine de la Maurette: For an authentic Provençal feast at a rustic wine estate. *noon-2pm Thu-Mon & 7.30-9.30pm Fri & Sat* €€

de l'Estérel (p135). But take advantage of the olive groves at **Moulin de Callas** *(moulindecallas.com)* at the foot of town, where four generations of the Bérenguier olive-growing dynasty stretches back to 1928.

Admire the old waterwheel, learn about olive-oil production and purchase the excellent oil in the shop, which also carries an array of regional soaps, honeys and other products. In-depth tours and tastings must be prearranged (some are free, others very reasonable).

Rosé All Day
Châteaux, domaines and Haut-Var vineyards

Don't miss sampling Var rosés, a staple at lunch tables across Provence. A rosé from the Var tastes of the rocky clay soil and the two winds that sweep the landscape: the bit of sea breeze sneaking up from the coast and the mistral slamming down from the north. Choosing from more than 300 regional vineyards may leave you feeling overwhelmed, but here's a start.

If your time is short, just go to **Maison des Vins Côtes de Provence** *(maison-des-vins.fr)*, 2.5km southwest of Les Arcs-sur-Argens. It's a one-stop shop: learn about and buy (at producers' prices) Côtes de Provence wines, including those made at local cooperatives. Each week 16 of the 800 wines from 250 wine estates are selected for tasting (for free!).

Just south, begin with **Domaine des Beaucas** *(domainedesbeaucas.com; tasting from €10)*, a chance to drive the vineyard-carpeted valley beyond the thundering **Cascades de l'Aille**. Jaunting 23.5km west of the falls, history, art and fine wine merge at **Commanderie de Peyrassol** *(peyrassol.com; tastings from €20)*. Our choice? A bottle of Le Clos Peyrassol Rosé from 2022, the year the vineyard was certified organic, over a light lunch at its bistro. Reserve ahead for a Thursday evening concert in July and August.

If you're getting tired, stay over after your tasting at organic winery **Domaine Rabiega** *(rabiega.com; tastings from €20)*, in a hamlet 5.5km southwest of Draguignan.

Travelling with family? Push on like the warrior you are and reserve a *visite ludique (*fun tour; *adult/under 10 €20/ free)* at **Château Nestuby** *(nestuby.com; tastings from €6)*, 24km north, which includes a treasure hunt in the vineyard. You can stay there, too, or head into nearby Cotignac (p145).

MEET THE HERMANN'S TORTOISE

The western Hermann's tortoise (*Testudo hermanni hermanni*) is an endangered species found in small pockets of the Mediterranean coast: it mainly lives in Italy, Sardinia and Corsica, but you can still find a number of them living in the Var – notably in **Grimaud** (p128). Outside the village, near the Pont des Fées, is one good place to look.

The tortoise is fairly small – they only grow 7cm to 18cm long – but the distinct black-and-yellow pattern on its shell makes them easy to recognise (assuming they're not camouflaged in the underbrush). Want to get to know them better? Visit the tortoise sanctuary, **Village des Tortues** *(tortupole.fr)* in Carnoules.

EATING IN TOURTOUR & LORGUES: OUR PICKS

| **La Table**, Tourtour: High-concept French classics in a cosy restaurant with a small covered terrace. Open year-round. *lunch & 7.15-9pm Wed-Mon* €€ | **Bar des Ormeaux**, **Tourtour:** Sidle up to the bar for a draft beer or eat cafe classics in the central square, chatting with residents. *6.30am-11pm* €€ | **Ô P'tibouren**, Lorgues: Fried mussels many ways, plus composed salads and rich meats, street-side in the centre of the village. *9am-10pm* €€ | **Chez Bruno**, **Lorgues:** If truffles are divine, then Chez Bruno is their high temple on an 18th-century estate. *noon-2pm & 7-10pm mid-Jun–Sep, shorter rest of year* €€€ |

DRIVING VILLAGES DE CARACTÈRE

String together a highlight reel of fabulous hill villages, each with their own character, as you cruise the gorgeous Var highlands.

START	END	LENGTH
Entrecasteaux	Seillans	78km; 5hr

Start with a wander around gorgeous ① **Entrecasteaux**, its giant 17th-century **château** the centrepiece of formal gardens perching dramatically along the river. Bear right along the D31 and drive another wiggly 6km to ② **Salernes**, where handmade terracotta tiles called *terres cuites* (literally 'baked earth') have been manufactured since the 18th century. The tourist office has a list of workshops to visit.

From Salernes, pick up the westbound D2560 and subsequent D560 to ③ **Sillans-la-Cascade**, a gem of a fortified village with a **waterfall** (p147). Then it's 9km north along the D22 to ④ **Aups**, a village that's ground zero for Haut-Var's famous truffles (p147). From here, it's a genuinely stunning 10km drive southeast past olive groves and lavender gardens to the 'eagle nest' gold-stone village of ⑤ **Tourtour** (p148), a great lunch stop. From December to January you can see olives being pressed in its 17th-century *moulin à huile*, or in summer there are art exhibits.

Six kilometres further east along the D51 you'll encounter Ampus; continue east 9km to ⑥ **Châteaudouble**, an astonishing village clinging to a cliff of the Gorges de Châteaudouble and River Nartuby. Just 7km east is ⑦ **Bargemon**, a village with a maze of medieval streets and ramparts to stroll. Finally finish in ⑧ **Seillans**, a scenic 12km drive east, an irresistibly pretty village with cobbled lanes coiling to its crown.

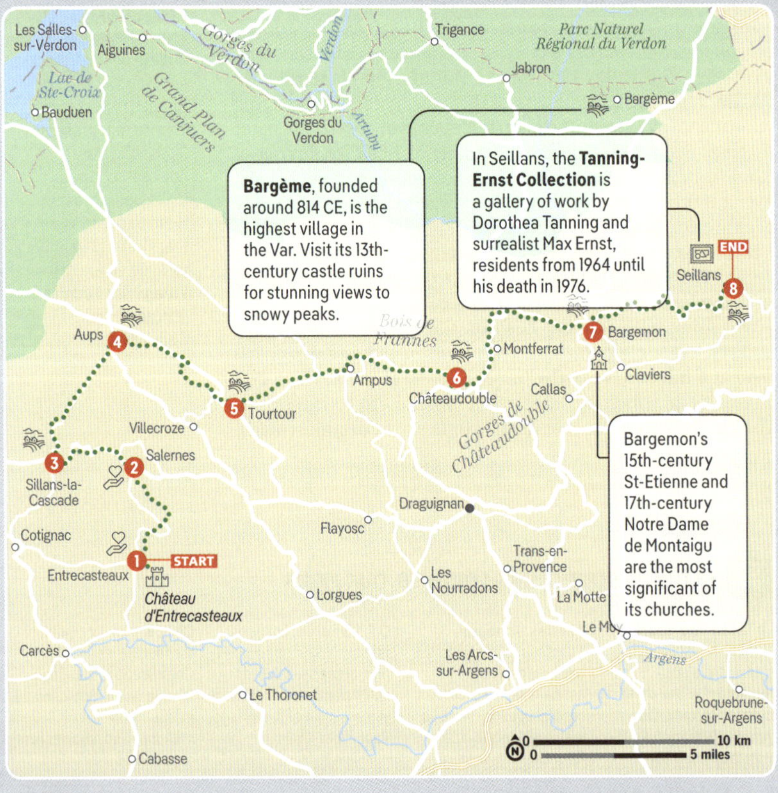

Bargème, founded around 814 CE, is the highest village in the Var. Visit its 13th-century castle ruins for stunning views to snowy peaks.

In Seillans, the **Tanning-Ernst Collection** is a gallery of work by Dorothea Tanning and surrealist Max Ernst, residents from 1964 until his death in 1976.

Bargemon's 15th-century St-Etienne and 17th-century Notre Dame de Montaigu are the most significant of its churches.

Abbaye du Thoronet

Marc Chagall Mosaic in a Hallowed Chapel

The charms of Chapelle Ste-Roseline

Art lovers should make a beeline for **Chapelle Ste-Roseline**, 4.5km east of Les Arcs-sur-Argens, where a 1975 mosaic by Marc Chagall illuminates this 13th-century Romanesque chapel. The church also contains a crystal shrine holding the corpse of St Roseline (1263–1329), who experienced visions and was said to curtail demons. Concerts are held here in July and August.

Cistercian Monastery Simplicity

Exploring Abbaye du Thoronet and beyond

The simplest but most beautiful of 'The Sisters' – a trio of great Provençal Cistercian abbeys, including Silvacane and Notre-Dame de Sénanque – **Abbaye du Thoronet**, built between 1160 and 1190, is a masterpiece of sacred architecture. You'll see how remarkable its ultra-austere style is: pure proportions and the subtle fall of light and shadow. There's so much to see, but highlights include the graceful cloisters, church, chapterhouse, lavabo and cellars. Definitely fork out for the enlightening €4 audioguide. It's 14km from Lorgues, a fantastic valley drive through beech and oak woods.

If you'd like to keep going, visit the modern **Monastère Notre-Dame du Torrent de Vie** (bethleem.org) next door and buy ceramics made by the nuns, before stopping in to **Royal Abbaye de la Celle**, a 12th-century Benedictine Romanesque abbey, 24.6km southwest.

RESOURCES FOR CYCLING THE VAR

The Haut-Var makes for idyllic cycles, through vineyards, down hidden valleys. Resources abound on websites (visitvar.fr; provenceverte.fr) and in tourist offices. Look for the thick booklet with routes called *Le Var à Vélo*, which rates the difficulty of each ride and makes suggestions for families.

Bobby at **Coti's Bike** (@cotisbike_cotignac83) in Cotignac rents both e-bikes and classic bikes, and can give you ideas.

One of our favourites is through **Vallon Sourn**, where the swift waters of the Argens have cut a picturesque canyon from the soft rock. It's also a haven for walking, canoeing and wild swimming.

If you're doing the latter, a scenic drive/ride from Correns, north on the D45 towards Châteauvert, will get you there.

BEST HIKES IN THE MASSIF DE LA STE-BAUME

The Gorges du Caramy: An 8km hike along the River Caramy, flanked by the cliffs. Especially great in autumn.

L'Abîme de Maramoye: Easy 5km hike to a ravine, with an unobstructed view and nontechnical path for all hikers.

Trou Zéro: From Bastide Blanche to the gaping rock at Trou Zéro, this 11km hike explores several old ruins.

Aiguilles de Valbelle: A 14km loop with trail signs, passing below the striking limestone formations of the Aiguilles de Valbelle, some of which are more than 15m high.

Grotte de Ste-Marie-Madeleine

Hike to the Venerated Cave of Mary Magdalene

Pay homage to a Catholic saint

Mary Magdalene is said to have spent the last years of her life in a small cave 950m up a cliff face in Massif de la Ste-Baume, now called **Grotte de Ste-Marie-Madeleine** *(saintebaume .org/grotte; admission free)*. Wear strong shoes for the sweaty but worthwhile 40-minute climb along a forest trail from La Ste-Baume. Its entrance offers a breathtaking panorama of Montagne Ste-Victoire, Mont Ventoux and the Alps. Dominican Friars have developed the grotto as a place of pilgrimage for over 700 years, and house pilgrims in **Hostellerie de la Ste-Baume**.

After, you can drive the 21km northwest to **Basilique Ste-Marie-Madeleine**, the largest Gothic church in Provence, located in workaday city **St-Maximin-la-Ste-Baum**. There, in the crypt, you'll find her relics, including her skull.

ABSORBING MONASTERIES

If you love monasteries, seek out **Monastère de La Verne** (p130) in the nearby Maures mountain range, or go further afield to **Abbaye Notre-Dame de Sénanque** (p240), famous for its lavender fields.

Spend the Night in an Eco-Village

Party, feast and sleep at a revived hamlet

The main region around **Montrieux-le-Vieux** *(montrieux.org)*, due north of Toulon, has been inhabited by religious communities for centuries. A group of socio-democratic investors bought one of the monks' old hamlets and created this *eco-lieu* (eco-village). Dine in an airy dining room overlooking the garden, and, in summer, a patio close to the river serves as a small *guinguette*, an outdoor bar/restaurant serving local beers, lemonade and sodas. The chefs use as much produce from their garden as possible. Flea markets and impromptu concerts mean a visit is full of surprises. Unwind by staying over in one of the pastel B&Bs or at the small hotel.

Places We Love to Stay

€ Budget   €€ Midrange   €€€ Top End

St-Tropez
Map p121

Hôtel Le Colombier €€ Immaculately clean, near place des Lices.

B Lodge Hôtel €€ Muted tones and rooms with balconies and Citadelle views are fabulous.

Hôtel Ermitage €€ Self-consciously retro, with sweeping views over town.

Hôtel Lou Cagnard €€€ Lovely jasmine-scented garden patios and welcoming feel. Open year-round.

Hôtel Byblos €€€ Perennial favourite among Hollywood A-listers, with a Michelin-star restaurant.

Presqu'île de St-Tropez

La Vigneraie 1860 € Tents and caravans camp off Plage de Pampelonne, beside vineyards. Basic apartments, too.

Le Refuge €€ Rustic house off Plage de Gigaro. Humble rooms and studios open onto terraces.

Hôtel Bellovisto €€ Gassin hotel's charm is due to the cafe-clad square with panoramic view out front.

Near Bormes-les-Mimosas

Hôtel California € Vintage hotel in Le Lavendou, with clean rooms for travellers on a budget.

La Villa Thalassa €€ Comfortable B&B with three bedrooms, plus a cute wooden caravan. Pool with sunset view.

Le Relais des Maures €€ This inn, tucked just off the D559, has homely guest rooms, some with sea views.

Fréjus & St-Raphaël

Hôtel Les Calanques, Les Issambres € Family-run three-star above its own quiet cove.

Hôtel L'Aréna, Fréjus € Provençal decor, with garden, pool and restaurant.

Hôtel le 21, St-Raphaël €€ Small, plain hotel; handy for both the train station and centre.

Hyères
Map p137

Lilou €€ City-centre, comfortable with a restaurant, small pool and parking.

Hôtel Les Orangers €€ Casual, clean hotel around a shady courtyard and convenient to the centre.

Presqu'île de Giens

Hôtel Le Méditerranée € Pleasant little hotel at Hyères' racing track and near a beach.

Camping à la Ferme le Pradeau € Small campground with access to Plage du Pradeau.

Camping Bernard € Shaded by eucalyptus trees, access to Plage de la Marquise and a boules terrain.

Hôtel Bor €€ This Scandi-tinged, palm-fringed hotel is a stylish place to stay.

Le Lodge des Îles d'Or €€€ Luxe resort back from Plage La Bergerie with light-filled rooms.

Île de Porquerolles

Villa Ste-Anne €€ Inn on the square with terrace overlooking the *pétanque* pitch.

Les Mèdes €€ Traditional rooms and self-catering apartments, with terraced garden and pool.

Le Mas du Langoustier €€€ Splashy inn with its own private beach, Michelin-starred restaurant.

Sanary-sur-Mer & Bandol

Hôtel de la Tour, Sanary-sur-Mer € Charming, fin-de-siècle hotel with large rooms, some with awesome portside views.

Key Largo, Bandol €€ Small place on the point between the port and Renécros beach is one of the better options.

Splendid Hôtel, Bandol €€€ Stone mansion dripping with boutique charm, smack on the sea at Renécros beach.

Haut-Var
Map p146

La Petite Nice, Barjols € Old-fashioned luxury decor with a charming garden.

Hôtel des Deux Rocs, Seillans € Atmospheric village inn with patio restaurant.

Camping de Correns Le Grand Jardin, Correns € Small family-friendly campground with access to the river.

Camping Les Fouguières, Carcès € In wine country, this family-oriented campground offers bungalows and shady sites by River Caramy.

Hotel La Falaise, Cotignac € A bright, clean and spacious hotel right in the heart of the village.

Mas de l'Olivette, Cotignac €€ Lovely proprietors welcome you so warmly to their tiny B&B that it feels like home.

Hotel Lou Calen, Cotignac €€€ Swank vintage-modern guest rooms, abundant gardens and a pool, with warm service.

Above: Calanque d'En-Vau (p173); Right: Rice cultivated in the Camargue (p195)

Researched by
Michael Frankel

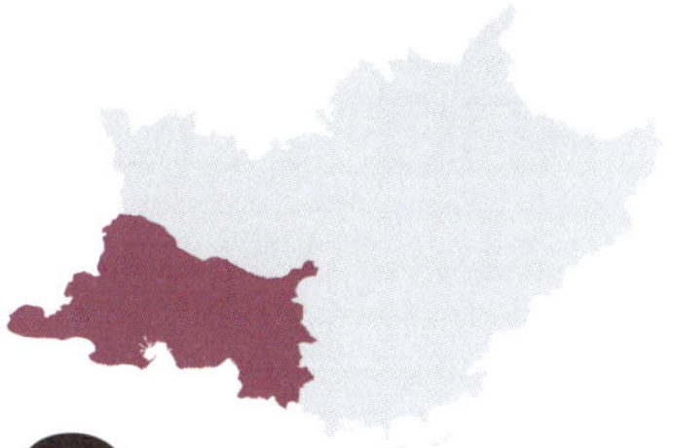

Bouches-du-Rhône

FOLLOWING THE RIVER TO THE SEA

This is a region that veers from enthralling city life to the gentle murmuring of the Mediterranean.

When you find yourself awash in the region's famous light, it becomes clear why so many artists have been magnetically drawn here for centuries, seeking to unlock something bigger than themselves. This land epitomises springtime, having inspired great post-impressionist painters Cézanne and Van Gogh to create their seminal works.

As the mistral wind howls down the Rhône Valley toward the sea, slamming the wooden shutters of homes throughout the night and clearing the skies for what feels like endless sunshine, it creates a climate that is not only inviting for travellers but also ideal for farming.

Sampling the fresh produce nurtured and grown here will be an essential part of your journey, especially in the bustling markets and endless stretches of vineyards. The region's palpitating heart is Marseille, France's second-largest city, known for its vibrant cultural energy.

Beyond the urban landscape are pine-swaddled coastal uplands cut by breathtaking *calanques* (coves). Inland you'll find the still-thriving Roman towns of Aix-en-Provence and Arles. At the mouth *(bouche)* of the River Rhône lies the timeless beauty of the Camargue wetlands, which are home to thousands of migratory birds.

Whether exploring nature, driving the countryside roads or sprawled on the beaches, absorbing the rhythm of the cicadas' cries, the Bouches-du-Rhône offers a sensuous Mediterranean experience waiting to be discovered, sparkling gloriously beneath the sun.

BARMALINI/SHUTTERSTOCK

THE MAIN AREAS

MARSEILLE
Cosmopolitan urban sprawl meets unspoilt beaches. **p160**

AIX-EN-PROVENCE
Elegant heart of Provence.
p178

ARLES
Roman ruins and modern art.
p188

STES-MARIES-DE-LA-MER
Seaside village in the Camargue. **p198**

Find Your Way

The Bouches-du-Rhône *département* is well connected by air, road, rail and sea to the rest of France and the Mediterranean beyond. In the countryside a car is best, though you can generally get around without one.

THE GUIDE

BOUCHES-DU-RHÔNE

Arles, p188
A slow-paced Roman town with a preserved grandness that goes back centuries. Food, drink and nightlife reflect the untamed soul of Camargue life.

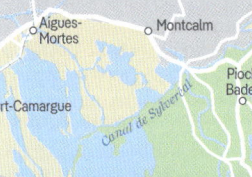

Stes-Maries-de-la-Mer, p198
A tiny fishing village in the Mediterranean backwaters that comes alive in spring and summer and is home to a spectacular parade every May.

CAR
Driving in this region is a joy, though parking can be a pain – especially in Marseille and Aix. If you plan on exploring tiny villages, far-flung vineyards or the Camargue, however, plan on renting a car.

TRAIN
Both Marseille and Aix connect to Paris, Lyon and Avignon via TGV, while slower services head west (to Montpellier) and east (to Nice and Italy). The regional train west along the Côte Bleue has spectacular views.

BUS
The local bus network is inexpensive and has regular and extensive services across the region, including multiple connections from Marseille airport.

Aix-en-Provence, p178
The heart of Provence is a place of refined elegance: fountains, narrow streets, high-end shopping and plenty of green spaces.

Marseille, p160
A cutting-edge city transforming itself for a new generation. As historic as it is fun, and home to some of the most unspoilt coastline in France.

Plan Your Time

This region is easiest to navigate if you base yourself in one place: Marseille for city life and the *calanques*, Aix for classic rural Provence or Arles for art, Roman ruins and the Camargue.

Ferry dock, Île d'If (p168)

Pressed for Time

● With only a day or two, sticking to just one place: **Marseille** (p160) makes sense if you want to explore this dynamic cultural melting pot, which presents a unique take on modern French life, with easy escapes along the coast.

● Well-heeled **Aix-en-Provence** (p178), meanwhile, is the opposite experience: think elegant architecture and high-brow culture, surrounded by prosperous farms, independent vineyards and charismatic stone villages perched on hillsides.

● For more art, plus the region's best Roman ruins, riverside **Arles** (p188) is a lovely base, with direct access to the wild and wonderous wetlands of the **Camargue** (p198) beyond.

SEASONAL HIGHLIGHTS

Winters are usually mild, but a mistral wind can change that in a second. Spring and autumn are blissful, summers hot and crowded.

MARCH
On the third weekend in March, the raucous **Carnaval de La Plaine** (p161) brings joy and protest to Marseille.

APRIL
Early spring harvests make their way to stalls around the region, with local produce on display on market days.

MAY
Members of European nomadic communities, including Roma, Manouches, Tziganes and Gitan travel to Stes-Maries-de-la-Mer on 24 May, ending their annual **pilgrimage** (p198).

A Long Weekend in Marseille

● Breakfast at the **Hôtel Belle-Vue** (p203) on the port before a ferry to the **Château d'If** (p168) or the **Îles du Frioul** (p169).

● Spend the evening in **cours Julien** (p160), the epicentre of social life, before dinner at **Les Babines de Mars** (p172) in the Longchamp neighbourhood.

● Next morning, embark on a walking tour of the old **Panier neighbourhood** (p170), then lunch at the cafe in the **Jardin du Pharo** (p171) before an afternoon winding your way along the **Corniche Kennedy coastline** (p165).

● Day three sail out to **Les Goudes** (p166), kayak to **Les Calanques** (p173) or take the train along the **Côte Bleue** (p176).

More than a Week

● In Aix-en-Provence, visit **art museums** (p178), drive out to scenic **vineyards** (p186) and climb up Cézanne's muse: **Montagne Ste-Victoire** (p184).

● In nearby Arles, walk through **Roman ruins** (p190) followed by a visit to the **Fondation Vincent Van Gogh** (p189) or the cutting-edge **Luma Arles art gallery** (p188).

● A day out in **Les Alpilles** (p196) delivers a true village experience with stunning treks. From here, head into the Camargue, where you can **ride white horses** (p193), **birdwatch** (p200) and trek to the **wild beaches** (p194) of the Rhône Delta.

● A final stop in **Stes-Maries-de-la-Mer** (p198) is perfect for coastal cycling and sunlounger life.

THE GUIDE

BOUCHES-DU-RHÔNE

JUNE	JULY	AUGUST	SEPTEMBER
Potentially the best time of year to go wine-tasting in Provence: students are still in school, airfares are lower and the heat is more bearable.	**Les Rencontres d'Arles** (p188) is an internationally renowned annual photography festival held throughout the city.	Peak heat and peak life: Marseille is on holiday with the residents enjoying a summer of excess.	Visit Mouriès in Les Alpilles for a celebration of the green olive season.

Marseille

BOATING | CUTTING-EDGE CULTURE | MEDITERRANEAN CUISINE

GETTING AROUND

Marseille has two metro lines, two tram lines and an extensive bus network. Bus, metro or tram tickets are available from machines in the metro, at tram stops and on buses. In general, however, Marseille is a delight to explore on foot.

From April to the end of September, the maritime shuttle crossings from the Vieux Port can also take you to L'Estaque and Pointe Rouge.

Sign up to the Levélo public e-bike network to navigate the city by bike *(levelo. ampmetropole.fr)*

☑ TOP TIP

'This is a city where we like to joke. It's what we call *t'emboucaner*. If we make fun of you, it's to make you feel at home. Don't take yourself too seriously here and you'll do well.' – JC, manager of Le Trois Quarts bar in the Camas.

Marseille has an edge. France's second-largest city puts its arms around you as a drunken friend would – passionately and deliriously. It is a city that revels in its status as France's underdog. As you explore its hidden corners it will reveal a beauty that is difficult to capture in photographs: an urban sprawl interspersed with pockets of inspiring nature that must be experienced in person. Since it was founded by the Greeks in 600 BCE the tremendous influx of immigration in this port city has never ceased. In Marseille, North and West Africans live shoulder to shoulder with a vast Corsican community, only a skipping stone's throw from northern Italy and Spanish Catalonia.

Greater Marseille is divided into 16 *arrondissements*, which are often indicated in addresses. The city's main thoroughfare, La Canebière, stretches eastwards from the Vieux Port towards the train station, a 10-minute walk away. Just uphill is Le Panier, the oldest neighbourhood in the city.

Cours Julien & La Plaine
Mix with the locals

Sooner or later, you'll end up on the **cours Julien** (known locally as 'le cours Ju') for a drink, and for good reason. As a pedestrian area slathered with street art and bohemian yearnings, this is the home of some great bars and restaurants, which remain open day and night. Wander the narrow side streets, packed with bookshops, galleries and tattoo parlours, until you reach the noisy and elongated main square, a destination for a solid night out, and a microcosm of the city itself. You are likely to hear boom boxes blasting, guitars strummed and African drums pounding as soon as the sun comes out.

Place Jean-Jaurès, also known as La Plaine, is another vast square surrounded by bars and restaurants. For years it has been the battleground for left-wing militants and artists. Closed for urban renewal before the pandemic, it reopened

Market, Noailles

LA CARNAVAL DE LA PLAINE

Every third weekend in March, the raucous **Carnaval de La Plaine** is held on place Jean-Jaurès. An explosive but joyful affair, the square fills with samba beats and chants for one big party that's essentially an anti-capitalist protest rooted in paganism.

As part of the fight against gentrification, neighbourhood residents dress up in themed costumes and dance, get merry and set fire to effigies of their political rivals.

Be prepared to be covered in flour and insults if you don't look the part.

If you do look the part, have your wits about you. Without fail, the event ends in a confrontation with the French riot police: a custom that can easily be avoided by heading home or to a bar before night falls.

to mixed emotions in 2021, with some claiming the square had become too controlled and sanitised. Unlike many public areas worldwide, however, it has been redesigned with skateboarders in mind, with long smooth runs and no anti-skate guards in sight. Buzzing day and night in the spring and summer months, it remains a beating heart for locals escaping the tourist traps, whether in the bars or in the public seating areas beneath the trees. La Plaine is only a 10-minute walk east from cours Julien.

African Food in Noailles

Travel your taste buds

Like Naples in Italy, Marseille is an anomaly in Europe: the poorest residents live in the centre of town, rather than on the outskirts. Noailles, a majority African neighbourhood, is only minutes from the Vieux Port.

As with any community, life revolves around the market square. The **Marché des Capucins** is where all the action happens. Sit outside the **Cafe Prinder** *(6am-6pm)*, an establishment serving strong cups of coffee since 1925, and bear witness to the square's energy. You are just as likely to hear Arabic as you are French as the locals come out to shop for essentials.

The long **rue d'Aubagne** acts as the neighbourhood's main artery. It was the scene of a terrible tragedy in 2019 when two buildings collapsed, killing the inhabitants within the walls of their own homes. The neighbourhood has refused to forget it.

Taking the **rue Longue des Capucins** is essential to understanding where you are. In this narrow street, it's easy to believe that you're in a North African souk. Pyramid-shaped piles of spices, halal butchers, fresh fish on ice and the aroma

MARSEILLE

● SIGHTS
1. Basilique Notre-Dame de la Garde
2. Cathédrale de la Major
3. Cours Julien
4. Jardin du Pharo
5. Palais Longchamp
6. Place Jean-Jaurès
7. Plage des Catalans
8. Vallon des Auffes

● ACTIVITIES
9. Capitaine Coco
10. Eco-Calanques
11. Le Bateau Jaune
12. Les Barquettes

● SLEEPING
13. Hôtel Belle-Vue
14. Hotel Peron
15. La Relève
16. Le Ryad
17. Les Appartements du Vieux Port
18. Les Bords de la Mer
19. Mama Shelter

● EATING
20. Amandine
21. Baussens Emmanuel
22. Belleville/Mer
23. Caterine
24. Chez Gilda
25. Chez Yassine
26. La Jungle
see 35 La Kaz Kreol
27. Le Bistrot Plage

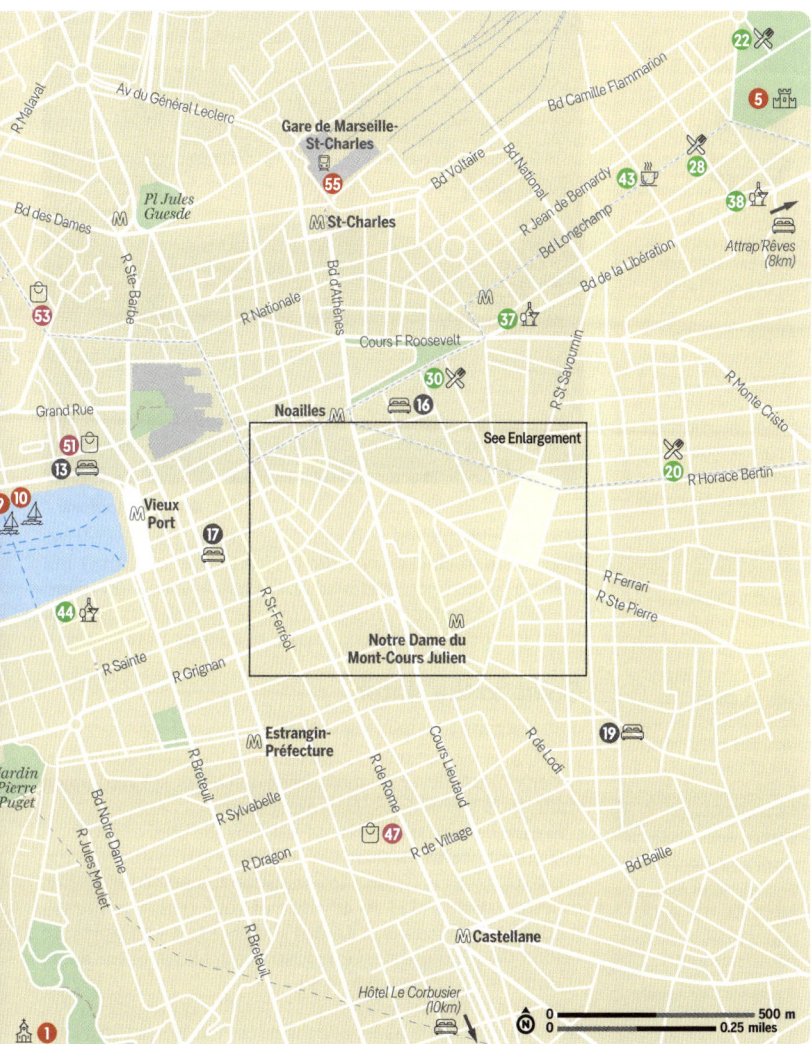

28	Les Babines de Mars
29	Limmat
30	Limon
31	Mama Ghana
32	Razzia
33	Restaurant Le Fémina
34	Vanille Noire

● **DRINKING & NIGHTLIFE**

35	Bar des Maraîchers
36	Cafe Prinder
37	Grand Bar du Chapitre
38	Ivresse
see 15	La Relève
39	Le Bar de la Plaine
40	Le Bar du Peuple
41	Planète Livre Marseille la Passerelle
42	PMU le blabla
43	Pollux
44	The Queen Victoria

● **ENTERTAINMENT**

45	OM Boutique

● **SHOPPING**

46	Bière de la Plaine
47	Camara
48	Jiji la Palme d'Or
49	Maison Empereur
50	Marché des Capucins
51	Michel Fauveau
52	OLAB
53	Photo République
54	Savonnerie Marseillaise de la Licorne

● **TRANSPORT**

55	Gare St-Charles

LOCAL TIPS FOR NOAILLES

Sadia Chellah, Algerian-born owner of **Le Bar du Peuple**, is passionate about her neighbourhood. As she describes it, 'Noailles is the place where people arrive. I love that we now have flower shops in the neighbourhood and tourism.'

These are some of her favourite spots:

OM Boutique: There is only one team in this city: Olympique de Marseille. Get your shirts here.

Maison Empereur: This hardware and homewares store was founded in 1827; it's one of the oldest in France. A great place for anything your kitchen would need.

Jiji la Palme d'Or: Enough North African bowls, baskets and rugs to make your home feel loved.

Baussens Emmanuel: The only place to buy pork in the whole neighbourhood. It's been there a long time.

Orange Vélodrome

of rotisserie chicken will send your senses into overdrive. Vegetarian or chicken *pastilla* (a North African pastry) and *kesra* (a round semolina bread served hot) are must-try items, as is West African *bissap* juice (a type of hibiscus). Do note that pickpockets have been known to operate in this area.

Going to the Match
Join the fiercely chanting crowds

Olympique de Marseille is the only top-level football club in the city. You will see it emblazoned on chests, sprayed up on walls, in shop windows: OM, everywhere.

To experience a sports event fuelled by the kind of ear-shatteringly unbridled passion you are unlikely to witness again, book your tickets (from €15) online at the official club site, billetterie.om.fr, way in advance of your trip. The French football season begins in August and ends in May. Games are held in the league almost every weekend, played at the home stadium every other week or so.

It is best to request seats around the halfway line, in either of the stands that run alongside the pitch. The fierce Ultra supporters position themselves behind each goal, lighting flares as their cries fill the air. Tickets in hand, it is easy to take a walk from the centre of town up to **Orange Vélodrome**, OM's

EATING AROUND COURS JULIEN: TOP SPOTS

Chez Gilda: Come here to eat fried seafood and drink white wine with the local skateboarders. *7.30-11pm Tue-Sat* €€

Limmat: The perfect lunch spot: Mediterranean food with a great view from the top of the stairs. *noon-2.30pm Mon-Fri, 7-10.30pm Wed-Fri* €€

Caterine: Unpretentious and yet gastronomic French cuisine that's served in a canteen-style setting. *noon-3pm & 7.30-10pm Tue-Fri* €€

Planète Livre Marseille la Passerelle: Attracts an international crowd keen on its vast range of natural wine who subsequently discover its food. *4.30pm-midnight Mon-Sat* €€

impressive 67,000-capacity stadium. The stadium begins to fill one or two hours before kickoff, with fans arriving early to take in the atmosphere. Beer and pizza are available and compared to the Premier League in England, the prices are very affordable. If you really want to look the part, buy a team shirt or scarf from the **official club shop** on La Canebière before you go. *Allez l'OM!*

The Best Urban Beaches
Catch some rays on *les plages*

Leave the Vieux Port behind for the **Corniche Kennedy**, which winds its way east along the coast. This is where many visitors first fall under Marseille's spell, bedazzled by the intense, raw energy of the sea, the endless sunshine glinting off the Med and the spectacular coastal beauty. Your first stop will be the crowded **Plage des Catalans** – home to volleyball and the rare sight of sand. Winding further out of town, you'll find the private club **Le Bistrot Plage** (*bistrot-plage.fr, 10am-10pm, €25 per day*), and can settle into its famous orange sunloungers to enjoy tapas as you oil up. As the road bends to the left, head down to the **Port de Malmousque** – a marina from another era where people bring wine and then glide out into the waters from the rocks at sunset. Bronzed and exhilarated: this is how the locals do it. Next is the **Anse de la Fausse Monnaie**, situated directly below one of the city's most exclusive restaurants, **Le Petit Nice** (*passedat.fr/fr/le-petit-nice, noon-9.30pm Tue-Sat*). This is where the best-looking, tattooed and nearly naked go to show themselves off and admire each other while pretending to read books on philosophy. It's hot. For a more standard beach, but much farther, you can always head to the vast **Plages du Prado**. It's family orientated, has a famous skate park and yes, there's sand.

Eco-Friendly Cruises on the Med
Take to the water

There is no more joyful escape than to take to the waters around Marseille. At the Vieux Port you can find Fanny's *barquettes* at **Capitaine Coco** (*capitainecoco.fr*) to experience the immediacy of the sea on a 1960s Provençal leisure vessel. You will help run up the sails, learn about biodiversity and enjoy a vegetarian lunch. It is an intimate and hands-on affair that can be geared towards educating children if you

---

WHAT IT MEANS TO BE A FAN

Gabriel Chiesa, member of Olympique de Marseille football supporters club:

You don't need religion when you have football in your life, but living in France's second-largest city, where we suffer with inequality and corruption, it is even more important to have a voice.

Our role is to to push the team to win, but filling the stadium with chanting and smoke helps us also to live in the moment. It is a time when we are united as a city and can truly express who we are, win or lose.

The terraces were once filled with fascists but it was our duty to remove them and create a safe environment for everyone, no matter their creed or colour, to come and wear our colours of white and blue.

 EATING IN NOAILLES: BEST AFRICAN RESTAURANTS

Chez Yassine: No-nonsense Tunisian restaurant with long lunch queues – for good reason. *11.30am-9pm Tue-Sun* €€

La Jungle: Serves massive plates of Cameroonian food. It's as much a party as it is a restaurant on weekends. *noon-midnight* €€

Mama Ghana: West African food prepared with love. Also a great spot to watch televised sports events. *noon-11pm Wed-Sun, noon-9pm Mon & Tue* €€

Restaurant Le Fémina: Eat couscous prepared by an all-female kitchen staff. An Anthony Bourdain favourite. *noon-2.30pm & 7-11pm Tue-Sat, noon-2.30pm Sun* €€

WHY I LOVE MARSEILLE'S BEACHES

Michael Frankel, writer

No one I know lives by the sea in Marseille; such people exist, of course, I just don't know them.

The coast is where we head when we need to cool off from the summer heat or escape the police sirens and industrial noise of the city.

I go to all the beaches I have suggested here (p165) and which one I choose is dependent on the mood I am in. Sometimes I might just walk along the corniche and find a private rock – a jagged little place of isolation where I can contemplate or just soak up the sun before plunging into the crystal waters.

In that moment, there is no flight, no fight, no negative ions. All static disappears.

have them. Prices begin at around €80 a head, with a full day for four people at €540. She will meet you at the Vieux Port at the end of Rue de la Prison.

Eco-Calanques *(eco-calanques.com)* is another small company run by local guides. Its eco-trawler is partly solar powered, and Thibault will entertain passengers with stories about the city's history as he takes you out to the most tranquil bays. While the Mediterranean is blessed with calm, warm waters in summer, the mistral wind may postpone excursions in winter. The day rate begins at €125 and includes lunch and the use of masks and snorkels to splash about in the *calanques*.

Based near the Mucem museum, **Les Barquettes** *(les barquettes.com)* also has a traditional 1970s fisherman's boat converted to a pleasure vessel, but its pride and joy is its sailing boat, a replica of a historical ship from 1903. It holds 20 people and the €110 ticket for a 3½-hour sunset tour is not only worth it for the blissful experience but includes an apéritif too. They will pick you up at an allotted time right alongside the MUCEM.

Dive into Les Goudes
Seafood at the end of the world

A common insult in Marseille is 'Go throw yourself in the Goudes', but Les Goudes is easily one of the area's highlights: a tiny fishing village locked in time, with access to spectacularly rugged coastlines. Its proximity to the **Parc National des Calanques** (p173) means the village is afforded the same legal protection; thus, there has been little development here. For now, the bygone era remains.

There has been a shift since **Tuba Club** arrived, a hotel so exclusive it's almost impossible to book one of its only eight rooms. It is possible to make reservations to have a drink on the rocks after 5pm. In the heart of the village is **L'Esplaï du Grand Bar des Goudes**, a rowdy seafood restaurant and bar. As you rub shoulders with those who grew up in these narrow streets, eating fish that has practically leapt out of the sea and onto your plate, you'll be face to face with all the local pride you can take.

The walk to the **Baie des Singes**, an old smuggling cove, is a surreal sun-beaten experience – don't miss it. The restaurant has sunloungers at €25 for the day. It's beyond picturesque.

Bus 19 and then 20 will get you close to Les Goudes year-round. From the end of April to September, boats leave from the Vieux Port – you will need to switch ferries in Pointe-Rouge.

DRINKING IN MARSEILLE: BARS FOR BEFORE THE MATCH

Brasserie du Stade: A quick jog from the Vélodrome stadium and an institution among fans. *noon-8pm*

The Queen Victoria: A veritable English pub in the Vieux Port that's an obvious choice before heading to the match. *11.30am-2.30pm & 6pm-midnight*

Le Bar de la Plaine: If you don't have tickets but still want to watch along with fervent fans on a large screen, this is the place. *8am-1am*

Emile Brasserie: Only 10 minutes' walk from the stadium, this is an elegant enough brasserie that would not look out of place in (dare I say it) Paris. *6am-10.30pm Mon-Sat*

Bottles of Pastis

Discover the History of Pastis
The art of the apéritif

Pastis is the apéritif of choice in many parts of southern France, and it's easy to spot: a milky-looking concoction served in a tall glass that adorns outdoor tables across Provence.

In 1932 in Marseille, Paul Ricard developed his aniseed-and-liquorice-based liqueur (*pastís* means 'mix' in Occitan) after absinthe was banned in France out of fear that it caused hallucinations and madness.

Since then, it has become a drink that is synonymous with the city. Ricard may now be part of a multinational conglomerate based in Lille, but there are still independent producers in Marseille where you can arrange a visit.

The distillery **Cristal Limiñana** *(cristal-liminana.com)* offers tours and tastings for €3. After hearing an in-depth history of anise and the family business, which dates back to 1884, take a walk through the factory to see the automated whir of bottles being filled, capped and packed at surprisingly close range.

The independent brewery **Bière de la Plaine** *(Distillerie de la Plaine; instagram.com/distillerie_de_la_plaine)*, only in operation since 2019, also has a pastis operation. Make contact via Instagram for a tasting session. It's €40 but you

RESPECTING NATURE ON THE WATERS

During the pandemic, the world saw wildlife return to places from where it had receded. The brutal impact of our civilisation on the natural world became evident as Marseille's lockdown encouraged biodiversity to thrive. This included sights of dolphin activity and of the rare fin whale – the world's second-largest mammal.

Now that the city is back on its feet and pleasure craft and maritime transport are at full throttle again, it is advised to act responsibly if you're fortunate enough to encounter such graceful creatures.

Keep a distance of at least 100m from the animals and even further if calves are present. Never feed the animals and, of course, avoid swimming with them.

DRINKING & EATING AROUND MARSEILLE: COASTAL BARS

Le Cabanon de Paulette: Sunbathers retire to flirt and dance on this terrace overhanging the Med. *10.30am-11.30pm in summer*

Sunset Bar: A simple bar on the corniche, perfect for a drink after a swim at sunset. Get a pastis and a tan. *6.30-8.30pm Mon-Sat*

Restaurant La Baie des Singes: There's better food to be found in Les Goudes, but these views can't be beaten. Get a drink on a lounger. *noon-9pm in summer* €€

Nautic Bar: Staring into the Calanque de Morgiou with a glass in hand, you will not want to go back to the city in a hurry. *noon-10pm Tue-Sun* €€

A MAN OF THE PEOPLE

Eric Signoret is one of the most recognisable faces of Les Goudes and has been the owner of the only convenience store for kilometres around for nearly 40 years:

I prefer to say 'no comment' when I am asked about how life is changing in Les Goudes. We feel that we are being pushed to the side of our own lives, not by tourism – tourists have always been welcome here – but by politicians. They tow our cars and make changes they do not fully understand. Visit Les Goudes from town, but do so on foot, by bike, boat or bus and avoid using an app to rent a house here. We welcome you to visit us.

get to take a bottle home. Those who shy away from aniseed can always mix the liqueur with sweet syrup. *Un perroquet* is mint-flavoured, *une tomate* is mixed with grenadine and *une mauresque* tastes of almonds. *Santé!*

Escape to the Château d'If
Island life

For a quick and easy trip out to sea, hop on the Frioul-If ferry to Marseille's closest islands: the Île d'If (for historians) and the Îles du Frioul (for nature lovers).

Commanding access to Marseille's Vieux Port, the **Chateau d'If** *(chateau-if.fr; adult/child €7/free)* was immortalised by Alexandre Dumas in his classic 1844 novel, *The Count of Monte Cristo*. At the 16th-century island prison with three towers, one giving a great view across the bay, you can wander unaccompanied or visit with an audio or guided tour; the contrast between the cells for the wealthy and the dungeon pit strikes

🍸 DRINKING IN MARSEILLE: BEST PASTIS BARS

Bar des Maraîchers: Listen to '80s radio hits with owner, Serge, who features in his own hilarious fresco of the last supper. *3pm-2am*

Grand Bar du Chapitre: A young crowd in a leafy square at the top of the main thoroughfare, La Canebière. *10am-12.30am*

PMU le blabla: Super cheap and one of the best sun traps protected from the wind in the city. *6.30am-9pm*

La Relève: In the Endoume neighbourhood. Pastis can still be fancy and here it's served with great food and music. *8am-10pm Mon-Sat 9am-5pm Sun*

Chateau d'If

a tone. This is the ferry's first stop; it's 20 minutes from the Vieux Port. It's another 15 minutes to the next stop, the Port du Frioul, your entry point to two of the **Îles du Frioul**, Pomègues and Ratonneau, which are connected by a dam.

Attacking the unspoiled jagged rock of **Pomègues** is liberating. Following the seawall after you dock will lead to the Fort de Caveaux, leaving you lost at sea on an uninhabited island, revisiting ghosts in the bunkers of WWII. Finding a spot to feel utterly alone with the swooping seabirds is easiest in spring.

The island of **Ratonneau** has a few small shops and restaurants and is popular for its beaches and tiny village. There's a chapel that resembles a Greek temple and the ruins of the Hôpital Caroline, which once housed quarantined travellers, but the highlight is the St-Estève beach, where you can swim safely, protected from the wind.

The ticket office and pier for **lebateau** ferries *(lebateau-frioul-if.fr; one/two islands return €11.10/16.70)* is at the Vieux Port.

MEAN CUISINE

Max Tuckwell, co-owner and chef at **Ivresse** (p172) wine bar *(instagram.com/ivresse.lacave)*

There is nothing better than to use pastis to finish a deep, rich caramelised sauce made from frying mullet or snapper with prawn shells, onions, fennel and garlic over a medium to high heat in a thick pan. Pastis contains over 50 local herbs and spices that are essential to this region's cuisine, including coriander, savory, sage and star anise. Use the pastis to deglaze the sauce once it starts to stick to the bottom of the pan. After reducing the bisque, strain it through a fine sieve, to separate it from the shell and bones. Serve that sauce over steamed Châteaurenard cabbage leaves, and add prawns. It's delicious!

EATING IN LES GOUDES: OUR PICKS

Chez Paul: Serves seafood in the heart of the village and popular with locals. *noon-2pm Wed-Sun, 7.45-10pm Mon-Fri, 8pm-10pm Sat-Sun* €€

La Grotte: Incredibly refined settings in the Port de Callelongue just outside the village. *noon-2.30 pm & 7.30-11pm Mon-Thu & Sat, noon-3pm & 7.30-10.30pm Sun* €€

Gelateria des Goudes: An Italian family business serious about their 1950s-style ice cream. A brioche ice cream sandwich is the one. *11am-8pm* €

Au Bord de l'Eau: In the small port of Madrague Montredon, the perfect spot to watch the fishermen deliver your lunch. *hours vary* €€€

LE PANIER ON FOOT

Discover the oldest and some of the most charming parts of the city founded by the Phoenicians in 600 BCE.

START	END	LENGTH
Hôtel Belle-Vue	place de Lenche	2.5km, 1hr

The Vieux Port, all boats and bars, is Marseille's central point where you begin beneath the historic ① **Hôtel Belle-Vue** (p203).

Walking away from town, turn right at ② **passage Pentecontore**, taking the steps up through the arch. This is a great spot to sample ice cream from ③ **Vanille Noire**, renowned for its charcoal-coloured vanilla flavour.

Not far from here is the steep, narrow corridor of steps of ④ **rue Beauregard** and rue des Moulins, now emblazoned with street art. These lead to ⑤ **place des Moulins**, once home to windmills in the 17th century. Today, it offers serenity no matter the time of year.

Descending the ⑥ **rue des Muettes** and ⑦ **rue du Refuge** takes you into the heart of Le Panier. 'The Basket' is Marseille's oldest quarter, the site of the original Greek settlement and nicknamed for its steep streets and buildings.

Make your way along ⑧ **rue des Pistoles** and ⑨ **rue du Petit Puits** via rue Antoine Becker, to come to the ⑩ **Cathédrale de la Major**.

If you time this walk for sunset the square will deliver a blazing view. Below on ⑪ **bd Jacques Saade** is a line of tapas bars, another perfect sunset stop before you settle for an evening in the buzzy ⑫ **place de Lenche**.

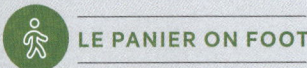

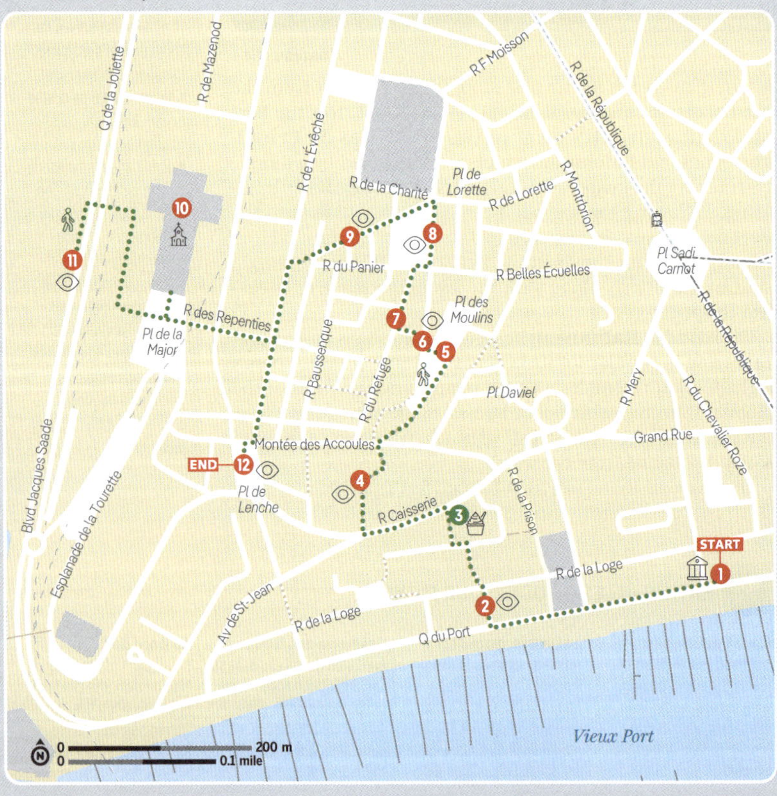

When facing the port, get in line at their large booth on the left. The Château d'If is closed on Mondays.

Another way to get here is with the **Le Bateau Jaune** *(lebateaujaune.com; adult/child from €40/35)* in the Vieux Port, which organises snorkelling and diving trips around the islands.

Capture a City of Views
Happy snapping

Luckily, Marseille is not only blessed with the kind of light that has made painters and writers flock to its shores for centuries, but it also has views that would inspire any photographer. Here are the best spots to capture that iconic moment for would-be Henri Cartier-Bressons armed with a 35mm film camera or smartphone.

Marseille has a sense of gravitas from the top of the grand steps of the **Gare St-Charles** train station. Its statues, palm trees and historic street lamps dating back to 1848 are the perfect foreground for the sweeping views across the city, inspiring a confidence that adventures have only just begun. The **Basilique Notre-Dame de la Garde** stands imperiously in the distance.

It is essential to trek for the views – note the football pitch beneath the apartment blocks below – and to explore the village-like neighbourhoods of Endoume and Vauban, which evoke a Marseille from another era. When walking from the Vieux Port towards the coast, cross a bridge on the left-hand side that looks down on the **Vallon des Auffes**. This colourful village of fishermen's houses, bars and typical Provençal boats is where the corniche starts and makes another perfect snap.

The **Jardin du Pharo** is not just 5 hectares of rare green space. The views of the old port from here give a perspective the Phoenicians would have had when they first arrived. Snap the boats returning to the city at sunset. There is a clear view from here of the Mucem museum, which has exhibited countless contemporary photographers and has its own spectacular views from Esplanade J4.

Back in town, at the top of the graffitied stairs of **cours Julien** (p160), click away to capture the gritty urban views Marseille revels in.

LIGHTS, CAMERA, ACTION!

Eric Pelloni is the owner of original movie poster store Cinésud on cours Julien *(cinesud-affiches.com)*:

When you think of Marseille in cinema, you naturally come to *The French Connection* and its sequel featuring Gene Hackman; they are classics. One particularly iconic scene takes place on the roof of the Chateau d'If. Many great movies have been filmed in Marseille. *Mémoire d'un Flic* and *Le Marginal* are also excellent gangster movies. But there is *37°2 Le Matin* – (also known as *Betty Blue*) and *Marius et Jeannette,* which are erotic, romantic, funny – they are particularly French. In recent years *The Bourne Identity* and *Stillwater*, both starring Matt Damon, have showcased the city. He must love coming here. That, and our magical light.

 EATING IN MARSEILLE: WHERE TO PACK A PICNIC

Razzia: A wildly popular lunchtime sandwich maker for the masses near cours Julien. *8.30am-4pm Tue-Fri, 9.30am-4pm Sat* €

Limon: Vegetarian favourite and an extravagant twist on North African and Mediterranean flavours. *11.45am-3pm Mon-Fri* €

La Kaz Kréol: House-baked Creole bread with big fillings. The white fish sandwich is incredible. *noon-9.30pm Tue & Thu, noon-10.30pm Wed, Fri, Sat* €

Amandine: Pastries that are as good as they look, for those obsessed with cream when passing through the Camas neighbourhood. *7am-7.30pm* €€

CLEANLINESS IS CLOSE TO GODLINESS

Following the cholera outbreaks of the early 1830s, which claimed thousands of lives in the city, a plan was devised to improve public health by channelling water from the Durance River in the Alps. By 1869, the Palais Longchamp was opened to the public as a 'hymn to water', celebrating this remarkable engineering feat.

Marseille's iconic soap (savon de Marseille) also played a significant role in reducing infant mortality and the spread of contagious diseases during the 19th century.

Originally made with olive oil and free of colouring and perfume, it now comes in various shapes and smells. The **Savonnerie Marseillaise de la Licorne** on cours Julien is an excellent place to purchase it, and offers free daily tours of its factory.

Palais Longchamp

The Longchamp Neighbourhood
Bohemian quarters

Parts of Marseille look much as they did decades ago. It is easy to imagine walking the same streets as Fernando Rey in *The French Connection* (the 1970s noir thriller). But rapid changes are afoot. The global pandemic accelerated many young people's desire to move closer to the Med for a slower pace of life and more sunshine, attracting newcomers to the city. Unsurprisingly, housing prices over the last few years have been soaring, particularly in the desirable district of Longchamp.

The centre point of Marseille's most chic neighbourhood is the sublime **Palais Longchamp**, an outrageous 19th-century palace with monumental fountains gushing in celebration of fertility and the arrival of water to the city. Its green and pleasant gardens host an international jazz festival every summer and are perfect for lazing around in. This magnificent building also houses the Musée des Beaux-Arts (home to 17th- and 18th-century art), the Muséum d'Histoire Naturelle and an observatory.

As you walk down the long bd Longchamp and its parallel backstreets, a proliferation of bars and restaurants takes centre stage. Despite the slogans and rallying cries of a highly organised left-wing community protesting gentrification in much of Marseille, there seems to be more refurbishment than ever in this neighbourhood that has always housed the upper classes.

 EATING & DRINKING IN LONGCHAMP: OUR PICKS

Ivresse: Easily the hottest candle-lit date spot in town. Small food plates, natural wine and perfect service. *6pm-11pm Mon-Sat*

Belleville/Mer: Simple, no-frills dishes with the local crowd on the patio. A friendly spot that is the place to be on Sundays. *8am-10.30pm Wed-Sun* €€

Pollux: Coffee lovers unite. Choose anything from a rare bean espresso to a Vietnamese iced coffee. Fancy brunch too. *8.30am-5pm Mon-Fri, 9.30am-3pm Sat & Sun* €€

Les Babines de Mars: A dedication to working with local products and fish from the port has helped Les Babines settle straight in. *11am-11pm Mon-Fri* €€

Beyond Marseille

To truly appreciate Marseille, cut loose from its intense energy and explore the nature that surrounds it.

Places
Les Calanques p173
La Côte Bleue p176

The beauty of leaving Marseille is the overwhelming contrasts that come at you so quickly. The welcome shock at sudden bursts of birdsong or the light breaking through the pine trees in spring will have you breathing easier. Lavender fields, ancient villages and winding mountain climbs offering views to the valleys below are everything you dreamed Provence could deliver.

Head inland to the Provençal countryside, famous for its idyllic charm, or cut yourself off from the world on far-flung beaches on the savage and yet increasingly fashionable coastline that extends in both directions from the city. Either way, the possibilities of vast horizons of time and space are endless.

Les Calanques

TIME FROM MARSEILLE: 1½hr

Outdoor adventures in the Parc National des Calanques

It feels like a miracle to find a refuge like the **Parc National des Calanques** only a short distance from Marseille. In parts of this diminutive 85-sq-km patch of scrubby promontories, it's easy to believe you're miles from civilisation. Then a twist in a pine-clad gully reveals the entirety of France's second metropolis spread out within apparent touching distance; the *calanques* (bays) appear almost as its uninhabited suburbs.

But with their light-shifting geometry, rich plant and animal life and idyllic hidden coves, Les Calanques are so much more than that. They are beloved of the Marseillais, who come for the sun and to hike over pine-strewn promontories, mess about in boats and generally refresh their souls.

Of the many *calanques* along the coastline, the most easily accessible are **Calanque de Sormiou** and **Calanque de Morgiou**. Remote inlets such as **Calanque d'En-Vau** and **Calanque de Port-Miou** take dedication and time to reach,

GETTING AROUND

Without a boat, you'll have to drive, cycle or take public transport to visit Cassis and the nearby *calanques*. Be warned that roads are rough, parking scarce and the going slow. In peak summer season, the municipality recommends arriving by bus. In the other direction, the train along the Côte Bleue is cheap and allows you to drink wine with your lunch.

BEST KAYAK & PADDLEBOARD RENTALS

Destination Calanques Kayak: Get out there from the heart of Les Calanques. Choose the long picnic tour, but book in advance as they are hugely popular. April to October.

Calanc'O: Stand-up paddleboarding takes core strength, beginners! But don't worry, the friendly guides make sure these trips are as informative as they are fun. April to October.

Expénature La Ciotat: Kayak with fun guides to the nearby *calanques* and the Île Verte, in La Ciotat, east of Cassis. Expert guides in spelunking (the exploration of caves). All year.

Raskas Kayak: Over 20 years of guiding kayaking trips to the *calanques*; located in eastern Marseille. The full-day option will leave you happily exhausted. All year.

either on foot or by kayak. Note that overland access is often limited from June to September due to fire danger; always check first.

There's no shortage of outdoor activities here: hiking, kayaking, stand-up paddleboarding, swimming, diving and rock climbing are all incredible. You'll find guides and gear rental in both Marseille and Cassis. From October to June, hiking trails lead through the maquis (scrub). Marseille's tourist office leads guided walks and has an excellent hiking map of the various *calanques*, as does Cassis' tourist office.

For access by public transport take bus 19 from Marseille's Castellane bus station down the coast to its terminus at La Madrague, then switch to bus 20 to Callelongue. Note that the road to Callelongue is only open to cars on weekdays from mid-April to May and closed entirely from June to September.

For the most up-to-date info on the park, activities and, most importantly, access, download the Mes Calanques app.

EATING IN CASSIS: BEST POST-BEACH RESTAURANTS

Le Poisson Rouge: Modern creative cuisine that has its focus on local wine-makers and a good time. *7.30pm-11pm Tue-Sat* €€

La Maison de Jo et Gaby: Friendly wine cellar. The charcuterie plates reflect just what the Med has to offer. *10am-1pm & 5-11.45pm Tues-Sun* €€

La Presqu'île: Come here for crisp white tablecloths and a Michelin star paired with great bay views. Reserve. *9.30am-11pm Tue-Sun* €€€

Chez Poulette: Fried seafood or subtle Asian fusion served by the owner. Nice to eat with the locals. *noon-2.30pm Wed, Thu, Sat, Sun, 7-10pm Thu-Sat* €€

Calanque d'En-Vau

Clambering down to paradise

The small port of **Cassis** has lost some of its charm over the years, but the coastline beyond is another story. The village is the perfect staging point for excursions to the **Calanque d'En-Vau**, which lives up to any hyperbole you wish to throw at it. From Cassis, make your way to the **Calanque de Port-Miou** on foot (30 minutes) or, alternatively, park in the Presqu'île car park. This is the start of a difficult, unshaded hike, but it's worth every stretch of sinew. Expect it to take a solid 1½ hours from here.

The first stop is the **Calanque de Port-Pin** for a quick dip. It takes at least 20 minutes to get here as you keep the water to your left and the boats below. From Port-Pin, there are two paths to the Calanque d'En-Vau. Take the blue-coded coastal path, which is longer (around one hour) but more rewarding. Arriving at the cliffs, you'll be glad you made the effort.

Clambering down to the beach is tricky for newbies; you can easily tell who's local, as they look like mountain goats when

WHAT IS A CALANQUE?

Calanques are coastal geological features typical of the Mediterranean region. These picturesque coves, formed in limestone and famously located between Marseille and Cassis, are characterised by steep cliffs rising above vibrant turquoise waters.

When the sun shines, the small beaches within these narrow bays, made up of either pebbles or fine sand, attract crowds.

Escaping to them has become a way of life for city dwellers, leading to various regulations protecting the natural sites. Access to the *calanques* by car can be challenging, and most routes are closed between June and October as the arid conditions during this period place the parks at a high chance of wildfires. The strong mistral winds that can sweep through the area further intensify the risks.

THE GUIDE

BEYOND MARSEILLE BOUCHES-DU-RHÔNE

 EATING IN NIOLON & L'ESTAQUE: OUR PICKS

L'Hippocampe l'Estaque: Extremely quaint, with a reputation that is almost folkloric. Go for a whole fish. *noon–2pm Tue-Sun, 7.45-10pm Fri & Sat* €€

La Pergola: Perched above the port of Niolon and the kind of peaceful lunch in the shade that the region promises. Book ahead. *9am-11pm Mon-Sat, 9am-6pm Sun* €€

Auberge du Mérou: Small guesthouse in Niolon that has a restaurant proud of its bouillabaisse and panoramic views. *11.30am-3pm & 7.30-11pm* €€€

Chez Magali: This kiosk in l'Estaque has been serving sugar-coated *chichis* and authentic panisse for over 80 years. Burn your lips and tongue and be happy. *10am-8pm* €

Côte Bleue

CALANQUE DE L'ÉVERINE

On leaving the train station at Niolon on the Côte Bleue line, turn left and continue walking. After 200m, take the path left into the valley; the path on the right leads up to the Fort de Niolon. This will take you under the last arch of the viaduct above the Calanque du Jonquier. You are now on the **Sentier des Douaniers**, a pleasant but occasionally steep coastal trek that passes beneath a shaded canopy.

From the station, it's around an hour's walk to the gorgeous **Calanque de l'Éverine**. The reward is a cove with crystal clear waters and only the gentle lapping of the Med and birdsong to keep you company.

scampering down the cliffs. If you arrive with good footwear and take your time the descent is fine, though if you suffer from vertigo, this is not for you. Ideally, plan on arriving by late morning and bring enough water and food for the day.

Cassis is 30km east of Marseille and is best reached by car in low season. At other times of year, taking the train (30 minutes) is advised as you may not be able to find a parking spot. From the Cassis train station, take the M1 bus to the centre of town (15 minutes).

La Côte Bleue

TIME FROM MARSEILLE: **15-30min**

Ride the rails along La Côte Bleue

Heading west from Gare St-Charles, Marseille's train station, is the spectacular **Côte Bleue** (Blue Coast) railway. A 15-minute journey (€3) takes passengers to **L'Estaque**; the views from the train window are the same as the ones that once inspired the impressionists. From L'Estaque's train station it's only a 10-minute walk to the port, where you can sample the regional delicacies of panisse (chickpea fritters) and *chichi*

EATING AROUND CARRY-LE-ROUET: OUR PICKS

Rest'o Cap Rousset: The sound of sun-worshippers flinging themselves into the *calanque* below as the ice cubes clink in your glass. *8am-9.30pm* €€

La Cale: Stop for great pizza if you are gently trekking between Carry and Sausset-les-Pins. Stunning views out to the Calanque de la Tuilière. *10am-10.30pm* €€

MyPitchu: Relaxed beach bar on the sand in Sausset-les-Pins serving fish fresh from the sea. *9am-11.45pm Mon-Sat, 9am-5pm Sun* €€

La Villa Arena: For a gastronomic experience rather than fish and chips, this 17th-century mansion restaurant will serve food for your eyes. *noon-9.30pm Tue-Sat* €€€

(similar to Spanish churros), both staple ingredients of the Mediterranean. Eat them in paper cones at the *barraques à chichis* (historic food stands).

The **Alhambra cinema** *(alhambracine.com; €7)* is a short cab ride away. Since 1928, it has been standing in a leafy square that's also home to **Denis Bar** *(8.30am-9.30pm Mon-Sat, 11am-1.30pm Sun)*. The bar feels like fishermen and artists have patronised it for a century and is perfect for a drink before a VO film (*version originale* films are screened in their original language).

The real gem, however, is further up the coast. Another 15 minutes on the train past L'Estaque brings you to **Niolon**, where you'll feel as if you've been transported to a Provençal village. Follow the crowd to make your way along the rocky path to the **Calanque du Jonquier** and swim in the shadow of the spectacular arched viaduct as you gaze across the calm waters back towards the city. Pretty unbeatable.

Coastal walks of Carry-le-Rouet

Only 30km west of Marseille, **Carry-le-Rouet** is another pearl on the Côte Bleue rail line, with its charming port, fragrant pine trees and perfectly rough-hewn inlets. The train from Gare St-Charles is around €6, and the 35-minute sea-view trip passes in the blink of an eye.

However, renting a car allows more freedom to stop in places along the way. You can drive along roads where limestone rises all around you, and long-horned goats nibble on scrub, but parking will never be easy. The first three Sundays of February are the subject of a grand celebration when seafood fanatics descend into the port for the **Oursinades**, a tasting festival offering an abundance of sea urchins considered the best in the Med. If you're not crazy about urchins, everything else pulled from the ocean, including shellfish platters, is also available.

At any time of the year, the jaggy promenade from the port to Sausset-les-Pins is the perfect coastal stroll, with no shortage of places to stop and take it all in. The beaches are more pebbly than sandy, but the waters are transparent. Every summer during July and August, the **Parc Marin Côte Bleue** *(parcmarincotebleue.fr)* organises free guided tours on the Plage du Cap Rousset, including a wetsuit, snorkel and mask. To book, see *en.otcarrylerouet.fr*.

PRICKLY DELIGHTS

Sea urchins, those spiny invertebrates that always seem to position themselves exactly where you want to put a foot down in secluded coves, are a prized epicurean speciality in this part of the world. Don't believe us? Wait until you see how locals slurp them up with gusto along the coast.

The outer, alien-looking body of black spines is first cut with scissors, revealing the tender, pumpkin-coloured flesh. This part is usually eaten with bread or a squirt of lemon on a teaspoon, but you can also mix it with scrambled eggs or serve it with a pancake. If you enjoy oysters and mussels, you'll find the experience is not all that different.

Aix-en-Provence

HISTORIC ARCHITECTURE | FRESH MARKET PRODUCE | VINEYARD VISITS

GETTING AROUND

Ask any local and they will tell you that Aix is tiny and you should walk everywhere. The local bus service *(aixenbus.fr)* to the edge of town is a good alternative; tickets are easily purchased on board. Hire bikes *(aixpritvelo.com)* in the centre of town.

The sun magically lights up centuries-old mansions while fountains gurgle in small squares, hidden at the end of narrow streets. Locals stroll by dressed in understated elegance and stare at you from stylish cafe terraces, coolly sipping espresso. Aix (pronounced like the letter X) is a caricature of French life – that there are no surprises is part of its charm.

It is a city to drift through and observe: precisely what Baudelaire was getting at when he coined the term *flâneur*. But to wander the urban landscape and do nothing is not nothing at all. It is to become part of your surroundings as you take your time. As a university city, Aix is elegant and welcoming, and the streets are arteries for a flood of international students.

Whether you've come to shop, indulge in gourmet meals or use it as a base to venture out into the countryside, Aix will gently guide you on your way.

Celebrate Cézanne

Aix's most famous son

Cézanne's post-impressionism significantly influenced contemporary art of the 19th and 20th centuries. Born in the city and having studied in the Musée d'Aix, now known as the **Musée Granet** *(museegranet-aixenprovence.fr; adult/child €6.50/free)*, he struggled for recognition for most of his career. Today, his paintings, capturing its landscapes and its people, have become synonymous with the city itself.

Aix celebrated its famous artist and his legacy in 2025 with a busy calendar of events, especially around the reopening of the renovated **Bastide du Jas de Bouffan** *(cezanne2025.com/sites-de-cezanne/bastide-du-jas-de-bouffan; adult/child €9.50/free)*, his family home, and his final studio, the **Atelier des Lauves** *(cezanne2025.com/sites-de-cezanne/atelier-des-lauves; adult/child €9.50/free)*, also renovated.

☑ **TOP TIP**

Being chic is part of cafe culture and an expensive pair of sunglasses are essential to the Aix wardrobe. People do not sit across from each other on the terraces but face outward instead, covertly watching who is coming down the street.

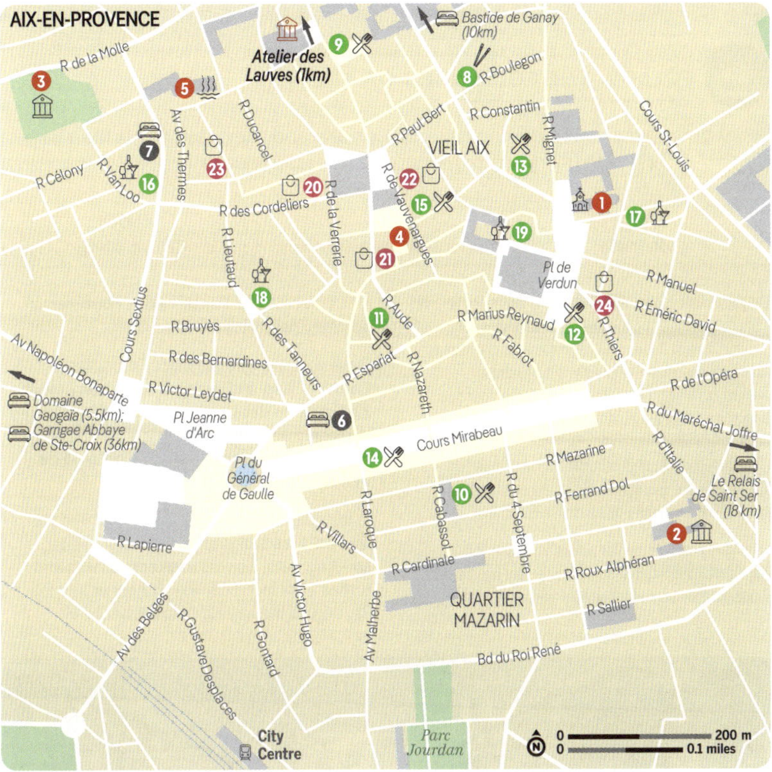

AIX-EN-PROVENCE

- **SIGHTS**
  1. Église de la Madeleine
  2. Musée Granet
  3. Pavillon Vendôme
  4. Place Richelme
- **ACTIVITIES**
  5. Les Thermes Sextius
- **SLEEPING**
  6. Hôtel des Augustins
  7. Hôtel Escaletto
- **EATING**
  8. Atelier du Mochi
  9. Brasserie de L'Archevêché
  10. Café Caumont
  11. Drôle d'Endroit
  12. Le Coude à Coude
  13. Les Macarons de Caroline
  14. Maison Béchard
  15. Maison Weibel
- **DRINKING & NIGHTLIFE**
  16. Back to Bac
  17. La Méduse
  18. Le Bouddoir
  19. Le Forum
- **SHOPPING**
  20. La Cave du Félibrige
  21. Onatera
  22. Panier des Sens
  23. Parfums de la Bastide
  24. Rose et Marius

To be in his studio is like snooping into someone's life. As luminous sunlight pours through the windows, painting tools and still-life models are positioned as if the artist has just left, and his hat is still hanging on a hook. He produced iconic paintings of Montagne Ste-Victoire from this studio until his

Continues on p182

EATING IN AIX: BEST PÂTISSERIES

Maison Weibel: Draws visitors but also an essential address for Aix's residents. *7.30am-7pm* €€

Maison Béchard: Best for *calissons* (regional treats made from almonds) and candied fruit. *8am-7pm Mon-Fri, 8am-8pm Sat* €€

Atelier du Mochi: vegan gooey, gummy Japanese rice cakes. A sensation. *10.30am-7.30pm Mon-Sat* €€

Les Macarons de Caroline: Freshly made macarons daily, even savoury ones. *9.30-7pm Tue-Sat* €€

FOLLOW THE FOUNTAINS OF AIX

What better way to explore the historical streets and alleyways of Aix than by using 17 of its most striking water monuments as reference points?

START	END	LENGTH
La Rotonde	place des Quatre-Dauphins	2.5km, 40min

Begin at the iconic ❶ **Fontaine de la Rotonde**. This magnificent fountain is adorned with sculptures of lions, swans, mythical creatures, and three women, representing justice, agriculture and the arts. Take the narrow rue Espariat to ❷ **Fontaine des Augustins**, splish-splashing above the din. Take a left onto rue de la Couronne, then right on rue Benardines to ❸ **Fontaine Séraphin Gilly**, a harmonious corner behind the Église du St-Esprit.

Forging up rue de Tanneurs you'll reach ❹ **Fontaine Altius**, surrounded by bar terraces. Continue on to rue Lieutaud and right onto place de Cardeurs to ❺ **Fontaine des Fontêtes**: all spouting gargoyles and cherubs.

Make your way through place Forum des Cardeurs' bars and restaurants to Jean Amado's ❻ **Fontaine des Cardeurs** from 1977. Veer right into place de l'Hotel de Ville, a vibrant flower market half the week, to the ❼ **Fontaine de l'Eau Bénite**.

In the adjacent place Richelme you'll find the ❽ **Fontaine Sanglier**: a bronzed wild boar spurting water from its nose onto snakes and turtles at its feet. Follow rue Chabrier and rue Jaubert all the way along to the peaceful

Fontaine d'Albertas

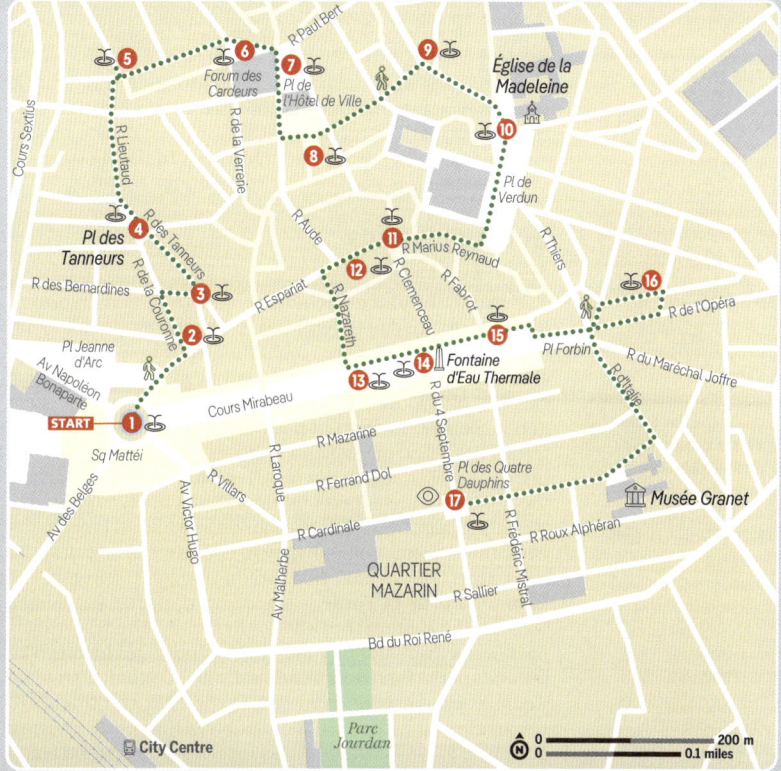

Fontaine des Trois Ormeaux. Then turn right onto rue de Montigny and head to place des Prêcheurs.

Here we find the most impressive **Fontaine des Prêcheurs**, an obelisk with a white eagle perched atop, next to the Église de la Madeleine.

Continuing past the Palais de Justice, take a right on rue Marius Reynaud to the so-subtle-it's-barely-there **Fontaine Marcelle Drutel** on the place St-Honoré.

It's a small hop down rue Espariat to **Fontaine d'Albertas**, an audacious monument to great wealth.

Now head towards the cours Mirabeau via rue Nazereth to **Fontaine de Neuf-Cannons**, once a watering hole for livestock and now overgrown with greenery enjoying the warm water that's sourced from a natural spring.

Turn left and you'll quickly reach the famous **Fontaine Moussue**, a rock covered in a thick green moss, making it something between an inanimate object and a living thing.

Close by, the **Fontaine du Roi René** depicts a 15th-century king holding grapes, which must be a sign that you are due a glass of wine by now.

Onwards to my favourite, **Fontaine de la Mule Noire**. It has two little heads delicately spitting into a trough. Check those eyes!

Make your way back down onto the cours Mirabeau and head via rue d'Italie past Musée Granet on rue Cardinale to the final fountain, **Fontaine des Quatre-Dauphins**: four spouting dolphins in the heart of the glorious Mazarin neighbourhood.

THE OPTICAL ILLUSIONS OF VICTOR VASARELY

While Cézanne inspired modern movements including cubism and was called by Picasso the 'father of us all', Aix is also home to the undisputed father of op art: Victor Vasarely.

Just 4km west of the city is the **Fondation Victor Vasarely** *(fondationvasarely.org; adult/child €15/9)*, a cavernous 1970s hyper-contemporary building of glass and metallic geometric blocks.

An architectural masterpiece, it has 16 interconnecting, hexagonal galleries purpose-built to display and reflect the patterning of this Hungarian-French artist's 44 acid-trip-ready, floor-to-ceiling geometric artworks.

It is a world of anamorphic patterns within seven galleries, each containing six works of art.

Continued from p179

death – views you can enjoy for yourself from the peaceful gardens outside. From there, as the birds coo and the breeze shakes the leaves in the trees, it is easy to understand that it is not only nature that inspires but that tranquillity is essential to the creative process itself.

For more, check out the self-guided app In the Footsteps of Cézanne *(cezanne-en-provence.com/en/app-cezanne)*.

Gourmet Picnics

Bread, wine and a blanket

The market in **place Richelme**, open from early morning until lunch Monday to Saturday, is the town's premier spot for quality local produce: you'll find fresh bread, speciality *saucissons* (sausages), the usual cavalcade of hard and soft cheeses, plus vibrantly coloured fruit and vegetables, jams and tapenades. In short, it has everything you would expect from a Provençal market and is the perfect spot to find picnic inspiration. For regional wines, try **La Cave du Félibrige**: the folks here are experts in natural and biodynamic wine. It's only a short walk from the market and like all French cavistes, they are more than happy to educate you on the stuff.

For green spaces that turn bright orange in autumn, the **Promenade de la Torse** is a wide-open space a half-hour's walk to the southeast of cours Mirabeau. Wooden bridges pass over a lively stream inhabited by ducks and herons. The grounds of the **Pavillon Vendôme**, only 10 minutes from La Rotonde, are everything you would expect Aix-en-Provence to be: manicured gardens in the shadow of historical opulence built by a love-sick Duke. It's as regal a setting as you could wish for for what is now an art museum. **Parc Jourdan** is a city park the locals are likelier to use to play boules and where many workers and university students eat sandwiches at lunchtime. What it lacks in beauty is made up for with local authenticity.

Thermal Waters

Luxuriate like a Roman

There comes a time on any road trip when you have to scrub yourself free of the tension of travelling, whether you've just arrived and want to wash your problems down the plughole or pause your journey for an afternoon of indulgence.

DRINKING IN AIX: BEST BARS

Le Bouddoir: Lively terrace on place des Tanneurs hosting an international crowd that merges effortlessly with those eating tapas next door. *8am-1am Mon-Sat*

Le Forum: Old-school brasserie with leather banquettes. Friendly, local feel and decent cocktails too. *8am-midnight Mon-Sat*

Back to Bac: Karaoke bar with good cocktails. Come with friends and howl at the moon. *5pm-2am Mon-Fri, 3pm-2am Sat & Sun*

La Méduse: Candle-lit intimacy with tiny food plates in Aix is not expected to come cheap but here it's worth it. A wine bar in wine country. *5pm-midnight Mon-Sat*

Market, place Richelme

Aix-en-Provence, originally known as Aquae Sextiae in Roman times, is a great place to immerse yourself in the healing powers of water, reconnecting your body and mind. It's easy to appreciate the significance of the modern spa **Les Thermes Sextius** *(thermes-sextius.com; from €58),* built atop the Roman baths of **Aquae Sextiae**, which can be seen beneath glass floors on arrival. Romans settled wherever they found natural springs, and their public baths were a fundamental part of everyday life. Much like the modern gym, this was not only a place to exercise and relax but also to socialise with people of all classes, strike deals and gossip.

The indulgence of steam and massage is a timeless combination. As you lie beneath the vestiges of the Roman empire, within its ancient walls surrounding the pool, you can absorb the sun in peace or choose from one of many hands-on treatments that will loosen those knots.

If a day in a spa in Aix isn't enough, quiet town **Gréoux-les-Bains** has countless options and could be the place to slip off to. It's only an hour's drive northeast towards the famous lavender fields of Lavensole.

THE JUICE FROM THE FRUIT

Isabelle Moulin is a stallholder at the place Richelme market:

I live 5km from Aix. Everyone who has a stand in the market is local and holds a licence. Tourists will always visit us but this market is vitally important to the people of Aix.

Market day on Tuesday, Thursday and Saturday means everything sold here is grown within 20km of the city. We pride ourselves on being organic. My apple juice, for example, has no sugar and no pesticides and is made from only the ugly fruit.

Here you not only have the best products that are always in season, you have a taste of our culture too.

EATING IN AIX: OUR PICKS

Café Caumont: For refined tea and cakes overlooking the gardens of the Caumont Centre d'Art. *10am-6pm Oct-Apr, 10am-7pm May-Sep* €€

Le Coude à Coude: Fancy little plates for young lovers in a candle-lit cave that goes way beyond intimate. *noon-midnight Tue-Sat* €€

Brasserie de L'Archevêché: Near Aix's IEP university, the lunchtime terrace buzzes with students under the shade of plane trees. *8am-11pm Mon-Sat* €€€

Drôle d'Endroit: Those who know head for a narrow alleyway in the heart of Aix for a great twist on regional and vegan produce. *hours vary* €€

Beyond Aix-en-Provence

The gastronomical treasures found in Aix hint at what lies beyond.

Places
Le Tholonet p184
Salon-de-Provence p185

GETTING AROUND

Although exploring by car is the most practical, there is a real road cycling culture in these parts. Cycling all the way to Montagne Ste-Victoire is not for beginners, but with an e-bike you can definitely go a long ways. Rent one in Aix at Aixprit Vélo. If exploring by car, look for a farmhouse rental rather than a standard hotel for the full-on rustic experience.

As a city that flaunts its abundance of water in its many fountains and stupefies with the excesses of nobility, Aix's connection to the countryside remains clear. Aromas in town suggest the wide-open spaces of lavender fields and the profusion of thyme. This is a land of wine, olive oil and bread, which are so much more than staples. In Provence, these things are given by the earth but brought to us with a sense of history, refinement and skill. The journey through the countryside and to the smaller villages allows travellers to experience for themselves what a privilege it is to live simply with the land, from Montagne Ste-Victoire to the Palette appellation vineyards to the olive trees of Salon-de-Provence.

Le Tholonet

TIME FROM AIX: **15min**

Hiking through Cézanne's landscapes

Provence is a hiker's dream. Climbing to the summit of **Montagne Ste-Victoire** seems like the obvious trek as it rises in the distance, but it can be excruciating – especially in the heat. A great alternative, especially for lovers of art and nature, is a ramble in Cézanne country. A 3½-hour hike from Le Tholonet with an expert guide can be booked at Aix's tourist office or online *(aixenprovencetourism.com; adult/child €29/19)*.

Le Tholonet provides the perfect starting point with its waterfalls, windmills, cafes and restaurants. Here, you are at the mountain's base, with the hike eventually taking you through the right angles of the Bibemus quarries and beneath the pine trees. This is the rock that Aix and its monuments

EATING IN SALON-DE-PROVENCE: OUR PICKS

Chadiyo: Hearty Provençal cuisine. The squid-ink risotto is a must, as is anything on the dessert menu. *noon-2.30pm Wed-Sun, 7pm-10.30pm Thu-Sat* €€

Bastide Chez Mus: Classic fancy brasserie in one of the nicest squares in Salon. Perfect for lunch on the terrace. *7.30am-midnight Mon-Fri, 8am-midnight Sat* €€

L'Atelier de la Cheffe: Delicate plates of artistic, inventive and extremely affordable food, if you choose the simple menu. *noon-1.15pm Thu-Sat, 7.30pm-9pm Tue-Sat* €€

La Fille De: Seriously fine wines and plates so well dressed that you feel guilty demolishing them. *noon-1.30pm & 7-9.30pm Tue-Sat* €€

were carved from, and the place where Cézanne had a stone house built so that he could immerse himself in his work. As you climb the terrain of dark earth and loose stones, the views take you into the shapes and colours of his paintings. The summer treks that set off at 6pm offer magical light.

Reaching the plateau offers the panoramic vistas that Cézanne made famous in his oil paintings and watercolours. You'll need plenty of water, especially in the arid summer months when forest access may be restricted to protect the region from fires. Check updates before you set out on *risque-prevention-incendie.fr/bouches-du-rhone*.

Salon-de-Provence

TIME FROM AIX: 1hr 🚆, 30min 🚗

A different sort of tasting

Olive oil is considered a sacred symbol of eternal life and has been used to signify health, beauty, wisdom and peace since ancient times. As recently as King Charles' coronation in London, oil from hand-picked olives in Jerusalem was used to anoint him.

The key to the Mediterranean diet is that olive oil pours as freely as wine. It is produced and consumed with the same passion, so much so that it remains in the bones of the inhabitants of this sun-drenched basin long after they have died. The French, Spanish, Italians and Greeks all receive honours in olive oil competitions, but when it comes to France, the oil of Provence – in particular Salon-de-Provence – is considered the best.

Salon is less than an hour's drive northwest of Aix, and the **Mas de Bories** *(masdesbories.com; tour €10)* olive grove, with its historical dry stone structures, is the ideal stop for anyone interested in the small-scale production of olive oil. It is easy to arrange a tour Monday to Saturday. When the owner, Claire, talks of her connection to the land, living a life with meaning and her constant search for quality, you feel it. The process from tree to bottle, taking in the super-modern extraction press, is a true education; once you taste it, you'll likely take some home.

THE CULTURE OF PÉTANQUE

Stephane Bromberger, local wine expert:

I don't play *pétanque* every day but as someone born and raised in Aix it is a pleasure to indulge in a game now and then on a late summer's afternoon. The only place I play is on the clay grounds next door to Le Relais Cézanne in Thalonet.

This is the oldest *pétanque* club on the planet. I will meet with a few friends and grab a few drinks to the sound of the cicadas in the trees. This is our real regional game.

We also play a card game called Contrée and that, more or less, says everything about the pace of life we live.

 EATING AROUND MONTAGNE STE-VICTOIRE: OUR PICKS

Le Relais de Saint Ser (p203): Panoramic views at sunset from this great hotel restaurant. *10am-5pm Wed & Thu, 10am-11pm Fri & Sat, 10am-6pm Sun* €€€

La Table du Boucher: Huge slabs of oozing beef or charcuterie plates to devour with a cocktail in hand. Carnivores only! *hours vary* €€€

Le Relais Cézanne: Perfect spot to relax before or after a hike up to the Bibemus quarries. The patio across the street gets lively on weekends. *10am-11pm* €€

Ancora Pizza: Where the Aixois drive out for pizza, even when they're already spoiled for choice in town. *noon-10pm Mon-Sat* €€

DRIVING TOUR

A Tour of Aix's Vineyards

The countryside that spreads out from Aix-en-Provence in every direction is rich with wineries and notable grape-growing areas. Take a road trip to sample the vintages produced around Montagne Ste-Victoire, where the hills and valleys shelter the vines and the volcanic earth gives life. This tour can easily be driven in a day.

❶ Domaine des Masques

Head east from Aix-en-Provence on the D17 for 13km, turning south on the rue du Bayon, where a secluded vineyard appears at the end of a potholed track. The landscapes here are as lovely as any in the French countryside. Pass a long line of cypress trees, park the car and then enter a small tasting room to sample a few whites, reds and rosés.

The Drive: Return to the D17 and continue east, turning southeast onto the D56C; the Domaine des Diables is only 14km away, but it's a 20-minute drive.

❷ Domaine des Diables

Thoroughly modern and tasting-friendly, this is the place to learn about rosé wines: the paler and greyer they are, the more delicious. Don't be fooled by the branding; this vineyard has no desire to be on the supermarket shelf. It's a small production of the highest quality. On a tour of the vineyard, you'll learn more about its organic, sustainable wines.

The Drive: Continue south to the D7, then turn west. It's a further 15km (20 minutes) to the next vineyard.

Vineyards, Domaine des Masques, below Mont Ste-Victoire

❸ Château Simone

Wine has been grown here for longer than history records, and this vineyard still produces 80% of the wine bearing the Palette AOC. Vines surrounding the handsome, honey-coloured, eponymous château and gardens produce grenache, syrah, cinsault, mourvèdre and the 'secondary varieties' that, fermented in barrels in a 16th-century cellar dug by monks, become Simone's award-winning wines.

The Drive: It's a short 5km drive north to Château Cremade on the D64E (route de l'Angesse).

❹ Château Cremade

This tiny 9-hectare winery manages to cultivate 25 different grape varieties, many ancient and rare, producing highly respected, AOC-protected whites, rosés and reds. It once hosted Cézanne and Émile Zola; expect a friendly reception and be sure to ask to visit the wine cellar, which feels genuinely historical. Try the fruity Palette reds.

The Drive: One kilometre north is the village of Le Tholonet.

❺ Le Tholonet

Roman ruins, 17th-century castles, windmills and hiking trails that can take you to lakes and mystifying quarries await in Le Tholonet. Finish the day in some of the popular yet tranquil family-run restaurants on a typically Provençal patio or play a game of *pétanque* with a glass of pastis in hand.

Arles

ROMAN HISTORY | MODERN ART | PEACEFUL SQUARES

GETTING AROUND

Arles is well connected by train to Avignon, Marseille and Nîmes. Buses leave for Stes-Marie-de-la-Mer and St-Rémy de Provence. Getting around town is easy on foot and bicycle.

Your arrival in Arles is bound to be rocked by its historic legacy. The power of Rome lies beneath your feet, and there is a glory to this town that belies its village intimacy. Indeed, Arles backed Julius Caesar when he wrestled for power and defeated its ancient coastal rival, Pompey's Marseille.

And then there is its place in the history of art. Writers have flocked to the city to write in the shade, and some of Van Gogh's finest works were conceived here. Nearly a century and a half later, the contemporary art world continues to boldly uphold the French ideal of straddling both the future and the ancient past at the same time.

Art and refinement effortlessly go hand in hand. It seeps into your whole experience as you wander the city, with history spiralling out before you at its own pace, a bastion in the vast, wet flatlands of the Camargue.

Capital of Art

Steel, glass and amphitheatres

Frank Gehry and Maja Hoffmann's Tower rises over the city limits, reflecting the south's famous light. It's a steel-and-glass testament to contemporary art and a billionaire-funded funhouse. To be within the walls of **Luma Arles** *(luma.org/en/arles.html; adult/child €15/free)* is to be within its sweeping dream. As a statement, it demands we consign Van Gogh and Gauguin to the past, ushering in a spangly new future in its cutting-edge studios, galleries and performance spaces.

Arles has long been synonymous with the arts: its photography school, the **École Nationale Supérieure de la Photographie**, is one of the best on the planet, and each year the city welcomes **Les Rencontres d'Arles** (July to September), an annual photography festival that began in the mid-1960s.

☑ **TOP TIP**

Set your alarm to before the city comes to life. Wandering the narrow alleys and ancient Roman vestiges at dawn is a form of time travel.

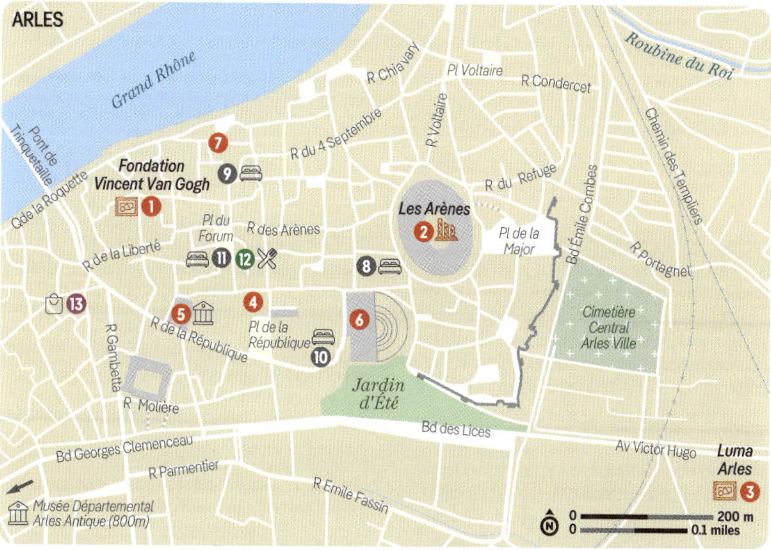

ARLES

	HIGHLIGHTS		SIGHTS		SLEEPING		EATING
1	Fondation Vincent Van Gogh	4	Cryptoportiques	8	Hôtel de l'Amphithéâtre	12	Le Tambourin
2	Les Arènes	5	Museon Arlaten	9	L'Arlatan		SHOPPING
3	Luma Arles	6	Théâtre Antique	10	Le Cloître	13	Maison Genin
		7	Thermes de Constantin	11	Le Nord-Pinus		

It celebrates the big names, discovers new talent and has the art world out until dawn on the festival's big 'Night of the Year' – a raucous international gathering that brings up to 150,000 people to the city.

Arles hosts countless arts festivals, and new art galleries are popping up at every angle. Rather than an appreciation of culture, some locals claim that the modern art world, with its huge branding and foreign investment, is simply a Trojan horse for gentrification, arguing that art's function is to change the world rather than be patronised by the wealthy who can afford it.

The **Fondation Vincent Van Gogh** (fondation-vincent-vangogh-arles.org; adult/child €10/free) does more than pay homage to one of the great masters by showcasing some of his most famous work that he produced while living in the city. By staging temporary exhibitions and seminars and keeping a contemporary eye on what has come before, it puts Van Gogh's time in the city into context.

To return to the 1st century CE, visit the **Museon Arlaten** (museonarlaten.fr; adult/child €8/5), a 15th-century mansion built around the remains of the Roman forum, which displays Provence's arts and crafts from across time.

Continued on p191

BULL BY THE HORNS

Charlie Laloe is the owner of Le Tambourin in Arles:

We live a life linked to the bull, an animal central to our fiestas, spirit and food. Matadors have always drunk here; it's always been a local's place. When people walk in, they are instantly attracted to the images on the wall. Bull meat is much less fatty than everyone imagines. It's because these animals live in the fields. They work.

ROMAN ARLES ON FOOT

Walking the streets of Arles, originally known as Arelate, its significance as centre of the Roman empire is overwhelmingly clear.

START	END	LENGTH
Les Arènes	Cryptoportiques	3km; 30min

Start at ❶ **Les Arènes** (p191), a well-preserved amphitheatre (90 CE) that hosts huge concerts and regional bull-racing competitions. It once hosted chariot races and gladiators fighting to the death, with as many as 21,000 spectators in attendance. Following the fall of Rome, the amphitheatre became a defensive fortress and over centuries, a 'town within a town' grew up within its walls.

The amphitheatre is only a stone's throw from the ❷ **Théâtre Antique d'Arles** (1st century BCE), which also remains part of contemporary cultural life as a well-curated concert venue. Walking 20 minutes across town, passing through the grounds of the ancient circus, brings you to the ❸ **Musée Départemental Arles Antique**, which houses impressive archaeological remains, including a marble statue of Augustus found between the pillars of the theatre in 1750.

A quiet walk along the Rhône's banks leads you past the ❹ **Thermes de Constantin**; peek into the old Roman baths built for Emperor Constantine's private use in the 4th century.

As you return to the place de la Forum, the Nord Pinus hotel's facade merges into the remains of the old entrance to the underground chambers of the ❺ **Cryptoportiques**, which once made up the foundations of the forum.

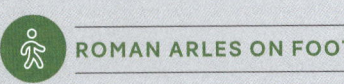

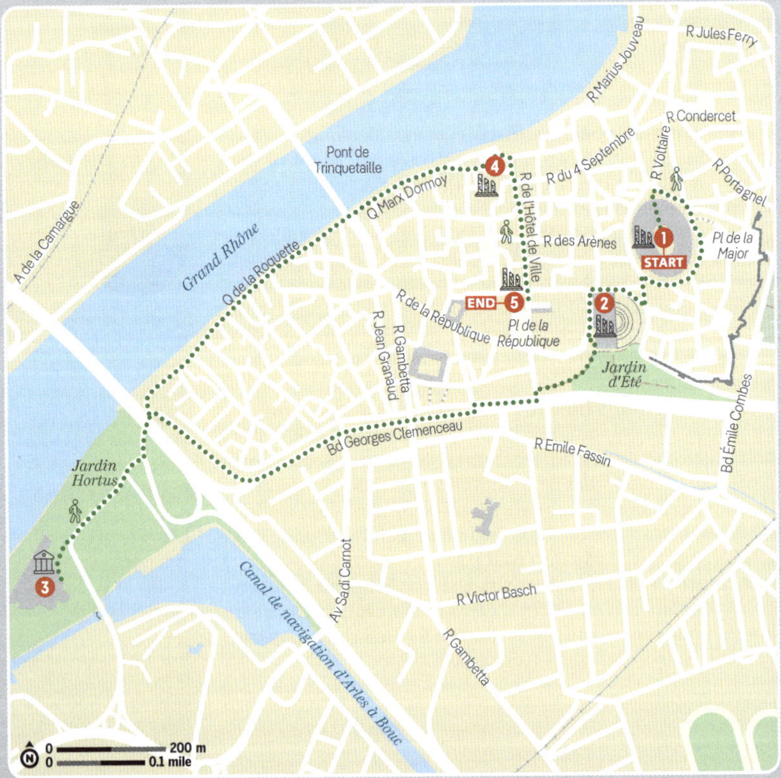

Continued from p189

Life of a Bull
The symbol of the Camargue

Unlike in Spain, here it is the name of the bull on the arena posters, not the bullfighter *(le raseteur)*. The bulls (known here as *les bious*) stamp and snort as the stars of the **Course Camarguaise**, a bloodless competition held in arenas around the city from July to October.

The Cocarde d'Or, in **Les Arènes**, is the main event. The bull spends 20 minutes in the arena as the *raseteurs* show off by dodging and ducking it (rather than attempting to harm it). The following three months are spent grazing in the fields.

In summer the villages of the region come alive to celebrate the bull as king by throwing joyous parties known as *abrivados,* historically the occasion when the strongest and fiercest bulls would be transported from their fields to the arenas.

Although the bulls are not harmed in the competition, many argue that the animals still suffer stress and that the spectacle should be avoided.

On the other side are the *gardians*, the Camargue cowboys, herders of the semi-feral cattle and horses in the Camargue's wetlands, who dream that their bulls will bring them honour. Bulls are selected by temperament at three years of age; the rest are sent to the abattoir to be butchered. Those chosen may have a career in the ring lasting up to 15 years before a peaceful retirement.

After their death, they are buried in an almost sacred ritual facing the sea. Bulls that do not have bronze statues to commemorate their greatness in the ring are likely to end up as part of the regional cuisine: *gardiane de taureau* is Provençal bull stew, a slow-cooked, comforting dish made with red wine and enjoyed in the winter months with Camargue rice.

SHADOWS & LIGHT

Delphine Manjard is the owner of Librarie du Palais, an independent photography bookstore, gallery and publisher in the centre of Arles (librairiedupalais.fr):

Arles is a city that resonates with artists due to its vibrant community – we make sure to help each other out. The people of Arles take pride in their city's heritage but are also unusually warm and welcoming to outsiders. Unlike cities like Venice, where outsiders are not welcome at all, Arles has a history of artists passing through and becoming part of the local culture.

My aim is to promote young, emerging artists and help tell their stories while also bridging their work with the vintage books we offer. We are proud to be the oldest bookstore in France, having printed books for Louis XIV 500 years ago.

 EATING AROUND ARLES: WHERE TO EAT BULL

La Chassagnette: If you want to splurge on a special meal, it should be at this Michelin-starred former sheepfold. *noon-1.30pm Thu-Mon; 8-9pm Sat & Sun* €€€

Maison Genin: Arles' outstanding artisanal butcher and deli since 1877. Cold cuts and *saucisson* served with a smile. *9am-12.30pm & 3.30pm-7pm Tue-Fri; 9am-1pm Sat* €€

Le Tambourin: More authentic than you might think, with many locals eating beneath the mounted bull heads all year-round. *8am-midnight Mon-Sat* €€

La Telline: Eat like a cowboy in what feels like a family home: a deep, rich stew and more than a few glasses of heavy red wine. *noon-1.30pm Fri-Sun, 7.30-9pm Thu-Mon* €€

Beyond Arles

To venture into the Camargue is to immerse yourself in another world that is distinct from modern France.

Places
Salin de Giraud p192
Albaron p195
Les Alpilles p196

The Camargue arises where the Petit Rhône and Grand Rhône meet the Mediterranean: 930 sq km of salt flats, saltwater lakes and marshlands, where the sea and the earth become one. The world here feels completely isolated: it is slow-go country, a timeless wetland chequered with salt pans and rice paddies. It is a land of ancient customs that go back so far that it's easy to suspect the Romans encountered a similar landscape to the one that still exists today. The Camargue is an adventure that extends to music and food. It is a place where you are forced to exert yourself and discover places that are as welcoming as they are alien.

GETTING AROUND

Touring the tiny roads criss-crossing this flat, wild region is best done by car or bicycle. Cycling from Arles into the Camargue requires long sleeves, long trousers, closed shoes and mosquito repellent. Rent bikes at VélocArles *(velocarles.fr)*.

Envia *(tout-envia.com)* runs the A50 bus that takes less than an hour from Arles to Stes-Maries-de-la-Mer for €1.

Zou! *(zou.maregionsud.fr)* runs buses to Les Baux-de-Provence and St-Rémy in under 45 minutes for €3.

Salin de Giraud

TIME FROM ARLES: **50min**

Wild beaches

Les Plages d'Arles are found as you follow the River Rhône out of the city and down to the sea. These are savage, windswept beaches that are atypical for the south of France and are as far from the crowded shores of the French Riviera as you could find. To get here, drive south out of Arles to Salin de Giraud, which is about 40km south of Arles and is your last chance to purchase water or provisions.

Following the D36D out of Salin to the route de la Mer, don't miss the car park on your right, where you'll find the **points d'observation des salins**, lookouts with views of the pink salt pans and a chance to see all manner of birdlife in their natural habitat as they feast upon various tiny creatures – a perfect stop for photos.

From here, the dusty drive to the **Plage de Piémanson** beach gets narrower to the point that you may doubt the road beneath you, but it's worth it. On arrival, the beach gives little indication nowadays of its Burning Man–style past when unlicensed parties lasted for days, unpoliced on the edge of the world. Part of the beach on the eastern side is still famously dedicated to nudists. Greeted by space and dunes, you can take your time to sink peacefully into the calm white sands

VIOLETTE FRANCHI FOR LONELY PLANET

Plage de Piémanson

WHITE WONDERS

The famous white horses of the Camargue are the first things that catch your eye as you drive into the flatlands. With short necks and thick manes, they are one of the oldest breeds of horses and the most visible of the glorious triumvirate of the Camargue's postcard-friendly animals (horses, bulls and flamingos). They have been bred to do a specific job, and to be brave, spirited and powerful. Living as semi-wild creatures, they also possess a sharp instinct for survival.

At the **Fête des Gardians** in Arles on 1 May, the day ends at the town's Roman amphitheatre, where the *gardians* demonstrate how they use their horses to round up bulls, displaying the dynamic grace of these iconic animals.

and just breathe, but do note that there is only a lifeguard station in the summer months.

Another way to get off the beaten track is to get back on it to another off-the-grid beach at the end of a potholed road. The kitesurfer's paradise of **Plage de Beauduc** makes the most of the ravaging embrace of the mistral winds, drawing in lovers of the sport from across the globe. More difficult to get to but somehow more populated, it rates highly as a place to lay down a towel with no phone signal for kilometres around.

Horseback riding in the Camargue

Livestock in the Camargue has a reputation for being at least half-wild, but riding the horses of the **Domaine de la Palissade** at the right time of day can be one of the most peaceful and authentic experiences you could find in the region.

Riding through the wetlands with the region's iconic flamingos swooping in low patterns all around you, you'll be left with the impression that this is how the Camargue has looked for centuries. Time disappears as you go deeper into the marshes along the trails, especially when the early evening sky glows red.

 DRINKING BEYOND ARLES: BEST REGIONAL VINEYARDS

Domaine Mas de Rey: A farmhouse dating back to the 12th century is the setting for a tasting that feels as much like an education. *10am-12.30pm & 2-6pm Mon-Fri*

Mas de Valériole: A real sense of family with lots of bull meat *saucisson* and regional cheese to accompany a very friendly tasting. *9am-noon & 3-7pm Mon-Fri, 3-7pm Sat*

Domaine de Beaujeu: Organic wines and rice. It is impossible to leave its *épicerie* empty-handed. *9am-noon & 3-7pm Mon-Fri, 3-7pm Sat*

Domaine Isle St-Pierre: This winery is also a great base for a popular hike on the opposite banks of the Rhone. Fantastic reds. *9am-noon & 2-6pm Mon-Sat, 9am-noon Sun*

THE FUTURE OF THE RHÔNE DELTA

The Rhône Delta, where the river meets the sea, is the largest delta in western Europe. But as the summers grow hotter and sea levels rise, life in the Camargue's marshes and lagoons faces an existential threat. An even more pressing problem than coastline erosion is that droughts have allowed the sea to push inland, destroying pastures and leaving the wetlands infertile.

Tourism has also played its part. Until 2012, these beaches acted as wild, overcrowded campsites that raged all summer. There are now more restrictions against pitching tents overnight. In the national park, the **Musée de la Camargue** has a great permanent exhibition highlighting how pressing the region's ecological issues have become.

The local guides are well informed and enthusiastic, and more than patient with first-timers. Do not be wary if you've never ridden a horse, but note children must be at least eight years old. On the three-hour trips down to the Plage de Piémanson (€70), more experienced riders will finally get to cut loose and gallop ecstatically down the hot sands.

Your guide's English is enough to keep you safe, but you will need a relatively good command of French to learn more about the local culture, flowers and fauna. There are more English-friendly schools near Stes-Maries-de-la-Mer but the terrain does not compare.

For English speakers, it is easiest to book through instagram.com/domainedelapalissade. Remember to bring mosquito repellent and wear long trousers and closed shoes.

EATING IN ST-RÉMY: OUR PICKS

Edù: Out of town and serene around the pond in the summer gardens; cosy in winter by the fire. Great pizza! *noon-2.30pm & 7.30-11.30pm Tue-Sat* €€

Gus: Big on seafood, this spot boasts the dynamics of modern presentation that its buzzy crowd laps up. *noon-2pm & 7-10pm Fri-Tue* €€

L'Aile ou la Cuisse: These old-school French plates rich with butter, fat and cream will transport you to the 1970s. An absolute institution. *noon-2pm & 7-10pm* €€

Chapeau de Paille: Proud Provençal cuisine served confidently and with grace. Authenticity sizzles on the dish. *11.30am-1.30pm & 7-8.30pm* €€

Horseback-riding tour, the Camargue

Albaron

TIME FROM ARLES: **30min** 🚆, **20min** 🚗

Discover rice cultivation in the Camargue

The Camargue is France's only rice region, producing nearly 100,000 tonnes of its three varieties annually. It may only be a tiny percentage of what is produced worldwide, but Camargue rice is nonetheless high quality. Blessed with water from the Rhône Delta and plenty of sunshine to help it grow, it also has the violent mistral wind arriving at just the right time to dry the grains after harvesting. None of the rice grown here is genetically modified.

Camargue red and black rice is not only slightly crunchier than other varieties, it also has more protein, fibre and vitamins. Importantly, rice cultivation is considered more beneficial to the local environment than salt harvesting, which is famously popular across the region.

NOSTRADAMUS' BIRTHPLACE

A plaque on 6 rue Hoche in St-Rémy commemorates where the famous prophet Nostradamus lived with his family. Born into a Jewish family forced to convert to Catholicism to escape the Inquisition, Michel de Nostredame's life in St-Rémy de Provence began to take shape when he was expelled from medical school. He chose to practice as a physician regardless.

Profound grief from having tragically lost his wife and children to one of the many plagues of his era led him to write grim predictions that would befall the earth, drawing on ancient Jewish mysticism and astrology.

The first book of prophecies was published in 1555. Some consider them vague noodlings and others divine foreseeings. He is said to have predicted wars, natural disasters and global upheaval for 2025.

 EATING IN LES BAUX-DE-PROVENCE & EYGALIÈRES: OUR PICKS

Restaurant de la Reine Jeanne: The most stunning vista in town. Go for the slow-cooked lamb above a tremendous drop. *8am-6pm Sun-Thu, 8am-11pm Fri & Sat* €€

Restaurant Le Mas d'Aigret: The ancient interior of a troglodyte dining room with a charming patio and surrounds. *noon-1.30pm & 7-8.45pm* €€

Le Café de la Place: Busy bar that has been the centre of village life in Eygalières for a good and a long time. Grab oysters and wine. *hours vary* €€

Restaurant L'Opale: Go on a sunny day to eat gently layered plates on a terrace among the trees in Eygalières. *noon-2pm & 7-9pm Tue-Sat, 11am-2pm Sun* €€€

Market, Les Alpilles

VILLAGES IN LES ALPILLES

The mountain range of the Alpilles is an understated destination where old French writers passed on to the next life and Hollywood stars still come wanting the semblance of a normal life. It could be the shady squares when spring has sprung, the colourful shutters of the homes or the treks into nature that make you stop and stare over and over again. Time slows down in this collection of unique villages – from Maillane to Le Paradou to Mouriès – with their customs and history that all reflect the generosity of Provence in bloom. For those who want to experience a quiet life, you won't find much better than this.

The **Maison du Riz** *(maisonduriz.com; adult/child €5/ free)*, less than half an hour's drive west of Arles, encourages travellers to visit its rice production centre or stay at its guesthouses. Here, you will see first-hand the Rozière family's way of life, where rice is treated with the same attention you would give to livestock. Their boutique sells all varieties of rice grown in the region, as well as rice-based beer, soaps and makeup. Local delicacies from this fertile region are also on sale, from the finest olive oil to bull sausage and terrines, making you likely to return bearing gifts.

Les Alpilles

TIME FROM ARLES: **35min**

St-Rémy dreams in the hills

Dutch post-impressionist Vincent Van Gogh's life has traced its way across Arles and the surrounding region. It is where he painted some of his most recognisable work. *The Yellow House*, *The Bedroom* and *Le Café de Nuit* all capture the atmosphere that still exists in the city.

In 1889, Van Gogh arrived in St-Rémy de Provence to commit himself to the Monastère St-Paul de Mausole, a psychiatric asylum, where he lived for a year.

His arguably most haunting work, *Starry Night*, a psychedelic and disturbing portrayal of the night swirling out of control, was one of over 150 paintings produced while battling with his mental health following his tragic act of self-mutilation.

The free, self-guided walk from **Musée Estrine** *(museeestrine.fr; adult/child €9/free)* in the centre of St-Rémy, signposted to St-Paul, includes reproductions of his works and snatches of his letters to friends and loved ones. Arriving at the **Monastère St-Paul de Mausole** *(saintpauldemausole.fr; adult/child €9/free)*, which retains an all-female art-therapy wing, one can imagine how an artist could be as prolific as Van Gogh in a haven such as this, resting between wild countryside and order. The intricate gardens at the right moment command a stillness and contemplation that one would expect from a Romanesque cloister.

The re-creation of his room on the first floor would be more moving if it were possible to experience it alone, and it is best to avoid visiting at all during the high season.

A pleasant 40-minute walk along the D5 takes you to to the **Lac de Peirou** where it is forbidden to swim, but beneath the limestone rocks and pine trees you can catch some peace in the reflection of the sky in soothing waters.

From Les Baux-de-Provence to Eygalières

Les Baux-de-Provence is the destination for views for days over the mountain range of Les Alpilles. Below, the tapestry of vineyards and olive and oak trees will give you feelings of nothing less than exaltation. The carved-up countryside with its sparkling swimming pools and rustic homes is as Provençal as can be, but Les Baux-de-Provence itself, with its fortified castle and hordes of tourists, may make you wonder if you've made your way to a Mediterranean Disneyland. To escape the crowds in the best possible way, take a hike. Once you have been mesmerised by the views from the rocks above the town you will be ready to descend into the valley. The **Val d'Enfer** hike is a 2½-hour loop that leads you past limestone caves – the remnants of troglodyte homes from the Neolithic era – and the **Carrières de Lumières** *(carrieres-lumieres.com; adult/child €16.50/14)* – a stone quarry that was turned into a cultural centre in the late 1970s, an outstanding cavernous chamber where music and spellbinding light projections have replaced the sounds of clacking rock.

Only half an hour's drive northeast will take you to **Eygalières**, a limestone village poking out from the top of a hill where calm is the order of the day. With the sweet smell of Mediterranean flora in the air, this is a place to wander to the sound of cicadas and gurgling fountains and to appreciate the soft-shoed rhythm of village life. Take to the winding streets and narrow alleys in a daze. On Friday mornings, the local market gives Eygalières a gentle buzz, with all the local cheeses, meats and wines you would expect on display, as does the antique market on the last Sunday of the month. La Banaste d'Eygalières organises summer events that bring the village to a standstill; antique collectors travel here from across the region to barter and poke about.

For great panoramic views and sacred energy, take the 2km walk to the **Chapelle St-Sixte**, painted by Van Gogh when he stayed in the asylum in nearby St-Rémy. The cypress trees can't help but remind you that this was once the site of an ancient Roman temple. To escape even further, a looping hike to Lamanon with scents of thyme and rosemary on the breeze will have the Alpilles embracing you.

LOCAL SAKE PRODUCTION

Olivier Sublett, producer of GuiSho, a sake (rice wine) made in the Camargue *(leguishu.fr)*:

I wanted to create something unique, different from pastis, wines and even the beers, which are typically associated with the Camargue.

Since we are the leading rice-producing region in Europe, I came up with the idea of making a sake infused with Provençal flavours.

This concept has even started to gain popularity in Asia. I'm proud to say that I have been awarded a Gold Medal at the International Awards in Hong Kong, and it's incredibly gratifying that Michelin-starred chefs are recognising my work.

My goal was to represent the Camargue in a forward-thinking and innovative way. By adding a twist to tradition, I believe we can make the world feel smaller and more connected.

Stes-Maries-de-la-Mer

CYCLE TRIPS | BIRD-WATCHING | WATERSPORTS

GETTING AROUND
Stes-Maries-de-la-Mer is easily explored on foot or bicycle. Envia (tout-envia.com) runs buses to/from Arles (Line 50, €1, 50 minutes).

Stes-Maries-de-la-Mer is wrapped up in its own mysticism, rendering it much more than just another Mediterranean coastal town with nice beaches. It has mesmerised Hemingway, Van Gogh and Picasso and served as a sacred site for Celts, Romans and Christians.

It is not uncommon to find tourists sitting on the terraces as the locals prop up the bar under bull heads mounted on the wall. There is a lot of bullfighting memorabilia on view; the bullring in town doubles as a popular summer concert venue.

Nowadays, the town centre resembles a Spanish seaside resort with bar after bar and restaurants at every turn. It is a place of postcards, stuffed flamingos, summer dresses and fish pedicures, but don't be put off. Each year on 24 May, it holds a celebration for the world's Roma community, who travel from all over to celebrate the spectacular Pèlerinage des Gitans.

A Pilgrimage to Notre-Dame-de-la-Mer
The veneration of Ste Sara

Stes-Maries-de-la-Mer has evolved from a fishing village to a town that revolves around its 12th-century Romanesque church, **Notre-Dame-de-la-Mer**, part holy site and part coastal fortress. Climb to the rooftop terrace for tremendous views. Even as a tourist destination, the church remains significant to the small community here and is likely the first site of Christianity in the Camargue.

In the crypt at the back and to the right, in a host of vivid-coloured materials draped across her form and bedecked in prayer beads, jewellery and a silver crown, is the statue of the patron saint of the Roma people, Ste Sara. According to local legend, she was the servant of Mary Magdalene, who landed here with Lazarus, Marie-Salomé and Marie-Jacobé after fleeing persecution in the Holy Land in 45 CE; they were all canonised after spreading the gospel. Sara-la-Kâli, or Sara the Black, is adored by her community of Roma, Manouches, Tziganes and Gitans, who amass here together for their

TOP TIP
The best way to enjoy Stes-Maries is by exploring its spectacular beaches and surroundings. Getting to know the locals is essential here; they know how to make the most of their region and will pull you into their experiences in no time.

STES-MARIES-DE-LA-MER

SIGHTS
1 Notre-Dame-de-la-Mer

ACTIVITIES
2 Le Vélociste

3 Trot'nalix

SLEEPING
4 Hôtel Casa Marina
5 Hotel Le Neptune en Camargue

EATING
6 Boho Beach
7 La Bohème by JF
8 La Casita

springtime pilgrimage, the **Pèlerinage des Gitans**.

This is a time for reunions, and the town comes alive with many people camping out on the streets and the beach – there was even a time when pilgrims slept next to the saint in the crypt, playing violins and singing into the night. Before the telephone, these disparate nomadic communities, who had no other way to stay in touch, would return to Stes-Maries each year to keep up with each other's lives. Their newborn children would also be baptised in the church in intense and noisy candle-lit ceremonies that have changed little over the centuries. When there are so many candles burning there is barely any oxygen in the crypt left to breathe as the *gitans* kiss the hem of the saint's dress and hold their babies up to plant a kiss upon her face.

Cycling the Camargue
Feel the wind in your hair

Coastal cycling is a unique rush. Pedalling away from town, the land turning into the sea before your eyes gives a feeling of liberation. Cycling in the Camargue between April and October combines great weather with a surreal landscape speckled with pink flamingos, wild horses and black bulls. While you can see all this through the car or bus windows, the connection with your surroundings is much more intimate as you cycle with the sea breeze in your hair. If you have the wind at your back, you'll speed off to discover the

OUTDOOR SPORTS

Le Vélociste: Helpful staff offering combined tours of bike and canoe or even switching onto horseback (levelociste.fr; €16 full day).

Trot'nalix: Electric and gravel racing bikes on the seafront. Perfect pick up and drop off for the 13km ride to the Gacholle lighthouse (trotnalex.com; €20 full day).

Lili Kitesurf: Learn to kitesurf on the famous beaches of Beauduc (lilikitesurf.com).

Manu Kayak: Paddle through the wetlands of Domaine de la Palissade (p193) (kayak-camargue.fr).

THE KING OF THE GYPSIES

Legendary jazz guitarist Django Reinhardt, hailed as the 'King of the Gypsies', was born into a Roma family in 1910. Among his remarkable works, 'Messe' was composed shortly before his death for the Pèlerinage des Gitans.

This unfinished piece still manages to capture the essence of a service that begins in a church and ends in the sea. Its orchestration, featuring accordion, violin and guitar, opens solemnly and ceremoniously. As the music unfolds, the swirling melodies reflect the emotional processions that symbolise the arrival of Sara and her companions by boat. The energy builds, evoking the *gardians* riding their horses into the sea, statues proudly held aloft, as the church bells ring loudly across town.

coast, far from peak season crowds. However, if you're fighting the severe mistral winds, at least be comforted that your journey back home will be considerably easier. The popular coastal dirt path out of town, straddling the marshlands and the sea, eventually leads to the solar-powered and uncrewed **Phare de la Gacholle** lighthouse, a great place to stop and use the picnic tables if you have packed a lunch. While it is a flat course all the way, you should be prepared to dismount and push through the sand for short periods towards the end. The joy is in the journey itself.

Bike rental staff in town are all tremendously helpful and will recommend cycling loops into the national park. Riding on the route de Méjanes will give you a real sense of open space. Be prepared to see *gardians* galloping on white horses as you follow the inlets inland. For those with limitless energy, some agencies combine tours that allow you to transfer from a bike to a horse or canoe. Those wanting to take it easier can rent an electric bike. If you have the energy to take things further, it is three hours northeast to Arles and 1½ hours northwest to the **Réserve Naturelle Régionale du Scamandre**, where you can cycle a loop around the lake *(camarguegardoise.com)*.

Bird-Watching in the Parc Ornithologique
Where flamingos fill the sky

If you're not a bird lover, a trip to the **Parc Ornithologique du Pont de Gau** *(parcornithologique.com; adult/child €8/5, binocular rental €5)* might turn you into one.

This nature reserve, 4km north of town on the D570, encompasses 60 hectares of wetland beauty and is home to over 200 species of migratory birds year-round. Explore the 7km of trails on foot and make use of the bird hides that allow you to approach the birds as if you're participating in a real-life wildlife documentary. Admiring the unreal beauty of flamingos swooping overhead or flocking together on the waters from your observatory or from deep grass is wondrous. Your ticket is for the day, so it's worth packing a picnic.

The park was devised as an almost artificial utopia for Camargue wildlife – some birds have given up migrating and live here full-time in inlets repopulated with the ideal flora and fauna to ensure they thrive. It is also a place that focuses on educating visitors to understand the fragile balance of the ecosystem, and is a good family excursion. In early autumn, you will enjoy pastel sunsets and flamingos at their pinkest, making for an unforgettable sight.

EATING IN STES-MARIES: OUR PICKS

La Casita: Authentic family restaurant that serves catch of the day *à la plancha* (grilled) near the bullring. *noon-2.30pm Tue-Sun, 7.30-10.30pm Tue-Sat* €€

Restaurant Chante Clair: Modern, popular choice: from *filet de taureau* and spaghetti in squid ink to huge vegetarian plates. *noon-3pm & 6-11pm Thu-Tue Apr-Nov* €€

La Bohème by JF: Well-established brunch spot serving great eggs and coffee that wouldn't look out of place in any major city. *11.30am-4.30pm Fri-Mon, to 2.30pm Tue* €€

Boho Beach: Fresh modern tapas with your feet in the sand in Stes-Maries' best beach bar. *summer; hours vary* €€

Beyond Stes-Maries-de-la-Mer

To immerse yourself in the Camargue is to connect with a unique and timeless way of life.

As your journey into the Camargue goes deeper, you learn more about life on the land as you swat the mosquitoes on your neck. Freezing in the winter and humid as hell in the summer months, it's here that the magical, almost psychotropic fever dream experience can open up to you. Where else can you find a world of knights, biblical characters and tireless animals populating the region with a freedom that cannot be tamed?

The fortified medieval town of Aigues-Mortes is an ideal base for exploring this region. It's actually located over the border from Provence in the Gard *département*, 28km northwest of Stes-Maries-de-la-Mer at the western extremity of the Rhône Delta.

Places
Aigues-Mortes p201

Aigues-Mortes TIME FROM STES-MARIES-DE-LA-MER: 30min
Walk the ramparts

On the edge of the Mediterranean, in the flat marshes of the Camargue, is the medieval town of Aigues-Mortes ('dead waters'). A UNESCO-protected World Heritage Site, it has sweeping views from its fortress walls of the peculiar pink salt pans stretching southwards, which have produced the region's famous salt for centuries. Built by Louis IX, this was where the French king's crusade set out in the 13th century, and with the citadel's towers and battlements you can well imagine the scene.

The first thing to do in town is walk the ramparts and climb the **Tour de Constance** *(aigues-mortes-monument. fr; adult/child €9/free),* which provides an education in how a walled city defended itself. Rambling along the 1.6km-long ramparts gives excellent views not only across the rooftops of the town but also out onto the pink waters. Climb higher

GETTING AROUND

The beauty of visiting such an untamed and almost trackless region is that you are at times standing alone in a place that feels far from civilisation. It goes without saying that car rental is the best way to navigate this remote part of the Mediterranean.

Rooftops, Aigues-Mortes (p201)

FLEUR DE SEL

The pink hues of Aigues-Mortes' surrounding salt pans are astounding from the ramparts. Even before Roman times, the marshes here were used to produce salt, and today **Les Salins du Midi** (visitesalinsdecamargue.com) continues to extract 500,000 tonnes of the stuff per year.

Water from the Mediterranean is pumped into the reservoirs and left to evaporate in the strong mistral winds; the crystallised *fleur de sel* is then shovelled into piles and left to bake beneath the hot sun.

You can ride the 30km around the pink waters (€22 with your own bike or rent an e-bike on site). Hiring a bike in town and cycling to the salt pans makes more sense. Race past flamingos tas they gorge themselves pink in the magical waters.

to the top of the tower, where the angles are a photographer's dream and the sudden tranquillity from its interior is a heart-opening surprise.

Tourists have replaced the marauding crusaders in the town, but you can happily walk its long, narrow and tightly packed streets, which always seem to lead back to the main square: place St-Louis. In peak season, Aigues-Mortes is bubbling with energy, its cafe and restaurant terraces full, but there remains a sense that the town is perfectly preserved – a bizarre rectangular world. Gothic church connoisseurs should spend a quiet moment in **Notre-Dame-des-Sablons**.

EATING IN AIGUES-MORTES: OUR PICKS

| **Restaurant l'Atelier de Nicolas**: Worth getting a reservation for its gastronomic pretensions. Subtle Asian fusion. *noon-1.30pm & 7-9pm Fri-Tue* €€€ | **La Goulue**: A highlight within the walls of the city. Food served with the energy of something to prove. *noon-2pm & 7pm-midnight* €€ | **Le Dit Vin**: Amazing wine cellar below your feet. Seafood or bull steaks – it's all local. *noon-2.30pm & 7-10pm* €€ | **Les Poissons d'Argent**: Barbecued fish in a friendly campsite on the Étang de la Marette. Anglers can have their own catches put on charcoal. *noon-8pm* €€ |

Places We Love to Stay

€ Budget €€ Midrange €€€ Top End

Marseille
Map p162

Mama Shelter € Budget with some style. This hotel can turn into a party with live music and a raucous bar on the weekend.

Hôtel Belle-Vue € Incredible views of the Vieux Port and a famous historical restaurant that turns into a jazz venue on Sundays. Great value.

Les Appartements du Vieux Port €€ Large, calm apartments with balconies, close to the Vieux Port. When you prefer to have a modern home-from-home.

La Relève €€ There are only four rooms, so book in advance for this '50s-inspired guest house that is attached to a very cool bar in the 7eme.

Hôtel Le Corbusier €€ A little out of the way, but this is a unique and historic monument to urban planning. Great pool on the roof.

Hotel Peron €€ Wes Anderson–style hotel with views of the corniche and beyond. Art deco from every angle and a friendly reception.

Le Ryad €€ North African–inspired hotel that has a sanctuary garden to drink fresh mint tea in after a long day.

Les Bords de la Mer €€€ Modern architectural lines that make it all about the views of the Plage des Catalans as you have breakfast. A statement option.

Attrap'Rêves: €€€ A bubble pod hotel in Allauch on the eastern outskirts of Marseille. Stare at the stars through a telescope in your transparent pod in the forest.

Aix-en-Provence
Map p179

Hôtel Escaletto €€ Friendly, modern spot close to the Roman baths and boasting a rooftop cocktail bar that goes late into the night.

Hôtel des Augustins €€ Incredible location just off cours Mirabeau with plenty of old-school Aixois ambience.

Domaine Gaogaïa €€ One for summer. Cocktails in the garden, and only 10 minutes from town but feels like a world away.

Le Relais de Saint Ser €€ At the foot of Montagne Ste-Victoire – the views from the restaurant are the best for miles around. Incredible food too.

Bastide de Ganay €€€ Quiet Provençal luxury with a saltwater pool in manicured gardens. Only a 15-minute drive into the centre of Aix.

Garrigae Abbaye de Ste-Croix €€€ Above Salon-de-Provence. Peaceful views across the Alpilles and blissful lazing by the pool.

Arles
Map p189

Hôtel de l'Amphithéâtre € Quaint sleeper in the heart of the city. No frills but plenty of character.

Le Nord-Pinus €€ Sleep where Hemmingway once did. This is a historic triumph of a hotel in the centre of town.

Le Cloître €€ Tasteful remodelling of a grand building, with a great summer roof bar and restaurant.

L'Arlatan €€€ An abundance of style and substance. The attention to each design detail is mind-boggling.

Stes-Maries-de-la-Mer
Map p199

Hôtel Casa Marina € A short hop from the sands and beach bars of Stes-Maries. Friendly and sparkly clean.

Hotel Le Neptune en Camargue € Small hotel that delivers charm, warmth and a huge breakfast.

Hôtel Les Arnelles €€€ A comfortably authentic experience in the wilds of the Camargue. Make the most of its stable to go for a horse ride at sunset.

Hotel Peron, Marseille

Researched by
Ashley Parsons

The Vaucluse & Luberon

MOUNTAINS, WINE & SUNSHINE

Dig deep into the many faces of the Vaucluse: sun-drenched hilltop villages, leisurely bike rides and scores of local markets.

One thing seems to lead to another in the Vaucluse. Start in Avignon, a city once home to successive popes and today home to the largest theatre festival in France. And then think bigger – nearby are the renowned vineyards that produce Châteauneuf-du-Pape. In the distance? That's Mont Ventoux, the giant of Provence and a dream challenge for many cyclists.

At the foot of the mountain is the village of Sault and its fields of lavender. Further south, the Plateau des Claperèdes is in bloom too, inside the wilds of the Parc Naturel Régional du Luberon. On the north side of the park are the red, yellow and orange ochres found in the cliffs and rock formations of the Colorado Provençal. And further west is Gordes, the most beautiful village in the world (seriously, it won a prize), which sits perched on a hill. Behind Gordes, the Monts de Vaucluse twist and roll, hiding smaller pastoral villages in their folds. At the bottom of those hills is L'Isle-sur-la-Sorgue, the French capital of antiques.

Back in the Luberon, chic villas and innovative restaurants sit below ruined châteaux, where nobility like the Marquis de Sade once retreated on holiday. And that's not the half of it. Even when you live in the Luberon, you can't do it all. But here are the best parts.

THE MAIN AREAS

AVIGNON
Dense medieval city with a flair for the stage.
p210

VENTOUX
The giant of Provence, with lots to discover.
p224

L'ISLE-SUR-LA-SORGUE
Canals and antiquing, history and style. **p229**

NORTH LUBERON
The wild side of the Luberon park.
p238

SOUTH LUBERON
Chic villages surrounded by vineyards. **p250**

For places to stay in the Vaucluse & Luberon, see p256

THE GUIDE

THE VAUCLUSE & LUBERON

Left: Abbaye Notre-Dame de Sénanque (p240); Above: Vineyards, Dentelles de Montmirail (p217)

Find Your Way

Reach Avignon by TGV and hire a car to discover the villages in Vaucluse, Ventoux or Luberon. There are lots of options for cycling trips, too.

BUS

The Zou! bus system serves the Vaucluse and Luberon. Comfy and clean, the bus is great for a day trip into town. For far-flung villages and to keep to your own timeline, though, it's better to have a bike or a car.

CAR

For day trips or excursions, consider BlaBlaCar (*blablacar.fr*), a widely used French ride-sharing app. Prices are reasonable and as long as your stop isn't too much of a detour, folks will usually take you all the way to your destination.

CYCLING

With endless backroad options, the Vaucluse and Luberon is one of the best cycling areas in France. Many villages now have a local bike-rental shop, and an e-bike can be a great solution for running short errands or side visits.

Ventoux, p224
Fields of lavender, gorges to hike and Mont Ventoux to cycle: nature and sports lovers will adore it here.

Plan Your Time

With so much to explore, it's impossible to see all of the Vaucluse and Luberon in one go. Plan at least a few days in the region.

Cycling, Mont Ventoux (p225)

Pedalling Provence

● For the leisure cyclist, hopping on an e-bike and cycling the **hill villages** (p242) on the north side of Luberon is unforgettable and accessible.

● A bit more sporty is the **Monts de Vaucluse loop** (p234) through the wild and fragrant hills.

● Or for a real challenge, set your sights on **Mont Ventoux** (p225). Wake up early, strap on your helmet and hop on the bike saddle to pedal up to the mythic summit, the giant of Provence. There are three routes up the mountain – which is the right one for you?

SEASONAL HIGHLIGHTS

Winters are usually mild, but a mistral wind can change that in a second. Summers are hot, but spring and autumn are blissful.

FEBRUARY
Peak truffle season. Visit the **Marché aux Truffes** (p218) in Carpentras to spot traders dealing in the black gold.

APRIL
The Luberon reawakens with spring; wild asparagus makes its way onto restaurant menus.

MAY
Warm temps mean hiking, cycling and climbing are at their best until the first heatwave hits, usually near the end of the month.

Four Days to Travel

- Arriving in Avignon, visit the **Palais des Papes** (p212) and go for a stroll around the old town.

- The next day, head to the **Dentelles de Montmirail** (p217) to taste the renowned Beaumes-de-Venise wine and watch the sunset over Mont Ventoux.

- Drive down to **L'Isle-sur-la-Sorgue** (p229) and hit the antique markets. Take a walk along the river's edge in L'Isle-sur-la-Sorgue or in Fontaine de Vaucluse.

- Wake up early for a sunrise visit to **Gordes** (p240), and then drive to the **Abbaye Notre-Dame de Sénanque** (p240), hidden away in a small canyon. Dine in **Venasque** (p234), on the other side of the Monts de Vaucluse, before returning to Avignon.

A Week in the Luberon

- Settle into your village of choice: maybe **Ménerbes** (p242), **Saignon** (p244) or **Bonnieux** (p243).

- Go for a walk in the **Forêt des Cèdres** (p253) before sunset. Get out early to visit the ochre hills and take a workshop at the Écomusée in **Roussillon** (p249).

- Rent a bike and cycle between Luberon villages like **Ménerbes** and **Lacoste** (p243).

- Discover **Lourmarin** (p251), where you can dine in an elegant and ecofriendly restaurant.

- Rent a vintage car and drive through the **South Luberon** (p250) in between vines and medieval châteaux.

JULY
The lavender is in bloom and theatre is in full swing for the **Festival d'Avignon** (p213).

AUGUST
Communities across the Luberon start to hold their annual *fêtes votives*, huge village parties.

SEPTEMBER
The *vendange*, or grape harvest, begins. In many villages, such as **La Tour d'Aigues**, there is a festival to celebrate.

DECEMBER
After the olive harvest wraps up in November, locals get ready for a Provençal Christmas with the famous thirteen desserts.

Avignon

PAPAL PALACES | PROVENCE PEOPLE-WATCHING | MUSEUM HOPPING

GETTING AROUND

Avignon is pretty straightforward to navigate. Many areas of the city centre are car-free, so it's best to park outside the city in a free car park like the **Parking de l'Île Piot** and grab a free shuttle into town.

Around the *rocade*, or walls of the city, is a tramway, which stops at the main station. A bike-sharing service called Vélopop' has nearly 30 e-bike hubs around the city and in nearby Villeneuve-lès-Avignon. Inside the city walls, a free electric shuttle connects the squares.

☑ TOP TIP

Need somewhere to stay during peak times? If there's not much on offer inside the walls of Avignon, don't turn up your nose at staying in Villeneuve-lès-Avignon, just on the other side of the Rhône. There are regular shuttles, and the city's bike-rental service Vélopop' has stations in Villeneuve.

Perched on the banks of the Rhône, Avignon is the gateway to Provence. Stop here at the beginning or end of a visit to get your city break. Inside the rampart-ringed old town, visitors can learn about the story of Avignon as a papal city, visit the numerous Provençal gardens or people-watch from one of the pedestrian-zone cafes and leafy squares. Many restaurants blend the French pastime of eating *en terrace* with seasonal menus that flaunt flavours from the rich agricultural plains alongside the Rhône and the Durance Rivers. And don't discount Avignon's museum scene: with half a dozen museums with world-class Provençal and Italian painting collections, as well as contemporary museums and galleries, Avignon is for lovers of the arts. In July, the city fills to bursting for the Festival d'Avignon. With theatre troupes walking the narrow streets in costume to promote their plays, the whole city feels like a stage.

Shop Around Avignon

Design comes first in Avignon's creative corners

Avignon's town centre hides some real treasures for design lovers, with a handful of independent boutiques offering colour, character and curation in place of big-brand sameness. Start on rue de la Bonneterie at **Bleu Mandarine**, a bright and welcoming boutique where Marie, the owner, stocks a playful mix of handmade jewellery, textiles, ceramics and accessories from local and European designers – and can tell you the story behind each piece.

A few minutes' walk away, **Mimi Vintage** on rue Galante is a small but beautifully curated hub of secondhand style. It's pricier than a thrift shop, but the pieces are in excellent condition, with a nostalgic flair that leans feminine and French.

Nearby, **CGFD** (*cqfd-avignon.fr*) is a sleek, Avignon-born concept store showcasing contemporary French designers – minimalist fashion, homewares and beauty brands with a focus on clean lines and quiet luxury. It's the kind of place where you'll want everything…even if you didn't plan to shop.

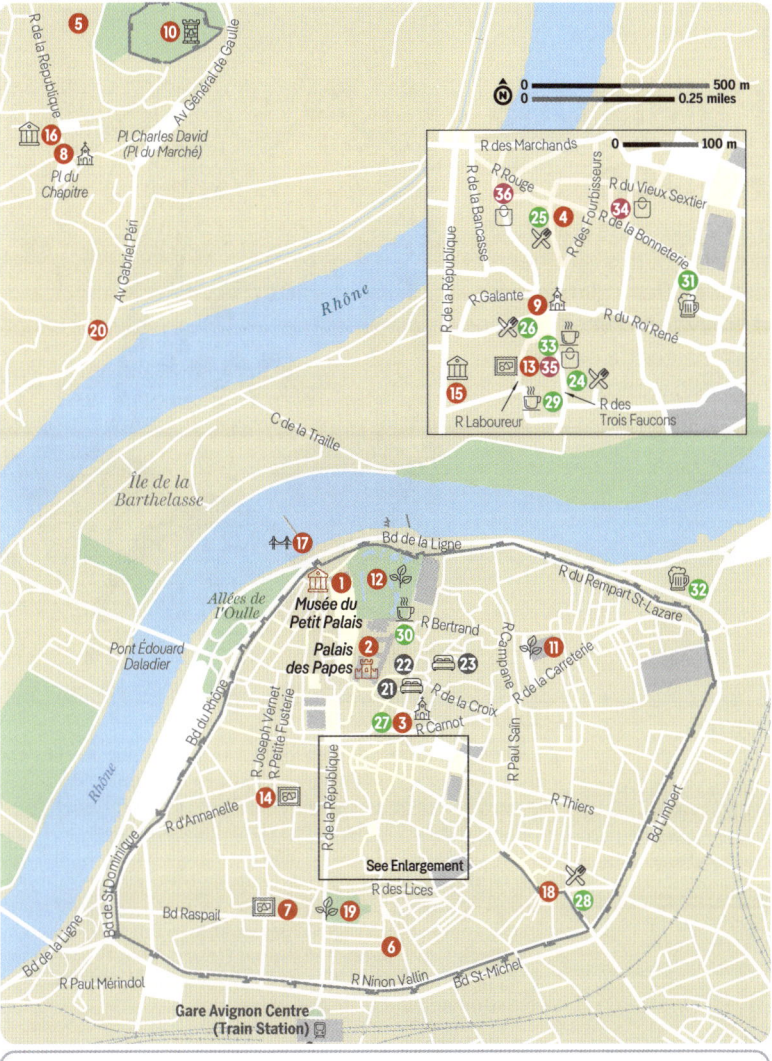

★ HIGHLIGHTS
1 Musée du Petit Palais
2 Palais des Papes

● SIGHTS
3 Basilique St-Pierre
4 Chapelle des Pénitents Blancs
5 Chartreuse du Val de Bénédiction
6 Cloître des Célestins
7 Collection Lambert
8 Collégiale Notre-Dame
9 Église St-Didier
10 Fort St-André
11 Jardin des Carmes
12 Jardin des Doms
see 10 Jardins de St-André
13 Musée Angladon
14 Musée Calvet
15 Musée Lapidaire
16 Musée Pierre de Luxembourg
17 Pont St-Bénézet
18 Rue des Teinturiers
19 Square Agricol Perdiguier
20 Tour Philippe-le-Bel

● SLEEPING
21 Hôtel La Mirande
22 La Banasterie
23 La Divine Comédie

● EATING
24 Fou de Fafa
25 Graines de Piment
26 Grand Café Barretta
27 L'Épicerie
see 5 Les Jardins d'Été
28 Numéro 75

● DRINKING & NIGHTLIFE
29 Buna Café
30 Café Roma
31 La Fabrique
32 La Scierie
33 Tulipe Café

● SHOPPING
34 Bleu Mandarine
35 CGFD
36 Mimi Vintage

TOP EXPERIENCE

Palais des Papes

The vast rooms and shady arcades of this 14th-century palace offer a glimpse into medieval life, when Avignon was the centre of the Catholic world.

TOP TIPS

● Buy tickets online to save time at the entrance, especially during the busy summer season and July theatre festival.

● Don't miss the Jardins du Palais, designed in the English style and accessible from the former apartments of the Pope – his place for wandering reflection.

PRACTICALITIES

● palais-des-papes.com
● adult/child €12/€6.50
● Mar-Oct 9am-7pm, rest of the year 10am-5pm

Rooms that Speak

From the moment you step into the echoing stone corridors of the palace, you're drawn into a journey that unfolds gradually. Each space reveals something different – a shift in light, a change in scale, a surprising view across the rooftops. Guided by the tablet, the experience brings to life vast halls like the Grand Tinel and more intimate cloisters and private chapels. The Great Chapel represents the largest covered space in the palace. Construction began in 1348 but was slowed by the Black Death pandemic. In the 14th century, the windows were of stained glass, the floors carpeted and walls covered with drapery dominated by green tones.

Fragments of Colour & Life

Tapestries and frescoes reigned as decor during the papal period in Avignon. In the Stag Room, delicate frescoes depict a papal hunting scene – a glimpse into the world of the Avignon popes. This was a court with its own rituals: scholars and scribes in heated debate, cardinals processing in crimson robes, feasts unfolding by candlelight in echoing halls. Elsewhere, such as the papal chambers, fragments of wall paintings and digital reconstructions suggest a setting once filled with pattern, fabric, ceremony and scent. Your imagination will have to fill in the rest.

In or Off: The Festival d'Avignon Unlocked
The play's the thing

The **Festival d'Avignon** is among the largest and most renowned festivals in the world for the performing arts. For three weeks in July, the otherwise calm and sometimes sleepy city of Avignon becomes a hive for the theatre world – shows are mostly in French, but some are in other languages or non-verbal.

The official festival, Avignon In (*festival-avignon.com*), takes place across the city, with its epicentre in the UNESCO-listed old town. Tickets go on sale in April and sell out fast, although resale tickets are advertised on a noticeboard at the box office in Cloître St-Louis. The unofficial fringe festival, Avignon Off (*festivaloffavignon.com*), runs during the same period. The difference between the two lies in the selection and promotion of performances: the In festival's selection is drawn up by a jury. The Off festival is more boot-strappy – troupes are responsible for signing up their piece for the festival, renting a theatre space and promoting their show. Want to see an acclaimed play? Check out the In. Want to see something more alternative? Go for the Off.

Provençal Gardens
A refuge of greenery

In and around Avignon are a host of Provençal gardens, which are a delight to wander. Inside the city walls, visit the **Jardin des Doms**, overlooking the papal palace and the city; **Jardin des Carmes**, a small, quiet garden outside the church of the same name; or the **Square Agricol Perdiguier**, previously the courtyard of an abbey.

Worth the trip across the Rhône, the **Jardins de St-André** and their 10th-century abbey in Villeneuve-lès-Avignon are a breezy way to spend a spring or autumn afternoon.

Art in Avignon
From the Gauls to the digital age

Stay cool in the dog days of summer with a visit to one, or several, of Avignon's superb collection of museums. They are all within easy walking distance of one another. At the top of the list is the **Musée du Petit Palais** (*free*), which was the archbishops' palace during the 14th and 15th centuries. Inside you'll find outstanding collections of primitive, pre-Renaissance

AVIGNON FESTIVAL VENUES

Setting the stage is key in performance, and Avignon has no lack of creative settings. Take the **Carrière de Boulbon**, located in a former limestone quarry outside the city, which is absolutely worth the trip if you can get tickets. But the most emblematic stages of the festival have to be those in former papal and abbey courtyards.

Wherever the popes went, vast construction projects followed. During their 100-year reign in Avignon, the popes commissioned the courtyards, gardens and chapels that are now home to some of the Festival d'Avignon's most unique theatres. Try to catch a play at the **Cour d'Honneur du Palais des Papes** (p212), the **Chapelle des Pénitents Blancs** or the **Cloître des Célestins**.

 DRINKING IN AVIGNON: BEST CAFES FOR PEOPLE-WATCHING

Tulipe Café: This small coffee and lunch spot has the best coffee in Avignon. Attached to the concept store and yoga studio Nid. *9am-5.30pm Tue-Sat, to 3pm Mon* €€	**Café Roma**: Just behind the Palais des Papes, grab a seat in the shade and people-watch. *noon-2pm & 7-10pm Tue-Sat, lunch Sun* €	**Grand Café Barretta**: In the same building as Avignon's first cafe is this sprawling terrace under a large plane tree. *8am-10.30pm* €	**Buna Café**: Not much for outdoor seating, though there are a few tables and chairs. This is one of the best spots for good coffee in Avignon. *8.30am-7pm Tue-Sat, 9am-3pm Sun* €

MEDIEVAL SITES

Tour Philippe-le-Bel: Climb this 13th-century tower to see the view French kings had of papal Avignon. The winding staircase is steep and narrow but the view of the rooftops, spires and river is a fair trade.

Collégiale Notre-Dame: This serene church in Villeneuve is considered one of the best examples of naturalism in the Gothic style.

Église St-Didier: This sturdy Gothic church rewards those who look beyond the obvious. Its stone nave leads to a remarkable 15th-century entombment of Christ, an outstanding example of early French sculpture.

Rue des Teinturiers: Avignon's most atmospheric street runs alongside an old canal, where 14th-century waterwheels still churn. It's now a shady, cobbled escape lined with artists' studios.

Musée Calvet

13th- to 16th-century Italian religious paintings by Old Masters. The most famous is Botticelli's *La Vierge et l'Enfant* (1470).

Tiny **Musée Angladon** *(angladon.com; adult/child €8/3)* harbours an impressive collection of realist, impressionist and expressionist treasures, including works by Cézanne, Sisley, Manet, Modigliani, Degas and Picasso – but the star piece is Van Gogh's *Railway Wagons*. Impress your friends by pointing out that the 'earth' isn't actually paint, but bare canvas.

The elegant Hôtel de Villeneuve-Martignan (built 1741–54) provides a fitting backdrop for Avignon's fine-arts museum, the **Musée Calvet**, *(institutcalvet.fr/en; free)* with 16th- to 20th-century oil paintings, compelling prehistoric pieces, 15th-century wrought iron, and the elongated landscapes of Avignonnais artist Joseph Vernet.

The **Musée Lapidaire** *(free)* is housed inside the town's striking Jesuit Chapel and is the archaeological collection of the Musée Calvet. There's a good display of Greek, Etruscan and Roman artefacts, but it's the Gaulish pieces that really draw the eye – including some grotesque masks and deeply strange figurines.

Finally, the **Collection Lambert** *(collectionlambert.fr; adult/child €12/5)* is Avignon's contemporary-arts museum. It focuses on works from the 1960s to the present. Works span from minimalist and conceptual to video and photography – in stark contrast to the classic 18th-century mansion housing it.

 EATING IN AVIGNON: BEST RESTAURANTS

Numéro 75: Chic restaurant in a *hôtel particulier* with an excellent Mediterranean menu and a stellar wine list. *noon-2.30pm & 7-10pm Mon-Fri* €€€

Graines de Piment: Affordable, tasty bistro on place de la Principale that gives disadvantaged youth a chance to gain work experience. *12.15-1.30pm Mon-Fri* €

Fou de Fafa: Four-course dinners at this Avignon staple, draw on Mediterranean and Provençal cuisines. Excellent wine list. *7-11pm Thu-Mon* €€

L'Épicerie: Classic French bistro with rustic decor in the heart of old Avignon. Plenty of hearty meat-based dishes; vegan options too. *noon-2.15pm & 7-10pm Thu-Mon* €€

A WALK THROUGH OLD AVIGNON

Stroll through Avignon's storied heart, where popes ruled, bridges broke and orchards still whisper medieval secrets.

START	END	LENGTH
Pont St-Bénézet	Ramparts	2.5km; 1½-2hr

Start from the ❶ **Pont St-Bénézet**, also known as the Pont d'Avignon. The bridge is unique in its inutility; over the centuries, arch after arch washed away during floods along the Rhône.

Cross the outer road and enter the walls of Avignon. Make your way to the shady ❷ **Jardin des Doms** (p213) with a view of Villeneuve-lès-Avignon to one side, and, as you work your way down the park, a view of Avignon to the other. Before leaving the garden, visit ❸ **Notre-Dame-des-Doms d'Avignon**. Here lies Pope Jean XXII, who anchored the papacy in Avignon during his lifetime, and his successor, Pope Benoît XII. Outside the Palais des Papes, visit the ❹ **orchards** (*vergers*), built by Pope Urban V. In a dedication to his childhood in the Cevennes, he spent large sums to maintain the orchards and nearby gardens.

Walk down the rue Banasterie to reach the ❺ **Basilique St-Pierre**. This flamboyant Gothic church begun in the 14th century is considered a good representation of the architecture and artwork of the period. Check out the ornately carved walnut door.

Finish your stroll by making your way back to the walls of the city. These ❻ **ramparts** were built during the reign of Pope Innocent VI in the 14th century to protect the city from English mercenaries during the Hundred Years' War.

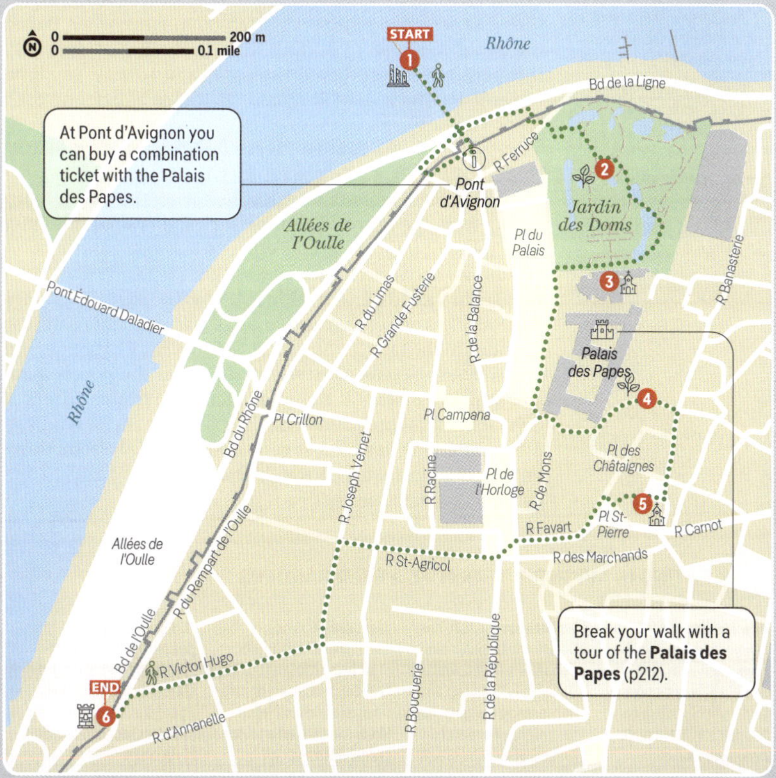

> At Pont d'Avignon you can buy a combination ticket with the Palais des Papes.

> Break your walk with a tour of the **Palais des Papes** (p212).

WORTH A TRIP: NÎMES

Not far from Avignon lies one of France's most impressive Roman cities: Nîmes. It's an easy and rewarding day trip from the Vaucluse, packed with monuments that still shape the city's rhythm today.

Start at the **Arènes de Nîmes**, a vast, beautifully preserved amphitheatre that once held up to 24,000 spectators – and still hosts concerts and events in summer.

A short walk away is the **Maison Carrée**, an elegant Roman temple so well preserved it almost looks new. Stroll the shady streets, browse the market, then pick up some picnic fare and make your way to the **Pont du Gard** (p220), en route back to Avignon.

Fort St-André

A Stone's Throw Away
Cross the river to explore Villeneuve-lès-Avignon

Begin your visit by getting a lay of the land. The climb to **Fort St-André** *(fort-saint-andre.fr; adult/under 26 €7/free)*, a 14th-century fortress atop Mont Andaon, isn't too difficult. Commissioned by King Philippe le Bel, this imposing structure was designed to assert French dominance when facing the papal Avignon – yes it's a little petty. But as you walk through its well-preserved ramparts and towers, you'll be rewarded with views of Avignon, the Rhône Valley, and even Mont Ventoux.

Indoors, visit the **Musée Pierre de Luxembourg** *(adult/child €4.50/3.50)*, inside a beautiful 17th-century *hôtel particulier*. Home to two notable works featuring the Virgin Mary dating from the 14th and 15th centuries, this small museum also holds an impressive collection of Baroque paintings.

Today an active artist and playwright residence, **La Chartreuse du Val de Bénédiction** *(chartreuse.org; adult/under 26 €8/6.50)* is one of France's largest Carthusian monasteries. Founded in the 14th century by Pope Innocent VI, the complex encompasses serene cloisters, chapels and the pope's mausoleum. Throughout the year, La Chartreuse offers a diverse cultural program, including performances, readings and exhibitions. It's almost certain there will be something on but if not, a walk through the monastery and to the gardens is worth the visit.

EATING IN AVIGNON: TERRACES & BEER GARDENS

Les Jardins d'Été: Open summers, with a visiting chef each year, this sweet little restaurant highlights local, organic food at La Chartreuse. *hours vary* €

La Fabrique: Craft-beer bar on the popular rue de la Bonneterie with a dozen beers on tap and homemade burgers. Good for catching a match. *10am-1.30am Tue-Sat* €

La Scierie: A community space that's great for families who want to enjoy a beer, a concert or an art installation and let the kids loose in an enclosed area. *hours vary* €

Le Tipi: This urban farm has a small cafe-bar perfect for grabbing a beer and visiting the gardens. Events weekly all year round. *9am-5pm Tue-Sat* €

Beyond Avignon

Within an hour from Avignon, you'll find Roman stones, Rhône wines, quiet lanes, and markets overflowing with Provence's produce.

The land around Avignon rewards the curious traveller. Head north for impressive Roman theatres in Orange and Vaison-la-Romaine, or veer east into the vine-striped foothills of the **Dentelles de Montmirail**. Villages like Gigondas and Beaumes-de-Venise pair world-class wines with views. To the south, the Pont du Gard stands tall over the Gardon River; it's an ancient architectural marvel, but also home to many nearby swimming spots. And Carpentras? Come in season for strawberries, truffles and a deep-rooted Jewish history that shapes the town's story. Whether you're sipping wine under a plane tree or wandering Roman paths, the rhythm slows as you leave the city behind.

Places

Châteauneuf-du-Pape p217

Carpentras p218

Orange p221

Vaison-la-Romaine p223

Châteauneuf-du-Pape TIME FROM AVIGNON: 30min 🚗
Wines with the Papal seal of approval

Even in the world of fine wines, Châteauneuf-du-Pape retains a special cachet. The village is located 18km north of Avignon, and its wine is arguably the best-known of the Rhône appellations, prized by oenophiles the world over.

As its name hints, the hilltop château after which the wine is named was originally built as a summer residence for Avignon's popes in the 14th century, but it's little more than a ruin now – plundered for stone after the Revolution and bombed by Germany in WWII for good measure. Nonetheless, the village itself is a perfect day trip for honeymooners to pick out a few bottles to take home and enjoy on anniversaries – this is a wine that keeps for a long time. To immerse completely while staying in the village, visit the **Musée du vin Brotte** *(museeduvinbrotte.com, from €8)*, which follows the history of a family's vineyard while giving a good insight into this prestigious wine.

If you're travelling with teens, **Château Fortia** *(chateau-fortia.com; tasting only/game €8/20)* runs a fun escape game in the vines. The clock is ticking as you follow the history of the domaine to gather the numbers needed for a code that unlocks a special reserve wine. A tasting visit awaits those who succeed.

GETTING AROUND

The easiest way to explore beyond Avignon is by car, especially if you want to spend time in villages, visit vineyards, or hit multiple stops in a day. Confident cyclists will find rewarding rides in the Dentelles de Montmirail and around Mont Ventoux. Public transport is limited but possible, with frequent trains from Avignon's central station to Orange or Carpentras and regional buses (Zou!) to Vaison-la-Romaine.

What Makes Châteauneuf-du-Pape Special?

The wine blends up to 13 varieties of grape: grenache, syrah, mourvèdre, cinsault, muscardin, counoise, vaccarèse, picpoul, terret noir, clairette, bourboulenc, roussane and picardon. Most other wines, even in France, are less complex.

Each winemaker has their own recipe. Each hectare parcel cannot produce more than 35L of wine; therefore, the grapes are all sorted and only the finest selected to use to make the wine.

Like other Côtes du Rhône wines, the Châteauneuf-du-Pape grapes are grown along the Rhône River, in clay soil topped with river rock, which absorbs the sunlight during the day and diffuses it at night, providing the roots with a constant temperature.

Carpentras
Capital of La Truffe

TIME FROM AVIGNON: **30min**, **45min**

Have a truffle lover in the family? Then a visit to the Carpentras truffle markets is a must. The Vaucluse region produces an estimated 70% of the black truffles in France.

Taking place from November to March, the Friday-morning **Marché aux Truffes** on place Aristide Briand is a far from the typically busy and buzzing markets of Provence. Here, secrecy and mystery reign as chefs and wholesalers haggle for the best deals of this rare mushroom.

Summer truffles are less sought-after but still have their fan club. From May to September, try summer truffles grated over salads, on top of omelettes or sliced, drizzled with olive oil and enjoyed on toast.

DRINKING AROUND AVIGNON: VINEYARDS TO VISIT

Château Mont-Redon: Three kilometres from Châteauneuf-du-Pape, Mont-Redon sits among sweeping vineyards. 9am-7pm Mon-Fri, from 9.30 Sat & Sun

Maison Ogier: Organic wines with lots of personality carried by the large proportion of grenache in the blend. 9.30am-6pm Mon-Sat, closed lunch

Domaine Usseglio Raymond & Fils: Family vineyard with a good selection of biodynamic wines and a friendly welcome (reservation required). hours vary.

Pavillon des Vins: Get in on the action and blend your own wine. Reserve for two people minimum at €45/person. 10am-12.30pm & 2-7pm Tue-Sat, 10am-12.30pm Sun

Carpentras Synagogue

Jewish Heritage in Provence

During the papal reign in Avignon in the 14th century, Provence's Jewish community found protection in the Comtat Venaissin, the modern-day Vaucluse region. Although Jews were initially welcomed into papal territory, by the 17th century they were forced into ghettos in Avignon, Carpentras, Cavaillon and L'Isle-sur-la-Sorgue, and many of the original synagogues were destroyed or left to ruin. The **Carpentras Synagogue** *(synagoguedecarpentras.fr; €7)*, in the centre of town, is the oldest synagogue (1367) still in use in France. Take a peek into medieval Jewish life in the subterranean level, where you'll see baths, a kosher abattoir and bread ovens. Visit Monday to Friday for self-guided tours, or arrange a guided tour through the tourism office. The synagogue's wood-panelled main level was rebuilt in the 18th century and is still a place of worship.

REGIONAL SPECIALITIES

Truffles: Black truffles are in season from November to March. St-Jean or summer truffles are in season from May to September. Don't miss a chance to try either.

Strawberries: The Carpentras strawberry has such a sweet and celebrated flavour that an entire guild and festival have sprung up to protect and promote the variety. In season from April to June.

Cherries: May sees market stalls overflowing with the *cerise des coteaux du Ventoux*. It's a protected cherry variety found only in this region.

Candied fruits: Historically the candied fruit market has been ruled by producers from the Luberon city of Apt, but a new wave of producers has made Carpentras a great place to find exceptionally good candied oranges, pears and even pineapples.

 EATING IN CARPENTRAS: OUR PICKS

Le Petit Serge: Shady wine and tapas bar attached to the fancier Chez Serge restaurant. It's not uncommon to find live music. *hours vary Thu-Sun €*

La Maison Jouvaud: This pastry shop has great *fruit confit* (candied fruit). Small dining room with quick bites. *Mon afternoons, 9am-7pm Tue-Sat, 8am-6pm Sun €*

Cercle 85: Chic restaurant with Mediterranean and Provençal dishes like Mont Ventoux pork or basil, and tomato confit prawns. *lunch only Mon-Wed, lunch & dinner Thu-Sat €€*

Brasserie É.Toq: New-wave *bistrot* open early till late with a clean-eating angle and outdoor seating. *7am-7pm Tue & Wed, to 11pm Thu-Fri, 8am-5pm Sat & Sun €*

TOP EXPERIENCE

Pont du Gard

Built in 60 CE, the **Pont du Gard** gives weight to Roman engineering. Fifty-two arches remain standing on this aqueduct halfway between Avignon and Nîmes. Rather than just stopping by on your way between cities, stay for an afternoon or night and explore the Gardon River and the villages around Pont du Gard.

TOP TIPS

- Go for a dip on the banks of the Gardon.
- Pont du Gard – beautiful but crowded, the beaches are right below the bridge.
- Collias – clear water, good beaches for picnics.
- Remoulins – near the town centre, this beach is easily accessible with fewer crowds.

PRACTICALITIES

- *pontdugard.fr/en*
- day parking €9, museum and expos €6.50-15
- 8am-midnight, museum hours vary

Architectural & Natural Heritage

The Pont du Gard and the Gorges du Gardon are both UNESCO-ranked sites and it's no surprise they're heavily visited. There is a walking trail on the *rive gauche* (left bank) side of the aqueduct.

If you're a fan of Roman architecture, it might be worth going on a guided tour to get a real sense of the construction and the human stories behind it. In July and August when it's very hot to visit during the day, consider a night visit. You'll be greeted with an enchanting surprise: light-and-audio shows that project artworks across the bridge.

Grab a Paddle

And pack a picnic: a day canoeing the Gardon River and passing under the Pont du Gard is a day well spent. The river flows down from the nearby Cévennes range.

The sparkling white beaches of the Gorges du Gardon are an ideal spot for a picnic. Several companies offer guided canoeing departures from nearby Collias. Shuttles will take you back to your car in Collias – nearly every company's last shuttle is at 6pm, so don't be late.

Other notable traces of Jewish heritage in the region include the **Synagogue of Cavaillon** and its Judeo-Comtadin Museum and the **Mikveh** (baths) of Pernes-les-Fontaines.

Wine Tasting in the Vaucluse

The French generally regard wines from the Côtes du Rhône region as table wines: not bad, but nothing special either. But not all Côtes du Rhône wines deserve their pedestrian reputation, and it'd be a shame to never taste a bottle of Gigondas, Châteauneuf-du-Pape, Vacqueyras or Beaumes-de-Venise.

All four of these appellations grow within a short drive of Carpentras (10 to 20km), making it the perfect city to start a wine tour. Growing in the limestone and ochre hills to the west, these are sun-drenched grapes that rely on water from the Rhône Valley. At the **Clos de Caveau** (closdecaveau.com; free) vineyard, go for a walk along the marked nature trail to learn more about the geology and climate of the vineyards below the sharp folds of the Dentelles de Montmirail, and then stop to taste the aromatic and powerful Vacqueyras wine in the cellar. In Gigondas, the **Caveau du Gigondas** (www.gigondas-vin.com) represents 100 small producers and offers free tastings.

Most vineyards also host tastings, but some go above and beyond to guide the senses: try **Domaine de Longue Toque** (gabriel-meffre.fr; from €10) for a detailed and personalised wine-tasting session. Wine lovers who've seen it all will love the organic and natural wine tastings at the **Domaine de Ferme St-Martin** (fermesaintmartin.com; €15) on the terraces above the village of Suzette. Accompanied by a sommelier, visitors are guided to a state of bliss before beginning a tasting of one of the finest wines in the region: Beaumes-de-Venise, famous for its *or blanc* (white gold) – sweet muscat wines, best drunk young and cold.

Orange

TIME FROM AVIGNON: 30-45min

Living Roman Heritage

Two sites may seem like a small reason to visit a city, but ancient art and culture lovers shouldn't skip Orange, 21km northwest of Carpentras. The UNESCO-protected **Théâtre Antique** (theatre-antique.com, adult/child €11.50/9.50), one of only three intact Roman amphitheatres left in the world (the others are in Syria and Turkey), is worth the visit alone. Its sheer size is awe-inspiring: designed to seat 10,000 spectators,

NO TICKET NO PROBLEM

Budget-friendly ways to explore Vaison-la-Romaine.

Window-shop on the cour Henri Fabre
Local pottery, Provençal linens and small galleries line this shady court in the new town.

Sip coffee on place Montfort
Cafe chairs sprawl beneath leafy plane trees on this mellow square for people-watching.

Cross the Ouvèze at sunset
The Roman bridge glows golden, with the medieval *cité* rising dramatically behind it.

Pick up picnic fare at the Tuesday market
Come early for strawberries, goat cheese, and just-baked *fougasse* (focaccia).

Wander rue des Fours at dusk
This narrow, stepped street catches the last of the day's light and there's often no one else at all.

EATING IN ORANGE: OUR PICKS

| **La Cantina**: Eat inside a natural cave near the Roman theatre. Generous portions for a fair price. *lunch & dinner, days vary* €€ | **La Grotte d'Auguste**: Also near the theatre, another cave restaurant has three-course menus starting around €25. *lunch & dinner Tue-Sat* €€ | **La Guinguette de la Colline**: Typical French fare at this laid-back outdoor restaurant, on the hill above the theatre. *dinner Tue-Sun* € | **Au Petit Patio**: Gastropub fare with a Provençal spin; try sweet potato tataki or a chocolate dessert with porcini mushrooms. *lunch Mon-Sat, dinner Mon, Tue, Fri & Sat* €€ |

Théâtre Antique (p221), Orange

it has a stage wall 37m high, 103m wide and 1.8m thick. You don't have to imagine how performances might have been in this theatre; the first two weeks of July, the **Chorégies d'Orange** opera festival takes place on stage. The rest of the year, book ahead for an Odyssée Sonore, an immersive light-and-sound performance that travels back in time to meet the gods and celebrities of mythology.

Orange's **Arc de Triomphe** lies less than 1km from the theatre. Once the entrance to the city of Arausio, as Orange was known in 35 BCE, the monument is so ornately decorated that scholars consider it to be an exemplary example of Roman art. Film fans might recognise it from *The Da Vinci Code*.

Day-trippers will also admire the 3rd-century mosaic *Aux Amphorettes* in the amphitheatre's **Musée d'Art et d'Histoire** *(theatre-antique. com, entry included with theatre)*.

Want to get an early start? The Thursday morning **market**, one of the oldest in Provence, dates back to the 15th century and sees more than 300 stalls weekly. For an out-of-the-ordinary lunch, reserve a table in one of the cave restaurants near the amphitheatre.

ROMAN RUINS

Gallia Narbonensis, or southern France, was the first Roman province established beyond the Italian Alps. See the amazing arenas, aqueducts and villas in **Arles** (p188), Glanum, **La Turbie** (p83) and at the **Musée d'Apt** (p244) in the Luberon.

Vaison-la-Romaine

TIME FROM AVIGNON: 1hr

Immersion in Antiquity

While Orange and Arles have the monumental Roman sites, Vaison-la-Romaine unveils more of the day-to-day Roman lifestyle. The modern city sits atop the old Gallo-Roman city of Vasio Vocontiorum, only parts of which have been excavated.

Visitor passes to the **Sites Antiques de Vaison-la-Romaine** *(www.provenceromaine.com, adult/child incl all ancient sites, museum & cathedral €9/4)* are sold for a 24-hour period, which is just the right amount of time to travel back to Roman days and follow the city's story through the Middle Ages. For younger visitors up to age 12, two of the main sites (Puymin and the Théo Desplans museum) are part of a grand treasure hunt – the game booklet is available for free at the museum.

Start at the ancient **Puymin** site, a former neighbourhood, where a hive of activity once buzzed in the shops and public squares. Also here is the huge **Maison à l'Apollon Lauré** – a manor with a feasting room, kitchen, private baths and more. Next, hit the **Musée Archéologique Théo Desplans** to admire a rich collection of marble statues and other objects. Imagine the sparks of joy and entertainment visitors must have experienced in the nearby 6000-seat theatre. Check online to see if your visit coincides with one of the regular concerts put on by the city.

No more daylight? Wander up to the spectacular walled, hilltop **Cité Médiévale** – one of Provence's most magical ancient villages – for dinner, before starting fresh the next morning with a sunrise visit to the 12th-century castle overlooking the valley. If possible, take a guided tour of the **Site Antique de la Villasse**, where local guides are adept at bringing the daily routines of residents back to life.

TOUR VINEYARDS WITHOUT A GLASS

Sometimes the best wine moments aren't about drinking.

Cycle the quiet roads between Beaumes de Venise and Gigondas, weaving through villages and climbing the hills through the vines.

Hike from Gigondas village to the Dentelles rock formations, an up-close view of the impressive scraggly peaks.

Discover tiny chapels that are perfect examples of Provençal Romanesque architecture like the Chapelle Notre-Dame d'Aubune in Beaumes-de-Venise.

Sketch in Suzette: the village is about as picture-perfect as it gets and the early/late light will make the ochre and green landscape glow.

Visit a festival: the Fête de la Vigne et du Vin takes place in May in Gigondas and the Provençal Fête Votive in Baumes de Venise is in September.

EATING IN VAISON-LA-ROMAINE: GOURMET STOPS

La Caillette: Delicious daily specials and local beers up in the medieval town. *10.30am-4pm daily* €

L'Arbre à Vins: Specialising in wines from the Rhône region, it serves homemade focaccia in the centre of the lower town. *10am-1pm & 3.30-11pm Tue-Sat* €

Bistro Du'O: Tidy design, private terrace and seasonal dishes put local ingredients and traditions in the spotlight. Reservations suggested. *lunch & dinner Tue-Sat* €€

Léone Artisan Glacier: Step back into town to try a scoop of homemade verbena ice cream. *12.30-6.30pm Wed-Sun* €

Ventoux Region

CYCLING BUCKET LIST | LAVENDER FIELDS | GORGEOUS HIKING

GETTING AROUND

A car is the easiest way to explore the region, especially for accessing remote villages, trailheads and scenic backroads. Drivers can loop around Mont Ventoux via Bédoin, Malaucène and Sault in a day, but it's worth slowing down. Cyclists flock here for the legendary summit climb, but there are gentler rides through lavender fields and forests. e-bikes make the hills more accessible, and rental shops are easy to find.

The rocky white peak of Mont Ventoux dominates the northern Vaucluse – a beacon for cyclists, hikers and road-trippers looking for Provençal panoramas. On the breezier eastern side, Sault is surrounded by lavender fields and limestone ridges, a quieter base for hiking and local food. Don't leave without tasting the nougat! At the foot of the mountain, Bédoin and Malaucène offer laid-back village life: morning markets, bike shops, cherry orchards and terrace cafes. Between the three, you'll find cool forests, gorges, Roman roads and endless options for getting outside. Whether you're here for the ride or the relaxed rhythm, the hills and plateau around Mont Ventoux run on fresh air.

Better than a Chocolate Factory
A tasty lesson in making nougat

Generations of Provençal children have enjoyed the sweet nougat made from sugar, honey and almonds that comes from the Vaucluse region. The oldest nougat-making shop is **André Boyer** *(nougat-boyer.fr)* in the centre of Sault. Keeping ancient recipes alive since 1887, its nougat is made with local lavender honey, which gives it a distinct flavour.

Don't know much about nougat? The André Boyer workshop hosts tours each Tuesday at 3pm *(€1; reservations advised)*. If you can't get a slot on the tour, here are the essentials: there are two types of almond nougat, *nougat noir* and *nougat blanc*. *Nougat noir* is made with caramelised sugar and dark lavender honey, while *nougat blanc* is made with egg whites and light lavender honey.

Cycling Mont Ventoux from Sault
The easiest way up

Ready to take on the challenge of reaching the summit of Mont Ventoux (1910m) without putting a foot down? This legendary mountain, which is often a part of the Tour de France, is a must-visit destination for cyclists. **Albion Cycles**

☑ TOP TIP

Shoulder seasons are best for visiting the Ventoux – summer is very hot and winter can be snowy.

(albioncycles.com), just outside the centre of Sault, rents both road bikes and e-bikes. The best time to cycle is in spring or autumn when the weather is mild. Winter can be chilly and windy, and summer can be extremely hot. Consider making a day of it – its about a 50km round trip but steep enough to slow you down during the climb. Pack a picnic lunch with a sandwich from the bakery **Aux Saveurs du Ventoux** next to the bike shop. Don't hesitate to add a homemade pastry to the picnic from the same shop – they're divine, and the sugar boost might help you reach the top.

The 25.7km route climbs 1152m in elevation and is the easiest of the three standard ascents of the mountain, taking cyclists through stunning lavender fields before the real work begins. It's a climb for sure, but if you need a distraction, just look around and see if you can spot a local bird of prey or a wild boar. Many portions of the road easily lend themselves to becoming an impromptu picnic spot. Once you reach Chalet Reynard, you'll have completed two-thirds of the climb. Smile for the freelance photographers just before arrival and grab their card to purchase a copy of the shot. At the top, drink a local beer, get comfy on your bike and check your brakes – the descent goes fast!

Continues on p227

HIKING THE GORGES DE LA NESQUE

For a classic walk that does not involve climbing Mont Ventoux, consider the Gorges de la Nesque.

START	END	LENGTH
Monieux	Monieux	10km; 3-4hr

This hike can be done in as little as a morning or it can be drawn out into a full-day trip. It's best in the spring or autumn, when the weather is mild and the foliage is at its most vibrant.

Start in ❶ **Monieux**, less than 10 minutes by car from Sault. Follow the ❷ **GR9**, a gradual climb that slowly leads up a hill. About 2km in, turn left on the ❸ **Sentier des Chapelles**. This gently descends to the D942 road, where there is ample room on the shoulder for walkers. It's worth detouring to the viewpoint ❹ **Le Castellaras**, from where you'll get a stunning view of the majestic Rocher du Cire cliffs.

Retracing your steps, descend into the Gorges de la Nesque, which was formed over millions of years as the Nesque River cut through the limestone rock. Here in the gorge, travellers will be surprised to find a troglodyte chapel: the ❺ **Chapelle St-Michel de Monieux**.

After exploring the chapel, continue back towards Monieux. The water levels in the gorge can vary greatly depending on the season so be prepared for different conditions. Before reaching the village, the trail goes by the ❻ **Plan d'Eau de Monieux**. In summer, a snack bar by the lake is open daily, and there's a small market on Sunday mornings. Just a few more minutes' hike brings you back to Monieux.

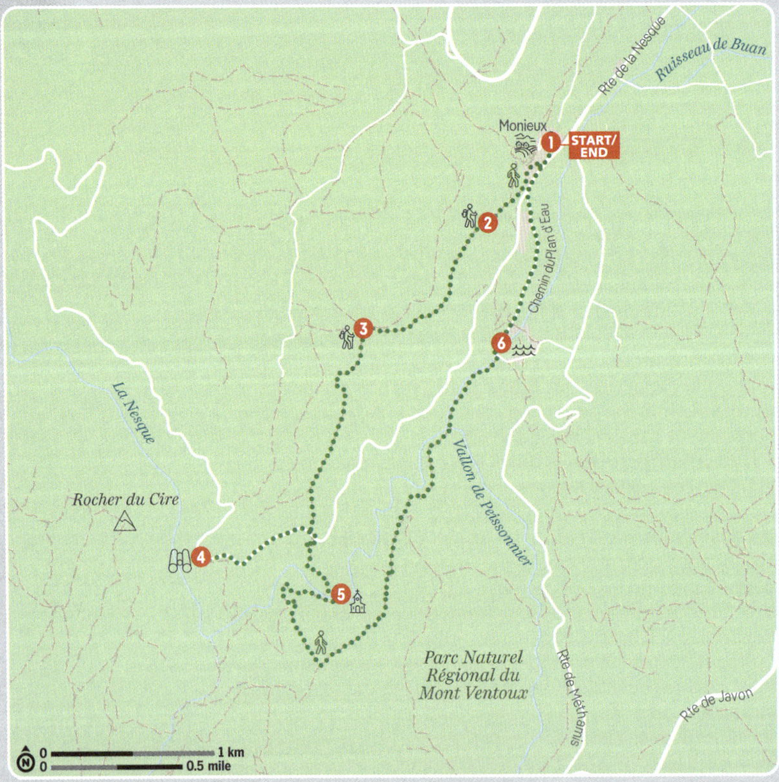

Continued from p225

Note that you can also ascend by car year-round, but you cannot traverse the summit from 15 November to 15 April, or in the case of lingering snow or dangerously high winds.

Cycling Mont Ventoux from Bédoin
The classic way up
On Mont Ventoux' southwestern flanks, Bédoin is a typical Provençal village that serves as the perfect starting point for cyclists climbing the peak. Rent a bike from **Bédoin Location** *(bedoin-location.fr)* in the village, from €25 per half-day. From here, the route to the peak is 21.3km, with an elevation gain of 1589m. The climbing grade is more consistent than the Malaucène route and the sights are more varied: it begins in the fields, climbs through forests, and then tops out in the moonscape of the wind-shorn summit.

Be sure to check the weather before departure – if the mistral wind is in the forecast, reconsider. This fierce wind, which sometimes reaches speeds of 250km/h, will definitely knock you off your bike. Bédoin is 30km west of Sault.

Cycling Mont Ventoux from Malaucène
The hard way up
Malaucène, 45km northwest of Sault, has deceptively lovely plane tree–lined streets, which hide the challenge that awaits: ascending Mont Ventoux along this northwestern route is considered to be the hardest route to the summit. To tackle this climb, rent a bike from **Provence Cycles** *(provence-cycles.com)*, from €49 per half-day. If you've decided on this route because it's the shortest (21.2km), don't think you're off the hook. You'll climb 1535m in elevation, passing a few strenuously steep sections that will put your endurance to the test. There are relatively few flat sections to give you a break.

The landscape on the northwest side of the mountain, which faces the Drome region, is different from the other routes. Conifer forests clothe the mountain slopes, and there is usually less vehicle traffic. Join the hundreds of cyclists who dream of cycling Ventoux three times – once from each direction.

Easy Walks Around Sault
Lavender-scented fields
For a family stroll, follow the **Chemin des Lavandes**, just below the village of Sault, in the direction of Mont Ventoux. The 5.3km lavender-strewn trail is well marked, and information panels periodically share the botanical properties, cultivation, harvesting and distilling techniques of the region's 'blue gold'.

Lavender fields and forests come together on a 10.6km intermediate loop from the centre of Sault through the **Bois du Défends** north of town. Start on the Ancien Chemin d'Aurel and follow the yellow hiking signs for Aurel village. The trail

---

WHY I LOVE MONT VENTOUX

Ashley Parsons, writer

I think of Mont Ventoux as a choose-your-own-adventure bike ride. There are three possible routes: from Sault, Bédoin and Malaucène. Each one is different, and each one presents its own challenge. Something about the difficulty of the climb and the encouraging applause from other cyclists at the top keeps me coming back. My favourite is from Bédoin – it's the classic way up, and the village has embraced the popularity of the ride. I find the Malaucène route to be the hardest, because the climb is inconsistent and it's harder to get a rhythm. No matter what, my number one don't-forget-to-pack item is a windbreaker for the ride back down – even in summer.

SCALE MONT VENTOUX ON THE GR4

The GR4 crosses the Dentelles de Montmirail before scaling Mont Ventoux's northern face, where it meets the GR9.

Both trails traverse the ridge. The GR4 branches eastwards to Gorges du Verdon; the GR9 crosses the Vaucluse Mountains to the Luberon. The essential map for the area is 3140ET Mont Ventoux, by IGN *(ign.fr)*. Bédoin's tourist office stocks maps and brochures detailing walks for all levels.

The Carpentras tourism office organises 24km sunrise hikes to the summit, but they can be grueling, with over 1500m of elevation gain. Departure is at 11pm – reservations, hiking boots and a headlamp are required for this €30 hike. Kids must be at least 12.

La Ferme aux Lavandes

loops back to Sault before it reaches Aurel, but if you have the energy, make the detour to visit the village's 12th-century church, perched on a hill.

Leaving from nearby Aurel, the 14.5km hike to the **Notre-Dame-des-Anges** chapel takes three to four hours and is nearly exclusively on trails and dirt tracks. Hike through lavender fields, pine forests and Provençal *maquis* or scrub, and make a day of it with a picnic lunch.

Lavender Hub

Soak up the lavender

The Plateau de Valensole is the top of many travellers' lists for lavender photos, but Sault and the plateau nearby is a hot spot for lavender too, without the crowds. Here, travellers will find working distilleries and ways to get closer to lavender essential oil production. **La Ferme aux Lavandes** *(la-ferme-aux-lavandes.com, adult/child €2.50/1.50)* is a working lavender and beekeeping farm with a charming outdoor cafe and relaxation area. For guided tours and to visit the distillery, you should call ahead: 06 82 93 52 09.

To level up in your lavender expertise and visit a distillery with plenty of activities (family-friendly!) you'll want to head to **Aroma Plantes** *(distillerie-aromaplantes.com)* nearby. It's open year-round and it's free to visit the plant library, gallery, lavender discovery room and hike, as well as the boutique. But it's worth booking ahead for a lavender soap-making workshop. For adults (€18) the workshops run on Tuesdays in summer, and for kids (€11) on Thursdays. And of course you leave with a soap or shower gel to bring the lavender memories home.

PICNIC PANTRIES

Sault's weekly Wednesday Provençal market has been running since the 16th century. Other not-to-be-missed markets in the region are in **L'Isle-sur-la-Sorgue**, **Arles** (p188) and **Aix-en-Provence** (p178).

L'Isle-sur-la-Sorgue

VINTAGE TREASURES | WATERSIDE CAFES | ART GALLERIES

L'Isle-sur-la-Sorgue is a destination for all the senses. The Sorgue River branches off into several canals throughout the village, and these canals play a key role in the town's identity. It's especially enticing in the springtime, when the village is in full bloom but the summer crowds haven't yet arrived. The town is best known for its antique *brocante* market that takes place every Sunday. All eras of vintage and contemporary finds turn up at the market, and the sellers are as passionate as they come.

For foodies, the Provençal market here is a delight for the palate. The market offers an array of local products, from tapenade to seasonal fruits, such as peaches, strawberries and cherries. For those who love to hike, a must-see is Fontaine de Vaucluse, a village situated at the foot of a cliff at the source of the Sorgue River.

A Stroll Around Town
Historic sites among the canals

The exceptional historic centre is contained within canals dotted by creaking waterwheels – the one by the tiny park at av des Quatre Otages is particularly photogenic.

In the very heart of the old town, the stately exterior of the **Collégiale Notre-Dame-des-Anges** shows no sign of the baroque theatrics inside – 122 gold angels ushering forward the Virgin Mary. Also of note is the 18th-century riverside mansion, **Campredon Centre d'Art**, a venue for seasonal contemporary art exhibitions.

Market Day
France's most bountiful region

The town of L'Isle-sur-la-Sorgue is a popular destination for travellers to Provence, and its market is one of the main draws. The market takes place year-round, with vendors setting up stalls on Thursday and Sunday mornings. It's a real pleasure

GETTING AROUND

L'Isle-sur-la-Sorgue's train station has connections to Avignon and Marseille. There is also a Zou! bus for intervillage travel, or try renting an e-bike to explore the surrounding countryside at a slower pace. The town itself is compact and walkable, with charming canalside lanes best discovered on foot. Parking in Fontaine de Vaucluse is crowded and expensive in summer – consider taking the bus to avoid the headache, especially on weekends or market days when traffic into the valley can back up. For those with a car, early arrival is key and carpooling helps. If you're travelling with kids, e-bikes or trailers might be less hassle in the end.

- **SIGHTS**
  1 Campredon Centre d'Art
  2 Collégiale Notre Dame des Anges
- **SLEEPING**
  3 Aux Heures Bleues
  4 La Magnanerie de l'Isle
  5 La Maison sur la Sorgue
  6 La Prévôté
- **EATING**
  7 Café de France
  8 Grand Café de la Sorgue
  see 6 La Prévôté
  9 Le 17 Place aux Vins
  10 Le Carré d'Herbes
  11 Les Coulisses
  12 Maison Moga
  13 Umami
- **SHOPPING**
  14 Acmaa
  see 17 Appel d'Air
  15 Blanc Kara
  16 Brun de Vian Tiran
  17 Dongier Antiquités
  18 Du Côté du Design
  19 L'Ile aux Brocantes
  20 Objets de Hasard
  21 Quai de la Gare
  22 Rives de Bechard
  23 Village des Antiquaires

to wander through the alleys and along the canals that run along the Sorgue, with the sound of the water providing a tranquil backdrop to the commercial bustle.

The market is a feast for the eyes and the taste buds, with colourful stalls selling fresh produce, flowers, artisanal crafts and delicious food. Some of the streets where the market stalls can be found include rue Carnot, rue Jean-Jacques Rousseau, rue de la République and place de la Liberté.

As you walk through the market, you'll be drawn in by the smells of freshly baked bread, lavender and grilled meats. You can sample local cheeses, jams and olive oil and pick up a handmade olive-oil soap to take home. The market is a great place to find unique gifts and souvenirs, such as painted ceramics, embroidered linens and handmade jewellery.

Antiquing in L'Isle-sur-la-Sorgue

Vintage finds await

If your manor house needs that perfect Louis XV chandelier, don't miss L'Isle-sur-la-Sorgue on weekends. It's home to one of the largest and most famous flea markets in France, with most of the antique dealers open Friday to Monday, with

☑ TOP TIP

Air-conditioning is becoming more common in French homes, but it's still somewhat rare. Copy the locals and respect a strict schedule of opening the windows at night to let in cool air and closing the shutters in mid-morning to keep out the sun and the heat.

Flea market, L'Isle-sur-la-Sorgue

Sunday being the biggest day. Twice a year, at Easter and in August, the city hosts an international Art, Antiques and Flea Fair, which attracts thousands of visitors.

You can find five main antiques villages along the canals of the Sorgue River. **Quai de la Gare**, located on av de la Libération, is home to galleries like Frédéric Bousquet and Cabanon Design. **Le Village des Antiquaires de la Gare**, located at 2 bis av de l'Egalité, is another great spot to browse. **Dongier Antiquités**, located at 15 esplanade Robert-Vasse, is a must-visit for antique lovers. **L'Ile aux Brocantes**, located at 7 av des Quatre Otages, is home to shops like l'Art et la Manière and Françoise Aillaud. And last but not least, **Rives de Bechard,** located at 38 av Jean-Charmasson, is another great option to explore for contemporary finds.

There are also a number of independent antique dealers scattered throughout town. **Objets de Hasard** is worth checking out.

Get Your Feet Wet

A canoe ride down the Sorgue

For a fresh-air adventure that's family-friendly, canoeing down the Sorgue is a must-do. Most of the canoeing companies are in Fontaine de Vaucluse, close to the source; we love **Kayak**

FARMERS' MARKETS

In Provence, there are two kinds of outdoor market: *marché Provençal* and *marché producteur*. The latter are similar to what are often called farmers' markets in English, meaning there's no middleman.

They only offer seasonal, local produce and are usually only open from June to November; there are dozens in the region. There are several close to L'Isle-sur-la-Sorgue.

Wednesday: Pernes-les-Fontaines (night market)

Thursday: Cavaillon (night market)

Saturday: Petit Palais

Sunday: Coustellet

More *marchés producteurs* can be found across the region. Check Provence Guide (provenceguide.com) for a comprehensive map and calendar.

 EATING IN L'ISLE-SUR-LA-SORGUE: TOP LUNCH SPOTS

Grand Café de la Sorgue: Popular spot with daily specials and an outdoor terrace overlooking the river. 8am-8pm €€

Café de France: Exactly what you want out of a cute French *bistrot*: antique mirrors and chandeliers with great pastries and sandwiches. 7.30am-8pm €

Le Carré d'Herbes: Cédric Brun's table serves an excellent weekday-lunch market menu outside under the arbour. *lunch & dinner Wed-Sat, lunch Sun* €€

Umami: This French fusion restaurant is excellent, with creative twists on French classics, such as *cassoulet* with maple syrup or scallop tart with yuzu. *hours vary* €€

CONTEMPORARY SHOPS

Appel d'Air: Modern antiques and objects with personality, with an emphasis on post-war lighting and ceramics.

Du Côté du Design: This store is for lighting professionals: here you'll find everything from 1950s industrial suspension lamps from Russia to cinema projectors recovered from American film studios.

Brun de Vian Tiran: Father and son foster a passion for collecting rare wools: from Arles merino to Kyrgyzstan ibex, infinite soft threads pass through their showroom.

Acmaa: A rotating associative gallery on place Xavier Battini where artists of all disciplines display their work. Frequent gallery openings – check their calendar.

Blanc Kara: Concept store near the centre of town, with on-trend furniture and textiles.

Kayaking, Sorgue River

Vert *(canoevaucluse.com)*. Riding on incredibly clear and pure water – the Sorgue springs from a mysteriously deep karst source – you'll be carried on the current downstream through tunnels of overhanging trees. Occasional gentle rapids spice things up, but this is more of a natural paddle than an adrenaline ride. The route ends near L'Isle-sur-la-Sorgue where you can dry off and hop back in the return shuttle. Operates from May to September, depending on water levels.

Relax and Get Close to the Water

Favourite local swimming spots

Looking for something even more low-key? Lounge on the banks of the Sorgue or find a great swimming spot for some relief on a summer afternoon. The most popular spot these days might be at the **Chemin Noir,** a small car park outside L'Isle-sur-la-Sorgue with direct access to the river. There are spaces for a picnic and the walk from the car park to the river

EATING IN L'ISLE-SUR-LA-SORGUE: TOP RESTAURANTS

Maison Moga: Sommeliers and cheese experts pair gourmet platters of cheese or charcuterie with the appropriate wine. *hours vary* €€

Le 17 Place aux Vins: Incredible local wine list and inventive tapas such as shrimp hot dogs, burrata with confit tomatoes or pulled pork polenta. *hours vary* €€

Les Coulisses: New *bistrot* and wine bar with live music on weekends and classic French *planches*, or charcuterie boards. *8.30am-midnight Tue-Sun* €

La Prévôté: Upmarket restaurant in the old town. Try the guineafowl with gnocchi or chestnuts with blackcurrant and smoked milk. *dinner Wed-Fri, lunch & dinner Sat & Sun* €€€

is only a few metres, so for a quick splash, it's not a bad choice. If you're up for a longer walk, there is a **parking lot** after the SPA (animal shelter) on the road connecting L'Isle-sur-la-Sorgue and Fontaine de Vaucluse. Once parked, walk along the field's edge to the river, and then down the path until you find a spot where you want take a dip. If getting in the water isn't the most important thing for you but you still want to soak up the chill vibes, the park at the edge of L'Isle-sur-la-Sorgue is the right spot: **Partage des Eaux** has a family-friendly park with a few shops and an ice cream stand.

Take a Day Trip to Fontaine de Vaucluse
The source of the Sorgue River

The village of **Fontaine de Vaucluse**, 12km east of L'Isle-sur-la-Sorgue, is known for its spring, which gushes out of a chasm at more than 90 cubic metres per second, making it France's largest karst spring and the fifth-largest on the planet. Consider this itinerary: starting off the day at 9am, head to any of the cute waterside cafes at the central roundabout to kick-start the day with a delicious cup of coffee. After that, hike up to the top of the cliffs from the Font de l'Oule. The hike is of medium difficulty and takes about an hour to reach the top.

Once at the top of the cliffs, celebrate with a picnic or snack and enjoy the view. Bring plenty of water, as the weather can be quite hot in the summer months. Afterwards, wander back to Fontaine de Vaucluse and hike 1km up to the source. The hike is a bit steep, but the view of the clear water is soothing and the chasm impressive.

After the hike, head down to the river near the Aire des Vergnes for a refreshing swim in the cold water. To be precise: the water temperature hovers around 14°C year-round. Time for an apéritif: sip on a cocktail before moving to a different restaurant for dinner. It's a tiny village with lots of options!

'DROWN THE DOG' BOATS?

In Provençal, the name of traditional fishing boats, *négo chin*, means 'drown the dog', due to their inherent wobbliness. Adapted to the shallow, clear waters of the Sorgue, they are manoeuvred with a long oar. Today, traditional net fishing is forbidden and the boats are used for pleasure.

Every year in mid-July, the Confrérie di Pescaïre Lilen, the local fishing guild that dates back to 1593, hosts La Pêche d'Antan festival, featuring these boats. There are traditional fishing-method demonstrations, races through the city's canals, boat rides and a floating market.

Occasionally, other floating markets pop up – check the town calendar online *(islesurlasorgue-tourisme.com)* or at the town hall. It's a celebration of river culture.

 EATING IN FONTAINE DE VAUCLUSE: OUR PICKS

Lou Fanou: Great for a coffee overlooking the river, and the trout tartare isn't bad either. *9am-11pm* €

Restaurant Philip: On the edge of the Sorgue, this award-winning restaurant gets busy quickly. Worth it for the location alone, but it can get busy. *10am-6pm* €€

La Vanne Marel: A charming *bistrot* with the best riverside seating, a relaxed atmosphere and stunning views of the surrounding cliffs. *noon-2am, closed Thu* €€

La Figuier: Reserve a table in advance at the best place in town. Dishes include *dorade au four* (baked sea bream) and *confit de canard*. *hours vary Tue-Sun* €€

Beyond L'Isle-sur-la-Sorgue

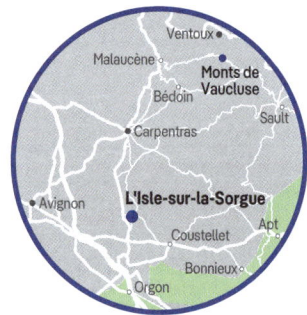

Venture into the Monts de Vaucluse to find tucked-away fountains, limestone ridges and sacred springs a short drive or bike ride from L'Isle-sur-la-Sorgue.

Places

Monts de Vaucluse p234

GETTING AROUND

There are a few Zou! buses connecting L'Isle-sur-la-Sorgue to nearby villages like Pernes-les-Fontaines and Saumane, but service is limited – check schedules in advance. For flexibility, a car is the best option, especially if you're visiting Venasque or hiking near Le Beaucet. Cyclists will find rewarding routes through the hills and forest roads, though gradients can be steep. Parking is generally easy outside high season, especially in smaller villages.

It doesn't take much to leave the bustle of L'Isle-sur-la-Sorgue behind. Just a short drive or a bike ride brings you into the Monts de Vaucluse, where forested hills hide centuries-old villages and quiet corners full of character. Pernes-les-Fontaines is a town of gently bubbling fountains and artisan studios; Venasque too has an artisanal twist, clinging to its cliffs with timeless grace. Saumane de Vaucluse guards a hulking château and sweeping valley views, while the wooded slopes beyond Le Beaucet lead to the hermitage of St-Gens, a cool, contemplative place that's at the heart of a local legend. Whether you're after culture, stillness or a scenic hike, this area is full of small discoveries that feel far from the crowds.

Monts de Vaucluse

TIME FROM L'ISLE-SUR-LA-SORGUE: **10-45min**

The château that shaped Sade

Explore the **Château de Saumane** (*adult/child €8/5*), a fortress-like manor perched above the valley that was once home to the Marquis de Sade's uncle. Young Sade – whose later writings on erotism, philosophy and radical freedom would coin the word sadism – spent part of his childhood here. The rooms, furnished with period weapons, maps and archives, offer a glimpse into aristocratic Provençal life and its darker corners. The architecture is striking: thick ramparts, stone staircases and views across pine forests and limestone ridges. A few panels hint at the Sade connection, but the atmosphere says it all. It's a moody, commanding place, and it's rarely crowded. The château was closed for renovation at the time of research; on the chance its reopening is delayed, even a stroll around the outside can spark one's imagination with bold ideas like Sade's.

CYCLING THROUGH THE MONTS DE VAUCLUSE

With 420m of altitude gain, this leisurely ride through the villages of the Vaucluse Mountains is best for intermediate cyclists.

START	END	LENGTH
Pernes-les-Fontaines	Pernes-les-Fontaines	27km; 2–3hr

Rent a bike from Vel'eau Loc in ❶ **Pernes-les-Fontaines**. Before starting, take a moment to admire the Notre-Dame gate. This ride takes cyclists through local fields where you can stop and admire the sheep or goats. The ❷ **Chèvrerie des Fontaines** has a small shop where you can sample local goat cheese.

Set your course towards ❸ **La Roque-sur-Pernes**, a Provençal village off the beaten path. The village square is welcoming and shaded, with the Fontaine du Renard and the church of Sts Pierre and Paul. Next, cycle through low-growing oak trees, looking for traditional stone shelters called *bories*. A small detour will take you to the ❹ **Borie de la Roque**, a particularly well-restored example open to visitors.

Continue cycling along the hill towards Le Beaucet, just on the other side of a small ravine.

From here, take the winding roads to ❺ **Venasque**. There are several local artisan shops and galleries worth a look. Reserve lunch at Le Petit Chose and be wowed by the local flavours like spring asparagus or summer cantaloupe. Plus, the balcony has a spectacular view of a wild gorge.

In ❻ **St-Didier**, cycle through the centre of town and take a moment to admire the Château de Thézan St-Didier. A few cafes decorate the central square. Return to Pernes-les-Fontaines, where you can attend the Wednesday evening farmers' market in the summer.

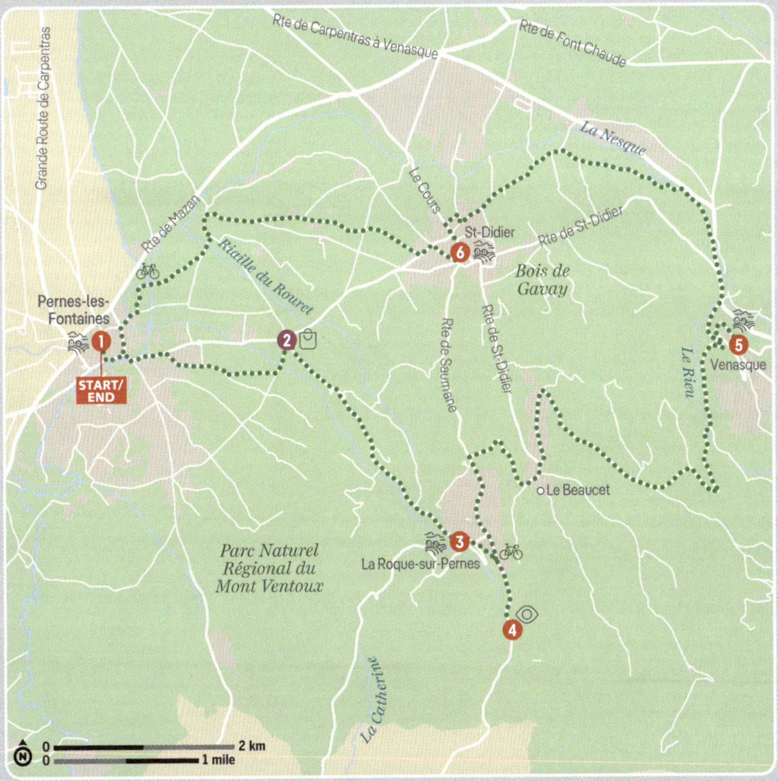

HIKING TOUR
Trek the Ermitage St-Gens

Starting from the quiet stone village of Le Beaucet, this 12km loop takes about a half-day, weaving through scrubland and folds of pale limestone to reach the hermitage of St-Gens. Along the way, you'll pass dry-stone shelters, curious rock formations and a legendary spring – all under the long gaze of Mont Ventoux in the distance.

❶ Le Beaucet

Start from the cobbled heart of Le Beaucet, a photogenic village tucked into a limestone bluff. Pop into the small chapel or just take in the view before setting off downhill. The forested path soon narrows between jagged rock outcrops, opening onto forgotten farmlands and ruined shepherds' shelters. This stretch already hints at the mix of mystery and geology that makes the trail so special.

The Hike: From Le Beaucet, descend through forest paths and cross the D247 to reach more open terrain. The limestone becomes more dramatic as you climb gradually (about 45 mins) towards the cliffs.

❷ Trogolodyte Ruins

As the trail flattens, look left – shallow caves and a crumbled troglodyte farmstead appear at the base of the cliffs. Next come dry-stone *jas* (old shepherds' shelters), perfectly nestled into the slope. These remnants of rural life tell a quieter story than the chapel ahead, but one etched into the stone.

The Hike: Continue uphill along the marked path to reach the high ridge. As you approach the rocky saddle, the landscape opens wide and the limestone formations become more and more interesting shapes.

Le Beaucet goat's cheese

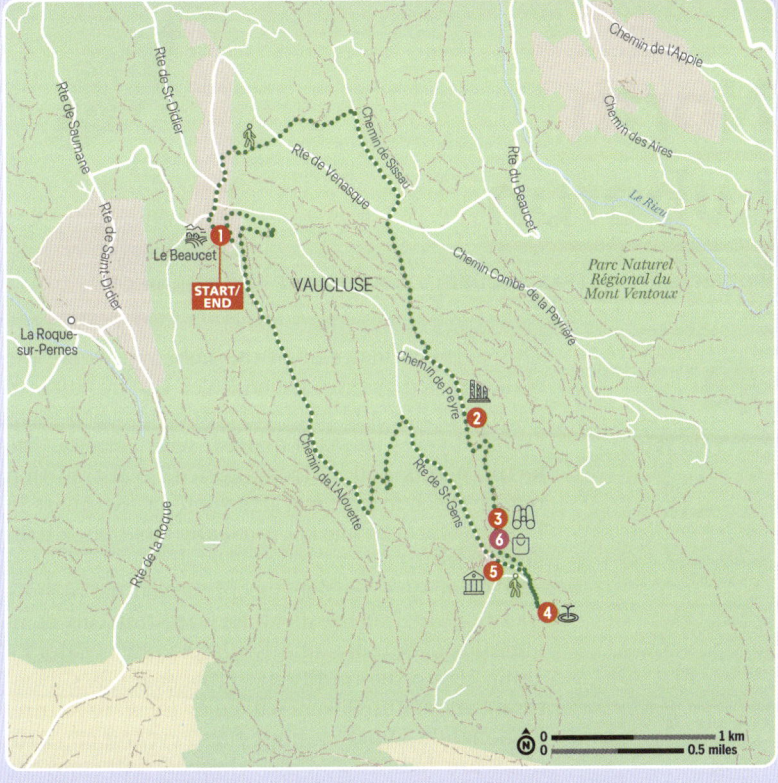

3 Demoiselle Coiffée

At 400m, this craggy outcrop offers panoramic views across the Combe de la Fontaine and towards the rooftops of Venasque. It's also home to the strange, eroded pillar known as the Demoiselle Coiffée – a limestone fairy chimney. The few steps to the peak of the rock might give you a little vertigo, but the view is even better from up high. Otherwise, stay below and continue the trail.

The Hike: From the ridge, descend steadily through forested slopes. After about 30 minutes you'll reach a few houses built into the cliff side.

4 La Bergerie

On the lower slopes of the descent sits a tiny goat farm where goats graze between outcrops and dry-stone walls. There's sometimes cheese, yoghurt or even ice cream for sale. Stop in or simply enjoy the gentle rural scene before continuing towards the sacred valley of St-Gens.

The Hike: A short, rocky climb leads into the ravine. The Fontaine de St-Gens and its chapel appear just beyond a bend in the path.

5 Fontaine de St-Gens

Pilgrims have visited this spring for centuries, drawn by the legend of St Gens, a hermit said to have performed miracles here. Today, water still flows from the source, pooling beside a small chapel.

The Hike: Head back down and take the left fork at the car park. The hermitage is a few minutes' walk following the signposts.

6 Ermitage St-Gens

Just below is the Ermitage St-Gens, built into the cliff face among cypress trees and silence. It's a tranquil, powerful place to pause – and the final reward before the trail loops back toward Le Beaucet.

North Luberon

HIDDEN HERITAGE | FARMHOUSE LUXURY | MARKETING MORNINGS

GETTING AROUND

Driving is the easiest way to get around, although a bus service does connect Cavaillon, L'Isle-sur-la-Sorgue and Manosque to Apt. There are many secure cycling lanes in the region, and with an e-bike there is hardly anywhere you can't go.

This is the wilder side of the Luberon, where the plains are fed by the Calavon River. On the flanks of the mountains and hills, villages established thousands of years ago still flourish with activity. The fertile plains and a strong agricultural tradition render the Luberon markets some of the finest in France – farm to market is usually less than a half-hour drive.

In some ways, tourism has preserved the region's traditions and the resilient, forward-thinking communities of Saignon and Reillanne offer visitors a glimpse into the traditional Provençal life. Adventurers and nature lovers will enjoy the Parc Naturel Régional du Luberon: hiking and cycling opportunities are endless, and rock climbers will enjoy the challenging cliffs in Buoux.

It's a region with memories waiting to be unlocked, and one of the best is a midsummer sunset over the lavender fields of Claperèdes, followed by a glass of rosé on the terrace.

Walking Along the Mur de la Peste

A dry-stone wall with an unnerving history

Just outside Cabrières-d'Avignon, a dry-stone wall snakes through the hills. It's a haunting reminder of Provence's 18th-century fight against the plague. Built in 1721, the **Mur de la Peste** stretched over 27km to keep infection from spreading north. Today, you can hike a peaceful loop through garrigue scrub and pine forest, following the wall as it crests ridgelines and dives into valleys. Along the way, you'll spot old watchposts, crumbling sections of wall, and wide views over the Luberon. The route is well signed and relatively gentle, making it ideal for families or history lovers looking to stretch their legs in quiet surroundings.

☑ TOP TIP

Summer is the high season in the Luberon, but the temperatures can be extremely hot. Plan your busy outdoor activities for the morning and leave time for a mid-afternoon siesta during the heat of the day.

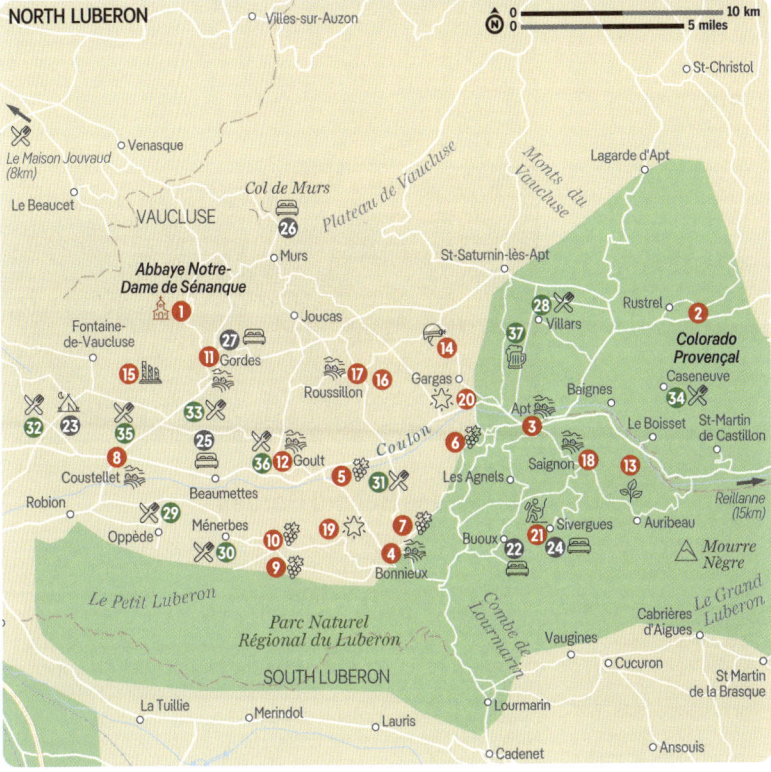

HIGHLIGHTS
1 Abbaye Notre-Dame de Sénanque
2 Colorado Provençal

SIGHTS
3 Apt
4 Bonnieux
5 Cave de Bonnieux
see 8 Cave du Luberon
6 Chateau de Mille
see 18 Château de Saignon
7 Chateau la Canorgue
8 Coustellet
see 12 Dolmen de l'Ubac
9 Domaine de Marie
10 Domaine des Cancélades
see 18 Église Notre-Dame de Pitié
11 Gordes
12 Goult
13 Le Potager d'un Curieux
14 Mines de Bruoux
15 Mur de la Peste
see 3 Musée d'Apt
16 Ôkhra Conservatoire des Ocres et de la Couleur
17 Roussillon
18 Saignon

ACTIVITIES
19 Carrières du Château de Lacoste
see 8 La Gare
20 La Maison du Fruit Confit
21 Mind Climbing
see 17 Sentier des Ocres

SLEEPING
22 Auberge des Seguins
23 Camping La Folie
24 Domaine du Castellas
25 Domaine Les Martins
26 Gite d'Étape de Murs
27 Les Milles Roches
see 17 Omma Luberon

EATING
28 Bar des Amis
29 Bistro Les Poulivets
see 12 Café de la Poste
30 Café du Progrès
see 3 Café La Félicità
see 3 Caillebotte Primeur
see 11 Clover Gordes by Jean-François Piège
see 4 Glacier Crêperie Le Tinel
see 4 JU Maison de Cuisine
see 24 La Table 1720
31 La Table des Amis
see 11 La Trinquette
see 22 L'Auberge des Seguins
32 Le Cabanon du Papi
see 17 Le Grappe de Raisin
33 Le Mas
see 11 Le Mas des Romarins
see 3 Le Saint Pierre
34 Le Sanglier Paresseux
see 11 Le Tigrr
see 3 L'Épicerie Verte Sesam Alain
see 3 L'Intramuros
35 Maison Balèti
see 17 Omma
36 Papotte
see 18 Un Jardin sur le Toit
see 3 Vin te Voilà

DRINKING & NIGHTLIFE
37 Ocria

SHOPPING
see 17 Comptoir des Ocres
see 3 Confiserie Marcel Richaud
see 17 Il Était une Flamme
see 17 Les Uns et Les Ocres

TRANSPORT
see 8 Luberon Bike Rental

Gordes

ARTISTS TO DISCOVER

Victor Vasarely: The grandfather of Op Art worked in Gordes for years. His bold, geometric canvases echo the architecture around him. Catch his work at the Vasarely Foundation in Aix.

Marc Chagall: Chagall often visited Gordes and Ménerbes, sketching Provençal scenes in the 1950s and 1960s. His works from the region turn up in travelling exhibitions – check in Avignon and Aix.

Nicolas de Staël: This Franco-Russian painter captured the Ventoux and Luberon landscape in blocks of textured colour. His time in Lagnes inspired late-period works – some are on display at the Musée Granet in Aix-en-Provence.

Pol Mara: A lesser-known Belgian pop artist, Pol Mara's dreamy, layered portraits are strikingly personal; the B&B Les Milles Roches was once the artist's home and workshop.

The Gorges Behind Gordes
The top sight, differently

If you're in the region, the 12th-century Cistercian **Abbaye Notre-Dame de Sénanque** *(senanque.fr, adult/child €8/4)* should be at the top of your list. The monks here support themselves by selling honey, lavender and essential oils to visitors. Unlike other abbeys in the region, they also open up their monastic home to visitors at certain times. Self-guided tablet tours are available for non-French speakers. If you're enchanted by the stone halls, the peaceful atmosphere and the spiritual connection, perhaps book a silent retreat for €40 per day and immerse yourself in the contemplative lifestyle of a monk.

The abbey is accessible by car but is also walking distance from **Gordes**. The most iconic hill village of the Luberon, Gordes seems to teeter improbably on the edge of the sheer rock faces of the Vaucluse plateau from which it rises. It's impossibly photogenic, but also impossibly crowded in peak season; walking a few kilometres out of town, however, is a peaceful diversion. The itinerary passes through Rouguière, Côte de Sénancole, the abbey, Ferme de la Débroussède and Les Boujolles. The route then continues to Croix des Baux, Les Grangiers and a beautiful viewpoint of Gordes before returning to the starting point. In total, the loop is 7km; expect to

EATING IN NORTH LUBERON: OUTDOOR DINING

Maison Balèti: Family-run restaurant in Cabrières-d'Avignon with Provençal fare and cocktail hour with charcuterie boards. *dinner in summer* €€

Papotte: Outdoor restaurant near Goult with a food truck and different vendors during summer. Burgers, sushi, Provençal fare. *Sat & Sun in summer* €

Le Cabanon du Papi: Outdoor wine and beer bar in Lagnes with a food-truck bar, pizzas and changing daily dishes. Reservations suggested. *dinner in summer* €

Le Mas: Lovely patio at this upmarket Gordes restaurant where you might enjoy a fine lamb with port, or freshly caught fish. *dinner Thu-Mon, lunch Sat & Sun* €€€

spend three hours, including a visit to the abbey. Follow the blue and green trail signs.

The hike begins with a slight climb up a hillside. Take a small path that descends towards the abbey if you want to see it from above or visit. Then, go back up and take the path that goes around the plateau above Gordes, which is both shaded and breezy.

Wine Tasting at a Co-op
Compare Luberon and Ventoux wines

Wine co-operatives are a great way for small farmers to pool their grapes and share the costs of turning them into wine. The Luberon was historically a region full of small farmers, and its communities came together at the end of WWI to create co-operatives that have endured, and grown, over the years. The wine produced by these co-operatives is still delicious, and the sale price is often lower.

The oldest wine co-operative in the Vaucluse region is the **Cave de Bonnieux** *(www.cave-bonnieux.com)*, which includes Bonnieux, Goult, Roussillon, Lacoste and Gordes. Among the recommended wines are the Les Safres white wine (Luberon) and the Domaine Bastide de Rodon red wine (Ventoux).

The second-largest co-operative in the area is nearby: the **Cave du Luberon** *(caveduluberon.fr)*. It celebrated its 100th anniversary in 2023 and offers one of the best affordable white wines in the region, Les Bories, a Ventoux that's perfect for a light apéritif under the trees while snacking on local tapenade. Rosé drinkers can try Ô de Léthé, while red wine enthusiasts will appreciate the complexity of Les Promises.

While tasting, be sure to ask which vineyards have apéritif nights – it's a Luberon summer pastime to visit a vineyard at sunset, taste a glass of wine and take a bottle home to accompany dinner.

Candied Fruit in Apt
The sweetest shopping trip

Apt has long been an important market town, dating back to the Middle Ages. The town's strategic location at the crossroads of several trade routes made it a centre of commerce and a destination for merchants from all over the region.

Today, the product everyone is after is *fruits confits* (candied fruits). The fruit is preserved in sugar syrup and then dried,

Continues on p244

LUBERON VERSUS VENTOUX

Luberon wines are grown in sandy, limestone-rich soil, which gives the wines a light and fresh character. The main grape varieties grown in the Luberon are grenache, syrah and mourvèdre. The wines produced here are generally lower in tannins than those from the Ventoux. They often have notes of red fruit, herbs and spices.

Ventoux wines are grown in rocky soil, which provides excellent drainage and helps to concentrate the flavours of the grapes. The grape varieties grown in the Ventoux are generally the same as in the Luberon, but because of the growing conditions, the wines produced here are fuller in body and higher in tannins. They often have notes of dark fruit, chocolate and leather.

 EATING IN GORDES: OUR PICKS

Clover Gordes by Jean-François Piège: You may recognise the stunning backdrop from *Emily in Paris*. The cuisine is a homage to braised dishes. *hours vary* €€€

La Trinquette: Stunning view. Regulars on the summer menu include Provençal aïoli and vegetable platters with chickpea sauce. *dinner Thu-Mon* €€

Le Tigrr: The more relaxed alternative to the renowned St-Tropez restaurant, this Asian-inspired restaurant puts flavour in the spotlight. *dinner in summer* €€

Le Mas des Romarins: Small snacking menu at this breezy hotel restaurant. Extremely affordable. Try a home-cooked pizza or a rabbit terrine. *hours vary* €

CYCLING TOUR

Pedalling the Luberon

With backroads galore, a wink to the agricultural fertility of the valley and twisty switchback turns to reach perched villages, cycling around the north side of the Luberon is the best way to experience what makes this region hum. It isn't just the chirping of the cicadas, but the constant movement of the entire ecosystem in tune with the seasons: from the farmers to the holidaymakers to the wildlife.

1 Coustellet

Forty years ago, the village of Coustellet was simply a crossroads, but today it's a commercial hub for the hilltop villages flanking it to the north and south. There are a few bike rental shops, such as **Luberon Bike Rental** *(luberon-bike-rental. com)*, where visitors can get equipped to hit the road.

The Ride: Follow the Calavon greenway east out of town. At Les Beaumettes (km 5), turn right onto route des Écoles to climb up to Maubec.

2 Ménerbes

It was a sleepy farming village at the foot of the Luberon range until Peter Mayle's bestselling *A Year in Provence* brought fame and new blood to the town.

The Ride: Head east out of town on the route de Bonnieux. After km 14, turn left onto route de la Valmasque and pedal up to the top of the hill, which leads down to Lacoste.

Pont Julien

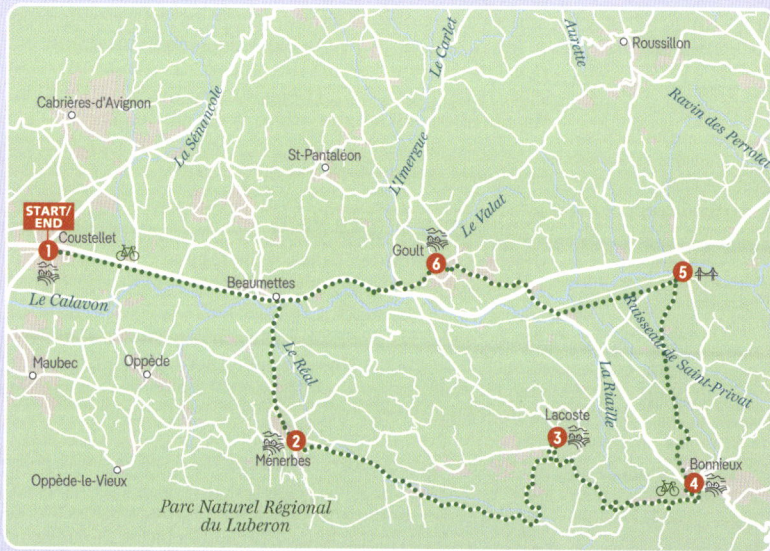

3 Lacoste

Perched on the east side of the hill, the village of Lacoste has been well restored thanks to a certain French billionaire (Pierre Cardin). An American art school has a satellite here and outdoor exhibitions sometimes decorate the town.

The Ride: Hold the course on route de Bonnieux. It's a short descent through cherry and olive groves, followed by another climb up to Bonnieux.

4 Bonnieux

This rival hill village is a bit more lively than Lacoste. Stop for a homemade ice cream at popular **Glacier Crêperie Le Tinel** (p239).

The Ride: Leave Bonnieux from the north and pick up the chemin de Gargas until it hits the D36. Turn right and then take the first left onto an unnamed road. On a map the road runs more or less parallel to the larger route du Pont Julien.

5 Pont Julien

This Roman bridge (3 BCE) is part of the Via Domitia, an important trade route linking Narbonne and Turin. Until 2005, cars were allowed to use the bridge, but today it is pedestrian or cyclist only.

The Ride: Pedal over the bridge and back, because to return you'll need to follow the Calavon greenway for a spell. Turn right on the D36, cross the river and the D900 roundabout to reach Goult.

6 Goult

A medieval village tucked behind a hill, Goult has loads of character and a tradition of fine dining. It's difficult to choose a restaurant, but try the cool garden and market menu at La Gaudina for a lunch fit for a cyclist.

The Ride: Leave Goult taking the direction 'Lumières', and then follow the Calavon greenway for the last 6km of the journey, taking you back to Coustellet.

LIVE MUSIC IN THE NORTH LUBERON

La Gare: Concerts all year long at Coustellet's former train station, now a cultural centre.

Les Musicales du Luberon: Regional musical association. Check the website for dates and artists (musicalesluberon.fr).

Carrières du Château de Lacoste: Cool acoustics in the former Roman quarry turned theatre. Hosts the Festival de Lacoste in July.

Café du Cours: The beating heart of the village of Reillanne, this live-music cafe draws visitors from all over.

Continued from p244

creating a delicious and long-lasting treat. Apt is considered the largest producer of candied fruit in the world, and you'll find a wide variety of flavours at the market, from apricots to figs to oranges. A visit to **La Maison du Fruit Confit** *(les fleurons-apt.com)* unveils the process; the shop is the best place to buy *fruit confit*. The oldest shop in town is the **Confiserie Marcel Richaud**, which is the only remaining shop to prepare the fruit by hand – its not glamour or glitz but it's great candied fruit at an unbeatable price.

Prehistory Starts Here
Discover the first residents of the region

For those interested in the prehistory of the Luberon region, start in Apt. The **Musée d'Apt** *(apt.fr/le-musee-de-l-aventure .html; adult/child €5/3)*, located in a former 18th-century mansion built on the remains of an ancient theatre, has a special collection on antiquity in the Annex Apta Julia, where the archaeological treasures of the region are presented.

Imagine discovering an ancient funerary chamber sealed off for nearly 5000 years. In nearby Goult, near the Calavon River, that's exactly what happened after days of rain flooded the local river. In 1994 the **dolmen de l'Ubac** was uncovered here, with the remains of up to 50 bodies inside. Because the site was so close to the riverbed and at risk of severe degradation, it was carefully excavated. A replica of the site is open to visitors 500m away from the original, near the old gare de Lumières.

Reach New Heights in Buoux & Saignon
Scale the Luberon cliffs

If you're looking for a thrilling adventure, climbing in Buoux is an experience not to be missed. These are some of the most famous limestone crags in Europe, and while the hard routes are *really* hard, beginners can get in on the action as well. It's not for the faint of heart, though – the area is known for its single-pitch sport climbs, with a lot of overhanging and sustained routes. **Mind Climbing** *(mind-climbing.com)* runs guided sessions for climbers of all levels. The best seasons to go are spring and autumn, when temperatures are cooler and the crowds are thinner.

DRINKING IN NORTH LUBERON: VINEYARDS TO VISIT

Domaine de Marie: Elegance and luxury are standard-bearers here; the wines are as opulent as the environment. *9am-6pm Mon-Sat, closed during lunch*

Domaine des Cancélades: Independent winemakers with reasonable prices. Fresh apricots, cherries and table grapes, too. *10am-6.30pm Mon-Sat*

Chateau la Canorgue: Near the Pont Julian, this vineyard was one of the first to go organic decades ago. *9am-6pm Mon-Sat, closed during lunch*

Chateau de Mille: With emblematic wines, this vineyard is a classic in the region, but that doesn't mean stuffy. Tours or even escape games with tastings. *hours vary*

Saignon

Above Apt, the village of Saignon oversees the valley. It was once an important centre for the production of wool and silk (many of the buildings in the village date back to this time period), but today Saignon residents live a peaceful routine, and the whole village oozes relaxation.

Wander up the streets to visit the **Château de Saignon**, a ruined medieval castle that sits at the top of the hill overlooking the village. Then weave back down to visit the cool interior of the **Église Notre-Dame de Pitié**. Built in the 12th century, the church features stunning Romanesque architecture and fading frescoes.

Small Village, Big Heart
Music and marketing in Reillanne

The intimate size of Reillanne, a small village in the Luberon Oriental, doesn't diminish its character and soul. Reillanne is a vibrant hub of social activity, largely thanks to the **Café du Cours** (*@cafedu coursdereillanne*). This cool cafe situated above the main square is a popular hangout

LOVE CANDIED FRUIT?
Apt was once the capital of candied fruit but today other artisans in the region give it a run for its money. Check out the competition at **La Maison Jouvaud** (p219) patisserie in Carpentras (it also has a branch in Isle-sur-la-Sorgue).

 EATING IN APT: OUR PICKS

Café La Félicità: Two mains per day: a Japanese dish, and an Italian one. *10am-6pm, Tue-Fri, 9am-4pm Sat* €

Le Sanglier Paresseux: An established classic. Seasonal mains might include sea bass tartare or duck stuffed with dried fruits. *lunch & dinner Fri-Mon, dinner Thu* €€

L'Intramuros: Calling the bar's rum and gin menu extensive is an understatement. Colourful vintage decor, and daily specials. *lunch & dinner Tue-Sat* €€

Vin te voilà: Small wine bar with a great local wine selection and hearty, seasonal appetisers, with lots of veggie options. *6-11pm* €€

ARTISANAL SHOPS

Bring home something beautiful from the land of ochres.

Comptoir des Ocres: Pick up small quantities of ochre pigment and gifts at this shop in Roussillon.

Les Uns et Les Ocres: Hidden in an alley in Roussillon, this little shop sells handmade pottery tinted with the natural pigments of the region.

Il Était une Flamme: Family-owned shop with all the good smells: handmade candles and diffusers in fresh natural scents like cedar, orange blossom and lily of the valley. Nice selection of authentic vials of *parfum de Grasse*.

for locals and visitors of all ages. The cafe's Friday night concerts have become the centrepiece of the village's social scene, showcasing the musical talent of both established and up-and-coming artists. The good news is that the village's music scene is due to expand. Rumour has it that a group of friends who frequent the Café du Cours have purchased the old Café de la Place nearby and transformed it into the **Multiverres** (multiverres.fr), which is set to host live music concerts every Saturday night. So, if you're a music lover, a weekend in Reillanne is all you'll need to get your fix. Come and experience the soul of the village through its music, food and friendly vibe.

After the music and dancing, shake off the Sunday morning blues with the **Grand Marché de Reillanne**. You can't miss it – the stands take over the centre of town. It's one of the most authentic places to buy local olive oil, lavender essence and farm-fresh eggs and chickpeas. Many of the vendors are producers themselves. Don't expect everything to look perfect, but do expect a great selection of organic and biodynamic produce. The beefsteak tomatoes are always full of flavour, which should be reason enough to make a stop here.

EATING NEAR APT: PICNIC OR DINE

L'Épicerie Verte Sesam Alain: Excellent little market with organic produce and a wide selection. *8.30am-1pm & 3.30-7.30pm Mon-Sat* €

Le Saint Pierre: A local favourite, this bakery and pastry shop uses high-quality bread flour. *hours vary* €

Caillebotte Primeur: Lots of organic fruit and veg, plus local specialities in this corner shop. *9am-12.45pm & 3-9pm Mon-Sat* €

Un Jardin sur le Toit: The best restaurant in Saignon. Try mains like braised pork cheek, chickpeas and carrot gel or octopus with saffron. *lunch & dinner Fri-Tue* €€

Plateau de Claparèdes

Into the Inner Luberon
Explore the Luberon mountains

The **Château de Buoux** outside the town of the same name is a peaceful and secluded spot in the Grand Luberon, perfect for those seeking tranquillity and natural beauty. Closed to the public for renovations, it serves more as a starting point for exploring the surrounding forests. There are several trails that lead through the nearby hills and forests.

If you keep climbing the road after Saignon, **Plateau de Claparèdes** will be your destination of the day. It's known for its stunning lavender fields and remoteness. Compared to the more famous **Plateau de Valensole** (p266), the Claparèdes is far less crowded, making it the perfect destination for those who prefer a more peaceful and relaxed atmosphere.

Visitors to the area can hike from the hamlet of **Sivergues** to explore the lavender fields and take in the stunning scenery. The hike offers a variety of terrain, from flat meadows to rocky outcroppings, and takes approximately two to three hours round trip.

LAVENDER: AN ESSENTIAL ESSENCE

Lavender lovers may already be familiar with the world-famous Plateau de Valensole, but the lavender-growing region stretches much further. Looking for the perfect souvenir? Popular items include soap, bulk lavender and essential oils, all of which you'll find throughout Provence.

Essential oils have a particularly high markup – a tiny vial can sell for €11 to €15. But if you have a number of gifts to buy, consider buying a bulk-sized bottle of essential oil at a local market. Reillane, Sault and Banon all have producers selling 500ml bottles for about €20, and you can transfer this yourself to smaller bottles – it's the perfect way to bring home a gift for everyone at an affordable price. Plus, you'll be supporting independent farmers.

 EATING IN NORTH LUBERON: COUNTRYSIDE EATS

L'Auberge des Seguins: The restaurant of this country-chic Buoux hotel serves simple lunches, hearty salads and desserts. *lunch hours vary Apr-Nov* €€

La Table 1720: In Sivergues, fixed-price menus, with sharing plates and micro-seasonal mains. Goat cheese and vegetables from the garden. *lunch & dinner* €€

La Table des Amis: With two Michelin stars, this Bonnieux restaurant is not cheap but it's unforgettable and brings technical finesse to its menu. *dinner* €€€

JU Maison de Cuisine: At Bonnieux's new Michelin-star restaurant, you might enjoy a trout from the Sorgue or dessert infused with basil. *lunch & dinner Fri-Tue* €€

PROTECTED LANDS

The **Parc Naturel Régional du Luberon** covers over 2500 sq km. It was created in 1977 to protect the region's natural and cultural heritage, and is home to a variety of wildlife, including wild boars, roe deer and red squirrels.

The cliffs in the park are also home to a variety of rare birds, such as the Bonelli's eagle, peregrine falcon and eagle owl. These birds can often be seen soaring high above the park.

The cutest animal to call the park home is the genet, which looks kind of like a ferret if a ferret had spots like a leopard and a mask like a racoon. Sightings are rare. The **Maison du Parc** (visitor centre) is in Apt (p241).

Parc Naturel Régional du Luberon

The lavender fields of the Plateau de Claparèdes are at their most vibrant in late June and early July, when the flowers are in full bloom. Wander through the fields and take in the sights and scents of the lavender, which has been cultivated in the region for centuries. On the drive home, stop at the **Auberge des Seguins** (p247) in Buoux for a drink.

Painting Workshops in the Ochre Hills
Where art and industry meet

The ochre of **Roussillon**, 13km west of Apt, has brought the region world fame. But for centuries myths have whirled around the village: that the cliffs are red because the lord of the city was tricked into eating his wife and subsequently threw himself into the void, or that the Titans built a fire cannon in a cave on Mont Ventoux, which burned the hillsides red for all eternity.

Admire the bright colours of the village houses and visit the **Ôkhra workshop** *(okhra.com, tours adult/child €10/7.50)*, located in the old factory at the Écomusée de l'Ocre. Sign up for a guided visit; in the summer, there is also a two-hour children's workshop to learn how to paint with ochre. The arts aren't only for kids, though – artists can treat themselves to an initiation to decorative painting. The six-hour workshop covers the basic techniques of painting and takes place monthly, depending on reservations. The pigments can be purchased in the shop to take home and continue the fun.

Engulfed by visitors during the high season, the **Colorado Provençal** *(coloradoprovencal.fr, per car/bicycle/pedestrian €8/3/2)* outside of Rustrel, 10km northeast of Apt and 21km east of Rousillon, is a former ochre and iron mine. A protected natural site displays the tracks, basins and pipes from the industrial era. Go early in the morning to avoid the heat and the crowds.

For fewer crowds, try an underground spot: the nearby **Mines de Bruoux** *(minesdebruoux.fr, adult/child €9.50/7.50)*, where you can don a helmet and visit the ochre quarries. The roofs of the tunnels reach up to 12m in height. Or go for a short hike on the **Sentier des Ocres** in Roussillon, to see the ochre cliffs dotted with bright green pine trees.

HEIRLOOM SEEDS

Think the local fruits and vegetables stop at the *melon de Cavaillon* (Cavaillon melon) and the *frais de Carpentras* (Carpentras strawberries)? Think again.

In Provence, 'agriculture ethnographer' is a real profession and seed saving here is alive and well. The region is home to many heritage varieties, like the small and square *poivrons de Lagnes* (Lagnes peppers), the delicious *tomate de Gigondas* (Gigondas tomato) or the adaptable *aubergine rond de Valence* (round Valencian aubergine).

You can snag a few plants or a bag of seeds at **Le Potager d'un Curieux** outside Saignon, or visit its stand at the **Marché d'Apt** on Saturdays. Otherwise, keep an eye out for ready-to-enjoy local varieties at *marchés de paysans*, which are local farmers' markets, particularly active in summer.

EATING & DRINKING AROUND ROUSSILLON: OUR PICKS

Bar des Amis: Don't miss the *hot dog du Luberon* or the grilled avocados in this *bistrot de pays* in Villars. *8.30am-1.30pm & 5.30-9pm Wed-Sat, 8.30am-3pm Sun* €

Ocria: The local microbrewery in St-Saturnin-lès-Apt, with a tasting room to enjoy the five types of organic beer. *hours vary* €

Le Grappe de Raisin: Balcony in the centre of Roussillon with cafe fare like steak, housemade chips and Provençal aïoli. *hours vary* €€

Omma: Be sure to reserve at this central Roussillon upscale *bistrot* with spectacular views and rapidly changing menus. *lunch & dinner Sat-Wed* €€

South Luberon

SUNNY ROSÉS | PROVENÇAL CHÂTEAUX | SOFT LUXURY

☑ TOP TIP
Obtaining restaurant reservations is a local sport in the Luberon. If you want to go to a trendy restaurant, no matter its price point, book a table well in advance.

The hot sun, rows of vineyards and dense villages define the South Luberon. The area tends to attract a chic vacation crowd, thanks to its proximity to Aix-en-Provence and the proliferation of excellent gourmet chefs who have taken up residence in the area. But there is an equilibrium here between chic tourism and down-to-earth activities. One of the standout markers of this equilibrium is the agro-ecology movement, spearheaded by renowned chef Nadia Sammut.

For those seeking a deeper connection with nature, a hike up to the Forêt des Cèdres is a must. This beautiful forest is filled with towering cedar trees and permits views of the surrounding countryside. Cycle or drive through the region and stop at one of the many Provençal châteaux to try to region's rosé. And after a day of exploring the land and the bounty it offers, nothing beats a leisurely stroll through Lourmarin.

GETTING AROUND
Driving is the easiest way to get around, although there are many secure cycling lanes in the region, and with an e-bike, there is hardly anywhere you can't go. ZOU! bus 909 connects Apt with Aix-en-Provence via Bonnieux, Lourmarin and Cadenet, 914 connects Apt with L'Isle-sur-la-Sorgue via Bonnieux and Goult, and certain 917 services connect Apt with Cavaillon via Roussillon and Gordes. Buses are infrequent.

Visit Museums in Ansouis
Learn something while indulging

While the Luberon is the more laid-back and relaxed side of the range, you can still make a visit here educational! Visit the **Musée des Arts et Métiers du Vin** *(adult/child €5/free)* in Ansouis, an interactive wine-tasting experience where you can learn about the six generations and more of the vineyard at the Château Turcan. Also in the village, tucked into a vaulted cellar, the **Musée Extraordinaire** *(musee-extraordinaire.fr; adult/child €4/2)* is a wonderfully eccentric private museum, where artist Georges Mazoyer displays his collection of underwater treasures, coral sculptures and surreal, maritime-inspired art. It's quirky and colourful and lends itself to reflection on the unknown worlds underwater.

- **HIGHLIGHTS**
1 Forêt des Cèdres
- **SIGHTS**
2 Ansouis
3 Château de Sannes
see 9 Château du Grand Pré
4 Château Fontvert
5 Château La Verrerie
6 Cucuron
7 Lourmarin
8 Musée des Arts et Métiers du Vin
see 2 Musée Extraordinaire
9 Vitrolles-en-Luberon
- **SLEEPING**
10 Aux Deux Fontaines
11 Camping Les Chênes Verts
12 Domaine de Fontenille
13 Domaine La Parpaille
see 9 Gite d'Étape de Vitrolles en Luberon
see 7 La Maison de Lourmarin
14 L'Auberge La Fenière
see 7 Le Moulin Lourmarin
15 Le Paradis Chambre d'Hôtes
see 2 Un Patio en Luberon
- **EATING**
see 14 Auberge La Fenière
16 Chez Lulu
see 2 La Closerie
see 7 La Maison de Gibassir
see 6 La Relève
17 La Source
see 9 Le Vieux Presbytère
see 2 Les Terrasses d'Ansouis
18 Maison Amore
see 6 Matcha Restaurant
see 6 Moris Restaurant
see 2 Pâtisserie Volpert
- **DRINKING & NIGHTLIFE**
see 7 La Maison Café
see 7 Le Bar du Moulin
- **SHOPPING**
19 À l'Ombre de l'Olivier

Lourmarin's Golden Hour

Go for a cocktail walk

As you pass through the Luberon massif via the deep, cliff-lined Combe de Lourmarin, the first village you'll strike is **Lourmarin**. Once a quiet farming town, it's now a chichi place, with streets lined with upmarket homewares shops and boutiques. Literary pilgrims might also want to peep into the town cemetery, the last resting place of Albert Camus, who was living nearby when he was killed in a car accident in 1960.

If you've got dinner reservations here, you could go out for a pre-dinner drink first. **La Maison Café** is a laid-back and intimate spot with classic cocktails at good prices. It's a great place for a spritz. **Le Bar du Moulin** is the chicest spot in town for a pre-dinner drink. It offers plenty of innovative cocktails, but its mojito with Provençal citrus is a must-try that will reinvent the drink for you.

MARKET DAYS IN THE LUBERON

No need to wait until the weekend to visit a produce market. With so many villages in the vicinity, there is one every single day of the week.

Prices are not always cheaper than the supermarket, but the products often come from nearby and are frequently sold straight from the farmer. Think like a chef: choose one of the in-season ingredients and make it the centrepiece of your meal.

Monday: Lauris, Cadenet

Tuesday: Lacoste, Cucuron, La Tour d'Aigues

Wednesday: Coustellet (summer nights)

Thursday: Mirabeau, Ménerbes

Friday: Lourmarin, Bonnieux

Saturday: Petit Palais, Apt

Sunday: Ansouis, Coustellet, Puyvert

Lourmarin

Road Trip Through the Hills
Queue up your Provence playlist

Just have one day in the South Luberon? Rent a vintage car and hit the road to discover the châteaux of the area and the unique character traits of each village. Start in chic **Lourmarin** – you can't choose a bad cafe as long as it's in the centre with good people-watching.

Get the car in gear and make for **Ansouis**. The part-fortified village's elegant history is still felt in the air today – Ansouis was previously a summer residence for the nobility of Aix-en-Provence. Ramparts, watchtowers and gateways ring the village's old centre, and it's also home to one of the rare Luberon châteaux that's open to the public; reservations are required.

Next on the route is **La Tour d'Aigues** and its Renaissance château, which today houses a *faience* (clay pottery) museum. Pick up local olive oil nearby at **À l'Ombre de l'Olivier** boutique. Nearby **Mirabeau** has a fascinating fortress, but it's more famous as the backdrop for the cult films *Jean de Florette* and *Manon des Sources*. If you watch any French film before or during your trip to Provence, one of these is ideal.

Continues on p254

EATING IN SOUTH LUBERON: ECO-RESPONSIBLE RESTAURANTS

Moris Restaurant: A top table in Cucuron. Dine on the patio where daily specials might include sole with sweet potatoes and passionfruit. *hours vary* €€€

L'Auberge La Fenière: In Lourmarin, with vegetarian and gluten-free dishes, using ingredients from the restaurant's garden. *lunch Wed-Sun, dinner Thu-Sun* €€€

Matcha Restaurant: Cucuron's modern health-oriented restaurant: the *plat du jour* might be vegetable Wellington or a homemade hot dog. *hours vary* €€

Chez Lulu: Enjoy a local fish of the day with roasted chard and fennel confit in this Lauris restaurant. *lunch & dinner Fri-Tue, lunch Wed* €€

A WALK IN THE FORÊT DES CÈDRES

Explore the **Forêt des Cèdres** and discover the beauty and diversity of nature.

START	END	LENGTH
Chemin de Recaute car park	Chemin de Recaute car park	14km; 4hr

Sprawling across a vast plateau in the Luberon mountain range, this forest was established from seeds that originated from the Middle Atlas Mountains in North Africa. To explore the area on foot, start at the car park located at the northern end of the ① **Chemin de Recaute**, northwest of the town of Lauris. The walk involves a total elevation gain of about 500m. It's a moderate trek that takes around four hours to complete at a leisurely pace.

As you begin your hike, follow the signs for the Forêt des Cèdres. To start climbing up, you can take the ② **Combe de Recaute**. During the hike, the path sweeps around and runs through the ③ **Vallon du Gros Ubac**, which is the shaded side of the mountain. At ④ **Vallon de Lare**, the path splits, and hikers turn left to climb up to the Forêt des Cèdres. Here begins the moment when you will be surrounded by towering trees and the invigorating scent of cedar.

Once you reach the ridge, follow the ⑤ **Sentier de la Forêt des Cèdres**, which winds through the impressive and shady forest. As you begin to descend, with ⑥ **Vallon de Sanguinette** on your left, the rocky path has a few technical switchbacks. At the split for Vallon de Lare, continue hiking straight south. You will see two paths: one on the left and one on the right. Take the left path down, which hugs a steep hill covered in scrubby forest. You'll pass through ⑦ **Vallon de Roumias** on your way back down to the car park.

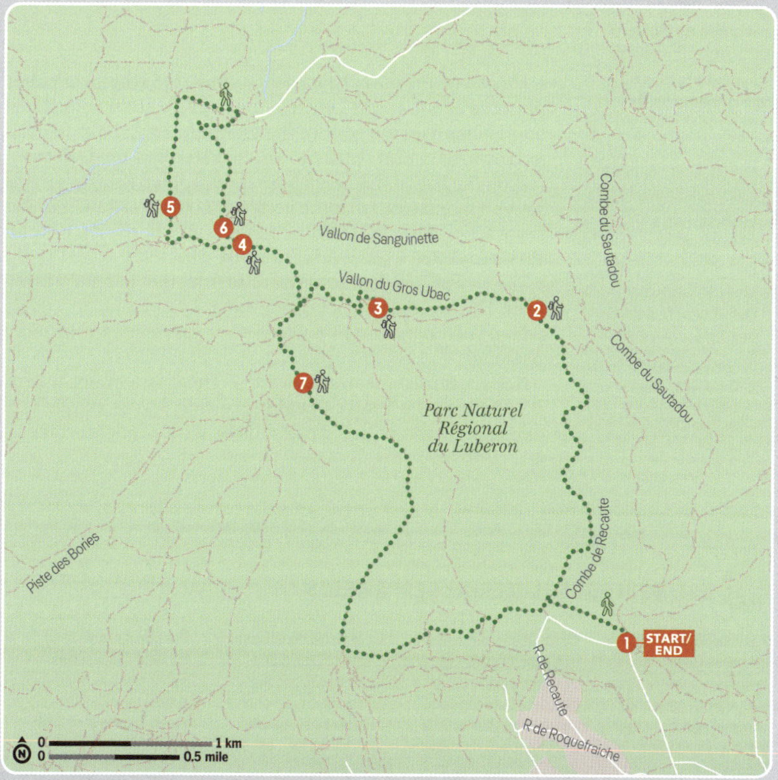

BEST ANNUAL EVENTS

Festival Vins & Passions: In late July, this is an elegant afternoon of wine tasting, small-plate dining and wellness, celebrating the region's viticultural heritage (*passion-luberon.com*).

Fête de la Musique: This takes place across France on 21 June but Lourmarin does a great job: open-air concerts, street performances and a bubbling atmosphere.

Marché de Noël: In Cucuran, the central pond and square are illuminated by the Christmas market, one of the cutest in the region. Don't expect too much snow.

Le Fascinant Weekend: At the end of the October, vineyards across the Vaucluse set up events for one last hurrah before winter. Expect anything – concerts, workshops, hikes and dinners.

Continued from p252

It's based on the novel *L'Eau des Collines* (1963) by local writer Marcel Pagnol. In the centre of town sits a statue of protagonist Manon on the edge of the fountain. You'll have to head northwards and inwards to reach **Vitrolles-en-Luberon**, last on the list, and less celebrated than other villages on this route. The château from the period of Louis XVI here is under renovation, but it's already possible to visit parts of **Château du Grand Pré** (*chateaudugrandpre.com, €12*).

The view of Montagne Ste-Victoire from the château is beautiful. The fact that it's being renovated by a passionate couple whom you might run into makes the experience all the more personal.

Need a refreshment afterwards? There is a sweet hikers' B&B named **Le Vieux Presbytère** that serves simple fare and cool drinks in this small village, with a quiet terrace.

EATING IN SOUTH LUBERON: BEST SWEETS

Pâtisserie Volpert: Inventive desserts like *le mistral*, a swirly treat with walnut ganache, caramel and *chou* pastry. In Ansouis. *8.30am-7pm Wed-Sun* €

Chez Jarry: In the heart of Cavaillon, this cafe and patisserie is the regional go-to for Yule logs and summer desserts. *8am-7.30pm Tue-Sat, to 1pm Sun* €

La Maison de Gibassir: Come to Lourmarin to try a *gibassir*, the anise-flavoured cookie, or a caramel-apple *lourmarinoise*. *6am-7pm Tue-Sun* €

Maison Amore: In La Motte d'Aigues, this patisserie has homemade products with a Provençal twist. Try the king cake in winter. *hours vary* €

Vineyard, Château La Verrerie

A Day of Wine and Wheels
Savour the Luberon naturally

Many of the grand homes of Provence have their own vineyards. These châteaux are in step with the times, with historic estates now embracing organic and biodynamic methods. For a leisurely wine-themed day out, explore by bicycle. Start near Puget at the **Château La Verrerie** *(chateau-la-verrerie.com)*, an organic vineyard that stretches into the flanks of the Luberon.

Several guided visits are available (reserve in advance), but if you've got the time and no lunch plans, the €65 visit to the vineyards and picnic lunch is worth it (and a great photo op).

Next pedal about 10km to the **Château Fontvert** *(fontvert.com)*, a small biodynamic vineyard with a passionate team that's anything but snobby. Smart cyclists will have brought saddlebags for the inevitable souvenir bottles. Another 45 minutes on the bike – around 10km – and you'll reach the last stop of the day: **Château de Sannes** *(chateaudesannes.fr)*, near Sannes. Taste a 1603 label rosé and check its calendar if visiting in summer, since there are plenty of sunset events.

NICE WHEELS

Looking to add some extra flair to your road trip? Why not rent a classic car for the day from **Yes Provence** *(yesprovence.com)* and drive in style.

While you may not have access to modern amenities like air-conditioning, the classic charm of a Citroën 2CV, Méhari, VW bug or even a VW minibus will more than make up for it.

And if you've been dreaming of cruising around in a classic Renault 4L, **Voitures Passion** *(voiturespassion.com)* near Aix-en-Provence has got you covered. Plus, with its convenient delivery service, you won't even have to worry about picking it up yourself.

EATING IN SOUTH LUBERON: OUR PICKS

Les Terrasses d'Ansouis: Carefully prepared Mediterranean dishes with sunset views from the terrace. *lunch & dinner Fri-Tue* €€€

La Closerie: Michelin-star restaurant in Ansouis with panoramic terrace and Provençal dishes. *noon-1.30pm & 7.30-9pm Mon, Tue, Fri, Sat, noon-1.30pm Sun* €€€

La Source: Cadenet's chic *bistrot* where you might find old-style French dishes, like a fish *ballotine* or marinated tuna with artichokes. *hours vary* €€

La Relève: *Bistrot*-style Provençal fine dining in Cucuron with a big wine list and exceptional seasonal dishes. *noon-2pm & 7-9pm Wed-Sun, noon-2pm Mon & Tue* €€

Places We Love to Stay

$ Budget $$ Midrange $$$ Top End

Avignon Map p211

La Banasterie €€ In the centre of Avignon, find yourself in one of those old, upmarket hotels you see in films – excellent service, interesting guests and tasteful design.

La Mirande €€€ Easily the grandest hotel in Avignon; you can pretend you're royalty here amid the luxurious 19th-century decor.

La Divine Comédie €€€ Theatre fans coming for the festival in Avignon can get a feel for old-world luxe in this private B&B.

Château de Varenne €€€ Decadent rooms in this sunny château near Villeneuve-lès-Avignon. A little on the pricey side but service and comfort are guaranteed.

Carpentras & Beaumes-de-Venise

Metafort €€ Can't hype this place up enough. Book the tiny house in the cave – you won't regret it. And order breakfast to enjoy on the terrace.

Domaine de Bellevue €€ Guesthouse (gîte) and rental cottage outside the village of Beaumes-de-Venise with budget-friendly rooms. Shady grounds, a small pond and the chic vintage style all add to the charm.

Mas l'Evajade €€ Farmhouse with regular rooms or the option to sleep in a huge wine-barrel-lined bedroom in the heart of the Domaine du Rocher des Dames vineyard in Beaumes-de-Venise.

Hôtel le Blason de Provence €€ A 15-minute drive from Carpentras, on the edge of the charming village of Monteux.

Mas Les Fleurs d'Hilaire €€ This 18th-century restored farmhouse has five stylish rooms, a garden and a pool.

Château Martinay €€€ Spend a luxurious night in this castle on the western outskirts of Carpentras.

Orange

Château du Mourre du Tendre €€ This guesthouse in the garden of the castle grounds is surrounded by Châteauneuf-du-Pape vines; there's pool access too. Don't miss the wine tastings.

Grand Hôtel d'Orange €€ Pretty and modern hotel in the centre of Orange. You can feel like royalty without the high price tag.

Ventoux Region Map p225

Aurel Inattendu € Comfortable, no-frills wooden roulotte (caravan), overlooking lavender fields.

La Bastide de la Loge €€ House rental a few kilometres outside Sault on the plain below Mont Ventoux.

Maison Leonard du Ventoux €€ In the centre of Sault, a large B&B of five rooms with great linens and a private garden and just two steps from shops and cafes.

Parcel Tiny House €€ On an alpaca farm outside Barroux, a cute tiny house with an enormous bay window to watch the goings-on of the farm.

L'Isle-sur-la-Sorgue Map p230

La Magnanerie de l'Isle €€ Character-filled guesthouse in a former industrial building in the heart of the historic centre.

Mas la Vitalis €€ Magali's B&B consists of two inviting bedrooms in a calm, restored farmhouse outside the town.

La Prévôté €€ Five-bedroom B&B with large, comfortable rooms and Provençal views.

Aux Heures Bleues €€€ B&B in the centre of L'Isle-sur-la-Sorgue with a boho yet chic design.

La Maison sur la Sorgue €€€ Historic boutique hotel with sumptuous suites and a hidden garden with a small stone pool.

Monts de Vaucluse

La Bergerie Pradel € Smart hotel in a renovated 16th-century villa surrounded by forests. Close to Le Beaucet.

Le Cabanon des Secrets €€ In La Roque-sur-Perne, this cool B&B made from stone is great for week-long stays.

Villa Chante Coucou €€ In the hills above Fontaine de Vaucluse, this is worth it for swimming with a view over the cliffs. Good value for the location and more than comfortable.

Enamoura €€€ This charming artsy vacation home in Saumane fills up quickly, but it's like staying in a spread from an architecture magazine.

North Luberon Map p239

Gite d'Étape de Murs € Simple dorm-style lodging, from €30 without dinner (€51 with dinner).

Camping La Folie € Simple, choose-your-own pitch campground near Lagnes.

Les Milles Roches €€ Trendy, artsy guesthouse in Gordes. Rooms or a home for up to six people, designed with light, simplicity and style.

Auberge des Seguins €€ Secluded B&B with a pool and view of the cliffs of Buoux. Restaurant and cafe on site.

Domaine du Castellas €€€ Farm converted into a luxury hotel in Sivergues. Community dining and loads of activities.

Domaine Les Martins €€€ Quiet guesthouse with lovely gardens near Gordes. It's an expensive area but a good deal for the calm and beauty.

Omma Luberon €€€ Stick around Roussillon after the crowds go home and enjoy the best views of the ochre hills from this classy hotel's windows.

South Luberon Map p251

Gite d'Étape de Vitrolles-en-Luberon € A great budget option for families or groups, this homestay offers half-board and a quiet stopover.

Camping Les Chênes Verts € Small lakeside campground near the Étang de la Bonde; it's basic but not expensive and it's kid-friendly.

Aux Deux Fontaines €€ A favourite spot – Provençal chic in Vaugines with great decor and an attentive but not overbearing host. Get the breakfast for homemade jams.

La Maison de Lourmarin €€ Chic rooms in this small house in the centre of Lourmarin. Laundry and kitchen available.

Un Patio en Luberon €€ In the centre of Ansouis, a beautiful stone B&B with spacious beds and bathrooms.

Domaine La Parpaille €€ Sunny, simple design in the countryside near Cucuron.

Le Paradis Chambre d'Hôtes €€ Secluded little B&B near Vaugines with a nice pool surrounded by greenery.

Domaine de Fontenille €€€ Bathed in decadence, with a touch of well-being. Friday nights are for barbecues in the garden. About 2km northwest of Lauris.

L'Auberge La Fenière €€€ Comfortable rural hotel near Lourmarin linked to the Michelin-starred restaurant and farm of chef Nadia Sammut.

Le Moulin Lourmarin €€€ Popular boutique hotel in the centre of Lourmarin; large bright rooms are a safe bet.

La Mirande, Avignon

For places to stay in Alpes-de-Haute-Provence, see p282

Above: Moustiers-Ste-Marie (p262); Right: Lavender field, Plateau de Valensole (p266)

Researched by
Ashley Parsons

Alpes-de-Haute-Provence

FROM ALPINE VALLEYS TO LAVENDER FIELDS

The Plateau de Valensole, Gorges du Verdon and the southern Alps enchant photographers and the outdoorsy alike with their uniquely dramatic landscapes.

The Alpes-de-Haute-Provence is a largely rural region, extending from the gentle hills of the eastern edge of the Luberon all the way up to the jagged high peaks of the Alps along the Italian border. Visitors tend to concentrate in the adventure-rich Gorges du Verdon and the sunflower- and lavender-speckled fields of the Plateau de Valensole in the southern part of the *département*, but there's so much more to discover. Try out rural village life in Banon, enjoying goat cheese preserved in chestnut leaves. Gaze at distant galaxies from one of the observatories. When you find the time to pull your nose out of a Giano book, get to know the tastes and flavours of his home in Forcalquier.

Cloaked in snow well into springtime, the mountains of Haute-Provence are divided by six main valleys, connected by some of the highest and most hair-raising road passes anywhere in Europe – an absolute must for road-trippers and outdoor enthusiasts. Head up north to the Ubaye Valley for some of the region's most unforgettable scenery. The uncrowded and unpretentious ski resorts here are great for families or adventurers in the winter, and in summer, the seven mountain passes that lead out of the valley are busy with cyclists and cars following the hairpin switchbacks all the way up to the top of the world.

THE MAIN AREAS

MOUSTIERS-STE-MARIE
Iconic gorges and
dreamy lavender. **p262**

UBAYE VALLEY
Ski resorts and
mountain vibes. **p276**

ALPES-DE-HAUTE-PROVENCE

Find Your Way

One of the largest regions in France, the Alpes-de-Haute-Provence doesn't have a big urban hub. The A51, which links Aix-en-Provence with Grenoble, connects to Digne-les-Bains via the N85.

Moustiers-Ste-Marie, p262
One of Provence's prettiest villages dazzles with its pastel facades, cliffs and centuries-old ceramics.

Ubaye Valley, p276
An underappreciated alpine haven, come here to ski, cycle or hike in the resort towns of this remote landscape.

CAR
Driving remains the most practical way to explore this large region. In Ubaye Valley in winter, be sure to have snow tyres or chains. Heavy snowfall means the highest *cols* (passes) are usually only open between May and September.

BIKE
This is a great cycling region with many backroads and villages that are usually within 10km of the next town. Rent a bike or e-bike during your stay and use it for short treks and day trips.

Route Napoléon (p268)

Plan Your Time

Short on time? Focus on the Gorges du Verdon for an outdoor adventure or make for the high peaks in the Ubaye Valley.

Pressed for Time

- Hike the ridge above **Moustiers-Ste-Marie** (p262) and visit the ceramic workshops. Spend a day exploring the **Gorges du Verdon** (p264) by foot, raft or bicycle. In early summer, pass through the **Plateau de Valensole** (p266) to see the lavender in bloom. Discover the forests around **Banon** (p271) and the Lure mountain, or the hills around **Forcalquier** (p272).

Five Days to Travel

- Drive the **Route Napoléon** (p268) through the Verdon, Dignes-les-Bains and onwards. Deviate from the main route to stay a night or two in **Banon** (p271), going for hikes during the day and spending the evenings **watching the stars** (p272). Detour again up to **Barcelonnette** (p276) to explore the Ubaye Valley: cycle, raft or hike your way through this amazing landscape.

SEASONAL HIGHLIGHTS

SPRING
Spring varies by altitude: always check temps and the snowpack in the mountains before setting off.

SUMMER
Lavender everywhere: visit the Plateau de Valensole; by July, the mountain passes in the Ubaye Valley open.

AUTUMN
Hike the Gorges du Verdon or the Lure mountain. It's the perfect time to admire the canyons and seasons.

WINTER
Hit the slopes in the Ubaye Valley. Ski on- or off-piste for adventure without the crowds and glitz of the northern Alps.

Moustiers-Ste-Marie

ADVENTURE HUB | ARTISANAL WARES | RUSTIC DINING

GETTING AROUND

Traffic gets crazy in the Verdon during high season. Best to park your car as soon as possible in Moustiers-Ste-Marie or La Palud and get around by bike, foot or raft. Bus 450 runs from Moustiers-Ste-Marie through La Palud to the departure point of many hikes, and on to Castellane. Hikers can reserve the Navette Blanc-Martel (navette. parcduverdon.fr) for drop-off and pick-up at the start and exit points of the famous hike of the same name.

The area around Moustiers-Ste-Marie sits at the crossroads of ancient trade routes linking the Alps to the Mediterranean – today's landscapes are shaped as much by human passage as by natural forces. The chic and laid-back village of Moustiers-Ste-Marie is ranked one of the most beautiful villages in France. Long celebrated for its fine faience pottery, the town is tucked at the base of towering limestone cliffs. Dramatic cliffs are a theme in the area; few sights in Provence can match the Gorges du Verdon. It's at the top of many visitors' to-see lists, and rightly so. Fighting for the top of that list is the nearby Plateau de Valensole, where the famous lavender fields extend beyond eyesight. Road-trippers can hit these sights and even more by driving the Route Napoléon through the region.

Moustiers-Ste-Marie from Above
The ultimate sunset spot
Suspended between the cliff walls above Moustiers-Ste-Marie is a golden star. Legend says the original was hung by a knight in 1210 in honour of the Virgin Mary. Climb above the village to get a better view of the star and the Gorges du Verdon in the distance. There are two ways to reach the path (the Sentier de la Chaîne): by foot or by electric mountain bike.

By foot from the centre of town, pick up the trail at the Parking Haut, which leads to the Chemin de Courchon (the old Roman road). After 1.5km, pick up the Sentier de la Chaîne until you reach the star. This is a steep hike not recommended for young children.

By electric mountain bike, take the main road out of town towards Puimoisson. Turn right towards En Naups and Le Castillon. The route passes above Le Castillon and hugs the hill until it comes back around nearly full circle to Moustiers-Ste-Marie, just on the other side of the hill. After the

☑ TOP TIP
Consider visiting from April to November – many spots in the region close up shop for the winter.

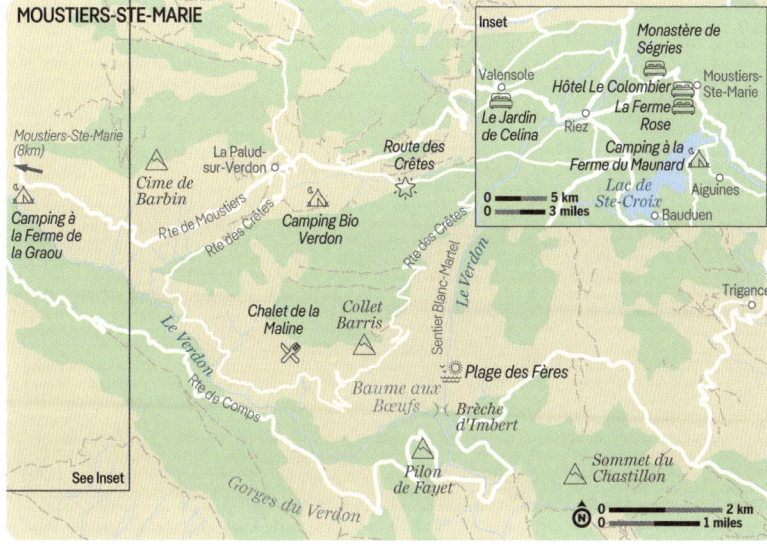

campground, turn on the bike's motor to help you climb up to the top of the hill via the old Roman road. It's marked with yellow-and-white VTT (mountain bike) trail signs.

Ceramics in Moustiers-Ste-Marie
From royal households to your table

A craft practised in Moustiers-Ste-Marie since the Middle Ages, the decorative faience (glazed earthenware) made here once graced the dining tables of Europe's most aristocratic houses. Typical decoration of faience pieces includes scenes in shades of blue; *aux guirlandes*, which is usually a single scene in the centre of the dish, surrounded by garlands; and *grotesques*, which usually incorporate animal or even some fantasy figures. Seven workshops still sell ceramics today, including **Atelier Serrailler**, **Atelier Soleil** and **Atelier Bondil**. For antique masterpieces, visit the small **Musée de la Faïence** *(adult/child €5/free)* adjacent to the town hall.

Path to the Ste-Croix Lake
A hidden beach accessible by foot

Set off from Moustiers-Ste-Marie on foot in the cool morning, taking the chemin de Quinson out of town, and turning left onto chemin de Peyrengue, a winding trail through olive groves and eventually a dirt path across open fields. After about 1½ hours, the turquoise shimmer of Lac de Ste-Croix appears, and

LAVENDER FAR & WIDE

For more perfectly symmetrical rows of lavender, check out the village of **Sault** (p224) in the Vaucluse and the **Plateau des Claparèdes** (p247) in the Luberon.

Continues on p266

TOP EXPERIENCE

Gorges du Verdon

Provence's own Grand Canyon: few places in Provence feel as untamed as the Gorges du Verdon. This deep limestone canyon stretches between Moustiers and Castellane, with turquoise water below and cliffs soaring high above. Hike, swim, paddle or cycle – there are countless ways to explore. Spring and autumn bring fewer crowds and cooler air, perfect for outdoor adventure.

DON'T MISS

Sentier Blanc-Martel

Route des Crêtes

River rafting

Canyoning tours

Le Palud-sur-Verdon

Birdwatching

Hike the Sentier Blanc-Martel

This 16km one-way trek from Chalet de la Maline to Point Sublime is one of France's most legendary hikes. Named after the first geologists to explore the canyon, the trail hugs the cliffs and drops down to the riverbed, with ladders, tunnels and dizzying views along the way. It's demanding but not extreme – suitable for fit beginners with proper footwear. Book the **Navette Blanc-Martel** *(navette.parcduverdon.fr)* in advance for transport to the trailhead and pickup at the end. Hikers should carry plenty of water, snacks and a torch for the tunnel. Get an early start to avoid the heat and crowds.

PRACTICALITIES

● Avoid visiting in winter – trails close and roads can be icy. In summer, use e-bikes or shuttle buses to dodge traffic.

Cycle the Route des Crêtes

This 24km balcony road loops out from La Palud-sur-Verdon, rising over 650m in elevation and offering heart-stopping views straight into the canyon. Originally designed for motorised day-trippers, parts of the **Route des Crêtes** are now restricted or closed to vehicles on select days, giving cyclists a stretch of silence and space. The ride is challenging but manageable with an e-bike – rentals are available in La Palud. Spring and autumn are the best times to ride, with cool weather and lighter traffic. Stop at *belvédères* (lookouts) along the way, where vultures and climbers share the same dizzying vertical playground. A helmet, water and good brakes are essential.

Raft the Verdon River

From April to June, when the river is flowing strong, rafting the Verdon is a wild, splashy ride through limestone corridors and rolling rapids. Most trips depart from Castellane, on the gorge's eastern end. Rapids range from easygoing to intense (Class I to IV), making this a good fit for both beginners and adrenaline junkies. Book ahead with a certified company such as **Yeti Rafting** *(from €40/person)* – gear and guides are included. Minimum age varies by route (usually 7 to 16), and all participants must be able to swim. It's a half-day adventure that takes you deep into the canyon, with moments of calm water to catch your breath between the thrills.

Try Canyoning in the Gorge

Canyoning in the Verdon means jumping, sliding and rappelling through chutes of clear river water, surrounded by towering cliffs. It's a full-sensory way to explore the gorge – part obstacle course, part wilderness immersion. You'll need to swim and scramble over rocks, but no experience is required. Outings depart from Moustiers-Ste-Marie and La Palud, with gear provided: wetsuits, harnesses, helmets and ropes. All you need are grippy shoes and a sense of adventure. For non-French speakers, it's easiest to book through the **tourist office** in Moustiers-Ste-Marie.

DO LOOK UP

The Gorges du Verdon is home to one of France's most impressive bird populations, including griffon, cinereous and Egyptian vultures. These massive birds ride the thermals above the cliffs, often visible from Route des Crêtes or trail lookouts. Bring binoculars and look for their broad wingspans and slow, soaring flight – especially active on warm afternoons with rising air currents.

TOP TIPS

● Go early, stay late. Morning light is best for photography; late afternoon brings fewer crowds and golden cliff glow.

● Skip weekends in summer. The roads clog fast – aim for midweek if you're visiting in July or August.

● Rent an e-bike. A game-changer for the Route des Crêtes, especially if you're not a seasoned cyclist.

● Wear real shoes. Trails can be rocky and slippery; sandals are a mistake.

● Buy the hiking map. Tourist offices stock the best Verdon trail maps in English.

● Picnic at Point Sublime. It's popular, but for good reason – the views really are that good.

Cycling, Route des Crêtes

CHAPELLE NOTRE-DAME DE BEAUVOIR

Flanked by two cliffs, the **Chapelle Notre-Dame de Beauvoir** is located in a peaceful area above Moustiers-Ste-Marie. Built between the 12th and 16th centuries, the chapel is partially Roman, partially Gothic in style. Follow a winding staircase up to the chapel for epic views over the surrounding plains; it's about a 20-minute climb from the centre of town.

Allegedly, the chapel has special powers. There were a number of cases recorded in the 17th century of villagers bringing stillborn infants here, only for them to come back to life long enough to receive their baptism.

On 8 September, Mass at 5am celebrates the nativity of the Virgin Mary, followed by flutes, drums and breakfast on the square.

Continued from p263

with it, the peaceful boat-rental base of **La Cadeno**. Here, you can slip off your shoes and wade into clear, calm water, then stretch out on the shores. It's a quiet escape, just far enough to feel earned.

Experience Sustainable Lavender Visits

Lavender is the new green

Dive into the new face of ecologically responsible lavender production by visiting an organic lavender farm on the **Plateau de Valensole**. To start with, look for the lavender fields that have let golden grass grow up between the rows of purple – these farms are doing their part to preserve the soil for the next generation. Many farms are open year-round to guests, but run special tours during the harvest season. And

EATING IN MOUSTIERS-STE-MARIE: OUR PICKS

Les Tables du Cloître: Stone interior with a local, rustic menu of dishes like rabbit or wild mushrooms. *noon-2pm Wed-Sun, 7-8.30pm Sat & Sun* €€

La Grignotière: Trendy breakfast and brunch place in the centre of Moustiers with a laid-back shady terrace. *9am-6pm Wed-Sun* €€

Ferme Ste-Cécile: Enjoy specialities by chef Patrick Crespin between Moustiers and the Gorges du Verdon (not vegetarian friendly). *hours vary* €€

Chalet de la Maline: Restaurant attached to the Club Alpin Français, with a terrace overlooking the Gorges du Verdon plus local beer. *hours vary* €

Lavender farm, Plateau de Valensole

no visit would be complete without trying some lavender-based products straight from the source, such as essential oils, soaps and perfumes produced on-site using sustainable methods.

The lavender fields of Valensole are usually the highlight of a photography tour of Provence. Visit in late June or early July, but no later. During this time, the fields are alive with colour and fragrance, providing a stunning backdrop for your photos.

To get the perfect shot, you'll have to get up early – sunrise has the longest 'soft-light' period, which reduces shadows and harsh glare. Don't go tromping in the fields, but tread carefully between rows – these are precious crops for local farmers.

What to wear? Consider colours that will complement the lavender fields. Soft pastels, earthy tones and neutral colours work well in this setting.

Avoid wearing bright colours that may clash with the lavender or draw too much attention away from the landscape's natural beauty.

LAVENDER FARMS ON THE PLATEAU DE VALENSOLE

La Ferme du Riou: This organic farm runs distillery visits during the harvest season and farm visits year-round.

Lavande Bio Berenger: Organic producer with a cabin in the fields during harvest season. Otherwise, stop at the shop in Valensole.

Lavandes Angelvin: Runs distillery visits during high season and guided visits on Tuesdays at 3pm.

Terraroma: Very photogenic lavender and almond farm, with a few sunflower fields to complete the mosaic.

Les Lavandes d'Isabelle et Sébastien: Techincally off the plateau and closer to Manosque, this little family lavender farm is less crowded and has a small boutique to find your favourite products.

 EATING IN VALENSOLE: OUR PICKS

Le Jardin de Celina: In a chic farmhouse setting, this standout table pairs creative Provençal cuisine with serious wine and a cosy garden. *hours vary seasonally* €€

Comptoir de Valérie: Good *bistrot* to grab summer dishes like a tomato and burratta salad or local melon with cured ham. *noon-2pm Tue-Sun, 7.30-9pm Fri & Sat* €

Maison de Marius: This charming spot is also an *épicerie* (gourmet grocer) where you can stock up on local treats. *8.30am-12.30pm & 3.30-6pm Mon-Sat, 9am-12.30pm Sun* €€

Café des Arts: On the other side of the Plateau de Valensole is the much less crowded Puimoisson and its Café des Arts. *7am-3pm Sun-Tue, 7am-10.30pm Thu-Sat* €

HIKING TOUR

Route Napoléon: Alpes-de-Haute-Provence Segment

In 1815, Napoléon Bonaparte marched this way on his dramatic return from exile – on foot, with just a handful of men. In the Alpes-de-Haute-Provence region, the modern Route Napoléon connects Castellane to Sisteron, a drive that rewards curiosity over speed. You'll pass gorges without railings, cafes without menus and ridgelines without people. This isn't the quickest route north – but it's the one you'll remember. Sure, you could do it in 2½ hours – but why not take 2½ days instead?

❶ Castellane

Castellane is a lively (for the region) crossroads town and the ideal launch point for this alpine leg of the Route Napoléon, if you're coming up from the Alpes-Maritimes (see p81). Before driving away, climb the path to **Chapelle Notre Dame du Roc**, perched high above the tiled rooftops, for a sweet view and a moment of calm. Back in town, stock up on picnic fare or linger over coffee on the square before heading into wilder country.

The Drive: From Castellane, get on the D4085 heading north. At Barrême, you turn left and the road becomes the N85. Signs for the Clue de Chabrières appear after about 40 minutes.

❷ Clue de Chabrières

Not far outside Castellane, you'll reach this small limestone gorge. The Gorges

Chapelle Notre Dame du Roc

ROUTE NAPOLÉON

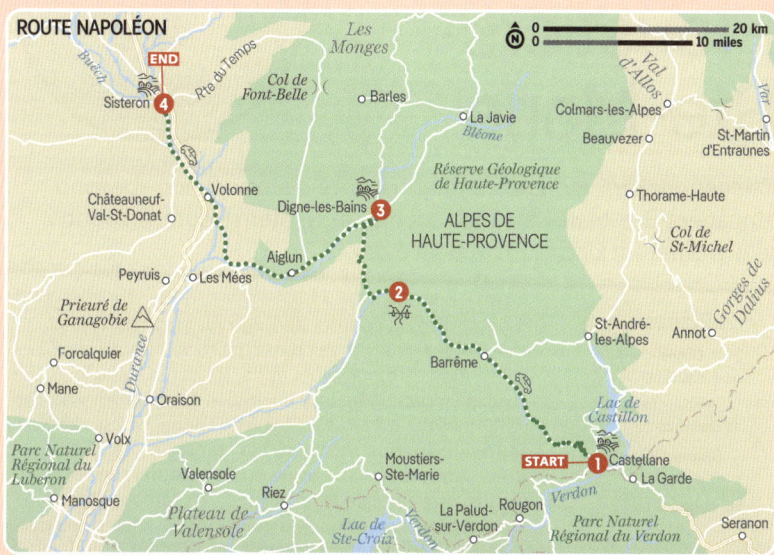

du Verdon get all the glory, but this spot on the road is impressive all the same, especially when you imagine that armies once passed through here.

The road threads through sheer rock, twists and tunnels, and shadows constantly move across the cliffs. Maybe it was the windy weather the day I drove through but there is a strange intimacy here, as if you're driving inside the bones of the mountain. There are no major sights, but that's the point.

The Drive: Just a quarter of an hour further up the N85, you'll arrive in Digne-les-Bains.

3 Digne-les-Bains

Take a spa break at the **Thermes de Digne-les-Bains** *(spadehauteprovence.com; adult/child from €19/11)* if you need it, but the really special thing to explore in Digne-les-Bains is the **Maison Alexandra David-Néel** *(alexandra-david-neel.fr; adult/child from €8/free)*.

This isn't a formal museum, but the house of France's most fascinating female explorer, preserved almost as she left it, filled with Tibetan textiles, manuscripts and souvenirs from her solo travels through early 20th-century Asia.

The Drive: Back on the N85 you'll reach the Vallée de la Durance and see signs for Sisteron via the highway (A51), or you can choose to stay on the N85 for the scenery.

4 Sisteron

Crowned by a citadel and flanked by jagged limestone cliffs, Sisteron marks a threshold between the Alps and Provence. It's also the place to eat: lamb from the surrounding hillsides is the local pride, often roasted or grilled with wild herbs.

Walk it off on a short hike in the **Monges** massif just east of town. One of France's least-visited mountain ranges, it offers solitude, sweeping views, and a chance to hear nothing but the wind.

Beyond Moustiers-Ste-Marie

Cheese-makers, stargazers, shepherds and storytellers – beyond Moustiers-Ste-Marie, the high country of western Haute-Provence tells a different kind of Provençal story.

Places
Digne-les-Bains p270
Vallée de la Durance p271
Banon p271
Pays de Forcalquier p272

Get out of Verdon country and into the rural rhythm of Haute-Provence. From the towering rock formations of Les Mées to dinosaur footprints in the Réserve Géologique, the landscape wears its history openly. In Forcalquier, visit the distillery or the home of writer Jean Giono, whose novels captured the soul of this land. For stargazers, St-Michel-l'Observatoire offers a glimpse far beyond the region. Banon is all about earthy pleasures – its famous chestnut-wrapped goat cheese is just the beginning. Hike through oak and pine, tuck into a leisurely lunch, then stretch out under a tree as the sun settles.

GETTING AROUND

You'll need a car to explore this region properly – buses are infrequent and many villages are off the grid. The main access route is the A51 motorway, which runs north–south between Sisteron and Manosque. Manosque also has the nearest main train station, with regular TER services to Marseille and Aix-en-Provence. From there, it's a short drive into the hills, where winding departmental roads link tiny villages, forests and wide skies.

Digne-les-Bains

TIME FROM MOUSTIERS-STE-MARIE: **50min**

Marvel at the tracks of time

Into rocks? Then the **Réserve Géologique de Haute-Provence** *(geoparchauteprovence.com)* should be on your list. Limestone cliffs, volcanic rocks and sedimentary layers are present in the region and highlighted throughout the park, which encompasses 18 sites. The park also contains several important paleontological sites, with fossils dating back to the Triassic period. Just 3km north of Digne is the impressive **Dalle aux Ammonites** (Ammonite Slab), containing over 1500 fossilised ammonites.

Early dinosaurs once roamed here and their footprints are preserved in the sedimentary rock. Visitors interested in exploring the area can book a guided tour in English. To visit the entire park, you'll need a car and a full day.

Need something more recent than a million years ago to hold your attention? Across from the Reserve Géologique, you'll find works from the **Route d'Arte Contemporain**, a Franco-Italian initiative that brings contemporary art to rural spaces.

Vallée de la Durance

TIME FROM MOUSTIERS-STE-MARIE: **1hr**

Hike the Pénitents Trail

Les Pénitents is a hiking trail that traverses the landscape above the village of **Les Mées**, 26km west of Digne. The hike takes up to 3½ hours, is well marked and begins in the centre of the village. Along the way, you'll pass a long and striking band of puddingstone (conglomerate) cliffs, which formed millions of years ago through sedimentation. It looks like a bunch of river stones cemented together and formed into a series of rocky pinnacles.

If you prefer the mythical explanation (it's got a bit of French cynicism...), the cliff is made of the monks of the Lure mountain, who were petrified by St Donat during the Saracen invasions as punishment for falling in love.

The hike takes you through a varied landscape, including dense forests, rolling hills and rocky outcrops, and has striking views of the village and the surrounding countryside. There's parking near the trailhead.

Feel the calm of a working abbey

A visit to **Abbaye Notre Dame de Ganagobie** is less about checking off a site and more about slipping into stillness. Set high on a little plateau, the monastery overlooks the vast Durance Valley – a view that hushes you without trying. Lions, griffins, warriors and abstract patterns sprawl across it in bold, red-and-black forms. Scholars say it's a moral allegory. Others see echoes of Eastern influence. Whatever the truth, its strangeness is part of the draw. The monks live here still. Visitors are welcome, even to stay the night – quietly.

Banon

TIME FROM MOUSTIERS-STE-MARIE: **1hr 20min**

Visit on market day

There is no cheese more cottage-core than Banon AOP, a soft goat cheese wrapped in chestnut leaves. Named after the small village of Banon, the cheese was made as early as the Middle Ages, though it may be older still. A typically French story attributes the death of Roman emperor Antoninus Pius to indigestion: allegedly, he gorged himself on too much Banon. A strong flavour radiates from this raw goat's milk cheese, but the most distinctive feature is the packaging. The cheese is preserved by wrapping it in chestnut leaves that have been soaked in *eau-de-vie*, a type of brandy made from fruit.

THE RULES OF FOSSIL HUNTING

From stone tools to fossilised sea creatures, the Alpes-de-Haute-Provence is full of surprises underfoot.

If you stumble on something curious – a worked flint, a fossil imprint – pause before pocketing it. It's not finders keepers in France. In fact it's illegal to take home fossils or artefacts. If you are lucky enough to find something interesting, here's what to do:

Leave it be: moving it can erase crucial context.

Snap a pic: take photos and note the exact location.

Report it: contact the Réserve Géologique or the local *mairie* (town hall).

 EATING IN THE VALLÉE DE LA DURANCE: AFFORDABLE DINING

| **Le Bistrot Gaby**: Come here for local and seasonal dishes without pretension; wonderful attention to detail. Near St-Auban. *noon-1.30pm & 7.30-9.30pm Fri-Tue* €€ | **La Trattoria**: Outside Malijai, this pizzeria has great pies and frequent live music. Stop on a road trip or come for dinner. *11am-2.30pm & 6-10pm Tue-Sat* € | **Le Rocher**: In the centre of Les Mées, this new restaurant has surprisingly chic dishes, an affordable *semigastro* (gastro-pub). *noon-1.30pm Tue-Sat, 7-9pm Thu-Sat* €€ | **Maison Ferrante**: In the middle of Digne-les-Bains, this patisserie is a dainty tea room with divine desserts. *hours vary Tue-Sat* € |

MEET THE GOATS YOUR CHEESE COMES FROM

Le Petit Troutouil: At this farm 7km from Banon in Simiaine-la-Rotonde, Valérie still milks her goats by hand each day at 6.30pm. Buy her AOP Banon cheese on the farm or at the Banon market on Saturdays.

Fromagerie GAEC du Grand Jas: Near St-Michel-l'Observatoire, this farm shop is open 8am to noon and 3pm to 7pm daily. In summer it's possible to organise group tours.

Fromagerie Domaine de la Haute Lèbre: In Revest-du-Bion, pick up Banon cheese and other fresh and aged goat cheeses.

Banon cheese is typically only produced during the summer months, when the goats are grazing in the lush mountain pastures. The cheese is then left to mature for several weeks before it is ready to be enjoyed. It is often served as a dessert cheese, paired with fresh fruit and a crisp white wine.

The cheese's fame has likely helped keep the village of Banon so dynamic, despite its isolation. The weekly market is a must-visit, taking place every Tuesday and Saturday morning in the town square. Here, visitors can find fresh produce, artisanal cheeses and handmade crafts from local vendors.

The village is also home to the popular blue bookshop, **Librairie le Bleuet** *(lebleuet.fr)* which is a must-visit for bibliophiles. Each May, the village hosts a Fête du Fromage and a literature festival, which is sure to be a good time.

Chestnut heritage

Each autumn, the hill village of Revest-du-Bion, 13km from Banon, celebrates its centuries-old chestnut culture with a lively village *fête*. A staple in the region's culinary culture, it features stalls piled with roasted marrons, handmade preserves, chestnut flour, liqueurs and cakes such as *gâteau à la châtaigne* (chestnut cake). The scent of woodsmoke drifts through the streets as locals share recipes and tastings. Outside the festival, you can still find chestnut products in local markets, especially in Banon and nearby farms. Chestnut trees once fed whole communities and they're still part of daily life.

Pays de Forcalquier

TIME FROM MOUSTIERS-STE-MARIE: 1hr

Stargazing in Provence

Clear skies and low light pollution combine to make the Alpes-de-Haute-Provence a destination for stargazing. One of the best places to observe the distant galaxies is at the **Centre d'Astronomie de St-Michel L'Observatoire** *(centre-astro.com; adult/child €7/4.50)* outside the village of St-Michel-l'Observatoire, a scientific research centre that is open to the public. Here, you can join guided tours and peer at the stars through telescopes with the help of experienced astronomers. English-speaking nights are held in the summer.

Another option is to visit the **Observatoire Astronomique de Puimichel** *(adult/child €20/10)*, a little further away, in Puimichel, where you can learn about the workings of the observatory as well as explore the night sky with telescopes. Reservations need to be made at the Manosque tourist office.

EATING & DRINKING IN BANON: IN THE HEART OF TOWN

Café de l'Union: With the ambiance of an old-fashioned French cafe, it's the bar of the village. *7am-midnight* €

La Suite...: *Bistrot* food done right: homemade fries, a house burger and seasonal appetisers, plus local beers – try the lavender-infused lager. *hours vary* €

Les Vins au Vert: A Banon staple, this well-curated wine bar offers local and international wines with charcuterie and cheese boards. *10am-3pm & 5.30-11pm Tue-Sun* €€

La Table de Panturle: The fancy restaurant in town, where chef Rippe has a rotating menu with restrained choices, all excellent and usually local. *hours vary* €€

MOUNTAIN BIKING THE LURE MOUNTAIN

Hills made for an e-bike tour: explore the flanks of the Lure mountain.

START	END	LENGTH
St-Étienne-les-Orgues	St-Étienne-les-Orgues	42km, 3½hr (e-bike), 5hr (regular)

Once old grazing country, this side of the Lure mountain is now heavily forested. But stone tracks, small spring pastures and the occasional *jas* (shepherd's hut) still mark the way. This isn't just a ride with big views. It's a slow journey through a lived-in mountain, shaped by animals, weather and the people who have worked it for centuries.

From ❶ **St-Étienne-les-Orgues**, climb gently into dense beech forest. Early in the ride, a short detour leads to ❷ **Notre-Dame de Lure**, a 12th-century chapel once used as a rest stop by monks and later, shepherds.

Above the forest, wide pistes and open meadows carry you steadily to the summit. At 1826m, the ❸ **Sommet de Lure** offers vast views over the Alps and the Durance. From there, descend along the ridge, then past ❹ **Cairn 2000**, where the terrain begins to soften.

On the lower slopes, you'll pass ❺ **Jas Neuf**, one of several traditional dry-stone shelters used during summer transhumance. Wide tracks and single-track paths lead through gullies and valleys toward the village of Cruis.

There, the ❻ **Auberge de l'Abbaye** *(hotel-restaurantcruis.fr)* makes a perfect final stop – serving local lamb, mountain cheese and a crisp glass of rosé. The last stretch back to St-Étienne is short and gentle.

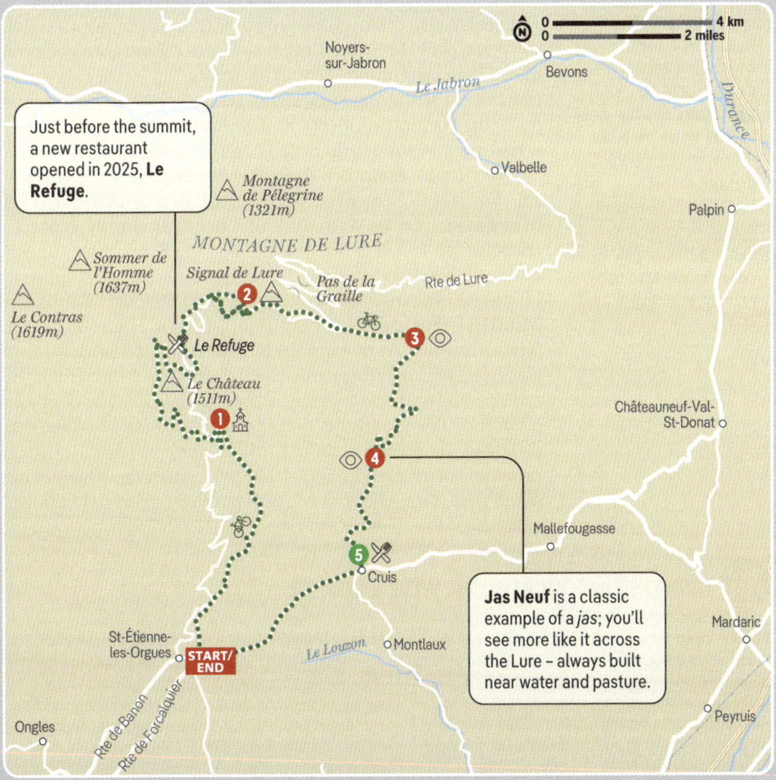

> Just before the summit, a new restaurant opened in 2025, **Le Refuge**.

> **Jas Neuf** is a classic example of a *jas*; you'll see more like it across the Lure – always built near water and pasture.

VILLAGE HOPPING

True to its *paysan* (farmer) past, the western part of the Alpes-de-Haute-Provence is marked by frequent villages with a tight and tidy centres, surrounded by rolling fields.

This makes the region perfect for village-hopping by electric bike or car – usually you're never any more than 10km away from the next village.

For example, from Banon, it's easy to explore the perched village of Simiane-la-Rotonde, the flourishing **Jardin de l'Abbaye de Valsainte**, or a bit further down the road, the mysterious Lure mountain.

All year round, each village helps you to explore Provençal culture, countryside and gastronomy.

For those who prefer to stargaze on their own, clear skies across the region offer plenty of opportunities to see the stars, and some planets, such as Venus and Jupiter, with the naked eye.

Walk up an appetite

The plan: hike to work up an appetite. The starting point: the village of Revest-des-Brousses, 20km from Forcalquier and home to **L'Auberge de la Petite Casserole**, a *bistrot de pays* (a rural restaurant where great-value meals are made with local produce). The well-marked hike takes two to three hours and covers about 13km of rolling terrain, weaving in and out of forests and fields. While on the trail, hikers might spot birds of prey circling above the fields. The loop starts and ends at the town square, leading to Aubenas-les-Alpes before circling back to Revest-des-Brousses for a much-anticipated lunch. The bistrot offers a nice selection of local spirits and a fresh menu every day. Reservations are recommended.

Giono's Provence

Jean Giono was a French writer who was born in the Provençal town of Manosque, and is known for his stories that celebrate the nature and beauty of the region. The **Centre Jean Giono** *(centrejeangiono.com; adult/child €6/4)* in Manosque's lovely old Hotel Raffin, is dedicated to his life and works, showcasing exhibitions that capture the essence of Giono's Provence. The centre also offers guided tours of Giono's home for French speakers, providing an intimate look into the author's personal life and the inspirations behind his works. The house was under renovation at the time of writing but expected to be finished in 2026. For nature lovers and literature enthusiasts alike, a visit here is a must-do in the beautiful region of Provence.

Love Giono's approach to Provence? His former farm outside Forcalquier has been transformed into a B&B called **La Margotte** (p283). Writer's block begone; Giono wrote *Le Hussard sur le Toit* (The Horseman on the Roof) in this house.

Giono waxed poetic about Provençal olive oil many times in his essays. Also in Forcalquier you can see the old oil mill, the **Moulin à Huile de Gouvan**, and taste AOC Haute-Provence olive oil produced in Lurs. In bygone days, the olive oil mill was used to crush the olives to make a paste from which the miller could extract the juice. After letting it sit, the water and oil in the juice separated, and the olive oil on the surface was collected. Giono wrote about the first *pompe à l'huile* (olive oil brioche), a common holiday treat, with such mouthwatering detail that you might find yourself purchasing one on impulse!

DRINKING IN FORCALQUIER: WINE & COFFEE

Le Bas-Alpin: Don't miss this wine bar in the centre of town, with a great selection of wines – including some natural wines – and tapas. *noon-2pm & 6-10pm Thu-Mon*

Château St-Jean lez Durance: With a tasting room and patio parties, this vineyard specialises in IGP Alpes-de-Haute-Provence. *9am-noon & 2-6pm Mon-Sat*

Maison Neseli: A new wine shop in Mane with frequent tastings. Rare wines from around the world plus gourmet coffee, olive oil and spirits. *hours vary*

Forcafé: Forcalquier's cafe for espresso lovers – a place to chat about coffee with French coffee lovers. *9am-12.30pm Mon-Thu, 9am-6pm Fri*

Distilleries et Domaines de Provence

Immersion in the herbs

Tucked into Forcalquier's old convent, the **Artemisia Museum** *(artemisia-museum.fr; adult/child €6.70/4.30)* is all about the power of plants. I came here familiar with the Provençal trifecta: rosemary, thyme and oregano, hoping my cooking horizons would be opened. The museum is also a working university, and oriented more towards the medicinal than the culinary: here you can smell dozens of plants and herbs from the Provençal fields to the foot of the mountains, fresh, dried and transformed into oils and remedies. Exhibits trace the long history of gathering and distillation in Haute-Provence. Come with time to spend: I got to see a working still, touch raw ingredients, and even try blending my own scent.

Spirited away

Can you identify the local ingredients in the spirits at the **Distilleries et Domaines de Provence** *(distilleries-provence.com)*? The easiest to identify will be the Pastis Henri Bourdin, with its strong anise flavour. But the most original remains the Farigoule, a thyme liqueur with a herbal punch. Another surprise might be tasting the *vin de noix* (walnut sweet wine). If you like sweet, you'll also like the comically named RinQuinQuin, made with Provençal peaches. Practise your Provençal accent by adding a twangy 'g' at the end. A tour of the copper stills and steeping jars doesn't take long; a tasting might take a little longer.

PICKING YOUR OWN HERBS

Xavier Lemonde, Director of the Artemisia Museum
@artemisiamuseum

Strolling through the Provençal hills, you don't need to look far to find the plants that define the region's scent and flavour.

Many grow wild: resinous thyme, rosemary and savory *(sarriette)* thrive in the sun-baked garrigue. Look closer and you'll spot mugwort *(Artemisia vulgaris)*, part of the same plant family as *génépi*.

Other finds include the twisted trunks of juniper trees *(genévriers)*, whose berries lend their punch to gin, and cade, a native juniper whose oil is still used in traditional soaps and salves. Even the names – *herbe de St-Eloi, sarriette, romarin* – sound like a Provençal poem.

 EATING IN FORCALQUIER: OUR PICKS

Ma Nine: Stylish restaurant with a terrace and balanced dishes like meatballs and pickled vegetables. Local and vegetarian options. *hours vary* €€

Lo Pichotome: Crispy thin-crust pizzas with fresh ingredients and local beers, on a relaxed patio. *10.30am-2pm & 6-10pm Tue-Sat* €

Le Bel Ecrin: Chic spot with a charming patio and menu that lets the Provencal trio – tomatoes, squash and aubergine – shine. *noon-2pm & 7.30-9.30pm Thu-Mon* €€

Pamparigouste: Upscale restaurant at the Couvent des Minimes Hôtel et Spa in Mane, with an emphasis on tradition. *12.15-1.30pm & 7.15-9.15pm* €€€

Ubaye Valley

WILD WATERS | HIGH PASSES | ALPINE ESCAPE

Tucked into the southern Alps near the Italian border, the Ubaye Valley feels like a world apart. Its heart is Barcelonnette, a lively little town with a curious twist: a strong Mexican influence, born from 19th-century French migrants returning back to the valley, still shapes its architecture, cuisine and festivals.

The valley itself is framed by seven high passes, making it a key stop on the Route des Grandes Alpes. It's a dream for cyclists and motorbikers, but also for white-water rafters, hikers and skiers. Pra Loup and Le Sauze offer solid snow without the crowds of the northern Alps, while summer brings trails, open-air concerts and local cheese on every menu.

There's a fiercely independent energy here; it's alpine, yes, but not like anywhere else. The Ubaye Valley makes an impression: wild, proud and slightly unexpected.

Try Cheeses from Ubaye
Prepare a fondue Ubaye-style

Wherever you go in the French Alps, you'll find a version of the holy trinity of cheese dishes: *tartiflette, raclette* and *fondue*. In the Ubaye Valley, fondue takes on a local twist. Head to the **Coopérative Laitière** *(fromagerie-ubaye.com)* in Barcelonnette, where you can choose a custom mix of *meule, miche gavotte* and *carline*.

The co-operative also produces excellent *tomme de chèvre* (goat cheese), creamy *bleu d'Ubaye*, and *tomme au Génépy*, a mountain cheese often baked and served over potatoes. Don't miss market day in Barcelonnette (Wednesday and Saturday), when the town buzzes with stalls selling cheese, cured meats and crusty loaves – perfect for a DIY picnic.

Whether you're cooking in a chalet kitchen or just looking for something to snack on after a hike, the valley's cheese reflects the land it comes from: alpine, seasonal and full of character.

GETTING AROUND

There's no train to Barcelonnette – the closest station is in Gap, about 1½ hours away by bus or car. Most visitors arrive by car via the D900 or the scenic Route des Grandes Alpes. To explore the valley's villages, passes and trailheads, having your own vehicle is essential. Buses run in summer, but service is limited. Cycling is popular, though the climbs are steep.

☑ TOP TIP

The southern Alps are less bling-bling than the northern resorts, with a laid-back attitude and pride in the local traditions. This is a region where actions speak louder than words; locals are welcoming but not overly outgoing.

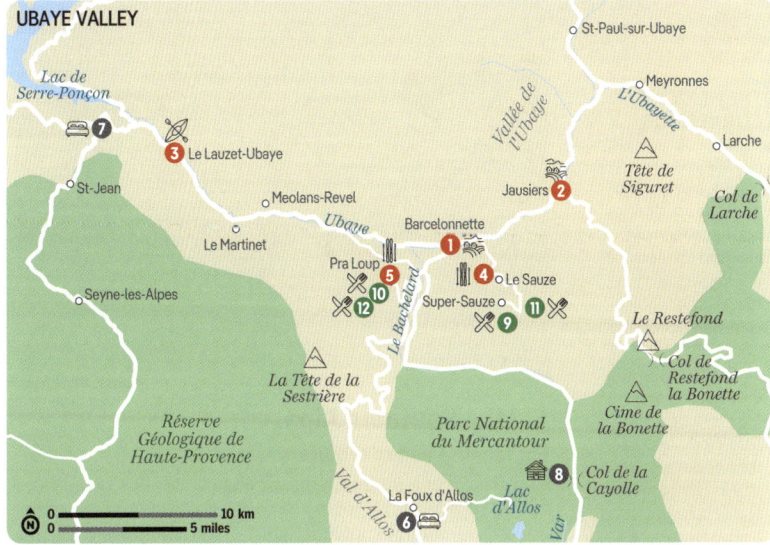

Barcelonnette: C'est la Fête
Secluded town with diverse celebrations

The **Fête des Mortes** is an annual celebration in Barcelonnette, taking place on the first two days of November and sharing similarities with Mexico's *Día de los Muertos*. This vibrant event has a long-standing history in the city, ever since emigrants from Barcelonnette to Mexico returned in the late 19th century. The festivities include colourful parades, street performances, traditional rituals and offerings.

In addition to the Fête des Mortes, the nearby town of Jausiers hosts the **Fête de la Transhumance** in early June each year to mark the beginning of the grazing season in the high pastures. Visitors alike can witness this impressive migration as they explore the surrounding woodlands and pastures, taking in the views of the Parc National du Mercantour. The festival also showcases local cuisine, traditional music and cultural activities.

Rafting the Ubaye River
Splash your way downstream

Late spring to autumn, rafters of all levels come to the Ubaye River above Barcelonnette for an adrenaline rush. Depending on the combination of rainfall and snowmelt, rafters will leave from Jausiers, Barcelonnette or further down the river. Age and experience are important too: starting at four years old, children can give baby-raft a go, but they need to be older to try the class IV rapids. Book an excursion with the team at **Anaconda Rafting** *(anacondarafting.com)* to race down the river in a raft, two-person kayak or hydrospeed, a type of miniature raft.

● SIGHTS
1. Barcelonnette
2. Jausiers

see 1 Musée de la Vallée

● ACTIVITIES
3. Anaconda Rafting
4. Le Sauze
5. Pra Loup

● SLEEPING
see 1 Hôtel Azteca
see 4 Hôtel l'Équipe
see 2 La Bousquetière
6. L'Attrapeur de Rêves
7. L'Auberge
8. Refuge de la Cayolle
see 2 Villa Morelia

● EATING
9. La Cabane à Jo
10. La Dalle en Pente
11. Le 2100
12. Le Peguieou
see 1 Villa Lorenzo
see 2 Villa Morelia

● SHOPPING
see 1 Coopérative Laitière de la Vallée de l'Ubaye
see 2 Maison de Pays

● TRANSPORT
see 1 Cycle Ubaye Sports
see 1 Sport Moto

THE MEXICAN CONNECTION

Mexican colonial-style homes, a celebration of Día de los Muertos and more than one Mexican restaurant in this small mountain town – what's going on in Barcelonnette?

In the 19th century, emigrants who'd left the region to seek their fortune in the New World returned, their pockets bursting thanks to a successful textile business they'd built in Mexico. This new bourgeoisie built around 50 'Mexican villas' from 1880 to 1930.

Drop into the Villa La Sapinière, which is home to the **Musée de la Vallée** *(museedela-vallee.fr; adult/child €5/3)*. The exhibition follows not only the entrepreneurial Barcelonnettes in Mexico, but the comings and goings of the valley communities between Italy and France, and the travels of notable locals around the world.

Skiing, Pra Loup

Ski the Southern Alps
For families and adventurers

The Ubaye is a hidden winter hotspot. Besides being home to two popular ski resorts, the valley has a microclimate that ensures abundant snowfall, which makes it an ideal destination for skiing enthusiasts.

Pra Loup, the larger of the two stations, is 9.5km southwest of Barcelonnette and has an extensive network of pistes spanning 180km, with an elevation ranging from 1600m to 2575m. With 80% of its runs higher than 2000m, Pra Loup is guaranteed a longer season, even during mild winters. In addition to skiing, the resort also has three marked ski touring trails, providing access for adventurous skiers to ascend towards higher summits for a more exhilarating experience. There are two main areas: Pra Loup 1500 (sometimes called Les Molanes) and Pra Loup 1600 (with more infrastructure and nightlife). Together they form the southern Alps' largest snow-sports destination, and in summer the lifts haul mountain-bikers and hikers up to the summit.

Le Sauze, a mere 5.5km southeast of Barcelonnette, is another skier's playground with 65km of runs and 1000m of elevation gain, topping out at 2400m. The resort also has five marked trails for snowshoeing, providing a more relaxed way of exploring the valley's winter landscape.

Apart from skiing and snowshoeing, the valley also has the usual run of other winter activities, including snowmobile rides, sledding, ice skating and the spa.

EATING & DRINKING IN THE UBAYE VALLEY: OUR PICKS

Villa Lorenzo: Clothilde and her team mix alpine and Provençal dishes, in a chic and comfortable environment. Reserve ahead. *lunch Tue-Sat, dinner Thu-Sat* €€

Villa Morelia: Reserve a table at this Mexican villa in Jausiers, with tall bay windows and spectacular dishes that change nearly daily. *hours vary* €€€

Maison de Pays: On the outskirts of Jausiers, come here for a selection of local cheeses from the co-operative to take on a picnic or bike ride. *9.30am-noon & 2-6pm* €

Brasserie des Hautes Vallées: The local microbrewery in St-Paul-sur-Ubaye; tasting rooms and fabulous alpine views. *10am-12.30pm & 2-6pm Mon-Fri*

Mush in the Mountains
Follow the paw prints

Glide through snow-covered meadows behind a team of eager pups on a dog-sledding adventure in the upper Ubaye Valley. At **Banquise Traîneau** (*banquisetraineau.fr*), near St-Paul-sur-Ubaye, you can either ride as a passenger or try your hand at mushing with guidance from seasoned mushers. Tours range from short family-friendly rides to longer, more immersive outings. It's a chance to experience the incredible bond between mushers and their dogs.

Hike to the Lauzanier Lake
Family-friendly hike to a glacier-fed lake

Leaving from the car park named the Vallon de Lauzanier, it's one of the most accessible hikes in the region – no steep climbs, just soft meadows, glacial streams and a steady sense of ascent. In early summer, the landscape bursts with wildflowers and the sound of marmots whistling from the rocks. The lake itself is still and glassy, set beneath jagged ridgelines near the Italian border. At 9km round trip, it's family friendly and appropriate for casual hikers. Have more time or energy? The trail continues deeper into the Parc National du Mercantour, but many choose to stop at the lake. Go in early summer for the best light and fewest crowds.

Spend the Night in the Mountains
Sleep under the clear night skies

In the upper Ubaye, mountain *refuges* (huts) aren't just overnight stops – they're part of the adventure. With a highly ritualised arrival process – shoes off, *refuge*-provided crocs on – you'll dine with hikers and alpinists on traditional alpine fare when you book the *demi-pension* package. From the hamlet of Maljasset, you can access directly the **Refuge CAF de Maljasset** (*chaletmaljasset.ffcam.fr*), basecamp for glacier lakes and wild peaks. Spend the night, and then allow four to five hours on foot to reach **Refuge du Chambeyron** (*refugeduchambeyron.ffcam.fr*), tucked below the jagged Brec de Chambeyron. On the other side of the valley, **Refuge de la Cayolle** (*refuge-delacayolle.fr*) is a 1½-hour hike to the Lac des Garrets and the Mercantour frontier. All three offer beds, hot meals and alpine silence under a starry sky. Book ahead, pack light, and sleep a little closer to the stars.

BEST ALPINE ACTIVITIES IN UBAYE

Sylvain Boudou (*@sylvainboudou*) is a mountain guide in the southern Alps.

As a guide, the southern Alps will always be a special place for me. Here are my favourite activities by season.

Winter: Ski touring in the high Ubaye and ice-climbing in the Vallon de Maljasset.

Spring: Mornings are for ski touring; in the afternoon, it's warm enough to go rock climbing in a T-shirt on the valley floor.

Summer: Mountaineering rules. There are summits and ridges suitable for all levels of mountaineers, and there are no queues like in the northern Alps.

Autumn: Climbing takes over again, and the skis come out of storage and get tuned up for winter.

 EATING IN THE UBAYE VALLEY: PISTE-SIDE EATS

La Cabane à Jo: Ski-in, ski-out restaurant with a variety of dishes. No need to reserve, service runs continuously, so you won't be pushed from your table. *hours vary* €€

Le 2100: Ski-in, ski-out with excellent burgers and a few local dishes like *tourtons* (cheese pastries), but not very vegetarian friendly. *hours vary* €€

Le Peguieou: At 2365m, a ski-in, ski-out spot with stunning views. Book a special dinner (€85) and arrive by skidozer for an incredible *raclette* and live music. *hours vary* €€€

La Dalle en Pente: The place to be if you want to eat, snack or have an après-ski drink on the runs in Pra Loup. Big patio with lots of sun. *hours vary* €€

HELP ME PICK:

Riding the High Passes

Whether you're a Lycra-clad climber, an e-biker in search of views, or a motorcyclist chasing curves, the Ubaye Valley's high passes deliver the sensations you're looking for. There are seven mountain passes, each with its own character, gradient and reward. Some feel like forgotten corners of the Alps, others like mini–Tour de France stages. Here's how to pick the right one for your ride.

What to Ride if You...

... have big goals

For pure elevation, head to the **Col de la Bonette**. At 2715m, it's often billed as the highest paved road in France. The climb is long but steady, and the views open up with every turn. The real summit is a loop above the actual pass. It's been featured in the Tour de France, and for good reason.

... are after the perfect shot

The **Col de la Cayolle** is one of the most beautiful climbs in the southern Alps. It's quiet, remote, and in summer marked by grazing sheep or, if you're lucky, a few whistling marmots. It offers a gentler gradient through high alpine meadows, gorges and wildflower-dotted slopes. Hairpin turns wind through postcard-perfect backdrops, and you'll want to stop for photos more than once. It's a top pick for early-morning or golden-hour rides when the light turns the rocks gold.

... love fast descents

The **Col de Vars** is for cyclists who like a good pay-off. The climb itself is smooth and satisfying, it's the descent steals the show: fast, sweeping curves on excellent tarmac, with long sightlines and no nasty surprises. Just watch for traffic on peak summer afternoons.

... want to see Italy

Cyclists can ride **Montée de Ste-Anne** and spot the Italian border. It's the legal (and scenic) alternative to the **Col de Larche**, which is officially closed to bikes for safety reasons (but you'll likely see cyclists on the route anyway).

The climb is no slouch, but you're rewarded with wide views and a real sense of crossing terrain. For motorcyclists, the Col de Larche itself is a stunning route with plenty of space to lean into curves.

... need some easy wins

The **Col de Pontis** is short but sharp, with a leg-breaking start and panoramic reward. Meanwhile, **Col St-Jean**, at the valley's western end, offers a longer but more forgiving climb through forest and pasture.

These passes are rarely busy and normally ideal if you're warming up, short on time, or just want a ride without traffic or fuss. They're also great e-bike territory.

Col de Larche

Col de la Bonette

HOW TO

Rent Locally	**Best Time to Ride**	**Bring Layers**	**Need Repairs?**
Cycle Ubaye Sports in Barcelonnette offers road bikes, e-bikes and advice on current conditions and routes.	June to September is safest – passes open late and can see snow even in early summer.	It can be 30°C in Barcelonnette and 5°C at the top. Windbreakers and gloves are a must.	For moto issues, head to **Sport Moto** in Barcelonnette – quick, friendly and used to travellers in a bind.

Earn bragging rights

Cycling in the Ubaye Valley is all about long climbs, wild landscapes and the feeling that you've left the busy Alps behind. Most passes average a steady 6 to 7% grade, with occasional bursts into 8 to 9% (sometimes higher), enough to get your legs burning, but rarely brutal.

Road conditions are usually excellent, traffic is light outside high season, and the scenery is always worth it.

To do this challenge, I based myself in Barcelonnette and rode a different col every day. Stronger riders can ride up two or three a day for a real alpine challenge. If that sounds like too much, an e-bike makes things easier without spoiling the experience.

Motorcyclists will find these roads just as rewarding, with wide turns, minimal potholes, and steep switchbacks.

Cyclists chasing bragging rights can try to tackle all seven passes and earn the Brevet des 7 Cols. Sure, it's not a real diploma, but for cyclists who love climbing, it's a badge of honour. Details at the Barcelonnette tourist office.

Places We Love to Stay

€ Budget €€ Mid-range €€€ Top-end

Moustiers-Ste-Marie
Map p263

Camping à la Ferme de la Graou € Stellar views over the Verdon and shady sites. There's no electricity or hot water, but it's a great, close-to-nature budget option.

Camping à la Ferme du Maunard € Right on the lake, this is a clean, calm, family-friendly campground.

Camping Bio Verdon € Located on an organic vegetable farm run by Jean-Marc, who is also a rock-climbing guide, this is a great campground with lots of space, clean toilets and good vibes.

Hôtel Le Colombier €€ Set among olive trees and lavender fields, this charming hotel offers modern rooms with private terraces, a heated pool and tennis courts, all within a short walk of the village centre.

La Ferme Rose €€ This boutique hotel, set in a former farmhouse, boasts uniquely decorated rooms filled with vintage artefacts, lush gardens and a relaxed ambience, perfect for a serene getaway.

Hôtel La Forge €€ This friendly village hotel offers simple, comfortable rooms and a restaurant with terrace seating – perfect after a day exploring the Gorges du Verdon.

Le Jardin de Célina €€€ Stylish yet relaxed, this boutique guesthouse has a pool, spa, and restaurant – with lavender fields just beyond your terrace. A serene base for exploring the plateau.

Monastère de Ségriès €€€ A former Cistercian monastery turned secluded guesthouse, this peaceful retreat offers simple charm, shady courtyards and nature all around – perfect for walkers, writers or quiet weekends.

Digne-les-Bains

Les Eaux Chaudes € Three-star campground, great for families with a pool and shady trees to pitch a tent. For cyclists or hikers it's an especially good deal. Option to recharge electric cars too.

Hôtel Villa Gaïa €€ A welcoming 19th-century manor turned small hotel, with just 15 rooms, mountain views and hearty half-board meals served in the garden.

Le Grand Paris €€ A shabby-chic hotel in downtown Digne with a lovely patio and spacious, if a little dated, rooms. Also has a pair of studio apartments to rent by the week.

Ecolodge La Pastouliere €€ New eco-friendly former farm north of Dignes, restored by Gloria and Regis. Comfortable rooms and good prices that attract hikers of the GR69 but also cyclists, bikers and other outdoor lovers.

Banon

Camping l'Épi Bleu € Good budget option near Banon for families who want central access to visit the region and comfortable amenities in the campground. It's possible to rent caravans or quaint little mobile homes. Kids will love the waterslide.

Auberge de l'Abbaye €€ In the heart of Cruis near Banon, this family-run inn offers nine comfortable rooms and a restaurant serving traditional Provençal cuisine. Guests can enjoy a terrace and easy access to the historic 13th-century St-Martin church next door.

Villa Morelia, Ubaye Valley

La Bousquetière, Ubaye Valley

Lou Jas des Parpalhouns €€ A cosy stone cottage for two to four, or a farmhouse for six to seven, with views and a private terrace. Weekly rentals only – perfect for slow stays near Banon's lavender trails.

Pays de Forcalquier

Bergerie La Beaudine €€ Quiet, relaxed and full of Provençal charm, La Beaudine is a peaceful bastide on a leafy hillside above Forcalquier, with a pool, garden hammocks and homemade breakfasts.

Jardin de l'Abbaye de Valsaintes €€ Get an intimate experience at the rose, dry and vegetable gardens at the old abbey. Sleeping in basic but comfortable rooms, you'll get the peace of the gardens when the day visitors have gone home.

La Margotte €€ Once the home of Jean Giono, this warm, book-filled B&B offers simple rooms, garden views and quiet inspiration just steps from literary history.

Le Couvent des Minimes €€€ A former 17th-century convent turned luxury spa hotel, this serene hilltop retreat blends historic stonework with refined service, gardens and a dreamy L'Occitane spa.

La Maison des Chapitres €€€ This 15th-century *hôtel particulier*, first the residence of art curator David Galloway, now offers five distinctive guest rooms and hosts cultural events in the heart of Forcalquier.

Ubaye Valley   p277

La Bousquetière €€ Set in a tranquil hamlet near Jausiers, this charming guesthouse occupies an 18th-century farmhouse. It offers three spacious guest rooms and a separate *gîte* (cottage).

Hôtel Azteca €€ An art deco–inspired hotel in central Barcelonnette offering uniquely decorated rooms, a spa and easy access to local attractions.

Hôtel l'Équipe €€ Located just 100m from the ski slopes in Le Sauze, this is a family-friendly hotel with comfortable, mountain-style rooms.

L'Auberge €€ Simple, comfortable rooms and a restaurant serving generous local dishes. With rustic decor and adorned with various old objects, it's off the beaten track on the road into Ubaye Valley.

La Posada €€ A nice guesthouse with mountain views, five comfy rooms, homemade breakfasts and direct access to trails. Ideal for slow stays in a wild, upper Ubaye Valley location.

L'Attrapeur de Rêves €€ This eco-conscious guesthouse blends comfort with nature: sparkling rooms, organic meals and a peaceful garden with sweeping alpine views.

Villa Morelia €€€ Set within a 1-hectare park, this 4-star château hotel offers elegant rooms with 360-degree mountain views, a gourmet restaurant and an outdoor pool.

TOOLKIT

The chapters in this section cover the most important topics you'll need to know about in Provence & the Côte d'Azur. They're full of nuts-and-bolts information and valuable insights to help you understand and navigate the region and get the most out of your trip.

Arriving
p286

Getting Around
p287

Money
p288

Accommodation
p289

Family Travel
p290

Health & Safe Travel
p291

Food, Drink & Nightlife
p292

Responsible Travel
p294

LGBTIQ+ Travellers
p296

Accessible Travel
p297

How to Visit Markets
p298

Nuts & Bolts
p299

Language
p300

Cycle path at Pont St-Bénézet (p215), Avignon
LUCENTIUS/GETTY IMAGES

Arriving

Aéroport Nice Côte d'Azur is an important intercontinental gateway to the region, and Aéroport Marseille Provence is connected to many European destinations as well. Avignon, Aix-en-Provence and Marseille are connected to Paris on the TGV high-speed rail network. Many services continue along the coast to Nice, but at a slower pace.

Border Crossings

As France is part of the Schengen zone, there are no formalities to complete when crossing land borders from elsewhere in the EU. ID checks at the Italian border at Menton are rare.

Visas

Travellers from the UK, Canada, New Zealand, the US and Australia can stay up to 90 days in any 180-day period with no visa. See schengenvisainfo.com for updates.

Wi-Fi

Follow the prompts to connect to free, untimed wi-fi at both Nice and Marseille airports. Marseille St-Charles and Nice Ville train stations also offer free wi-fi.

Tax Refunds

Non-EU residents can claim VAT refunds on purchases made in France over €100 in value at self-service machines called PABLO or at Interchange offices at Aéroport Nice Côte d'Azur.

Public Transport from Airport to City Centre

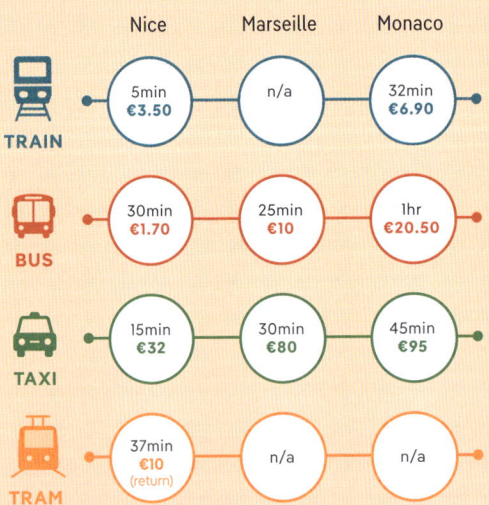

	Nice	Marseille	Monaco
TRAIN	5min €3.50	n/a	32min €6.90
BUS	30min €1.70	25min €10	1hr €20.50
TAXI	15min €32	30min €80	45min €95
TRAM	37min €10 (return)	n/a	n/a

EUROPEAN TRAVEL INFORMATION AND AUTHORISATION SYSTEM (ETIAS)

Towards the end of 2026, the European Commission's new electronic vetting system – European Travel Information and Authorisation System (ETIAS) – will begin operation. Nationals from 59 non-EU, visa-exempt countries, including the UK, US, Canada, Australia and New Zealand, will have to fill in a pre-arrival online form. Once approved, travellers will be able to remain up to 90 days out of any 180-day period in 30 European countries. Applications can be made online and cost €7 and your ETIAS will remain valid for three years, or until your passport expires, whichever comes first. For updated information, see *etiasvisa.com*.

Getting Around

You can't beat the value of the combined Zou! train and bus regional network when travelling between the main tourist centres. Elsewhere, it's best to have your own wheels.

TRAVEL COSTS

Car rental
€50-60/day

Petrol
**Approx
€1.90/litre**

E-Bike rental
€40/day

Train ticket Nice–Marseille
From €40

Bikes & E-Bikes

From breezy coastal tracks to pro-level mountain passes, the region is a cyclist's dream. Both road bikes and e-bikes are readily available to hire in most towns. Nice *(li.me* and *getapony.com)*, Monaco *(monabike.mc)*, Marseille *(levelo.ampmetropole.fr* and *li.me)* and Avignon *(velo-grandavignon.fr)* have user-friendly public bike and e-bike share schemes.

Taxis & Rideshares

You can't just hail a taxi in the region; when in doubt, there will always be a taxi rank at the train station. Uber is a well-established rideshare platform in the bigger cities. Note Uber can drop off but not pick up in Monaco. The app Taxi Monaco is the principality's alternative.

TIP

French carpooling app BlaBlaCar is the country's favourite app for connecting drivers with travellers heading in the same direction. See *blablacar.com*.

USING PUBLIC TRANSPORT

Both Nice and Marseille's bus and tram networks use a contactless card system. Buy Nice's **Ma Carte** onboard buses for €2 (plus the cost of a single fare, €1.70), using cash only or at ticket booths at tram stations. In Marseille, you can pay using your bank card. Tap on when boarding. There's no need to tap off.

Speed Limit

The motorway speed is 130km, except in the Alpes-Maritimes where it drops to 110km. Motorways, called *autoroutes*, are toll roads. Be aware of speed cameras, roadworks and traffic jams and other obstacles. To calculate the best route, use a navigation app like Waze *(waze.com)*.

Parking

Parking in big cities and tourist destinations is becoming increasingly difficult, although new park-and-ride options are springing up. Many towns offer 30 minutes to an hour of free metered parking but a ticket is still required. As a general rule, street parking, if metered, is free between noon & 2pm and in the evening.

Peak Hour

During peak commuter times, the motorway exits around Aix-en-Provence, Toulon and everywhere between Nice and Antibes can be gridlocked; expect the same around Monaco. Between Menton and St-Tropez, local English-speaking radio station *106.5 FM Riviera Radio* provides live traffic updates.

DRIVING ESSENTIALS

Drive on the right.

Priorité à droite means you must yield to vehicles entering from the right.

.08
Blood alcohol limit is 0.08%.

Money

CURRENCY: EURO (€)

Credit & Debit Cards

Many, but not all, businesses accept credit or debit card payments. That said, always carry a small reserve of cash, particularly in small towns or in the markets. Small businesses may ask for a minimum spend to pay with card. Tap payments are authorised up to €50.

Digital Payments

It's increasingly common to use your phone's digital wallet to pay for things in France. Still, it's worth having an alternative mode of payment at hand (cash, physical credit or debit card) for occasions when the facility is not available, such as at petrol station pumps and toll booths.

ATMs

There is no shortage of ATMs, known as *distributeurs automatiques de billets* (DAB), particularly in more populated areas. However, bank charges may apply to withdraw cash – check with your bank.

Obtaining cashback at a supermarket or another point of sale is not practised in France.

HOW MUCH FOR A...

French Riviera Pass (48hr)
€40

Sunlounger on the beach
€20–65

Boat from Ste-Maxime to St-Tropez
€9

museum entry
Free–€18

HOW TO... Save Money

Order the *plat du jour* (daily special) at lunchtime.

Check out visitor's passes like the French Riviera Pass or Avignon City Pass. You can bundle up plenty of the main attractions for one flat fee – and get discounts on others.

Public transport passes work out cheaper than individual tickets if you're taking more than one trip by public transport.

COINS

Always keep some coins handy to pay for public toilets (between €0.50 and €1), a coffee, a cool drink or to buy a ticket on the bus.

TIPPING & HAGGLING

France doesn't have a tipping culture similar to the US; in fact, as is indicated by the phrase *service compris* on the bottom of your restaurant or cafe bill, a 15% service fee is already included. To show your appreciation for good service, however, a *pourboire* (gratuity) in the form of a few coins is always welcome.

Find a treasure at the **L'Isle-sur-la-Sorgue** (p229) or **Nice** (p63) antique markets.

Go ahead and bargain. Price tags are firm everywhere except in the popular *brocantes* and *marchés aux puces* (antique and flea markets).

Accommodation

Chambres d'Hôte

Whether surrounded by lavender in the Luberon or lemon trees in Menton, cosy *chambres d'hôte* are the French equivalent of B&Bs: a handful of guest rooms inside a private home. Breakfast is included in the nightly rate; rooms are usually doubles so families will need to book two. Amenities can vary; pools and parking are popular add-ons in Provence.

Gîtes

To live out your Provençal holiday dreams, nothing beats the romance of a stone *gîte*, a rural, self-catered cottage. Usually rented by the week in the summer months, or for shorter durations the remainder of the year, *gîtes* come in all shapes and sizes, from rustic barn conversions to sprawling villas with private pools, townhouses and mountain chalets.

Refuges & Gîtes d'Étape

Hikers bunk down in *refuges* (mountain huts) and *gîtes d'étape* (rest houses) dotted strategically atop mountains and beside lakes on popular trails. Facilities are basic, usually just bunkbeds in shared dorms and hot showers, but new friendships are often struck up over evening meals. Most shutter up outside of summer or open on reservation only. Booking in advance and sleeping bags (for *refuges*) are strongly recommended.

Camping

Wild camping is technically illegal in Provence and the Côte d'Azur, but there is no shortage of designated campsites across the region. Many lean towards the holiday-park definition of camping, with mobile homes and evening discos; *campings municipaux* (municipal campsites) can be smart options if you are looking for flat, uncluttered spaces to pitch a tent or park a campervan. Flashy glamping sites, including treehouses, are also popping up.

HOW MUCH FOR A NIGHT IN A...

chambre d'hôte
€60–200

mountain refuge
€20–30

hôtel de charme
€110 and up

Hôtels de Charme

Provence overflows with *hôtels de charme*, an unofficial definition for intimate, independently run hotels that offer a uniquely regional flavour. Expect sublime design, personalised service and a high-quality restaurant, all set inside character-filled buildings such as manors, *châteaux*, *priories* and *hôtels particuliers* (private townhouses) with manicured gardens and friendly hosts.

HIDDEN COSTS

All accommodation providers (including Airbnb) are obliged to collect a tourist tax on behalf of the local municipality. Exactly how much depends on the rating of the property: budget for a little over €1 per night extra for one-star establishments and around €4 when living it up in five-star glitz.

Bedding and towels aren't usually included in holiday-park-style campsites; if you don't bring your own, you can pay extra for a linen pack. Don't assume you'll find sheets in your *gîte* rentals either. An end-of-stay cleaning fee often applies, too.

Family Travel

Laze on a sunlounger at the beach while the kids play with a bucket and spade in the sand, or stretch out on the grass in one of the many gated parks and gardens – for sleep-deprived parents of young children in particular, the outdoor lifestyle and year-round sunshine of Provence and the Côte d'Azur provides a welcome, vitamin D–infused respite.

Reduced Rates

Children under four travel for free on the region's Zou! train and bus networks, assuming they sit on your lap. Nice's Ligne d'Azur network is free for under-4s. Admission is free for under-12s (and sometimes under-18s) at many state-run museums and sites; otherwise, a reduced rate applies for children's tickets. Keep your eyes peeled for family-entry tickets.

Eating with Kids

Most restaurants have a set-priced *menu enfant* (children's menu) at lunch and dinner; expect to pay between €10 and €12 for a meal with a drink and scoop of ice-cream for dessert. Dinner service rarely starts before 7pm. *Boulangeries* abound with all-day supplies of croissants, *pains au chocolat* and other delights for snack times.

No Change

Nappy-changing facilities are the exception rather than the rule in cafes and restaurants. Carry a changing mat and be prepared to improvise. Dedicated private breastfeeding spaces are almost non-existent.

Not So Pram-Friendly

The narrow streets that make the villages of Provence and the Côte d'Azur such a photographer's delight make pram-wrangling bumpy. Smaller, lighter prams, such as the fold-up types that fit on airplanes fare best on the cobblestones.

KID-FRIENDLY PICKS

Musée Océanographique de Monaco (p107)

Four floors of wonder, including a vibrant aquarium and mesmerising multimedia show.

St-Martin-Vésubie (p81)

Indoor fun at Vésubia Mountain Park and outdoor adventures in the majestic Mercantour.

Plage de Pampelonne (p124)

With a long curve of fine buttercream sand, there's no better beach in the region.

Gorges du Verdon (p264)

With rafting and rock climbing, canyoning and hiking, energetic teens are all set in this natural landscape.

CAMPING COOL

Camping in France can mean many things besides pitching a tent. As a general rule, campsites are hybrid holiday parks where you can pitch your tent, park your camping car or book a stay in a mobile home on site.

Since it can feel like the entire country migrates south in summer, the region overflows with options from the water's edge deep into the Haut-Var. Blessed with space and on-site facilities such as swimming pools, restaurants and play areas, they offer plenty of chances for kids to find playmates.

During the high-season months, most operate a weekday kids' club led by a trained team, as well as hosting lively evening shows.

Health & Safe Travel

HEALTH CARE

The French love their pharmacies and you are never far from one: a lit-up green cross indicates that a pharmacy is open. Call here first to treat cuts, infected insect bites, grazes and burns. Nice's Pharmacie Riviera (66 av Jean Médecin) is open 24/7. On Sundays, find out which one is open closest to you at 3237.fr. Dial 112 for an ambulance.

Hunting Season

Hunting is France's third-most popular sport and the hunting season – *la chasse* in French – runs from September to February. Signs reading *chasse en cours* are put up on forest tracks to make walkers, hikers and joggers aware that a hunt is underway, although it's probably best to postpone your planned outing for another day.

Forest Fires

Over a third of the Provence-Alpes-Côte d'Azur region is covered by natural forest, and sizzling heat can spark fires from early July to mid-September. *The Var* publishes daily fire-danger updates during summer on its social media accounts (see @Prefet83 on Facebook and X). The My Calanques app is similarly up to date.

ON THE BEACH

Never leave valuables unattended when in the water. Keep your eyes peeled for purple jellyfish; particularly during summer and autumn.

SWIM SAFELY

Green flag
Swimming authorised and supervised

Yellow flag
Swimming supervised. Limited or marked danger

Red flag
No swimming allowed

Red & yellow striped flag
Lifeguard supervision if first-aid post open

Purple flag
Pollution or other danger

Black & white chequered flag
Watersports zone; swim with caution

Petty Crime

Keep handbags and phones carefully guarded as pickpocketing is rife, particularly in busy tourist areas and on crowded trains of the Côte d'Azur. Lock your doors and wind up your windows while driving in bigger cities as thefts have been known to happen at red lights. Don't leave anything valuable on display in parked cars.

STORM ALEX

In October 2020, Storm Alex swept through the mountain communities of the Côte d'Azur, in particular the valleys of the Vésubie and the Roya. The force of the storm washed away homes and killed 10 people. Recovery has been slow, not least because of damage to the road infrastructure connecting these towns and villages to the coastline. As these communities rebuild, tourism is a key driver.

Food, Drink & Nightlife

When to Eat

Petit déjeuner (7–10am) French breakfasts are simple: a toasted baguette or croissant with coffee.

Déjeuner (noon–2.30pm) Lunch can be a baguette sandwich enjoyed on the run or a sit-down meal with a glass of wine.

Goûter (4pm) Timed for the end of school, this afternoon snack is a national sugar boost.

Dîner (7–10pm) Dinner is never rushed, with three courses (starter, main, dessert) and sometimes four (cheese).

Where to Eat

Brasserie Casual restaurant open all day with a menu of traditional favourites.

Snack Might have a couple of tables but mostly does take-away. Budget-friendly food to eat on the run.

Kiosk A roadside hut, often known for regional specialities such as *panisse* and *pan bagnat*.

Boulangerie Bakery for bread and pastries.

Pâtisserie Specialises in cakes of all sizes.

Cave A wine shop; can sell wine by the glass.

Bistrot de pays A rural restaurant where great value meals are made with local produce.

MENU DECODER

Entrée A starter or appetiser
Plat The main course
Dessert Dessert
Plat du jour Daily special
Formule A meal deal, usually in bakeries
Carte A menu
Menu Two or three courses at a fixed price
Fait maison Homemade
Menu dégustation A tasting menu (high-end restaurants)
Menu enfant Set-price kids' menu (meal, drink, dessert)
Viande Meat
Fruits de la mer Seafood
Légumes Vegetables
Glace Ice cream
Gâteau Cake
Boisson Drink
Pichet de vin A carafe of wine
Bouteille de vin A bottle of wine
Vin blanc White wine
Vin rouge Red wine
Vin rosé Rosé wine
Pression Draught beer
Démi 25cl draught beer
Carte des vins Wine list
Eau plat Still water
Eau pétillante Sparkling water
Carafe d'eau Tap water (free)

HOW TO... Order Rosé

Although it's synonymous with warmer months elsewhere in the world, it's always rosé season in Provence. This is the region that sparked the world's love affair with the pink drink. You can order it *au verre* (by the glass), *au pichet* (by the carafe; 25/50cl), or *à la bouteille* (by the bottle) from the *carte des vins* (wine list). A *pichet* costs less, but expect a more rustic wine. No one will bat an eyelid if you ask for a couple of *glaçons* (ice cubes) to be added in your glass – in fact, it's quite common to drink a *piscine de rosé*, or a glass of rosé wine served over a generous scoop of ice-cubes (you can also ask for a *piscine de vin blanc* if you'd prefer).

Côtes de Provence is the largest AOP (geographically defined wine-making area) in the region. Don't expect to find much rosé made anywhere else on the menu here, either.

HOW MUCH FOR A...

small pastry
€1.20-1.80

espresso coffee
€1.90-2.50

glass of wine
€3.50-8

pint of beer
€8

pizza
€10-17

plat du jour
€10-15

dinner at a Michelin-starred restaurant
€100 and up

single scoop of ice cream
€2.50

FROM LEFT: BBSTOCKIMAGE/
SHUTTERSTOCK, LIAMI/
SHUTTERSTOCK

HOW TO... Drink Pastis

Nothing screams summer in the south of France more than a highball glass of cloudy pastis, the anise-flavoured drink born in Marseille. For purists, there's only way to sip it: *à l'ancienne*. To prepare it just right, you'll need a 20ml shot in a tall glass, a carafe of water and a pot of ice cubes. For one part pastis, add five parts water to dilute the amber-coloured drink. Watch the liquid turn opaque as the water mixes with the spirit. Add ice cubes last – any earlier and it stops the release of delicate aromas.

Once you've got the hang of the basics, it's time to add a twist, so stock up on a collection of *sirops* (cordials). For a *mauresque*, add 10cl of *orgeat* (almond) syrup to your 20cl shot, before adding the water and the ice.

A *perroquet* shimmers green from a similar pour of mint cordial, while *la tomate* takes its name from the red colour the drink turns once a 10cl serve of grenadine cordial has been mixed in. Or go all out and swap the water for a can of Coca-Cola: et voilà, you've got yourself a *pétrole* (also called *mazout*).

MIXOLOGY

Across Provence, a new wave of craft distilleries is adding an artisanal twist to this classic drink. Marseille's Bière de la Plaine runs pastis-blending workshops near cours Julien. In Nice, keep your eyes peeled for the local Pastis de Nice.

COFFEE, TEA HOUSES & CAFÉ GOURMAND

Order *un café* (a coffee) and most people will assume an espresso, the shot of choice for kick-starting mornings or rounding off a meal. For an espresso with a dash of milk, ask for *une noisette*. As a blanket rule, the milk added to coffee, whether poured in cold, heated or frothed, is long-life.

On the menu, a cappuccino or a *café crème* (milk coffee) is often as adventurous as it gets. Thankfully, coffee culture is trickling through the region, and it's becoming easier to find a latte or flat white, or a quality brew to take away. An Australian owner has made Lorgues Cafe worth the detour when in the Var; Nice's **Café du Cycliste** (p077) is a similarly sure bet.

If tea is more to your taste, stop by a *salon de thé* (tea room). Chances are the setting will be wonderfully boho-chic, with hot drinks and accompanying sweet treats served up on mismatched china. Take your pick from a multitude of sachets of herbal teas *(tisanes);* tracking down a milky English tea is more difficult.

The restaurant menu conceals a sweet secret: a coffee and dessert combo called the *café gourmand*. An espresso (or *noisette*) is served with a selection of mini desserts of different styles, textures and colours; this pretty dish is made for indecisive dessert diners.

No *café gourmand* is ever the same; the selection changes daily, even in the same restaurant. And this variety is where, for most, the attraction lies.

Responsible Travel

Climate Change & Travel

It's impossible to ignore the impact we have when travelling; Lonely Planet urges all travellers to engage with their travel carbon footprint, which will mainly come from air travel. While there often isn't an alternative, travellers can look to minimise the number of flights they take, opt for newer aircrafts and use cleaner ground transport, such as trains. One proposed solution — purchasing carbon offsets — unfortunately does not cancel out the impact of individual flights. While most destinations will depend on air travel for the foreseeable future, for now, pursuing ground-based travel where possible is the best course of action.

The **UN Carbon Offset Calculator** shows how flying impacts a household's emissions

The **ICAO's carbon emissions calculator** allows visitors to analyse the CO2 generated by point-to-point journeys

Local Meets

See the region through local eyes on a walking tour with a city **Greeter**. In Avignon and surrounds, Sanary-sur-Mer, Marseille, Nice and Cannes, these passionate volunteer guides show you the lesser-known side of their cities. See *greeters.fr*.

Cyclists Only

Keep an eye on the *Cols Réservés* dates every summer, when legendary mountain passes such as Allos, Agnel, Izoard, Galibier and Granon are closed to traffic in the morning to allow cyclists the chance to tackle these summits without any other road traffic.

Up to three million visitors visit Marseille's *calanques* (coves) annually. To combat overtourism, **Calanque de Sugiton** and **Calanque des Pierres Tombées** are now restricted and must be booked in advance. See *calanques-parcnational.fr*.

Take your rubbish back to the mainland after a day trip to the Îles des Lérins; the two islands off Cannes no longer have any garbage bins after tourist trash led to a proliferation of rats.

Support Rural Bistros

Dig into local flavours at great prices at a *bistrot de pays*. Championed by an association created to attract diners to rural towns and villages, they can be found across the region. See bistrotdepays.com.

Too Good to Waste

Find nearby bakeries, supermarkets, cafes and restaurants selling 'surprise bags', or end-of-service food bundles for a heavily reduced price, by downloading the **Too Good to Go** app *(toogoodtogo.com)*.

Best Beach

Relax on a sunlounger at **Baia Bella** (p66; *baiabella.com*) in Beaulieu-sur-Mer, France's first carbon-neutral beach according to Allcot. Solar panels, recycled water, wooden furniture and seabed cleaning are some of the sustainable initiatives at play in the sun.

Water Fountains
Save on single-use plastic by carrying a reusable water bottle. In Nice, public drinking-water stations offer the choice of still or sparkling water. The app **Free Taps** *(freetaps.earth)* directs you to the nearest fountain.

Green Touch
Search unique stays and other experiences on the website of Mercantour Ecotourisme *(mercantourecotourisme.eu)*, an association grouping sustainably minded accommodation providers, restaurants, producers and artisans in the Parc National du Mercantour.

E-Dreams
Plug your electric car into charging points scattered across the region, from five-star hotels to campsites and at public networks operated by Eborn (Alpes-de-Haute-Provence, Var), Wiiiz and Prise de Nice (Alpes-Maritimes), larecharge (Bouches-du-Rhône) and Vauclus'elec (Luberon).

Solar Power
Enjoy a sunny serving of solar cuisine at Le Présage *(lepresage.fr)*, a 100% solar-powered restaurant in Marseille. The cuisine is made from seasonal, locally sourced ingredients and cooked in solar-powered ovens.

Say yes to **Uber Green** to ride in an electric or a hybrid vehicle for very little extra charge.

Dine at restaurants sourcing from local producers. Many menus specify the provenance of their ingredients.

A Changing Aesthetic
The purple explosion of blooming lavender fields is emblematic of Provence, but the image as we know it has to change. Rows of lavender with cover crops in between are the sustainable vision of the future.

RESOURCES

laclefverte.org
An international label for sustainable accommodation.

bienvenue-a-la-ferme.com
Your stay, meal or visit will support an independent farmer.

blablacar.com
Hitch a ride with France's incredibly popular rideshare app.

LGBTIQ+ Travellers

The French have long considered people's private lives just that: private. This laissez-faire attitude means that France is one of the most LGBTIQ+-friendly countries in the world. The rainbow flag flies high in Nice; it's more discreet in Marseille. There are also gay bars in Cannes, Aix-en-Provence and Avignon. As always, rural areas tend to be more conservative than bigger cities.

Nice Events

Nice is the undisputed hub of the LGBTIQ+ scene in the region. Plan your visit to coincide with one of the following community events. Glitter and confetti cover Nice in February during France's first queer carnival, **Lou Queernaval.** Expect live bands, energetic dancers, dazzling floats and drag queens. The queer film festival **In&Out** spans a week in April. Look for autumn editions in Cannes and Toulon. Crowds swarm Nice's main streets for July's **Pink Parade (Pride)**. The dress code is white for the Centre LGBT de Nice's loud and proud **Dolly Party** street fiesta in August.

BEST OF THE REST EVENTS

Pride spills onto the streets in June with **Marche des Fiertés** parades in Arles, Toulon and Avignon. July's **Pride Marseille** is 30 years strong; the day itself is now prefaced by two weeks of debates, exhibitions, workshops and shows. Queer acts take to the stage during summer's **Festival Off Avignon**. Autumn's **ZeFestival** LGBTIQ+ film festival takes over cinema screens in Nice, Marseille, Toulon, Avignon and Seillans.

Neighbourhood Watch

Painted in the colours of the rainbow flag, rue Bonaparte is Nice's LGBTIQ+ HQ. Despite a host of gay bars, gay saunas and gay-friendly restaurants, Marseille lacks a gay quarter – in fact, the city's first LGBTIQ+ centre *(centrelgbtqiamarseille.org)* only opened its doors in 2023. The city's underground music scene is anti-fascist and queer-friendly.

MONACO PRIDE

Monaco Pride is still in its infancy – 2022 marked the inaugural edition. The formal event lacks flamboyant flair, but it's a step in the right direction: in 2022 Monaco was called out by the European Commission against Racism and Intolerance (ECRI) for unjustified differences in treatment between same-sex and heterosexual couples. Monaco's first LGBTIQ+ association, Mon'Arc en Ciel *(monarcenciel.com)*, launched in 2024.

LOCAL RESOURCES

Find LGBTIQ+ friendly hotel listings on **Gay Sejour** *(gay-sejour.com)*.
Get out and about in the great outdoors with gay and lesbian hiking club **Rando's Provence** *(randosprovence.org)*.
Keep up to date with what's on by bookmarking LGBTIQ+ travel blog **Gay French Riviera** *(gayfrenchriviera.com)*.
LGBT+ PACA *(lgbt-paca.org)* groups all the local LGBTIQ+ associations, although it's more active on social media.

Nice Irisée Naturellement

Nice's gay-friendly venues carry the *Irisée Naturellement* (Naturally Iridescent) branding; browse the city's gay-friendly guide *explorenicecotedazur.com* for a list of theatres, bars, clubs, saunas and cruising bars.

Accessible Travel

Travel across Provence and the Côte d'Azur still presents accessibility challenges, although efforts are underway to make tourism more inclusive. Many *offices de tourisme* publish a comprehensive mobility guide in English.

Cobblestone Streets

High-walled medieval villages and city neighbourhoods often have uneven cobblestone streets not adapted for wheelchair use. Paved sidewalks frequently become car parking spaces or restaurant terraces.

Airports

Both Aéroport Nice Côte d'Azur and Aéroport Marseille-Provence provide a comprehensive range of services for travellers requiring special assistance; notify your airline of your requirements at least 48 hours before departure.

Accommodation

Lifts and accessible rooms are harder to find in older hotels and small B&Bs; however, bigger, brand-name hotels should have both. **Gîtes de France** *(gites-de-france.com)* filters B&Bs and self-catering accommodation by accessibility.

RESOURCES

tourisme-handicaps.org Accessible hotels, restaurants, tourist operators, hiking trails and nature sites are grouped under the label Tourisme & Handicaps.

zou.maregionsud.fr/en/accessibility Contact to arrange special assistance in advance on the region's trains. Bookings 48 hours in advance are essential.

info.urgence114.fr 114 is the French emergency number for the deaf and hard of hearing. Send a text message, connect through the website or download the app.

BEACH

Check for accessible beaches near you using the **Handiplage** website *(handiplage.fr)*; there are over 30 in the region. The better equipped are overseen by trained staff with equipment such as amphibious wheelchairs.

Female & Solo Travellers

Female and solo travellers should exercise the usual precautions when travelling Provence and the Côte d'Azur. Avoid walking alone through big cities late at night and early in the morning.

Car Hire & Transfers

Rent adapted cars for the duration of your stay through **Libertans** *(libertans.com)*. **MCMobility's** *(monaco-mobilites.mc)* fleet provides airport and train station transfers among its transport services.

BUS & TRAM

Ligne d'Azur's *(lignesdazur.com)* dedicated mobility service Mobil'azur offers an on-demand bus in and around Nice and nearby villages, including Villefranche-sur-Mer, Èze, Vence and into the Vésubie. Most buses and all trams have retractable platforms.

Grands Prix

The Automobile Club de Monaco reserves a grandstand for spectators with reduced mobility to watch the Monaco Grand Prix, Monaco ePrix and Grand Prix Historique de Monaco. Pre-registration is required through the **Monegasque Association of Motor Disabilities** *(AMHM; amhm98.com)*.

How to Visit Markets

Busy and brimming with colours, scents and flavours, markets are an essential ingredient in the intoxicating recipe for life in Provence and the Côte d'Azur. More than a chance to fill your basket with fragrant fresh produce, the market is a highly social occasion and a chance to catch up with neighbours and friends, as well as on all the local gossip.

On Special

Plan your shopping list around local specialities in season: summer screams sweet melons from Cavaillon and juicy strawberries from Carros while winter kitchens warm up with pungent truffles from Carpentras and candied chestnuts from Collobrières.

Inside Out

Covered food markets are a treasure trove of culinary delights come lunchtime, where you can feast on regional fare at wallet-friendly prices. Eat in at Monaco's **Marché de la Condamine**, or take away at the **Marché Forville** in Cannes.

Market Do's

Early bird catches the worm Arrive early for your pick of the produce. Vendors start to pack up around lunchtime. By 1pm, the scene can feel like the markets never happened.

BYO bag Do bring your own bags, whether a woven basket, canvas tote or reusable supermarket bag.

Small change Do carry some cash; the stallholders that accept cards often have a minimum spend.

Market Don'ts

Don't be afraid to ask for advice It's OK to let the stallholder choose your fruit and veg; perhaps a ripe melon for today and an avocado ready to be cut open tomorrow. Same goes for serving suggestions and cooking tips.

Bargaining Save it for antique and flea markets; haggling is a no-go at produce markets.

Night Markets

In July and August, Provence's *marchés nocturnes* kick off around 5pm. Expect food to eat on big communal tables, artisanal wares for souvenirs, live music and lots of smiles.

WHAT'S IN A NAME?

- **Marché provençal** As well as fruit and veg, you can pick up tasty tapenade, runny cheeses and spicy sausages for a picnic, fresh flowers or a floppy sun hat or new linen shirt here.
- **Marché des producteurs** Farmers market where zero-kilometre produce reigns.
- **Marché de nuit** Also known as *marché nocturne*, this market comes alive as the sun starts to set. Expect local arts and crafts accompanied by a live band and food trucks.
- **Marché à la brocante** Antique market; scour for a one-of-a-kind souvenirs on the cours Saleya in Nice and along the canals in L'Isle-sur-la-Sorgue.
- **Vide-grenier** Car boot sale.

Nuts & Bolts

OPENING HOURS

Banks open around 9am, close for lunch for at least an hour between noon and 2pm and for the day by 5.30 or 6pm. Can be closed Mondays.

Shops open at 10am and close around 7pm. Smaller boutiques may still close for lunch.

Retailers are increasingly opening on Sunday (usually from 11am), particularly shopping malls. Supermarkets usually open Sunday morning only.

Restaurant hours vary but most stop serving between lunch and dinner. Many close Monday.

Bars stay open until around 1am.

Smoking

Smoking is forbidden inside restaurants, cafes and bars as well as on public transport and near forests in summer. Certain beaches are now smoke-free.

Weights & Measures

France uses the metric system. Decimal places are indicated by commas, and thousands by points.

Public Toilets

Carry some small change to pay for public toilets, although some now accept card payments. Expect to pay either €0.50 or €1. In cafes, order a drink.

GOOD TO KNOW

Time zone
GMT+1

Country code
+33

Emergency number
112

Population
5.2 million

Electricity
220V/50Hz

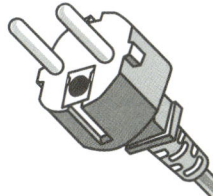

PUBLIC HOLIDAYS

Good Friday and St Stephen's Day are not public holidays in Provence and the Côte d'Azur.

New Year's Day 1 January

Easter Sunday & Monday Late March/April

May Day 1 May

WWII Victory Day 8 May

Ascension Thursday May (40th day after Easter)

Pentecost & Whit Monday Mid-May to mid-June (7th Sunday after Easter)

Bastille Day (Fête Nationale) 14 July

Assumption Day 15 August

All Saints' Day 1 November

Remembrance Day 11 November

Christmas Day 25 December

Monaco shares some public holidays with France. Differences include:

La Ste Dévote (27 January)

Corpus Christi Thursday (60th day after Easter)

Monaco National Day (19 November)

Language

Standard French is taught and spoken throughout France. This said, regional accents and dialects are an important part of identity in certain regions, but you'll have no trouble being understood anywhere if you stick to standard French.

Basics
Hello. Bonjour. *bon-zhoor*
Goodbye. Au revoir. *o-rer-vwa*
Yes. Oui. *wee*
No. Non. *non*
Please. S'il vous plaît. *seel voo play*
Thank you. Merci. *mair-see*
Excuse me. Excusez-moi. *ek-skew-zay-mwa*
Sorry. Pardon. *par-don*
What's your name? Comment vous appelez-vous? *ko-mon voo-za-play voo*
My name is ... Je m'appelle ... *zher ma-pel ...*
Do you speak English? Parlez-vous anglais? *par-lay-voo ong-glay*
I don't understand. Je ne comprends pas. *zher ner kom-pron pa*

Directions
Where's ...? Où est ...? *oo ay ...*
What's the address? Quelle est l'adresse? *kel ay la-dres*
Could you write the address, please? Est-ce que vous pourriez écrire l'adresse, s'il vous plaît? *es-ker voo poo-ryay ay-kreer la-dres seel voo play*
Can you show me (on the map)? Pouvez-vous m'indiquer (sur la carte)? *poo-vay-voo mun-dee-kay (sewr la kart)*

Signs
Entrée Entrance
Fermé Closed
Ouvert Open
Sortie Exit
Toilettes/WC Toilets

Time
What time is it? Quelle heure est-il? *kel ay til*
It's (8) o'clock. Il est (huit) heures. *il ay (weet) er*
Half past (10). Il est (dix) heures et demie. *il ay (deez) er ay day-mee*
morning matin. *ma-tun*
afternoon après-midi. *a-pray-mee-dee*
evening soir. *swar*
yesterday hier. *yair*
today aujourd'hui. *o-zhoor-dwee*
tomorrow demain. *der-mun*

Emergencies
Help! Au secours! *o skoor*
Leave me alone! Fichez-moi la paix! *fee-shay-mwa la pay*
I'm ill. Je suis malade. *zher swee ma-lad*
Call ... Appelez... *a-play*
  a doctor un médecin. *un mayd-sun*
  the police la police. *la po-lees*

Eating & Drinking
What would you recommend? Qu'est-ce que vous conseillez? *kes-ker voo kon-say-yay*
Cheers! Santé! *son-tay*
That was delicious. C'était délicieux! *say-tay day-lee-syer*

NUMBERS

1 un *un*
2 deux *der*
3 trois *trwa*
4 quatre *ka-trer*
5 cinq *sungk*
6 six *sees*
7 sept *set*
8 huit *weet*
9 neuf *nerf*
10 dix *dees*

DISTINCTIVE SOUNDS

Throaty r, silent h, nasal vowels (pronounced as if you're trying to force the sound 'through the nose').

Street Talk

What's up? Quoi de neuf?
Drop it/nevermind! Laisse-tomber!
I can't be bothered/am feeling lazy J'ai la flemme
Enjoy your meal! Bon app!
No way! C'est pas vrai!
Let's go/do it! C'est parti!
Perfect! It's good! Nickel
Oh god! La vache! (literally 'the cow')
Good luck/break a leg Merde
There you go/there you have it Et voilà

And if you want to swear French-style (or express your joy at a gobsmackingly gorgeous view, amazement or disbelief at something... the word is used in many different ways), simply say *Putain!*

DONATIONS TO ENGLISH

Numerous – thanks to the Norman invasion of England in the 11th century, some estimate that three-fifths of everyday English vocabulary arrived via French. You may recognise *café, déjà vu, bon vivant, cliché...*

Language Family

Romance (developed from the Latin spoken by the Romans during their conquest of the 1st century BCE). Close relatives include Italian, Spanish, Portuguese and Romanian.

Must-Know Grammar

French has a formal and informal word for 'you' (*vous* and *tu* respectively). It distinguishes between masculine and feminine forms of words, eg *beau/belle* (beautiful).

False Friends

Warning: many French words look like English words but have a different meaning altogether, eg *menu* is a set lunch, not a menu (which is *carte* in French).

Why Bother

You may be told of a cosy vineyard way off the tourist track, or discover that there's little merit in the stereotype about the French being rude.

WHO SPEAKS FRENCH?

French is an official language of 29 countries, including France, Belgium, Canada, Democratic Republic of the Congo and Vanuatu.

80 million speak French as their first language

50 million speak French as their second language

THE PROVENCE & THE CÔTE D'AZUR
STORYBOOK

Our writers delve deep into different aspects of life in the region

A History of Provence & the Côte d'Azur in 15 Places
A region that feels like a museum
Chrissie McClatchie
p304

A Spotlight on Niçoise Cuisine
The street food that's quickly becoming a fine-dining star
Chrissie McClatchie
p308

Facing into Le Mistral Gagnant
The story of the famous and fearsome wind of Provence
Ashley Parsons
p311

Beat the Heat in Marseille
La canicule, or 'heat wave', transforms Marseille in summer
Michael Frankel
p314

Les Arènes d'Arles (p190)

A HISTORY OF PROVENCE & THE CÔTE D'AZUR IN
15 PLACES

Mysterious cave paintings, Roman arenas, papal palaces, Belle Époque buildings and architectural marvels. In many ways, Provence and the Côte d'Azur feels like one large, open-air museum. By Chrissie McClatchie

WELCOME TO A corner of the world that brings the history books of your childhood instantly to life, starting with a slab of fossilised ammonites, 200 million years old, cast for eternity in the Alpes-de-Haute-Provence.

After that, the mysterious rock engravings that haunt the Vallée des Merveilles seem positively modern, until you learn they date back to between 1800 and 1500 BCE. Fast forward to the Greeks, who colonised Marseille in 600 BCE and brought with them wine, grapes and olives. The Romans weren't far behind and left the imprint of their grandeur in towns and cities across the region.

In the Middle Ages, much of the population fled to the hills, taking refuge in thick-walled hilltop villages that offered protection from invaders, while the papacy swapped Rome for Avignon. Wars and plagues followed, as well as Napoléon, who marched across the region to reclaim his throne in Paris. Then came the first tourists in search of winter sun and the Côte d'Azur was born.

Whether your favourite bedtime reading was stories of the earliest humans or more recent tales of power-hungry emperors or swapping city life for the Provençal idyll, Provence and the Côte d'Azur has it covered.

1. Réserve Géologique de Haute-Provence
WHEN OCEANS COVERED THE LAND

Over one hundred million years ago, the Alps were covered by a vast temperate sea. Today, a mammoth 230,000-hectare stretch of the mountain range is Europe's largest protected geological reserve: the Réserve Géologique de Haute-Provence. While the park stretches across three Provence départements (Alpes-de-Haute-Provence, Var, Haute-Alpes), its most emblematic site is just outside of Dignes-les-Bains in the Alpes-de-Haute-Provence. Known as La Dalle aux Ammonites (the Ammonite Slab), this wall is a geological marvel, with over 1500 ammonite shells from 200 million years ago frozen in time. The largest specimen is an incredible 70cm long.

For more on Réserve Géologique de Haute-Provence, see page 270

2. Vallée des Merveilles
ANCIENT ART

Over 40,000 mysterious petroglyphs – ancient pictures carved into rock – cover the red stones of the Vallée des Merveilles and give this narrow canyon its name: the Valley of Wonders. Much mystery surrounds the identity of the artists behind them, but what's not up for question is just how important these prehistoric etchings of animals, weapons, tools and even people are when it comes to giving us a glimpse into Bronze Age life in the region. You really need to plan for two days to do it justice; because access is limited unless you are accompanied by a qualified guide, this remains one of the Côte d'Azur's blissfully untouched sites.

For more on the Vallée des Merveilles, see page 84

3. Roman Arles
VENI, VIDI, VICI

Arelate (Arles) owes its ancient prosperity to Julius Caesar, who elevated the status of the town as a reward for its support when his troops plundered nearby Marseille in 49 BCE. Befitting its new status as a regional Roman darling, Arles welcomed high-society events like gladiator fights, chariot races and plays in its 20,000-seat amphitheatre and 12,000-seat theatre. Modelled on the Colosseum in Rome, Les Arènes d'Arles, as the amphitheatre is known, stands tall as the largest Roman monument in France. A block away, centuries of looting have taken their toll on the Théâtre Antique, but it's still a majestic setting for summer events.

For more on Roman Arles, see page 190

4. Théâtre Antique, Orange
PAX ROMANA

Louis XIV called Orange's Théâtre Antique 'the finest wall in my kingdom' but he owed his gratitude to the stability of the Roman empire, specifically during the reign of Augustus (27 BCE–14 CE), who commissioned the theatre's construction. A magnificent setting fit for an emperor, the ingenious venue was built to host 10,000 spectators. The natural acoustics are so superb that even those in the furthest corners could hear the action from the stage. In the centuries since, the site has been pillaged, used as a prison and a place of refuge. Today, it's under UNESCO protection.

For more on Théâtre Antique, Orange, see page 190

5. Monastère de la Verne, Collobrières
A REFUGE FROM THE WORLD

Just an hour from St-Tropez but a world away from the flash of paparazzi cameras, the Monastère de la Verne rises up on a ridge in the Massif des Maures, surrounded by little more than chestnut and oak trees. The 12th-century monastery is said to have been built on the site of a pagan temple to the goddess Laverna, who protected the brigands who took shelter within the mountain ranges' leafy folds. Three fires in three separate centuries couldn't drive out the monks, but the French Revolution did. Almost two hundred years would pass before another religious order moved in.

For more on Monastère de la Verne, Collobrières, see page 130

6. Palais des Papes
GAME OF THRONES

A series of seven French-born popes put Avignon on the map in the 14th century when they made the city on the Rhône the centre of the Roman Catholic universe. It may have been the seat of power for less than 70 years – during the Great Schism (1378–1417), rival popes resided at Rome and Avignon, denouncing and even

Petroglyphs, Vallée des Merveilles (p84)

excommunicating one another – but the papal presence can still be felt in the immense Palais de Papes, the largest Gothic palace ever built, as well as the prized red wine that flows through the cellars of nearby Châteauneuf-du-Pape, the site of the pope's summer residence.

For more on the Palais des Papes, see page 212

7. Palais Princier de Monaco
A HOLLYWOOD LOVE STORY

Set in their palace on Le Rocher, Monaco's oldest neighbourhood perched high above the Mediterranean Sea, the Grimaldis – aka the royal family of Monaco – stand firm as the longest-ruling royal family in Europe. Within these gilded walls, Prince Rainier III met Grace Kelly, Hollywood royalty, in 1955. But that's only part of the story that unfurls on a visit to the ornate Grands Appartements, or staterooms, the only section of the residence open to the public. A new chapter is being written as painstaking restoration works continue to bring sweeping Renaissance frescoes hidden under layers of paint for centuries back to the surface.

For more on Palais Princier de Monaco, see page 105

8. Route Napoléon
THE BEGINNING OF THE HUNDRED DAYS

In February 1815, Napoléon Bonaparte returned to home soil after fleeing exile on the Italian island of Elba. From Cannes, he set off on a route into the French Alps and then on to Paris. Once he arrived in the capital, just two and a half weeks later, he swept back to power in a legendary military comeback. The 325km path he took from the Côte d'Azur to Grenoble is now considered one of France's epic road trips, passing through destinations such as the potter's village of Vallauris that later inspired Picasso and the perfume-scented town of Grasse before flattening out on the alpine plains of the Alpes-de-Haute-Provence.

For more on the Route Napoléon, see page 268

9. Casino de Monte-Carlo
PLACE YOUR BETS

If you need an example of a building that changed the course of a nation's history, look no further than the Casino de Monte-Carlo. Built on an arid plateau dotted by olive trees, this Belle Époque beauty's opening in 1863 heralded the arrival of a new destination for Europe's elite – and a new direction for the tiny principality on the Mediterranean that had until then relied on agriculture as its main source of income. Not long after the casino threw open its doors, the similarly lavish Hôtel de Paris was inaugurated and the neighbourhood of Monte-Carlo was born.

For more on Casino de Monte-Carlo, see page 109

10. Barcelonnette
FROM THE ALPS TO MEXICO

In the early 19th century, a wave of young men left the villages of the Vallée de l'Ubaye in the Alpes-de-Haute-Provence in search of a new life in Mexico. They found success in the textile and banking industries, and many eventually returned to Provence with money to spend. And spend they did, building large villas as a visible testament to their wealth. Around 50 of these villas, mainly built between 1890 and 1930, still remain in Barcelonnette and Jausiers. Collectively, these elegant bourgeois residences are known around the valley as the 'Mexican villas'.

For more on Barcelonnette, see page 276

11. Nice
STROLL THE PROMENADE

During the late 19th and early 20th centuries, everyone from aristocrats to artists was drawn to the mild winters of the Côte d'Azur on doctor's orders – the sunshine was thought to cure tuberculosis in particular. Visitors returned every year for the colours, the light and the mild climate, making Nice's wide waterfront boulevards and Belle Époque gambling dens the place to be seen. At this time, winter was the high season in Nice, and the rich architectural legacy that remains has conferred a new distinction on the city: it's now a World Heritage–listed Winter Resort Town of the Riviera.

For more on Nice, see page 58

12. Villa Ephrussi de Rothschild
LIFESTYLES OF THE RICH AND FAMOUS

On the leafy millionaires' peninsula of St-Jean-Cap-Ferrat, the Villa Ephrussi de Rothschild is one of the Belle Époque jewels of the Côte d'Azur. Appearing like a two-tiered,

Villa Ephrussi de Rothschild (p74)

candy-pink wedding cake, the building brims with ornate architectural detailing and is framed by manicured gardens. Commissioned as a winter residence for Baroness Béatrice Ephrussi de Rothschild in 1912, it has rooms are filled with objects from her personal art collection. Just before her death in 1933, she bequeathed the villa and all its collections to the Académie des Beaux-Arts, which has maintained it as a splendid museum of the era.

For more on Villa Ephrussi de Rothschild, see page 74

13. Ménerbes
TOUJOURS PROVENCE
It's the classic tale: busy city professional throws it all away to embrace rural life in a new country. But Peter Mayle wrote the script when he swapped his advertising career in London for a ramshackle farmhouse in the Luberon. The book that followed – *A Year in Provence* – put the sleepy village of Ménerbes on the map and triggered a slew of copycat travel writers. But more than that, his work crystallised the concept of the Provençal idyll that still defines the region today and draws visitors in ever-increasing numbers.

For more on Ménerbes, see page 242

14. Luma Arles
FUTURE PAST
The chrome facade of Luma Arles can be seen from all angles, its 11,000 stainless-steel panels shimmering in chorus against the southern French sun. The Frank Gehry–designed structure rises 56m high (it's the tallest building for miles) and is a bold statement of the future in a place so often defined by its past – although the architect drew inspiration from both the artist Vincent Van Gogh and the Romans. The creative campus is a new hub for the arts as well as a centre promoting future-forward thinking about topics such as sustainable design.

For more on Luma Arles, see page 188

15. Mareterra
TRANSFORMING THE SEA INTO LIVEABLE LAND
Ever since it was forced to cede the majority of its land to France in 1861, leaving it with a territory around the same size as New York's Central Park, Monaco's ruling Grimaldi family have grappled with the question of how their principality can grow. The answer has come from looking out towards the Mediterranean Sea. Since 1907, Monaco has grown by a quarter thanks to land reclamation. In December 2024, the latest addition to the national map was officially inaugurated, called Mareterra. This six-hectare pedestrian neighbourhood is also Monaco's greenest, with nearly 1000 trees planted, as well as 9000 sq metres of solar panels and 200 EV charging stations, among other eco-initiatives.

For more on Mareterra, see page 108

Socca (chickpea-flour pancake), Nice

A SPOTLIGHT ON NIÇOISE CUISINE

The lesser-known street food that's quickly becoming a fine-dining star. By Chrissie McClatchie

IN EARLY 2024, while on assignment to review a hip new hotel opening in Dubai, I did a double take. On the menu at one of its many dining venues helmed by a clutch of star chefs was *pissaladière*, a tart of caramelised onions layered on a base of doughy bread.

Having lived in Nice for nearly two decades, for me this is a familiar street food that I pick up at my local markets on a Wednesday morning or as a *goûter* (afternoon snack) for my children after school from the boulangerie. Yet, like typical Niçoise cuisine – the cuisine of Nice – it's little-known outside of the region. Or so I thought.

Since then, I've seen the *pissaladière* appear on more menus in unexpected places, as well as other traditional dishes from the city, like *panisse* (chickpea chips) and *pan bagnat* (salade Niçoise in a bread roll). These finds serve to demonstrate the extent to which Nice's food culture is starting to gain the recognition that it deserves.

Nowhere can this culinary renaissance be felt more than in the city of Nice itself, where this street-food heritage is being elevated to fine-dining status. That means, for visitors, there's no better time to tuck into the taste and flavours of the Côte d'Azur.

Simple but Not Simplistic

With a preference for oils over butter, Niçoise cuisine feels more aligned to Italian cooking than France's traditional sauce-based culinary culture. This makes sense, considering the city's history: for years France and Italy have been engaged in a tug-of-war for its attention – until a line was drawn in the sand in 1860 and Nice became French once and for all.

Socca, essentially a savoury chickpea-flour pancake and the classic Niçois street-food snack, is a local take on a dish that exists around the world, including just across the border in Italy's Liguria, where it is known as *farinata*.

Others dishes are much more specific to the city, such as the popular *tourte de blettes sucrée*, a sweet tart made from a savoury ingredient, Swiss chard (a staple along this coastline).

At its core are the colourful vegetables and legumes that can survive in the poor, water-deprived soils of the Mediterranean coastline. The chickpea, or *lou cèe* as it is known in the local dialect, is a staple in salads and aioli as well as in *socca* and panisse

'It's a simple cuisine because it only uses local produce', explains Nice-based culinary historian Alex Benvenuto. 'But it's not simplistic. It is elaborate and respectful of flavours.'

Not only does eating Niçoise mean eating local produce and seasonal flavours – but it's also a cuisine that offers something for those who follow a vegan, vegetarian, gluten-free or plant-based diet.

Benvenuto was among the group that campaigned to have authentic Niçoise cuisine recognised in France's inventory of Intangible Cultural Heritage in 2019, alongside the country's bistros and cafes and *pétanque* (boules).

STORYBOOK

A Fine-Dining Twist

Socca, *pissaladière*, *panisse* and *pan bagnat* are all foods that can be eaten on the run – wholesome enough to keep hunger pangs at bay before (or after) a day at work.

Much of Nice's cuisine is still enjoyed in a casual street-food setting: you'll spot the queue at Chez René Socca *(rene-socca. foodjoyy.com)* before you see the entrance: this cheap and cheerful Vieux Nice institution is the classic Niçoise street-food stop.

Newcomer D'Aqui *(daqui-barbajuans. com)* in Port Lympia has made a splash as the spot for bite-sized *barbajuans* (fried raviolis considered Monaco's national dish) to eat in or take away, while Chez Pipo *(chezpipo.fr)* is the undisputed address for *socca* served piping hot from the oven. And, if you see the Cuisine Nissarde sticker displayed proudly at a restaurant's entrance, you know that their dishes respect local culinary traditions: perennial favourites include Chez Acchiardo *(@restaurantacchiardo)* and Le Safari *(restaurant safari.fr)* in Vieux Nice.

Yet away from these more traditional addresses, you'll increasingly find dishes from the Niçois repertoire on the city's *bistronomique* (a bistro serving top-quality food) tables. Opposite the beach on les Ponchettes, Babel Babel *(babelbabel.fr)* sprinkles homemade *za'atar* over panisse in a delicious twist, and dishes them up as a gluten-free alternative to chips. To nab one of 24 seats at the wonderfully rustic La Merenda *(lamerenda.net)*, where a rich, slow-cooked *daube* (beef stew) is served with a half-moon of crispy yet creamy panisse, you'll need to book in advance on its social media pages.

It's no surprise Niçoise cuisine is being embraced by the city's fine-dining chefs, says Rosa Jackson, who has authored the cookbook *Niçoise: Market-Inspired Cooking from France's Sunniest City* and runs Les Petits Farcis *(petitsfarcis.com)* food tours and cooking school in Vieux Nice. 'Because our ingredients are so beautiful, it's very easy to take them from a casual street-food or peasant-type cooking to something much more haute cuisine, and everything in-between', says Jackson.

Some of her favourite addresses include Pinpin *(pin-pin.fr)*, whose market-fresh menu includes its own versions of classic dishes like *les petits farcis* (stuffed vegetables) with its own twist, as well as l'Atelier *(l-atelier-restaurant-nice.com)*, which plates up *socca* with calamari and chorizo, among a host of other inventive toppings.

More than Salade Niçoise

Although Jackson says she's noticing a steady stream of visitors to the city in search of local culinary experiences after having picked up a copy of her cookbook, she says 90% of the people who come to her classes don't know what the word Niçois means.

'They've heard of salade Niçoise, but the international take is not quite what we eat here', she says.

If there's one dish from Nice that's travelled to many tables around the globe, it's this fresh salad full of crunchy flavours. Gordon Ramsey and Nigella Lawson are among the world-famous chefs to have put their spin on the classic salad. But it's a dish that's not without contention. 'Everyone seems to have a very strong opinion as to what should or should not go into a salade Niçoise', writes Lawson in her book *Nigella Express*.

And she's exactly right. Who first added potatoes? Should the tuna be fresh or tinned? Are there green beans in a veritable take on the dish? Should it just be eaten in summer?

The purists from the city say that a *veritable* salade Niçoise has mesclun salad, tomatoes, spring onions, celery, purple artichoke, green peppers, radish, tuna in olive oil, anchovy fillets, garlic, olive oil, eggs, basil and pepper, with permitted variants red wine vinegar, cucumber and broad beans.

Yet the beauty of Nice today is that new twists are not only permitted, but encouraged. So tuck in and enjoy the city's enchanting local cuisine.

> **IF YOU SEE THE CUISINE NISSARDE STICKER DISPLAYED AT A RESTAURANT'S ENTRANCE, YOU KNOW THEIR DISHES RESPECT LOCAL CULINARY TRADITIONS**

FACING INTO LE MISTRAL GAGNANT

Legends and superstitions still fuel the story of the famous and fearsome wind of Provence. By Ashley Parsons

DURING THE FIRST few hours of the mistral, a feeling of reassurance sweeps across Provence. A good wind has come to blow away the humidity and the clouds. Its arrival will bring clear blue skies and a brilliant sun that defines the picturesque Provençal landscape. Farmers are pleased for what it means for their crops, and people recount legends and sayings about the wind to each other. No one really has to listen, though; they've heard them all since childhood.

The mistral wind, renowned for its ferocity and persistence, has been an integral part of Provence's identity for centuries. The first mention of the mistral dates back to 700 BCE when it was described as a 'horrible force'. The Albique people, a Celtic tribe, believed that the wind was the child of Vintur, a Gaulish god, and an Albique woman.

In one legend, villagers barricaded the mistral inside a cave with planks made from century-old olive trees – a tree that notably resists the mistral's temper. When the mistral awoke, it warned the people that without its presence, desolation would befall the land. Mosquitoes would infest their fields, water would putrefy, and fevers would claim the lives of their children and elders. However, the villagers remained steadfast in their desire, and left the mistral confined.

The mistral turned out to be right, of course, and during a night of debate among the villagers, the wind spoke up and pledged to show clemency if the villagers granted it its freedom. It promised to not uproot fruit trees, dismantle rooftops or destroy the fences in the fields.

And so the villagers agreed to free the wind. When the last plank was lifted from the cave, the mistral rushed out and began to blow with all its might. The villagers stood frozen in place, uncertain of how to react. At that moment, a courageous child stepped forward and reminded the wind of its promise. Instantly, the ferocious gusts subsided.Text.

> **THE ALBIQUE PEOPLE, A CELTIC TRIBE, BELIEVED THAT THE WIND WAS THE CHILD OF VINTUR, A GAULISH GOD, AND AN ALBIQUE WOMAN.**

On the Second Day of the Mistral

Yesterday's laundry freshly put away, today people might wash their sheets or even a carpet. The incessant wind will dry wet linens on a line in less than an hour. But by

STORYBOOK

midday, weariness is starting to creep in. Born from the convergence of anticyclones and depressions, the mistral possesses a chilly and arid nature. It sweeps across the region with an average speed of 50 km/h, occasionally unleashing gusts exceeding 100 km/h.

With such an intrusive nature, it penetrates even the tiniest crevices, causing windows and doors to rattle. Dust devils whirl across the countryside, inciting a resigned frustration among inhabitants. The mistral's arrival is often met with mixed emotions. While it brings the challenges of strong gusts and unsettled weather, it also cleanses the air, providing clarity and vivid colours to the landscape. The wind's cooling effect on hot summer days is welcomed, as it offers respite from the scorching sun.

It becomes a dance of emotions – a waltz between joy and frustration, appreciation and annoyance.

Does it remind the inhabitants of their interconnectedness with nature and the challenges they must face? As the wind howls through the narrow streets, it weaves stories and bonds. Touching all aspects of life in Provence, where the forces of nature coexist with human existence, a simple wind shapes the character of the land and its people.

Protection from the mistral in Provence goes as far as to influence rural architecture: old Provençal *mas*, or farmhouses, are usually south facing, and there are few, often tiny, windows on the north side.

The Third Day of the Mistral

Shouldering a thick coat, one might meander to a village cafe while waiting out the wind. Across Provence, dozens of bars, tabacs and bistros bear the name of the mistral (*lou mistrau* – the master – in Provençal). This powerful wind not only shapes the physical environment but also plays a crucial role in the region's viticulture. The mistral's influence on vineyards is significant and beneficial. As it blows through the grapevines, it helps to dry the leaves, reducing the risk of fungal diseases such as mildew. This drying effect, combined with the wind's ability to prevent excessive humidity, creates favorable conditions for grape cultivation. A natural ally to the renowned vineyards of Provence, the mistral contributes to the production of high-quality Côtes du Rhône wines, including the famous Châteauneuf-du-Pape.

In the face of the relentless gusts, the Provençaux find solace in their cherished traditions. The local cafes and brasseries become sanctuaries where friends gather to find camaraderie and share their grievances over a glass of red wine or pastis. The clinking of glasses and the lively chatter form a symphony of frustration and resilience, echoing the spirit of Provence.

With a nod to the wind, to time and to nostalgia, the bar owner might play a Georges Brassens album, the one with 'Le Chapeau de Mireille' on it.

This action is with the hope that tonight the wind will calm, and that three days will not stretch into six. As it's said: The mistral that says 'good day' (starts in the morning) is here for 3, 6 or 9 days, but the mistral that says 'good evening' (starts in the evening) is here until tomorrow night. *(Le mistral qui dit «bonjour» (débutant le jour) est là pour 3, 6 ou 9 jours, alors que celui qui dit «bonsoir» (débutant le soir) est là jusqu'à demain soir.)*

> THE LOCAL CAFES AND BRASSERIES BECOME SANCTUARIES WHERE FRIENDS GATHER TO FIND CAMARADERIE AND SHARE THEIR GRIEVANCES OVER A GLASS OF RED WINE OR PASTIS.

Le mistral, Manosque (p270)
MASLENKA/SHUTTERSTOCK

Les Goudes (p166), Marseille
IMAGESOI/SHUTTERSTOCK

BEAT THE
HEAT IN MARSEILLE

La canicule ('dog days') is the annual heat wave that transforms Marseille in summer. By Michael Frankel

THE HEAT TRANSFORMS Marseille's personality in the summer and forces residents to adapt to a life outdoors.

This is a rebellious city, where people claim the streets as their own. When night falls, they commune in the thronging squares until late or lean over balconies and stare into each other's lives above the narrow passages. From the cobbles, you hear the intimate sound of a thousand living rooms: televisions on blast, erupting laughter, mangled conversations over music, the lonely scraping of chair legs on tiles or a fork across a plate.

All these sounds ring out from open windows after a day spent horizontal on the rocks and rare sand that lies at the edge of the gently agitated waters of the Mediterranean.

Summer in the City

Marseille's summer heat forces the molecules around us to vibrate faster as life slows down, altering what we choose to eat, the liveliness of our energy levels and the regulation of our sleep patterns. Over time, it begins to define who we are. It affects our bodies and minds as we wake up in a daze of late mornings to the sleepily hypnotic whirrings of a fan, stretched out on bed sheets, deeply tanned and still. The duvet will have long been packed away, forgotten and unimaginable. Reaching for water, the idea of anything touching your skin becomes abhorrent; even the proximity of another body radiating next to you can be too much.

Opening the shutters to blue skies and white light, we soon venture outdoors to a sun that scorches us, the heat punishingly reflecting up from the concrete that has absorbed as much as it can take. It's like living in a furnace with the temperature penetrating your existence the same way that gravity does: completely.

Yet, these summers force many of us to rise gratefully. If you visit in the months of July or August, be prepared to sweat. There is no escaping how close and hot it is, even indoors or in the shade. Large beads of perspiration pour from your body and explode at your feet, your brain sending blood racing to the skin's surface, regulating your temperature, to keep you cool, to keep you alive.

Showers are taken cold; inadvertently, you awaken the reptilian brain. Water spraying over your head and neck invigorates your system. Soon, you make your way to the coast to stare at the summer crowds that lie prostrate on the rocks or vividly coloured sunbeds as the temperatures

STORYBOOK

climb, causing your vision to become wavy and your brain confused. This may be what people describe as 'too hot' – when decisions are made that may not feel like your own. It is the point where your cognitive function becomes languorous as your body overheats.

Those not from Marseille may be taken aback to see the tanned, lithe bodies, semi-nude or completely naked in the sun. These bodies disappear into the waters to return energised, golden, wet. Where do you look? It becomes normalised; there is a timeless pagan connection to it all – worshipping the sun and its effects. Your afternoon can become meditative or even spiritual as you slowly become an offering to the gods, as wave after wave of infernal heat forces you to retreat into an inner world of glory. Thoughts get pushed away until you are only a voice saying, 'Wow, it's so hot'. You are incredulous as you suck from a bottle of cold beer. It can become a challenge, but out of your pores streams the cleansing of your inner world, allowing everything bad and unwanted to escape. You can sweat so much it is almost at a cellular level. Your body is a universe unto itself.

YOU ARE INCREDULOUS AS YOU SUCK FROM A BOTTLE OF COLD BEER. IT CAN BECOME A CHALLENGE, BUT OUT OF YOUR PORES STREAMS THE CLEANSING OF YOUR INNER WORLD.

Take to the Sea

You wait as long as you can before you plunge into the sea, unable to take any more of the sun burning into your skin. Diving into the Mediterranean can feel like being reborn, with the colours of the water and the stillness below. You get to let go of it all. Removing all static and connecting with your inner voice. It leaves you fortified, ready to brave the chaos of real life again, back to a sweltering city of a million people packed together with lots of personality on display. Back to a city that is reactive, provocative and as short-tempered as it is wildly expressive and bold, whether you like that or not. Marseille's character has been forged in fire.

In such sweltering heat, you are luckily forgiven for doing nothing. It would be impossible to expect anything from anyone in such conditions. Life is on pause; in the intensity of no future and no past, there is only the blistering moment. A long, hot summer where your ambitions become overridden, when all you need to do is lie down with your friends and laugh for days on end. To float through it in a haze. Everything becomes more straightforward and lighter, even what is found on your plate.

The spaces we love the most, where we go to escape the heat, are also those that are most at risk; preserving nature together is also preserving a whole culture. In the summer months, there is a ban on trips into the *calanques*, so it is essential to download the My Calanques app to keep you informed on navigating the region's most precious natural spaces.

The app encourages us to be responsible, report incidents and ask questions. The national park has become a tinderbox, rendered so arid that a single cigarette butt can destroy the biodiversity of acres of scrubland, the flames wildly driven on by the furious mistral winds.

The heat's effects on the ecology strike you the most as you return from the beach to see end-of-the-world images on the news, where nature has been eviscerated and entire regions destroyed. The weather reports become red maps and exclamation marks. There are interviews from families fleeing and crying, their tears salty tracks down soot-covered faces. Desperately, you watch people fighting the flames, as planes overhead drop tons of water and fire retardants. It's as regular as the summer itself and seemingly inescapable.

Marseille watches the news as the media reaches a boiling point. It is a city neglected by the state; it is the poorest in France and one of the poorest cities in Europe.

Summer was once the great leveller, where all you needed was a hat and a cold drink to survive. Now, it threatens to engulf us all.

INDEX

Abbaye Notre-Dame de Sénanque 40
accessible travel 297
accommodation
 Côte d'Azur & Monaco 114-15
 Var, The 153
 Bouches-du-Rhône 203
 Vaucluse & Luberon 256
 Alpes-de-Haute-Provence 282-3
activities 36-7, 46-9
Aigues-Mortes 201
Aix-en-Provence 34, 178-83, **179**
 drinking 182
 food 179, 183
 shopping 182
Albaron 195-6
Alpes-de-Haute-Provence 28-9, 259-83, **260**, *see also* Moustiers-Ste-Marie, Ubaye Valley
 accommodation 282-3
 festivals & events 261
 itineraries 261
 navigation 260
 travel seasons 261
 travel within 260
 Ubaye Valley, *see individual location*
ammonites 270
Ansouis 250
Antibes 94
apéro 11
architecture 11, 21
 Galimard factory 99
 Le Corbusier 76-7
 Molinard 99
 Pont du Gard 220
Arles 188-91, **189**
 food 191
 travel within 188
 walking tour 190, **190**
art 80, *see also* museums & galleries
arts and crafts 12-13
Atelier des Lauves 178
ATMs 288
Avignon 210-16, **211**
 drinking 213
 food 214, 216
 shopping 210
 tours 215, **215**
 travel within 210
 walking tour 215, **215**

Bandol 34, 144
Banon 28, 271-2
Barcelonnette 29, 277
Basilique Notre-Dame de la Garde 171
Bastille Day 57
beach clubs 124
beaches 30-1
 Baia Bella 66
 Calanque de Brégançonnet 141
 Calanque de l'Oustaou-de-Diou 141
 Calanque de Maubois 66
 Cap de Brégançon 132
 Castel Plage 66
 Coco Beach 66
 Crique des Pêcheurs 66, 111
 Iléo Porquerolles 141
 La Guérite 66
 La Réserve de Mala 66
 Les Plages d'Arles 192-3
 Plage Beaurivage 135
 Plage d'Argent 141
 Plage de Beauduc 193
 Plage de Cavalière 132
 Plage de Gigaro 126, 127
 Plage de la Bouillabaisse 126-7
 Plage de la Courtade 141
 Plage de la Darse 66
 Plage de la Fontanette 127
 Plage de la Madrague 129
 Plage de La Ponche 127
 Plage de l'Almanarre 139
 Plage de Notre Dame 141
 Plage de Pampelonne 127
 Plage de Port-Fréjus 135
 Plage de St-Aygulf 135
 Plage de Tahiti 127
 Plage des Catalans 165
 Plage des Marinières 66
 Plage des Sablettes 66
 Plage des Salins 127
 Plage du Langoustier 141
 Plage du Larvotto 111
 Plage du Lavandou 132
 Plage du Layet 132
 Plage du Midi 66
 Plage du Rayol 132
 Plage du Solarium 111
 Plage Keller 66
 Plage Publique de l'Opéra 66
 Stade Nautique Rainier III 111
 transport to 126
bicycle hire 287, *see also* cycling
bird-watching
 Parc Ornithologique 200
Gorges du Verdon 265
Presqu'île de Giens 139
boat hire 97
boating 10, 93
 Cannes 93
 L'Isle-sur-la-Sorgue 233
Marseille 165-6
 St-Tropez 133
 Toulon 143
Bonaparte, Napoléon 100
books 39, 272, 274
border crossings 286
Bouches-du-Rhône 154-203, *see also* Aix-en-Provence, Arles, Marseille, Stes-Maries-de-la-Mer
 accommodation 203
 festivals & events 158
 itineraries 30-1, 158-9
 navigation 156-7
 travel seasons 158-9
 travel within 156-7
boules 69
breweries & distilleries
 Bacho Brewery 101
 La Distillerie de Monaco 110
bullfighting 189, 191

calanques 14, 173-5
 boat tours 144
 Calanque de Brégançonnet 141
 Calanque de l'Éverine 176
 Calanque de Port-Miou 175
 Calanque de Port-Pin 175
 Calanque d'En-Vau 175
Californie 92
Camargue, The 189, 192-7
 white horses 193
 camping 289, 290
Cannes 32, 86-93, **87**
 drinking 93
 food 90
 tours 91, 98, **91**, **98**
 travel within 86
Cannes Film Festival 56, 90
canyoning 10, 46, 265

Cap Camarat
  lighthouse 126
Cap Moderne 77
Carpentras 26, 218
Carpentras
  Synagogue 219
car rental 287
Carrières de
  Lumières 197
Carry-le-Rouet 30, 177
Casino de
  Monte-Carlo 109
Cassis 30, 175
castles & forts
  Château de Bellet 69
  Château de Buoux 247
  Château de Crémat 69
  Château de
    Saignon 245
  Château de
    Sannes 255
  Chateau d'If 168-9
  Château du
    Grand Pré 254
  Château Fontvert 255
  Château Grimaldi 95
  Château La
    Verrerie 255
  Citadelle St-Elme 73
  Colline du Château 59
  Fort de Brégançon 132
  Fort du Pradeau 139
  Fort Royal 88
  Fort St-André 216
  Fort Ste-Agathe 140
ceramics 263
Cézanne, Paul 12, 178-9
Chagall, Marc 62-3,
  151, 240
chambres d'hôte 289
Chapelle du Rosaire 80
Chapelle Notre-Dame
  de Beauvoir 266
Château d'If 168-9
Châteauneuf-du-
  Pape 217
cheese 44, 271-2, 276
  Banon 271-2
  goat's cheese 272
  Ubaye 276

cherries 219
chestnuts 130, 272
Christmas markets 57
churches & cathedrals
  Abbaye Notre Dame
    de Ganagobie 271
  Abbaye Notre Dame
    de Sénanque 240
  Basilique Notre-Dame
    de la Garde 171
  Basilique Ste-Marie-
    Madeleine 152
  Basilique St-Pierre 215
  Cathédrale Notre-
    Dame de la
    Nativité 80
  Chapelle de la
    Miséricorde 122
  Chapelle Notre Dame
    de Vie 99
  Chapelle Notre-Dame
    de Beauvoir 266
  Chapelle Ste-
    Roseline 151
  Chapelle St-Sixte 197
  Cloître de la
    Cathédrale de
    Fréjus 135
  Collégiale Notre-
    Dame 214
  Collégiale
    Notre-Dame de
    l'Assomption 85
  Collégiale Notre-
    Dame-des-
    Anges 229
  Église de
    St-Tropez 122
  Église Notre-Dame de
    l'Espérance 92
  Église Notre-Dame
    de Pitié 245
  Église St-Didier 214
  Notre-Dame-de-
    la-Mer 198-9
  Notre-Dame-des-
    Doms d'Avignon 215
  Sanctuaire Notre-
    Dame-des-
    Fontaines 85
  Shrine of Our Lady
    of Graces 145
cinema 171
cliff-face dwellings 145
climate 20, 36-7, 294,
  311-13
climate change 314-16
climbing 244
coffee 293

Colorado Provençal
  27, 249
Corbusier 76-7
Corniche des
  Maures 133
Côte d'Azur 53-114,
  54-5, *see also*
  Cannes, Monaco, Nice
  accommodation 114-15
  beaches 66-7
  climate 56-7
  festivals 56-7
  itineraries 32-3, 56-7
  navigation 54-5
  travel seasons 62
  travel within 54-5
Cotignac 145
country code 299
credit cards 288
crime 291
cycling 46-9, 287
  Alpes-de-Haute-
    Provence (high
    passes) 280
  Camargue, the 199
  Col de la Madone 78
  Cols Réservés 294
  Île de
    Porquerolles 143
  Luberon 242-3, **243**
  Monts de
    Vaucluse 235, **235**
  Nice 59, 63, 78
  Route des Crêtes 265
  South Luberon 255
  Var, The 151

de Staël, Nicolas 240
Demoiselle Coiffée 237
Dentelles de
  Montmirail 217
digital payments 288
Digne-les-Bains 29, 270
disabilities 297
diving 47
  Côte d'Azur 102
  Corniche de
    l'Estérel 133
  Euro Plongée 133
dog-sledding 279
drinking 44-5, 122-3,
  166-7, 292-3, *see
  also* breweries &
  distilleries, wine
driving 287

driving tours
  Aix's vineyards
    186-7, **187**
  Esterel 98, **98**
  La Route du Mimosa
    134, **134**
  Three Corniches (Côte
    d'Azur) 82-3, **83**
  Aix's vineyards
    186-7, **187**
  villages de caractère
    (Haut-Var) 150, **150**

École Nationale
  Supérieure de la
  Photographie 188
electric car
  charging 295
electricity 299
emergencies 299
Ermitage St-Gens 237
European Travel
  Information &
  Authorisation System
  (ETIAS) 286
events, *see* festivals
  & events
Èze 33, 74

F

family travel 47, 113,
  129, 290
ferries 14
  Cannes 89
Festival d'Avignon 213
festivals & events 36-7
  Bravade de Saint-
    Tropez 128
  Bravade des
    Espagnols 128
  Cannes Film
    Festival 90
  Carnaval de La
    Plaine 161
  Carnaval de Nice 68
  Chorégies
    d'Orange 222
  Corso de
    la Lavande 41
  Dolly Party 296
  Festival d'Art
    Pyrotechnique 92
  Festival d'Avignon 213
  Festival de
    Ramatuelle 126

Festival des Jardins de la Côte d'Azur 17
Festival Off Avignon 296
Festival Vins & Passions 254
Fête de la Châtaigne 43, 130
Fête de la Libération 128
Fête de la Musique 254
Fête de la St-Pierre des Pêcheurs 128
Fête de la Transhumance 277
Fête des Gardians 193
Fête des Mortes 277
Fête des Vendanges 43, 128
Fête des Violettes 17
Fête du Citron 43
Fête du Fromage 43
Fête du Mimosa 94
In&Out 296
Jazz à Juan 97
Le Fascinant Weekend 254
Les Plages Électroniques 92
Les Rencontres d'Arles 188
Les Voiles de St-Tropez 128
Lou Queernaval 68, 296
Marche des Fiertés 296
Monaco Pride 296
Nice Jazz Festival 68, 296
Noël à Nice 68
Oursinade 43
Pink Parade (Pride) 68
Pride Marseille 296
ZeFestival 296
films 39
Fitzgerald, F Scott 103
Fondation Vincent Van Gogh 189
Fontaine de la Rotonde 180
Fontaine de St-Gens 237
Fontaine de Vaucluse 233
food 42-5, *see also individual locations*
cheese 44, 271-2, 276
cherries 219
chestnuts 130, 272
festivals 43
honey 148
itineraries 22-3
language 292
lemons 77
markets 22
Michelin star restaurants 45
Niçoise cuisine 308-10
seasons 45
street food 308
truffles 22, 44, 147, 218
football 18
forest fires 291
Formula One Grand Prix 104-5
fossil hunting 271
Fréjus & St-Raphaël 35, 135

gardens, *see* parks & gardens
gay travellers 65, 296
Giono, Jean 274
gîtes 289
gîtes d'étape 289
glacier 279
glassblowing 96
Gordes 26, 40, 240-1
Gorges du Loup 101
Gorges du Verdon 36, 264-5
Grasse 32
Grimaud 31
Grotte de Ste-Marie-Madeleine 152
Grottes Troglodytes de Cotignac 145

haggling 288
Haut-Var 145-52, **146**
drinking 147
food 147, 148-9
tours 150
travel within 145
health 291
heat waves 314-16
Hemingway, Ernest 103
highlights 8-23
hiking 46-9
Aiguilles de Valbelle 152
coastal hikes 75
Corniche de l'Estérel 133
Gorges du Caramy 152
L'Abîme de Maramoye 152
Lauzanier Lake 279
Le Tholonet 184-5
Les Baux-de-Provence to Eygalières 197
Les Pénitents 271
Massif de la Ste-Baume 152
Massif des Maures 131
Mont Ventoux on the GR4 228
Mur de la Peste 238
Nice Alps 84
Parc National du Mercantour 81
Plateau de Cavillore 103
Promenade Maurice Rouvier 75
Réserve Naturelle de la Plaine des Maures 131
Sentier Blanc-Martel 264
Sentier de Cap d'Ail 75
Sentier de Tirepoil 103
Sentier des Douaniers 176
Sentier des Fortifications Henri Layet 78
Sentier du Littoral 75, 125, 133, 144
Sentier Le Corbusier 75
Sentier Marin de la Pointe des Sardinaux 129
Sentier Nietzsche 76
Tour du Cap-Ferrat 75
Trou Zéro 152
Val d'Enfer 197
Vallée de la Durance 271
hiking tours
Ermitage St-Gens 236, **236**
Gorges de la Nesque 226, **226**
Pristine Île de Port-Cros 142, **142**
Route Napoléon: Alpes-de-Haute-Provence 268-9, **269**
history 18-19
architecture 307
Casino de Monte-Carlo 306
French popes 305
geology 304
Hyères 139
Mareterra 307
Mexican connection 306
Monaco's peaceful conquests 110
Monastère de la Verne, Collobrières 305
Napoléon 306
Nice 58, 65
Palais Longchamp 172
Palais Princier de Monaco 105-6
pastis 167
rock art 304
Roman Arles 190, 305
Romans 182-3
royal family 306
sun tourism 306
Théâtre Antique, Orange 305
Villa Ephrussi de Rothschild 306
honey 148
horses 193
Hôtel Belles Rives 103
Hôtel du Cap Eden Roc 103
hôtels de charme 289
Hyères 31, 136-9, **137**
drinking 138-9
food 138-9
shopping 138
hiking tour 142, **142**
travel within 136

Île de Porquerolles 140
Île de Port-Cros 143
Île du Levant 144
Îles de Lérins 88-9
Îles du Frioul 169
Irisée Naturelle 96
itineraries 26-35
see also individual locations

Jewish heritage 219-21
Juan-les-Pins 97

kayaking 47, 89, 174, 231-2
kids, travelling with, 47, 113, 129, 290
kitesurfing 46

La Côte Bleue 176
La Croisette 21, 90
La Ponche 122
Lac de Ste-Croix 263
land reclamation 110
language 39, 70, 292, 300
lavender 40-1
  Abbaye Notre-Dame de Sénanque 40
  environmental threats 41
  essential oils 247
  farms 267
  festivals 41
  Gordes 40
  lavandin 41
  museums 41
  Plateau de Claparèdes 41, 247
  Plateau de Valensole 266-7
  Sault 40, 228
  seasons 41
  sustainability 266
  Valensole 40
Le Beaucet 236
Le Suquet 90
Le Tholonet 184-5
lemon farms 77
Les Alpilles 196-7
Les Arènes 135, 189-91
Les Calanques 173-5

Les Goudes 166
LGBTIQ+ travellers 65, 296
L'Isle-sur-la-Sorgue 26, 229-33, **230**
  food 232-3
  shopping 229-30
  tours 235, 236-7, **235**, **237**
  travel within 229
Lourmarin 252
Luberon mountains 247

Mandelieu-La Napoule 94
Mara, Pol 240
Mareterra 108
markets 298
  Cours Saleya flea market (Nice) 63-4
  L'Isle-sur-la-Sorgue 231
  L'Isle-sur-la-Sorgue (Vaucluse & Luberon) 229-30, 231
  Luberon 252
  Marché aux Truffes (Carpentras) 218
  Marché de la Condamine (Monaco) 111
  Marché de la Libération (Nice) 64
  Marché des Capucins (Marseille) 161
  Marché Forville (Cannes) 92
  Marché Provençal (Antibes) 94
  Pêche Locale (Nice) 65
  place Richelme (Aix-en-Provence) 182
  Puces de Nice 64
  St-Tropez 122
  Var, The 147
Marseille 34, 160-72, 314-16, **162-3**
  drinking 168
  food 160-1, 164-5, 169, 171-2
  nightlife 160-1
  shopping 164
  travel within 160
  walking tour 170, **170**
Massif de l'Estérel 148
Massif des Maures 130
Matisse, Henri 62-3

medieval sites 214
Mediterranean Sea 10
Menton 33, 77
Mexican links 278
Michelin star restaurants 45
mimosa flowers 95
Mines de Bruoux 249
Mirabeau 252
mistral gagnant 311
Monaco 104-13, **106-7**
  drinking 108-11
  food 105, 108, 113
  travel within 104
  walking tour 112, **112**
Monaco Formula One Grand Prix 57
Monaco Open-Air Cinema 113
monasteries
  Abbaye du Thoronet 151
  La Chartreuse du Val de Bénédiction 216
  Monastère de la Verne 130
  Monastère Fortifié 89
  Monastère Notre Dame de Cimiez 63
  Monastère Notre-Dame du Torrent de Vie 151
  Monastère St-Paul de Mausole 197
  Royal Abbaye de la Celle 151
money 288
Mont Ventoux 224-5
Montagne Ste-Victoire 184
Montrieux-le-Vieux 152
Monts de Vaucluse 234
Mougins 32, 97
mountain biking 135
  Lure Mountain 273, **273**
Moustiers-Ste-Marie 29, 262-9, **263**
  food 266-7
  travel within 262
museums & galleries 12-13
  Artemisia Museum 275
  Bel-Air Fine Art 124
  Campredon Centre d'Art 229
  Centre Jean Giono 274

Écomusée Sous-Marin de Cannes 89
FAMM 21, **97**
Fondation Victor Vasarely 182
Fondation Vincent Van Gogh 189
Fragonard's Usine Historique & Musée du Parfum 99
Le Suquet des Artistes 92
Luma Arles 188
Musée Anglandon 214
Musée Archéologique 135
Musée Archéologique de St-Raphaël 135
Musée Bonnard 92
Musée Calvet 214
Musée d'Anthropologie Préhistorique de Monaco 113
Musée d'Apt 244
Musée d'Art et d'Histoire 222
Musée d'Art et d'Histoire de Provence 99
Musée d'Art Moderne et d'Art Contemporain (MAMAC) 64
Musée de la Faïence 263
Musée de la Lavande Luberon 41
Musée de la Marine 143
Musée de l'Annonciade 123
Musée de l'Histoire Maritime 128
Musée des Arts et Métiers du Vin 250
Musée des Explorations du Monde 92
Musée des Merveilles 85
Musée du Masque de Fer et du Fort Royal 88
Musée du Petit Palais 213-14
Musée du vin Brotte 217
Musée Estrine 196

Map Pages **000**

Musée Extraordinaire 250
Musée Granet 178
Musée International de la Parfumerie 99
Musée Jean-Honoré Fragonard 99
Musée Lapidaire 214
Musée Massena 58
Musée Matisse 63
Musée National Marc Chagall 62-3
Musée National Picasso 'La Guerre et la Paix' 97
Musée Océanographique de Monaco 113
Musée Picasso 95
Musée Pierre de Luxembourg 216
Musée Provençal du Costume et du Bijou 99
Museon Arlaten 189
Sites Antiques de Vaison-la-Romaine 223
music 39

national parks & reserves
Parc Marin Côte Bleue 177
Parc National de Port-Cros 141
Parc National des Calanques 166, 173
Parc National du Mercantour 81
Parc Naturel Régional des Préalpes d'Azur 96, 103
Parc Naturel Régional du Luberon 248
Parc Ornithologique du Pont de Gau 200
Réserve Géologique de Haute-Provence 270
Vésubia Mountain Park 81
nature 16
Nice 35, 58-72, **60-1**
drinking 72
festivals & events 68
food 62-4, 68-9

nightlife 65, 70, 72
shopping 64
travel within 58, 72
wine 69-70
walking tour 71, **71**
Niçoise cuisine 308-10
nightlife 292
Nîmes 216
North Luberon 238-49, **239**
food 240, 245, 246-7
nightlife 244
shopping 241, 246
tours 242-3, **243**
travel within 238
Notre-Dame-de-la-Mer 198-9
nudist colonies 144

Olbia 139
olive oil 148, 185, 274
Olympique de Marseille 164-5
opening hours 299
Orange 221
Orange Vélodrome 164
overtourism 76

paddleboarding 174
Palais des Papes 212
Palais Longchamp 172
Parc Marin Côte Bleue 177
parking 287
parks & gardens 17
Jardin Botanique du Val Rahmeh 77
Jardin des Doms 213, 215
Jardin Emmanuel Lopez 141
Jardin Exotique d'Èze 74
Jardin Serre de la Madone 7
Jardins de St-André 213
Jardins du MIP 101
Parc Princesse Antoinette 113
Roseraie Princesse Grace 113
pastis 167, 293
Pays de Forcalquier 272
perfume 75, 99

pétanque 185
Phare de la Garoupe 96
Picasso, Pablo 13, 95, 97, 99
planning
budgeting 221
car rental 255
clothes 38
costs 129, 287, 289, 293
etiquette 38
Provence & the Côte d'Azur basics 38-9
Plateau de Valensole 266
Plateau des Claparèdes 41
pointus 10
Pont du Gard 220
Pont Julien 243
Port de Ste-Maxime 129
Port Hercules 110
pottery 13, 252, 263
Princess Grace Irish Library 113
Promenade du Paillon 63
Provence & Côte d'Azur itineraries 26-35, *see also* individual locations
public holidays 299
public transport 287

radio 39
rafting 47, 265, 277
recycling 294
refuges 289
Reillanne 27, 245-6
Reinhardt, Django 200
Réserve Biologique des Monts d'Azur 103
responsible travel 294-5
Rhône Delta 194
rice cultivation 195
rideshares 287
rock art 84
rock climbing 46, 244
Roquebrune-Cap-Martin 76
Route du Mimosa 56, 94
Route Napoléon 96, 100

safe travel 291
Saignon 27
sailing 10, 95, 165-6
sake 197
Salin de Giraud 192-3
Salin des Presquiers 139
Salon-de-Provence 185-6
Sanary-sur-Mer 144
Sault 40, 227, 278
skiing 47-9, 278
smoking 299
snorkelling 47
snow 37, *see also* skiing
South Luberon 250-5, **251**
festivals & events 254
food 252
walking tour 253, **253**
stargazing 272, 279
Ste-Agnès 78
Stes-Maries-de-la-Mer 30, 198-200, **199**
food 200
St-Jean-Cap-Ferrat 74
St-Martin-Vésubie 81
St-Michel-L'Observatoire 28, 278
St-Paul de Vence 78
St-Raphaël 31, 135
strawberries 219
street food 45
St-Tropez 120-9, **121**
drinking 127, 128
driving tour 134, **134**
food 122-3, 129
nightlife 128
shopping 122-3, 124
travel within 120, 126
sustainability 294-5
swimming 46-9, 111
L'Isle-sur-la-Sorgue 232-3
safety 291

tax refunds 286
taxis 287
tennis 93
theatres & cinemas
Alhambra cinema 177
Avignon venues 213
Théâtre de la Mer 129
Théâtre Princesse Grace 113

Continued on p322

Continued from p321

thermal baths
　Aix-en-Provence 182-3
　Aquae Sextiae 183
　Gréoux-les-Bains 183
time zone 299
tipping 288
toilets 299
Toulon 35, 143
Tour de Constance 201
Tour des Templiers 136
Tour Philippe-le-Bel 214
Train des Merveilles 85
trains 34-5
travel seasons 20, 36-7, 56-7
travel to/from Provence & the Côte d'Azur 286
travel within Provence & the Côte d'Azur 287
Trogolodyte ruins 236
truffles 22, 44, 147, 218

Ubaye River 277
Ubaye Valley 276-81, **277**
　drinking 278
　food 278-9
　travel within 276
UNESCO sites
　Avignon 213
　Cabanon Le Corbusier 76
　Grasse 99, 101
　Nice 58
　Théâtre Antique 221-2

Vaison-la-Romaine 223
Valensole 28, 40
Vallauris 97
Vallée de Fontanalba 84-5
Vallée de la Durance 271
Vallée de la Roya 84
Vallée des Merveilles 84-5
Van Gogh, Vincent 12, 196
Var, The 116-53, **118**, *see also* Haut-Var, Hyères, St-Tropez
　accommodation 153
　itineraries 30-1, 119
　navigation 118
　seasons 119
　travel within 118
Vasarely, Victor 182, 240
Vaucluse, The 204-57, **206-7**, *see also* Avignon, L'Isle-sur-la-Sorgue, South Luberon, Ventoux Region
　accommodation 256-7
　festivals & events 208-9
　itineraries 208-9
　navigation 206-7
　travel seasons 208-9
　travel within 206-7
vegetarians & vegans 43-4
Vence 79
Ventoux Region 224-8, **255**
　shopping 224
Verdon River 265
Vieux Port (St-Tropez) 121-2
Villa Ephrussi de Rothschild 74
villages 15
　Alpes-de-Haute Provence 274
　Ansouis 252
　Banon 15
　Bonnieux 243
　Cassis 175
　Castellar 79
　Castillon 79
　Collobrières 130
　Cotignac 15
　Coustellet 242
　Eygalières 15, 197
　Fontaine de Vaucluse 233
　Gassin 127
　Gorbio 79
　Goult 243
　Grimaud 128-9
　itineraries 26-7
　Lacoste 243
　Les Alpilles 196
　Les Mées 271
　Loup River 101
　Lourmarin 251
　Ménerbes 242
　Moulins de Paillas 127
　Peillon 79
　Ramatuelle 126
　Reillanne 245
　Roquebrune 79
　Saignon 15, 244
　Ste-Agnès 15
　St-Martin-Vésubie 84
　Tourrettes-sur-Loup 17
　Villecroze 145
　Villefranche-sur-Mer 33, 73
vineyards 8-9
　Cave de Bonnieux 241
　Cave du Luberon 241
　Caveau du Gigondas 221
　Château de Bellet 69
　Château de Chausse 123
　Château de Crémat 69
　Château Minuty 123
　Châteauneuf-du-Pape 217-23
　Clos de Caveau 221
　Domaine de Ferme St-Martin 221
　Domaine de Longue Toque 221
　Domaine des Beaucas 149
　Les Maîtres Vignerons de la Presqu'île de St-Tropez 123
　Maison des Vins Côtes de Provence 149
　Mas de Pampelonne 123
　Vignobles de Ramatuelle 123
　Vineyards of Île St-Honorat 88-9
vineyard tours 223
visas 286

W

walking tours
　old Avignon 215, **215**
　Cannes art mural walk 91, **91**
　Forêt des Cèdres 253, **253**
　fountains of Aix 180-81, **81**
　Le Panier 170, **170**
　Monaco F1 112, **112**
　Roman Arles 190, **190**
　Vieux Nice 71, **71**
waterfalls
　Cascade de Sillans 147
　Cascades de l'Aille 149
watersports 10, *see also individual sports*
weather 36-7
weights & measures 299
wi-fi 286
wildlife 16
　dolphins 74, 167
　Egyptian vultures 265
　European bison 103
　flamingos 200
　heirloom seeds 249
　Hermann's tortoise 149
　sea urchins 177
　whales 74
　wolves 84
wind 311-13
windsurfing 138
wine 8-9
　Bandol 144
　Châteauneuf-du-Pape 217
　Luberon 241
　Rosé 292
　Ventoux 241
winter Olympics 21

"Few places feel as untamed as the Gorges du Verdon (p264). This deep canyon stretches between Moustiers and Castellane, with turquoise water below and cliffs soaring high above."

"With backroads galore and twisty switchback turns to perched villages, cycling around the north side of the Luberon (p242) is the best way to experience what makes this region hum."

All rights reserved. No part of this publication may be copied, stored in a retrieval system, or transmitted in any form by any means, electronic, mechanical, recording or otherwise, except brief extracts for the purpose of review, and no part of this publication may be sold or hired, without the written permission of the publisher. Lonely Planet and the Lonely Planet logo are trademarks of Lonely Planet and are registered in the US Patent and Trademark Office and in other countries. Lonely Planet does not allow its name or logo to be appropriated by commercial establishments, such as retailers, restaurants or hotels. Please let us know of any misuses: lonelyplanet.com/legal/intellectual-property.

Mapping data sources:
© Lonely Planet
© OpenStreetMap http://openstreetmap.org/copyright

THIS BOOK

The 12th edition of Lonely Planet's Provence & the Côte d'Azur guidebook was written and researched by Chrissie McClatchie, Alexis Averbuck, Michael Frankel and Ashley Parsons.

The previous edition was written by Chrissie, Michael and Ashley.

This guidebook was produced by the following:

Destination Editor
Annemarie McCarthy

Production Editor
Gary Quinn

Image Editor
Ania Lenihan

Cartographer
Anita Banh

Coordinating Editor
Bridget Blair

Assisting Editor
Karyn Noble

Cover Researcher
Kat Marsh

Thanks Lianna Cafolla, Melanie Dankel, Sally Davies, Alison Killilea, Kate Mathews

MIX
Paper | Supporting responsible forestry
FSC™ C021741

Paper in this book is certified against the Forest Stewardship Council™ standards. FSC™ promotes environmentally responsible, socially beneficial and economically viable management of the world's forests.

Published by Lonely Planet Global Limited
CRN 554153
12th edition – March 2026
ISBN 978 1 83869 935 2
© Lonely Planet 2026
10 9 8 7 6 5 4 3 2 1
Printed in China